Should the church – can the church – repent? H
responsible for the faults of past generations? If the
gizing' for everything imaginable, does she not risk
remarkable book, Jeremy Bergen displays a sure hand in addressing questions
like these. It is not political correctness bids the church repent, he argues, but
love of neighbor and fidelity to the Crucified. An important and timely study.

Joseph Mangina, Wycliffe College, Toronto School of Theology, Canada

This is a wonderful example of systematic ecclesiological inquiry that is disciplined *both* by faithful dialogue with the doctrinal tradition *and* by critical engagement with what churches and church people are actually doing. In the first part of the book, Bergen presents an immensely helpful analytic description and assessment of a wide range of concrete examples of acts of apology and repentance performed in recent years by churches, governments and other groups, together with their varied receptions. Reflecting upon this material in the second part, he constructs a bold yet deeply thoughtful ecclesiological proposal that deserves careful consideration, not least for its ecumenical benefits. Particularly significant is his proposal that the Church's continuity over time derives not from claims about some ideal or institutional element. Rather, he reworks the creedal 'communion of saints' – and sinners! – to argue that it is these practices of repentance and forgiveness, enabled by the Holy Spirit, that enable us both to appropriate our churches' pasts and be drawn up in Christ into the life of God. It is thus 'through repentance the Church may be granted a share of its own continuity in God's triune life', and thus truly *be* the Church.

Nicholas Healy, St. John's University, NY, USA

In a context in which churches, as well as national governments, are increasingly offering public apologies for past acts of injustice and failure, this book represents an important contribution. Rather than seeing ecclesial repentance as undermining the Church's reputation, or functioning as a self-serving public relations strategy, Bergen offers a theological account of how they help the Church be faithful to its mission. The discussion is attentive to both concrete historical failures of churches, as well as to the richness of the Christian theological tradition's treatment of reconciliation. The result is a sensitive reflection on the complexities and perils of public apologies, as well as a thoughtful appreciation for their potential to facilitate the healing of past wounds.

Christopher Craig Brittain, University of Aberdeen, UK

With grace, courage, and a discerning spirit, Jeremy Bergen offers an account of ecclesial repentance worthy of a pilgrim people, a church at once reconciled and always on the journey toward full reconciliation. Christian communities would do well to use this volume in a process of communal examination of conscience.

Margaret Pfeil, Department of Theology, University of Notre Dame, IN, USA

ECCLESIAL REPENTANCE

THE CHURCHES CONFRONT
THEIR SINFUL PASTS

JEREMY M. BERGEN

t&t clark

Published by T&T Clark International
A Continuum Imprint
The Tower Building, 11 York Road, London SE1 7NX
80 Maiden Lane, Suite 704, New York, NY 10038

www.continuumbooks.com

All rights reserved. No part of this publication may be reproduced or transmitted in any form or by any means, electronic or mechanical, including photocopying, recording or any information storage or retrieval system, without permission in writing from the publishers.

Copyright © Jeremy M. Bergen, 2011

Jeremy M. Bergen has asserted his right under the Copyright, Designs and Patents Act 1988, to be identified as the Author of this work.

British Library Cataloguing-in-Publication Data
A catalogue record for this book is available from the British Library

ISBN 13:   978-0-567-21432-4 (Hardback)
           978-0-567-52368-6 (Paperback)

Typeset by Fakenham Photosetting, Fakenham, Norfolk
Printed and bound in India by Replika Press Pvt Ltd

Cover art

Artist: Paul Roorda
Title: *Icon Lament*
Media: Slate tile, blood, ashes, gold leaf.
Date: 2009
Dimensions: 18 × 20.5 inches
www.paulroorda.com

Artist statement about Slate Roof series:

Using slate tiles from the leaking roof of an old church, I create images which examine the tension between faith and knowledge. In each slate tile, there is a hole, either found or cut. Just as the roof has failed as a barrier to the rain, the boundaries of faith have been penetrated and confidence in knowledge compromised. Combining the iconographies of the church and of science, the work in this series exposes the anxiety of a generation for which the idea of certainty has been eroded.

CONTENTS

Abbreviations	ix
Notes About Sources	xi
Acknowledgements	xiv
Introduction	1
Part 1: Counter-Witness and Scandal: Repentance for Historical Wrongs	15

Chapter 1: DIVISION AMONG THE PEOPLE OF GOD   17

    The Disunity of Christians
    Offences Against the Jewish People

Chapter 2: WESTERN COLONIALISM AND ITS LEGACY   57

    Offences Against Aboriginal People
    Slavery and/or Racism
    Apartheid in South Africa

Chapter 3: SEXUAL ABUSE, VIOLENCE, INJUSTICE   87

    Clergy Sexual Abuse
    War, Civil War, Crusades
    Women
    Homosexual Persons
    Relation to Science/Scientists
    Environmental Destruction

Chapter 4: DAY OF PARDON   115

    Preparation
    Theological Reflection: *Memory and Reconciliation*

  First Sunday of Lent, 12 March 2000
  Response, Debate, Reception

Part 2: Doctrine and Practice: Frameworks and Implications   151

Chapter 5: THE COMMUNION OF SAINTS   153

  The Church in Time: Robert Jenson on the Trinity
   God and Time
   Ecclesiology
  Communion, Forgiveness, Intercession
  Healing of Memories
   Remembering, Forgetting, Final Reconciliation

Chapter 6: SIN AND THE HOLINESS OF THE CHURCH   199

  Discourses of Sin and Holiness
   The Holy Church in Protestant Theology
   The Holy Church in Roman Catholic Theology
   A (Catholic) Theology of a Sinful Church
  Finding the Penitential Body in History
   Identity of a Penitent Church in Relation to Judaism
   Conforming the Body of Christ Over Time

Chapter 7: FORGIVENESS AND RECONCILIATION   243

  Sacrament of Reconciliation
   Contrition and Confession: The Examination of Conscience
   Penance
   Absolution
  Contributions of Repentance and Apology to Reconciliation
   Collective Responsibility
   Social Sin
   Forgiveness
   Apology and Reconciliation

Conclusion   285
Bibliography   289
Appendix   307
Index   333

ABBREVIATIONS

CDF – Congregation for the Doctrine of the Faith
CMC – Conference of Mennonites in Canada
EKD – *Evangelische Kirche in Deutschland* (Evangelical Church in Germany)
ELCA – Evangelical Lutheran Church in America
LWF – Lutheran World Federation
MR – Memory and Reconciliation: The Church and the Faults of the Past
NGK – *Nederduits Gereformeerde Kerk* (Dutch Reformed Church, South Africa)
RICSA – Research Institute on Christianity in South Africa
SBC – Southern Baptist Convention
TRC – Truth and Reconciliation Commission (South Africa)
UCC – United Church of Canada
UMC – United Methodist Church
WARC – World Alliance of Reformed Churches
WCC – World Council of Churches

NOTE ABOUT SOURCES

Full bibliographic information on ecclesial repentance primary documents, often both hard copy and online sources, is provided in the appendix. Shortened references appear in the footnotes. Citations from church documents are made to paragraph or section numbers, where available. While the appendix may appear to present a definitive list of events and documents, it reflects significant subjective judgement, as discussed throughout the book. Some entries are clearly 'ecclesial repentance,' others borderline, while others have undoubtedly been missed.

ACKNOWLEDGEMENTS

I have long been interested in public statements by the church. One of my distinct memories as a young boy at the 1983 Bethlehem, Pennsylvania joint assembly of the Mennonite Church and the General Conference Mennonite Church was seeing a group of Christians gather to hold an all-night public prayer vigil for peace, on the anniversary of the bombing of Hiroshima. I recall the very emotional debate at an assembly three years later about the denominational position on homosexuality. What the church says matters, and the world is indeed watching. I do thank my parents for dragging me to such conferences, instilling in me the convictions that the church is important, but also that if the church is to witness truly to the justice, peace and reconciliation of the gospel, its repentance may be needed.

I am grateful to those who read iterations of this book, posed provocative questions and offered insightful suggestions: Nicholas M. Healy, Joseph Mangina, Gilles Mongeau, Jeff Nowers, Margaret O'Gara, Anthony Siegrist, Jaroslav Skira, Rebecca Steinmann. Elements of Chapter 5 were presented at the LEST VI conference, Faculty of Theology, Katholieke Universiteit Leuven, Belgium. The Toronto Mennonite Theological Centre Fellows Group was especially important in shaping my general approach to this topic. This group has been a model of collegial engagement and a source of theological friendship. Special thanks are due to Joseph Mangina of Wycliffe College, University of Toronto, the supervisor of the dissertation on which this book is based, who supported the project even when I could not yet articulate what it was about and pushed me to probe more deeply into its theological implications.

Though I cannot name everyone who has shaped my theological thinking, I want to acknowledge the influence of three outstanding teachers, all deceased. Professor Carl Ridd (University of Winnipeg) exemplified to many the world-shaping power of a commitment to social justice. Professor George Vandervelde (Institute for Christian

Studies, Toronto), whose perceptive mind contributed to some of the official texts discussed in this book, taught me much about the nature and mission of the church, its vocation of unity and its Christological centre. Professor A. James Reimer (Conrad Grebel University College, University of Waterloo) taught many Mennonites, myself included, to nurture a 'dogmatic imagination' rooted in the classical theological tradition. The logic and structure of this book owe much to his influence.

I am grateful for institutional support during my research and writing from Emmanuel College, Toronto School of Theology, Massey College at the University of Toronto, the Social Sciences and Humanities Research Council of Canada and the Ontario Graduate Scholarship programme. Conrad Grebel University College provided me with the best possible incentive to complete the dissertation on time and gave me much needed support to turn it into the present book.

For many reasons, this book is dedicated to Rebecca.

INTRODUCTION

> There was a chair right in the middle in the front of the room, and one by one we came by the chair to sit down. I looked down, and saw all that black hair all around the chair, because there were other girls that were ahead of me. There were a lot of us that had long black hair. Now I think that must have been the beginning of the efforts in the residential school to cut me off from my *Indian-ness*. (Eva Louttit)

> When they punished me for speaking my language, they pulled my pants down and with a harvester belt this thick and that wide they strapped me on my bare bottom for every time they caught me speaking my language. That's why it's hard for me to communicate in the English language. I'm scared. I don't trust white people yet. I'm afraid you'll take the message, and you'll put it in your system. You'll judge it by your culture, by your English language, and its going to come back to us Indian people the same. (Mervin Wolfleg)

> The residential school closed in 1979. My boys disclosed sexual abuse in 1987, that one of the intermediate boys was sexually abusing them. One week before my oldest boy's court [date], he committed suicide. A year and a half later, my second son committed suicide. I had a hard time coming up here. I was scared, but I'm here now. (Elizabeth Hope Johns)[1]

At the second National Native Convocation, in 1993, Eva Louttit, Mervin Wolfleg, Elizabeth Hope Johns and dozens of other Aboriginal members of the Anglican Church of Canada gathered to tell painful stories of their experiences in Anglican-run residential schools. For decades, these schools were central to the Canadian government's policy of assimiliating Aboriginal peoples to the dominant culture. By 1920, Aboriginal children aged 7 to 15 were required to leave their homes to live in the schools, most of which were run by churches. The policy of suppressing Aboriginal culture, language and spirituality, was infamously summarized as 'killing the Indian in the child.' In addition to this cultural and spiritual abuse, many children were subject to harsh physical punishment, emotional neglect or sexual

---

[1] Transcribed from Anglican Church of Canada, *Dancing the Dream*, National Native Convocation, videocassette (1993).

abuse. The legacy of the residential schools includes poverty, addictions, domestic violence and suicide.

> I seem to have something I have to share with you. I was a student in a residential school. I was just sitting back there and I was counting the years of the bitterness inside me. Do you know it's 50 years I carried that burden? Somebody has to answer to this, this inhuman punishment that we got at that school. But my interest today . . . is that I want to hear the apology of the Anglican Church of Canada! . . . Apologize to our native people. (Ernest McGraw)[2]

After listening to these stories for nearly a week, Archbishop Michael Peers, Primate of the Anglican Church of Canada, rose and delivered an emotional apology on behalf of the church. He said, in part,

> Brothers and sisters, [t]ogether here with you I have listened as you have told your stories of the residential schools. I have heard the voices that have spoken of pain and hurt experienced in the schools, and of the scars which endure to this day. I have felt shame and humiliation as I have heard of suffering inflicted by my people, and as I think of the part our church played in that suffering . . . I also know that it is God who heals, and that God can begin to heal when we open ourselves, our wounds, our failures and our shame to God. I want to take one step along that path here and now. I accept and I confess before God and you, our failures in the residential schools. We failed you. We failed ourselves. We failed God. . . I am sorry, more than I can say, that we tried to remake you in our image, taking from you your language and the signs of your identity. . . . On behalf of the Anglican Church of Canada, I present our apology.[3]

Once there was no ecclesial repentance. Once church leaders did not acknowledge that the actions of their predecessors were wrong. Once churches did not apologize or seek forgiveness. Once churches did not confess that they failed God. Churches have changed courses may times. They have stopped doing one thing and have done something else in turn. But they have not usually gone the additional step of declaring that a previous course had been offensive to God and a counter-witness to the gospel. Churches have always recognized the sinfulness of all members, and confessed this in corporate worship. But they have not always named themselves as agents of sin. Moreover, in the apology for having run residential schools within a policy of assimilation (as distinct from abuse within them), Archbishop Peers was repenting not for malice, but for the honest *best intentions* of the Anglican Church in the late nineteenth and twentieth centuries. Indeed, hundreds of faithful Christians dedicated their lives to these

---

[2] *Ibid.*

[3] Archbishop Michael Peers, Anglican Church of Canada, 'A Message to the National Native Convocation' (1993).

schools and understood their work with Aboriginal people as a calling from God to serve the wider mission of the church. By what right did a church leader, with the benefit of hindsight, presume to repudiate their life's work? Nevertheless, the Anglican Church of Canada repented, and it is not alone.

Ecclesial repentance is the act in which church/denominational bodies make official statements of repentance, apology, confession or requests for forgiveness for those things which were once official church policy or practice. Most have been made by churches in North America, Western Europe and Australia. Churches have repented for the enslavement of people of African descent, as well as continuing racist attitudes and institutions. Statements of confession have been issued by some German and Japanese churches for supporting the war policies of their governments. An awareness of the Christian dimensions of anti-Semitism have led to apologies for silence or complicity during the Holocaust and to attempts to address theological anti-Judaism. A few churches have repented of the sinful or inadequate ways they have treated women or homosexual persons. Already in 1920 the Anglican Communion repented of its role in the disunity of Christianity; subsequent statements by other groups have acknowledged the sinfulness of church division and the need for mutual forgiveness for actions and attitudes among Christians past and present. In a 'Day of Pardon' service at the height of the 2000 Jubilee Year celebrations, Pope John Paul II asked God's forgiveness for a variety of sins committed in the name of the church.

The very fact that churches are repenting, and doing so publicly, necessitates careful theological assessment. Is it *possible*, theologically speaking, for a church to repent? Is it faithful? Or required? While the practice as it emerged in the twentieth century always intends some break with the church's historical past, it does so only by presupposing a deeper continuity. The Anglican Church of Canada was still the church when it did what it has since repudiated. Ecclesial repentance marks a wrestling with the past on the basis of numerous core Christian convictions about confession, forgiveness, reconciliation, holiness, the mystical bond among Christians over time and mission of the church.

These churchly actions have elicited considerable interest and controversy both within the repenting denominations and among the public at large. In part, this is due to a broader trend in which the collective apology is employed in political, legal and business spheres (while celebrities seek to outdo each other in offering profuse apologies for various misdeeds). Governments and nations debate if and when apologies should be offered for past wrongs and scholars assess what they mean.[4] Victims of historical injustices, or their heirs, quite rightly seek recognition of their suffering and correction, often in the form of apologies and reparations.[5] The nature of public interest in church apologies is complex, but is often linked to the pain, frustration or sense of hypocrisy that some people experience and ascribe to the church. That the church in particular, and Christianity more generally, is the source of more harm than good is a thesis plausible to many. Interest in ecclesial repentance is heightened by an expectation of the church's moral superiority, even purity, and thus the magnitude of its failures. Cynicism may be fed by the perception that church apologies are merely hypocritical 'public relations'. From a more constructive perspective, an apology may also be perceived as a practical way whereby a church commits itself to a certain course of action, such as a renewed relationship with Aboriginal people based on mutual respect.

This book is an attempt to make theological sense of ecclesial repentance. I ask two basic questions: What is this new practice? What does it mean? I then develop a theological framework in three distinct layers. First, ecclesial repentance is an exercise in which the church becomes more deeply cognizant of its concrete historical

---

[4] Key texts among the burgeoning literature on apologies, especially collective apologies, include: Nicholas Tavuchis, *Mea Culpa: A Sociology of Apology and Reconciliation* (Stanford, CA: Stanford University Press, 1991); Aaron Lazare, *On Apology* (Oxford: Oxford University Press, 2004); Elazar Barkan and Alexander Karn, eds., *Taking Wrongs Seriously: Apologies and Reconciliation* (Stanford, CA: Stanford University Press, 2006); Mark Gibney, Rhoda Howard-Hassmann, Jean-Marc Coicaud and Niklaus Steiner, eds., *The Age of Apology: Facing up to the Past* (Philadelphia: Pennsylvania University Press, 2008); Nick Smith, *I Was Wrong: The Meanings of Apologies* (Cambridge: Cambridge University Press, 2008); Jennifer Lind, *Sorry States: Apologies in International Politics* (Ithaca, NY: Cornell University Press, 2008); Danielle Celermajer, *The Sins of the Nations and the Ritual of Apologies* (Cambridge: Cambridge University Press, 2009). See also Jeremy M. Bergen, 'Reconciling Past and Present: A Review Essay on Collective Apologies,' *Journal of Religion, Conflict, and Peace* 2, no. 2 (Spring 2008), online journal: www.religionconflictpeace.org/node/52.

[5] See Roy L. Brooks, ed., *When Sorry Isn't Enough: The Controversy Over Apologies and Reparations for Human Injustice* (New York: New York University Press, 1999); Elazar Barkan, *The Guilt of Nations: Restitution and Negotiating Historical Injustices* (New York: Norton, 2000); Janna Thompson, *Taking Responsibility for the Past: Reparation and Historical Injustice* (Cambridge, UK: Polity Press, 2002); John C. Torpey, *Making Whole What Has Been Smashed: On Reparations Politics* (Cambridge, MA: Harvard University Press, 2006).

particularity. There is no church but the one (or ones – I discuss this tension below) that exists. Ecclesiology, the discipline within which this project proceeds, is thus not a theoretical discipline but an irreducibly historical and practical one, as Nicholas M. Healy has argued.[6] Second, I will show how ecclesial repentance both *reflects* and *reshapes* the church's identity by focusing on three classical doctrines – the communion of saints, the holiness of the church and the forgiveness of sins. For example, the belief that Christians are linked to one another through space and time (communion of saints) helps to explain how it is possible for the present church to repent for an action of the church centuries ago. At the same time, the implicit invocation of the communion of saints in repentance for the past suggests that this communion in some way includes those who have been harmed by it, even if they would not (or no longer) identify with the church. This double movement, from doctrine to practice and from practice to doctrine, echoes the way in which the repentance of a church is an act of both continuity and discontinuity. The turning away from a particular past may also imply the turning away from the theological convictions that have aided and abetted it, but this can only be done on the basis of a deeper continuity. Therefore, I aim to understand the dynamics of ecclesial repentance within the action of the triune God, the ultimate grounding of the church. In this third theological layer, I propose that ecclesial repentance be understood as a work of the Holy Spirit to conform the church to the body of Christ. Ultimately, I argue, the church's break with some elements of its past makes sense only if the church is grounded outside of itself, in the saving action of the triune God. Taken together, these three layers constitute a broad framework for thinking about this emerging practice.

While there is no other book-length study of the theological implications of ecclesial repentance, though particular apologies have generated many shorter reflections, several theologians have argued that the church ought to adopt a penitential attitude with respect to its past (and present) actions. They have argued this, for example, on the basis of the typological continuity of the church and the unfaithful Kingdoms of Israel and Judah,[7] the Christological constitution of the

---

[6] *Church, World and the Christian Life: Practical–Prophetic Ecclesiology* (Cambridge: Cambridge University Press, 2000).

[7] Ephraim Radner, *The End of the Church: A Pneumatology of Christian Division in the West* (Grand Rapids: Eerdmans, 1998).

church's vicarious action,[8] the church's status as a forgiven people,[9] the irreducibly human dimension of the concrete church,[10] the way in which such penitence binds the church to solidarity with the marginalized[11] or how a penitent church forms virtuous members.[12]

I understand repentance to refer to a practice within the Christian tradition (and the Jewish tradition, among others) whereby an individual or a group seeks to turn away from sin towards righteousness – taking responsibility for a particular wrong (confession), expressing remorse and pledging some kind of amendment. It is connected with notions of conversion and return to God. This pledge may involve concrete steps to set straight the historical record, ask forgiveness, repair the harm, promise not to repeat the offence and/or reconcile with offended groups. Repentance is, in some sense, 'before God', though if public, it is also before various human audiences. An apology, generally made to an individual or community, is frequently conceived as a secularized version of repentance – it is the most commonly used descriptor of these practices in the public media – as it does not necessarily presuppose the presence or action of God. And yet some churches explicitly apologize. A request for forgiveness may be explicitly or implicitly addressed to God, a human community, or both. Ecclesial repentance is my inclusive term for the church practice described in the chapters that follow, though elements such as confession, request for forgiveness or apology are sometimes used to describe either the whole or the part. Some churches make specific delineations about why they are repenting rather than apologizing and vice-versa, while others use the terms somewhat interchangeably. I set out with very approximate working definitions to avoid forcing actual instances into rigid theoretical categories and track the meanings that emerge.

Given that verbal or written statements of repentance are just one element in a larger process that may include conscientization, dialogue, institutional reform, judicial remedies, amendment of

---

[8] Dietrich Bonhoeffer, *Ethics*, trans. Neville Horton Smith (New York: Macmillan, 1955).

[9] Rowan Williams, *Resurrection: Interpreting the Easter Gospel*, rev. ed. (Cleveland: Pilgrim Press, 2002).

[10] Healy, *Church, World and the Christian Life*.

[11] Jürgen Moltmann, *The Church in the Power of the Spirit*, trans. Margaret Kohl (Minneapolis: Fortress Press, 1993).

[12] James Dallen, *The Reconciling Community: The Rite of Penance* (New York: Pueblo Publishing, 1986).

practice or reparations, it must be borne in mind that I am concerned in this project with a very discrete element in the larger processes of reconciliation. Though one may argue that words (such as a verbal apology) without deeds (such as reparations) are empty, I maintain that words *are* deeds though they are rarely if ever the only deeds required. My focus on statements of repentance does not imply that I have taken them to be the most important element in a church's wrestling with its painful past, let alone the only element.

In what sense is this repentance 'ecclesial'? Ecclesial refers to repentance by the church as opposed to personal repentance or that of other corporate actors. Moreover, repentance is ecclesial to the extent that it is officially sanctioned by a church body, bearing in mind that different ecclesiologies determine how speech in the name of a church is authorized. My focus is on what may be called 'denominations', not parachurch organizations nor ecumenical bodies, though some discussion of ecumenical statements is warranted, especially in the early stages of repentance for a given history. I examine primarily statements at the national or international, rather than provincial, diocesan or congregational levels, in full recognition that there is a debate in Catholic theology about the ecclesial status of national conferences of bishops and that some traditions on the Protestant side assert that the 'church' exists only at the congregational level. My criteria for inclusion create a bias in favour of Catholic and mainline Protestant churches, who have highly developed bureaucracies for making such statements at these levels, rather than traditions with a congregational polities. For example, though repentance is a prominent theme in Pentecostal theology and practice, I have found no instances of ecclesial repentance by Pentecostal denominations (though they may well exist), and have included no discussion of such actions by congregations.

I do not restrict my study to any one denomination or tradition. In part, this is because of the fact that the division of Christians is itself a significant failure of which churches are repenting. Even though I argue against a disembodied, ideal church, it is grammatically necessarily to employ the terms 'church' as well as 'churches'. I use the term 'churches' to refer to the empirical fact of diverse, non-reconciled Christian communities and 'church' to refer to the theological concept (which itself affirms the concrete historical dimension of the church). I am sensitive to the fact that a particular ecclesiology is already implied by the language one uses for Christian unity and disunity.¹³ I do not intend to promote a specific ecclesiology by inclusion of my criteria for this nor by my choice of words to describe them.

The scope of this book is partly delineated by what it does not include. I do not include apologies for individual wrongdoing, misconduct or criminal activity among church members or leaders. I exclude instances of reform or change in policy that might be taken as an implicit repentance or rejection of a previous position. For example, I do not take the fact that a church begins to ordain women as even implicit repentance for a past in which it did not do so. I do not delve into the particular history of which a church is repenting. I take penitent churches at their word regarding their account of a regrettable past, though sometimes the event of apology reveals competing versions of a particular history. I do not attempt to account why the late twentieth century has seen such a proliferation of apologies.¹⁴ I do not give historical or sociological accounts of the institutional decisions to apologize, nor assess whether they were 'successful',¹⁵ though I aim to contribute to an understanding of what 'success' might entail. I do not advocate any particular future act of repentance, nor examine the many calls for a church to repent. While my theological framework may indeed help churches think about whether and how to repent of a particular past, this book is not intended as a recommendation of repentance in any circumstance nor is it a manual for how to go about it.

Furthermore, I do not analyse the absence of repentance, aside from observing some striking gaps. Of all the ecumenical dialogues

---

¹³ Peter C. Bouteneff, 'Ecumenical Ecclesiology and the Language of Unity', *Journal of Ecumenical Studies* 44 (2009), 352–60.

¹⁴ Elazar Barkan argues that the end of the Cold War made possible new discourses of morality in international relations through which various national and ethnic groups sought to redefine and negotiate their identities through the rectification of past wrongs, *Guilt of Nations*, x–xii. More pessimistically, John C. Torpey diagnoses a society generally unable to think constructively about the future. '[R]ighting past wrongs tends to supplant the search for a vision of a better tomorrow. The reckoning with abominable pasts becomes, in fact, the idiom in which the future is sought.' 'The Pursuit of the Past: A Polemical Perspective', in *Theorizing Historical Consciousness*, ed. Peter Seixas (Toronto: University of Toronto Press, 2004), 251.

¹⁵ One notable attempt to gauge success was undertaken through extensive interviews with former students at Indian Residential Schools, Alain Paul Durocher, 'Between the Right to Forget and the Duty to Remember: The Politics of Memory in Canada's Public Church Apologies', unpublished Ph.D. dissertation (Graduate Theological Union, 2002).

or guidelines for Christian–Jewish dialogue, a great many do not include confession of wrongdoing, though my sustained discussion of the ones that do might suggest otherwise. These criteria turn my attention to some churches and not others, to some documents and not others. All these exclusions emphasize the fact that my starting point is the *given fact* of ecclesial repentance, and what this given fact implies about the nature and mission of the church.

The field of contemporary ecclesiology, within which I locate this project, is undergoing significant debate about the methods and sources to be employed, even about the kind of discipline it is. I take Nicholas M. Healy's account of ecclesiology as a practical–prophetic discipline as a point of departure and a basis for my methodological minimalism. He is highly critical of ecclesiologies overly concerned with methods and timeless theories, and is only secondarily (at best) interested in how such theories are put into practice. The 'blueprint' approach problematically construes the church as an ideal, abstract essence, as though the contingency of historical messiness is not the proper sphere of the church. Healy contends that ecclesiology ought to be a practical discipline that helps the church and its members to live out their Christian callings in specific contexts. Ecclesiology ought to be concerned with the church's historical, rather than theoretical, identity. Attention to the concrete church and the complexity of its historical character suggest that images such as 'pilgrim church' are particularly helpful as the church undertakes its mission here and now. While the church's identity does not hover 'above' its concrete action in history, the work of the Holy Spirit in the church, through the church – and in spite of the church – renders sociology unable to fully account for this identity.[16]

A project on ecclesial repentance is a contribution to this kind of practical–prophetic ecclesiology both because it starts with actual things that churches are doing, and because these practices are themselves attempts to grapple theologically with the church's historical identity. An analysis of such practices thus articulates an ecclesiology that can support the church's discernment about how its mission might include contrition for its past actions and points to what such actions reveal about the nature of a penitent church. If anything, starting from particular church statements disciplines my theological reflection to be rooted in what churches are doing now in relation to what churches have done in the past. Ecclesial

---

[16] Healy, *Church, World and the Christian Life*, Chapter 1.

repentance does not emerge fully formed and as a fully theorized 'blueprint', ready to implemented. Churches that repent, often for the first time, do so because they understand themselves to be called to do so, not because they have thought through all of the theological implications. When a practice of the church, which may indeed be the work of the Spirit, outpaces theology (often rightly so – the life of the church is prior to theological method[17]), the task of theology is to serve the church by helping it to reflect on this practice.

My consistent starting point is the given fact that churches are repenting for very particular past actions. I proceed from the premise that when a church claims to be repenting, then it is repenting. This key contention may seem alternately tautological and controversial. It names my bias to test the possibility that ecclesial repentance is a faithful response and even the work of the Holy Spirit in the church. It also names my rejection of the idea that what is 'really' happening is disconnected from what principal actors think they are doing but can be authoritatively known instead by an outside observer. It is certainly possible that though a church appears or intends to repent, it somehow fails to do so, perhaps because of mixed motives or lack of contrition (though what motive or contrition might mean on a personal level cannot be easily transposed to a collective actor like the church). I do discuss several cases in which an act of repentance was received as somewhat less than that. But, my initial posture towards the material is that a church which declares repentance should be given the benefit of the doubt.

This sympathetic starting point must be problematized along the way. To treat a church practice as a sign of the Spirit risks blessing whatever the church does. Healy contends that much church practices discourse fails to consider how practices may be distorted or misperformed, and thus fails to adequately form a community or to embody essential elements of the faith.[18] Regarding ecclesial repentance in particular, a prophetic/critical moment is essential because its own logic turns attention to the human and sinful dimension of the church. Ecclesial repentance presupposes precisely that some practices of the church *were* not (and presumably *are* not) consistent

---

[17] According to John Howard Yoder, '[T]he life of the community is prior to all possible methodological distillations.' 'Walk and Word', in *Theology Without Foundations*, ed. Stanley Hauerwas, Nancey C. Murphy and Mark Nation (Nashville: Abingdon Press, 1994), 82.

[18] Nicholas M. Healy, 'Practices and the New Ecclesiology: Misplaced Concreteness?', *International Journal of Systematic Theology* 5 (2003), 287–308.

with the gospel. It may be that in decades to come, churches will regard their past acts of repentance as tainted by sin and a scandal to the gospel. Through an engagement with various others – scripture, critics, prophets, and those who have suffered what churches have done – theology must guard against temptations to become insular.

At the outset, I name two possible criticisms of my proposal from quite different angles within the church and my strategies to respond to them. From a 'conservative' perspective (for lack of a better term), there may be suspicion that my pointing to the many failures of the church portrays it as a merely human institution, and one that is as bad as its many secular critics have long asserted. There may be suspicion that by describing and interpreting ecclesial repentance as a faithful church practice, my agenda is to call the church to repent for the next long list of sins, subject it to alien standards of political correctness, or simply disparage it as a ruin to be abandoned. I aim to address this concern by giving a thoroughly theological account of ecclesial repentance, grounding it in the saving action of the triune God. I do not believe the church is only a human institution, though by God's design it is certainly also that. I do not intend to undermine the church, but to help it be faithful in its mission. Nor do I intend to propogate a progressive view of church history that contrasts a dark past of sin with enlightened contemporary repentance. And while the novelty of ecclesial repentance as I have defined it cannot be denied, my arguments about sin in the church and sin of the church ought to unsettle any triumphalism of the present.

From a 'liberal' or 'progressive' perspective, there may be a concern that I have co-opted ecclesial repentance to the church's credit. The fact that any church came to recognize and confess the sinfulness of something it once espoused, whether the legitimacy of slavery or the abrogation of God's covenant with the Jews, might be taken as unwarranted attention to the church's faithfulness, especially given that I located this process in relation to Christ and the Holy Spirit. In this approach, which I also reject, the focus is on the positive fact that the church faithfully 'caught' its faults, rather than the tragedy and sin of the faults themselves. To draw an analogy to a case where an eleventh hour reprieve frees an innocent man from execution, the point is not to interpret this as proof that the system works but rather to highlight that it (almost) did not. Does my approach too quickly turn attention to the good the church is doing, in repentance, when justice for victims demands dwelling in the depths of the church's sin a bit longer?

I intend to be vigilant against this danger throughout the book. I will remind both myself and readers that repentance may indeed turn out to be primarily defensive *apologia*, rather than true contrition and pleading God's mercy. An act of repentance may essentially be a kind of risk management strategy by which the church attempts to 'get past' some painful episode, mitigate 'fallout', and quickly frame itself in the best possible light. This ultimately denies God as the source of forgiveness and healing. It denies the church's mandate to embody reconciliation in patience and in ambiguity, suffering the Spirit's work in the church and frequently in spite of itself. Even sincere words are not yet reconciliation itself.

Reconciliation, for nearly all of the histories that churches have been confronting, has some implication for renewed social relationships. Ecclesial repentance undermines itself if the suffering of those whom the church has harmed is rendered invisible. I acknowledge in advance that I will not give adequate space to the voices of those sinned against. By focusing primarily on the church statements, rather than on their effects and the response to them, I risk once again privileging the voice of the powerful, a dynamic usually underlying the need for confession in the first place. The identities and voices of those Aboriginal people whose 'Indian-ness' was cut off together with their braids of long black hair in the name of the gospel ought not to be silenced by the statement of apology that followed. Mervin Wolfleg's warning that '[y]ou'll judge [my words] by your culture, by your English language, and its going to come back to us Indian people the same' applies to this book. Testimonies to the betrayal of the gospel must remain to the wider church profoundly unsettling and profoundly *strange*. A church seized by the injustices it has promoted will be called to more than minor adjustments and new programmes, but to a radical and ongoing conversion in its common life. A study of ecclesial repentance deals not just with the 'data' of church statements, but with the reality of pain and the hope for healing.

The plan for the book is as follows. Part 1 describes ecclesial repentance by breadth (Chapters 1 to 3) and depth (Chapter 4). In Chapter 1, I examine repentance for sins broadly against the unity of the people of God, first against the unity of the church, and then against the Jewish people. The legacy of the Western colonial project, as manifest in oppression of Aboriginal people and African slaves, South African apartheid and ongoing racism is the subject of

Chapter 2. Chapter 3 addresses repentance with respect to clergy sexual abuse, war, crusades, women, homosexuals, science and the environment. Chapter 4 consists of a description and analysis of what may be the most complex instance of ecclesial repentance to date – Pope John Paul II's Day of Pardon during Lent 2000, including preparatory documents and subsequent debate and reception. My narration of actual practice identifies various points of theological tension and focuses them around three key issues that ecclesial repentance raises for ecclesiology, to be considered in subsequent chapters. First, how can repentance for acts of the church in the distant past have integrity and be meaningful? That is, are guilt and contrition for guilt, in some sense, burdens borne within and among generations continuously over time in the church? Second, how is sin present in and through the church; and what is the basis and nature of the church's holiness? Third, how does an act of ecclesial repentance fit into a larger context of forgiveness and reconciliation?

In Chapters 5 to 7 (Part 2), I show how each doctrinal locus helps us to understand how ecclesial repentance reflects the church's nature and mission, and how this practice in turn compels some reshaping of that locus. Through these appeals to the doctrinal tradition, I propose some Christological and pneumatological suppositions of ecclesial repentance. While I argue that these doctrines constitute a fitting and fruitful framework which responds to the issues raised in the first chapters, I do not claim that this is only or even the best possible way of approaching this emerging practice.

Drawing especially from cases of ecumenical repentance, I consider in Chapter 5 what the doctrine of the communion of saints discloses about the continuity of the church through time. How is the church that repents today the same church that committed an offence centuries earlier? I draw on Robert Jenson's account of the temporal nature of the church to locate ecclesial repentance in the interaction of the Holy Spirit and the *totus Christus* – the total Christ. Given the centrality of memory to the mediation of blessings and burdens throughout the communion of saints, I engage Miroslav Volf on the healing of memories, ecclesial identity and penitential history.

Chapter 6 explores the mark of the holiness of the church, and the related questions of sin *in* the church and the sin *of* the church. Despite the ecclesiological differences represented by the typically Protestant confession that the church itself sins and the official Catholic account of the church sinning strictly in its members, I argue that both discourses are unable to respond to the challenge of historical particularity posed by ecclesial repentance. I focus on repentance for sins against Jews and Judaism in order to pursue an instructive connection between form and substance, arguing that ecclesial repentance is an occasion for the church to recover a sense of its holiness as a radical gift of the Holy Spirit to the whole people of God, rather than an institutional or moral possession.

In Chapter 7 I analyse how ecclesial repentance grounds the church's mission of reconciliation in its reception of forgiveness. Since corporate acts of repentance are both like and unlike the (individual) sacrament of reconciliation, I explore this link in order to think through some implications for forgiveness and reconciliation from the perspective of those churches repenting of elements of the Western colonial project. Finally, I examine how church apologies both draw from and contribute to a wider discourse about collective apologies and social reconciliation.

Part 1

*COUNTER-WITNESS AND SCANDAL:
REPENTANCE FOR HISTORICAL WRONGS*

Chapter 1

DIVISION AMONG THE PEOPLE OF GOD

The church . . . questions itself. (French Catholic Bishops)[1]

Ecclesial repentance is a public act. By naming what has been a 'counter-witness and scandal' to the gospel,[2] a church repents before a watching world and pledges to address this past. When a church repents, it gives a official account of its own history, identifies sin within that history, assumes responsibility, seeks to repair and heal, and makes a public promise to not repeat the offence. When acts of repentance include an apology or a request for forgiveness, there is an explicitly dialogical moment in which the church awaits a response from those affected by its actions. Even if repentance is directed primarily to God, church leadership may work at making this act meaningful at a local level through education, programmes of reconciliation, or dialogue. The secular media reports with great interest cases of 'church apologies'; sometimes with sensitivity to the complexities involved, and sometimes with an air of smugness or cynicism: 'Nice sentiment, but two centuries too late!'

The public element of ecclesial repentance has implications for how to organize and interpret these acts. First, it is not necessary (nor possible) to name every single instance of ecclesial repentance. The territory is adequately surveyed if I include those acts of ecclesial repentance that have been sufficiently public to have entered into a wider discourse. Second, the public perception of an act as ecclesial repentance, or 'church apology', helps to indicate whether it ought to be included in this discussion. For example, according to standard definitions of apology, Pope Benedict did not really apologize for

---

[1] Drancy Declaration (1997).

[2] The phrase appears in Pope John Paul II, *Tertio Millennio Adveniente: Apostolic Letter on Preparation for the Jubilee of the Year 2000* (1994), no. 33.

clergy sexual abuse of children during his 2008 visit to the United States. He did not say 'sorry' or 'repent', for example, but rather expressed regret that the abuse happened. Yet, some commentators as well as some victims took his words as a true apology, while others denounced them as a failed apology. The 1945 Stuttgart Declaration of Guilt by the Evangelical Church in Germany was actually quite vague and expressed in a passive voice, yet was held up my many in the anti-apartheid movement as a true instance of church repentance that South African churches should emulate. At the very least, there is no simple threshold, no magic word or formula, by which one can distinguish a true statement of ecclesial repentance from something less than one. Third, the meaning of any particular act of repentance exceeds both a church's explicit intentions and the texts it produces. Though occasionally churches use 'apology' to describe their actions, this word and the broader discourse of collective apology may be invoked in the minds of church members or the general public, even if church leaders say explicitly that they are repenting or asking forgiveness, but not apologizing. Yet, if an act is received as an act of apology, what is implied by this concept nevertheless becomes relevant for assessing what the act is and what it means. This is all to say that the meaning of ecclesial repentance is negotiated through complex processes of intention, reception, dialogue and analysis.

Therefore, I have exercised judgement in my decisions to include some statements and not others. Attention to statements by national or international church entities results in bias in favour of Catholic and mainline Protestant churches, which have developed mechanisms and bureaucracies for speaking at those levels. Congregationalist, charismatic and Pentecostal groups are grossly underrepresented, and I cannot be certain whether this is because I have not examined the congregational level or because agents of these traditions have not engaged in repentance for historical wrongs. The literature I read is primarily North American and European, and thus my attention turns to those church actions discussed therein. If I have missed a great number of instances, it may be that my constructive arguments in Part 2 still hold, though elements of Chapters 1 to 3 may require revised narratives.

To classify ecclesial repentance is to begin to tell a particular story. The story of how different theological commitments or polities inform repentance would emerge by tracing the various ways that the United Church of Canada or the Roman Catholic Church, for example, have repented for a variety of particular pasts and even begun to develop a self-conscious 'tradition' of apology. Alternately, a story about the rhetorical significance of various forms of repentance would emerge from a focus on the similarities and differences among liturgical acts of confession, speeches, legislative resolutions, symbols and memorials of repentance, and requests for forgiveness in the context of dialogue.[3]

However, I believe the most compelling stories emerge with respect to the different pasts that the churches confront. The volume of statements wrestling with the divisions among Christians, the history of relations with the Jewish people and the legacies of Western colonialism, especially racism, already illustrates the churches' self-perception of the most significant ways they have compromised their mission in recent centuries. The point is not just that the church is repenting or that it has sinned, but that it repents for specific histories and has sinned in particular ways. The victims matter, injustices matter and the theological issues at stake matter, both for the sake of reconciliation and for the sake of reshaping a more adequate theology and practice.

The Disunity of Christians

The ecumenical movement in the twentieth century has been a call to conversion. The *Groupe des Dombes*, the unofficial but very influential French Protestant–Catholic dialogue, championed the radical conviction that the *church* stands in need of conversion. For spokesman Paul Couturier, ecumenism begins with a recognition of the sin of division and the fact that reconciliation is not simply a matter of human effort. He counselled his own Catholic Church to humility and truthfulness with respect to their responsibility for the history of division, followed by repentance and prayer.[4]

As Christians of various confessions began meeting face to face and recognizing true faith in each other, there emerged a shared sense of the tragedy, even sinfulness, of separation. A report from the first Faith and Order Conference (Lausanne, 1927) raised questions about the extent and location of that sin. It noted that some hold

---

[3] This is the general form used by Robert R. Weyeneth, 'The Power of Apology and the Process of Historical Reconciliation', *Public Historian* 23, no. 3 (Summer 2001), 9–38.

[4] Catherine E. Clifford, *The Groupe Des Dombes: A Dialogue of Conversion* (New York: Peter Lang, 2005), 17–18. The group began meeting in the 1930s, and initiated the Week of Prayer for Christian Unity.

all divisions to be rooted in sin, while others believe that divisions may reflect a faithful diversity of gifts. A middle way was proposed in which Christians might 'look back on the divisions of the past with penitence and sorrow coupled with a lively sense of God's mercy'.[5] In his sermon at the opening of the second conference on Faith and Order (Edinburgh, 1937), Archbishop of Canterbury William Temple spoke about how divisions obscure the witness of the one gospel and compromise the spiritual treasures of 'each party'. He was clear that sin lay at the root of these divisions. If the church preaches that Christ truly conquers sin and death, and establishes fellowship among people, its witness to the world requires that divided churches first receive Christ's healing for the sinful betrayal of that fellowship. The movement towards church unity must therefore be a 'matter for deep penitence'.[6] In these early statements, there is a reticence to assume or assign responsibility for wrongs more specific than generalized arrogance, uncharity or misrepresentation of others. Nevertheless, proceeding in a spirit of penitence became part of the explicit ecumenical discourse.

In his address to the First Assembly of the World Council of Churches (WCC) (Amsterdam, 1948), H. Richard Niebuhr argued that repentance is a general condition for recognizing the particular disorders of the church.[7] Niebuhr contrasted self-criticism as mere belief in the analytic capacity of the self with true repentance as an act of faith that turns to God.[8] The official report of the assembly states that estrangement from Christ, a plausible definition for sin itself, is the root of division. In its call for repentance, it links prayer for renewal in Christ with prayer for the unity of the church.[9]

The WCC's Second Assembly (Evanston, 1954) wrestled with a theologically complex Faith and Order document on 'Our Oneness in Christ and our Disunity as Churches'. That document describes a basic eschatological tension between the church's given unity in Christ's saving work, and the need to grow in unity in light of actual discord. This tension parallels the *simul justus et peccator* of the

---

[5] 'Lausanne: Final Report', First World Conference on Faith and Order (1927).

[6] 'The Opening Service', Second World Conference on Faith and Order (1937).

[7] H. Richard Niebuhr, 'The Disorder of Man in the Church of God', in *Man's Disorder and God's Design: The Amsterdam Assembly Series*, vol. 1, World Council of Churches (New York: Harper & Brothers, 1949), 80.

[8] *Ibid.*, 78.

[9] World Council of Churches, 'The Universal Church in God's Design: Report of Section 1', First General Assembly (1948), 80–1.

individual. The report maintains that church divisions arose from a sincere concern for the truth, as well as social/cultural factors. Yet, it warns that diversity becomes sinful if it compromises the unity of the church. This formulation moves the discussion about sinful division away from a narrow focus on the sinful acts of individuals. The document notes that individuals may have acted in good faith and in genuine search of the truth, yet contributed to a situation of division which is, as such, sinful. Recognition that undue attachment to church distinctives denies Christ's lordship over the church ought to bring all together before the cross wherein they rediscover their unity, even though it is a unity of lament and repentance. 'True repentance is the acknowledgement before God that we have sinned so as to be caught in the net of inexplicable evil and rendered unable to heal our divisions ourselves'.[10] The assembly recognized, as had Niebuhr, that repentance is not simply a tactic or tool for the repair of the church, but a radical confession that the church must turn to God for healing. Repentance cannot simply be what ecumenically minded people say when they get together. It involves a 'willingness to endure judgement' and new forms of 'active obedience', as affirmed by a subsequent Faith and Order conference.[11] It requires a commitment to reconsider the past and test where faithfulness demands obedience unto the death of even cherished traditions.

While framing the ecumenical impulse as penitent, these early conferences did not speak for the member churches. A call for repentance is not yet repentance itself. Self-reflective member churches would need to face this history of estrangement directly, the first of which actually did so prior to the Faith and Order Conferences. The 'Appeal to all Christian People', issued by the Anglican Bishops' meeting at Lambeth in 1920, together with proposed principles for union, had the tone of the somewhat diffuse call to repentance that would mark future multilateral statements. The bishops described their appeal as rooted in the work of the Holy Spirit to bind together 'in penitence and prayer . . . all those who deplore the divisions of Christian people', and the consequent compromise of the church's mission. But they went on to confess their share in the divisions,

---

[10] World Council of Churches, 'Faith and Order: Our Oneness in Christ and Our Disunity as Churches', Second Assembly (1954). These themes are central to Claude Welch's book on ecclesiology published shortly after the assembly, *The Reality of the Church* (New York: Scribner's, 1958).

[11] 'Final Report: Lund', Third World Conference on Faith and Order (1952).

which were caused by sinful 'self-will, ambition, and lack of charity', as well as unspecified legitimate causes.[12] The statement is notable as the first *confession* of the sin of division by an official organ of one of the divided churches.

Many leaders in the early ecumenical movement viewed organic church union, especially those from different confessional traditions, as a sign promising even greater unity. Unions such as the United Church of Canada (1925), the Church of South India (1947), and the United Church of Christ (1957), in which old denominations as well as non-essential beliefs and practices 'died', reinforced the motif of ecclesial conversion as death and new life. Reflecting the height of the WCC's vision of organic unity, the Third Assembly (New Delhi, 1961) declared:

> We all confess that sinful self-will operates to keep us separated and that in our human ignorance we cannot discern clearly the lines of God's design for the future. But it is our firm hope that through the Holy Spirit God's will as it is witnessed to in Holy Scripture will be more and more disclosed to us and in us. The achievement of unity will involve nothing less than a death and rebirth of many forms of church life as we have known them. We believe that nothing less costly can finally suffice.[13]

The churches which united as the Church of South India explicitly invoked repentance in their service of inauguration. Their Prayer of Confession included the following: 'We acknowledge, O Lord, our share in the sin and shame of divisions in Thy holy Church; we confess our prejudice and our pride, our lack of sympathy and understanding; and the feebleness of our efforts to secure all the riches of our inheritance in the saints.'[14] A similar confession inaugurated the Church of North India in 1970. The United Reformed Church (UK) described its formation as 'obedience to the call to repent of what has been amiss in the past and to be reconciled', and enshrined that conviction in its Basis of Union.[15] It is important to note that not all unions were marked with the explicit language of repentance.[16] However, the enthusiasm for organic church union in the 1960s was

---

[12] Lambeth Conference of Anglican Bishops, 'Appeal to all Christian People' (1920).

[13] World Council of Churches, 'Report of the Section on Unity', Third Assembly (1961), 117.

[14] 'Order of Service for the Inauguration of Church Union in South India' (1947).

[15] United Reformed Church, 'Basis of Union' (1972).

[16] For example, in neither the Basis of Union nor the Service of Inauguration of the Uniting Church in Australia, which was formed in 1977.

eclipsed by a move towards a vision of reconciled diversity, and by the impact of the Roman Catholic Church's official entry into the ecumenical movement.

Pope Paul VI's opening speech to the second session of the Second Vatican Council marked a first for Roman Catholic ecclesial repentance. Addressing representatives of 'Christian denominations separated from the Catholic Church',[17] he lamented the separation and invited a sincere dialogue free from polemics. He stated:

> If we are in any way to blame for that separation, we humbly beg God's forgiveness. And we ask pardon too of our brethren who feel themselves to have been injured by us. For our part, we willingly forgive the injuries which the Catholic Church has suffered, and forget the grief endured during the long series of dissensions and separations.[18]

His statement requested forgiveness from God, as would subsequent Catholic repentance statements, though notably it also asked pardon from human beings as well. The pope's speech was a qualified one; it implicitly repeated the accusation that fault also lies with the 'separated brethren' and granted only the *possibility* that Catholics may have done harm.

Yet, his statement clearly made possible a similar request for pardon in *Unitatis Redintegratio: Decree on Ecumenism*. In the article, which begins 'There can be no ecumenism worthy of the name without a change of heart', the Council Fathers confessed that each person is a sinner, and therefore also a sinner against the unity of the church. 'Thus, in humble prayer, we beg pardon of God and of our separated brethren, just as we forgive those who trespass against us.'[19] This passage was controversial – one Council Father opposed it, saying 'If someone is guilty, let him go find a good confessor!'[20] – even though it also contained an implicit accusation about the fault of non-Catholics in church division. Nevertheless, the inclusion of a request for pardon in a council document must be understood in

---

[17] According to a recent Vatican document, the pope was addressing the Orthodox churches of the East. International Theological Commission, *Memory and Reconciliation: The Church and the Faults of the Past* (2000), no. 1.1.

[18] Pope Paul VI, 'Speech at the Opening of the Second Session of Vatican Council II' (1963).

[19] Second Vatican Council, *Unitatis Redintegratio: Decree on Ecumenism* (1964), no. 7.

[20] Cited in Claude Soetens, 'The Ecumenical Commitment of the Catholic Church', in *History of Vatican II*, vol. 3, ed. Giuseppe Alberigo and Joseph A. Komonchak (Maryknoll, NY: Orbis, 1995), 272.

light of the overriding vision emerging from pope and council with respect to other Christians: dialogue.

Dialogue was the manner in which the Catholic Church, through Vatican II, proposed to engage with the world. Pope Paul's Encyclical Letter *Ecclesiam Suam* argued that the church's nature and mission is dialogical, grounded in God's loving 'dialogue of salvation' with all persons. In fact, only through internal and external dialogue does the church come to a deeper awareness of itself as church.[21] This openness to ecumenical dialogue was effectively a break with Pope Pius XI's prohibition of Catholic participation in ecumenical organizations. Requesting pardon of 'separated brethren' was a means by which to remove a barrier to dialogue and enter into a spirit of humility, openness and willingness to hear the other. In this light, the request for forgiveness paired with an offer of forgiveness may be interpreted as an example of the give and take of a true dialogue. But what is the nature and meaning of the trespasses that led to separation? These would be discussed in actual dialogues with other churches and, through an attempt to view history through the eyes of another, further repentance.

Shortly after the initiation of Catholic–Orthodox dialogue, clearly the top ecumenical priority emerging from Vatican II, Pope Paul VI and Ecumenical Patriarch Athenagoras I issued an historic Joint Declaration in 1965, simultaneously proclaimed at the Vatican and the Phanar in Constantinople on 7 December, that acknowledged the 'excess' of the mutual excommunications of 1054. They identified 'lack of understanding and mutual trust' as factors in the rupture of communion, and they pledged to remove from memory the sentences of excommunication that followed. Declaring mutual pardon, they indirectly asked God's pardon, affirming that God pardons those who pardon each other.[22] Pope and patriarch recognized that while the declaration does not end tensions between the Catholic and Orthodox Churches, it does promote the trust and mutual charity necessary for the *dialogue* that will lead to a restoration of fellowship.

The late 1960s witnessed a rise in bilateral dialogues between confessional groups at the world level (often called Christian World

---

[21] Pope Paul VI, *Ecclesiam Suam: Encyclical Letter on the Church* (1964).

[22] Pope Paul VI and Ecumenical Patriarch Athenagoras I, 'Joint Catholic–Orthodox Declaration' (1965). The documentary history of the dialogue preceding and following the Declaration is in E. J. Stormon, ed., *Towards the Healing of Schism: The Sees of Rome and Constantinople* (New York: Paulist Press, 1987).

Communions.) Much more so than multilateral conversations, bilateral dialogues facilitated the examination of the particular factors that gave rise to divisions in Christianity, and assessed the implications of theological points of disagreement. In addition, the Catholic Church preferred discussion with confessional groups at the world level.[23]

Dialogue between the Catholic Church and the Lutheran World Federation (LWF), established in 1965, soon led to confessions about the past. In response to a speech given by Cardinal Jan Willebrands, head of the Secretariat for Promoting Christian Unity, to its 1970 Assembly, the LWF responded with an apology (using the word 'sorry') for the 'offense and misunderstanding which these polemic elements [in Luther's writings and Lutheran theology] have caused our Roman Catholic brethren'.[24] The LWF statement noted the potential for research on Luther and the Reformation period to shed light on present differences. In a letter to Cardinal Willebrands several years later, Pope John Paul II echoed the importance of determining more precisely Luther's context and personal intention. Historical investigation can point out the sincere faith that motivated Luther. As long as such research seeks the truth for the sake of unity, the pope concluded, then the church must recognize fault wherever it is discovered.[25]

A 1985 report on Lutheran–Catholic dialogue locates confession and repentance in a framework of reconciliation. The reconciliation given in Christ calls for human reconciliation. It requires the mutual recognition of the same faith expressed in different forms, but also the naming of those 'differences that stem from error and weakness of faith and which cannot therefore be overcome without repentance, self-criticism and renewal'. This discernment requires honest dialogue.[26] In a section entitled 'Growth of Church Fellowship Through Mutual Recognition and Reception', several acts of Lutheran and Catholic repentance are cited as milestones in

---

[23] Harding Meyer, 'Christian World Communions', in *A History of the Ecumenical Movement, 1968–2000*, vol. 3, ed. John Briggs, Mercy Amba Oduyoye, and Georges Tsetsis (Geneva: WCC Publications, 2004), 103–22.

[24] Lutheran World Federation, 'Statement on the Visit of Cardinal Willebrands' (1970).

[25] Pope John Paul II, Letter to Cardinal Willebrands for the Fifth Centenary of the Birth of Martin Luther (1983).

[26] Roman Catholic/Lutheran Joint Commission, *Facing Unity* (1985), no. 48.

the transformation of perspective.[27] Through the lens of dialogue, gifts from the other tradition were recognized as important for all. Thus, the Catholics recognized the need of the church for continual reformation, and the Lutherans recognized the inadequacy of a narrowly interpreted doctrine of *sola scriptura*.[28] An openness to see the past penitentially through the eyes of the other was undoubtedly a key to the landmark statement 15 years later that differences on the doctrine of justification are no longer church-dividing and past condemnations do not apply to the present churches.[29]

A world-level dialogue involving Baptists and Reformed concluded in 1983 with a 'Day of Encounter' in Zurich, marked by a joint communion service and mutual confessions of sin. The Reformed statement confessed the church's deafness to the Spirit and its failure to recognize that Baptists and Mennonites also proclaimed the gospel. It named persecution, oppression, execution and banishment as injustices done by Reformed churches, and requested forgiveness from God and divine assistance in healing. The Baptists confessed that they have often closed their lives to blessings from other Christians and instead presumed a spiritual self-sufficiency. They confessed that their past actions have sown mistrust, and that they have often accepted these divisions instead of working to overcome them.[30]

While confessions or statements of regret in reports on bilateral dialogues cannot be simply taken as the position of the respective church bodies, their function and status may be considered in several ways. First, they may be commended for reception by the sponsoring bodies. Second, they may promise a particular action to undo the effects of the past. Third, they may indicate that confession and repentance will be coming at a further stage of dialogue. Fourth, they may invoke previous statements of repentance and apply them to a particular relationship. In all of these ways, repentance in bilateral dialogues begins to assume some ecclesial 'density'.

---

[27] *Ibid.*, no. 51.

[28] *Ibid.*, nos. 53–54.

[29] Lutheran World Federation and Roman Catholic Church, 'Joint Declaration on the Doctrine of Justification, 1999', in *Growth in Agreement II: Reports and Agreed Statements of Ecumenical Conversations on a World Level, 1982–1998*, ed. Jeffrey Gros, Harding Meyer and William G. Rusch (Geneva: WCC Publications, 2000), 566–82.

[30] 'Reformed Confession of Sin', delivered by the president of the Reformed Church of Zurich, and 'Baptist Confession of Sin', delivered by the president of the Swiss Union of Baptist Churches, Day of Encounter, 5 March 1983.

Illustrating the first two strategies, a 1990 report issuing from an international Baptist–Lutheran dialogue considered the Lutheran condemnation of 'Anabaptists'. In the report, Lutherans deplored the effect these statements had in the persecution of other Christians, and asked for forgiveness. They made a practical commitment to qualify these condemnations in the training of ministers. In turn, the Baptists deplored their own misrepresentations and attitudes of superiority towards Lutherans and asked forgiveness. Together, they recommended that churches from each tradition make use of the mutual statements of forgiveness in worship services.[31] A major 1990 report on the international Reformed–Catholic dialogue discussed the need for mutual forgiveness within the framework of the 'reconciliation of memories', a concept promoted especially by Pope John Paul II in which divergent accounts of the past 'may in time become a basis for new mutual bonding and a growing sense of shared identity'.[32] To this end, the document discusses the sinfulness of human beings to which the church is entrusted, and the particular errors made by both Catholics and Reformers in the past. Though there is disagreement about the precise relationship of sin, sinners and the church, there is agreement that human sinfulness harms the church's mission.[33] The church that responds to the call of ongoing conversion asks Christ's forgiveness and the forgiveness of those Christians from whom that church is separated. Illustrating the third strategy of repentance in bilateral dialogue, the report commends careful study of the history of the division, the status of mutual condemnations, and the further recognition of error and responsibility. Finally, the delegations to the international Mennonite–Catholic dialogue were clear that while they did not have authority to proclaim repentance, each side could invoke previously authorized statements of ecumenical repentance and assert their applicability to the present relationship.[34]

Pope John Paul II made numerous ecumenical overtures during his pontificate, many of which were in some mode of repentance.

---

[31] Baptist–Lutheran Joint Commission, 'Lutheran Condemnations of the Anabaptists in the 16th Century and the Relationship of Lutherans and Baptists Today' (1990), 38–41.

[32] Reformed–Roman Catholic Dialogue, 'Towards a Common Understanding of the Church, Second Phase, 1984–1990', no. 153.

[33] Ibid., no. 117.

[34] Roman Catholic Church and Mennonite World Conference, 'Called Together to be Peacemakers: Report of the International Dialogue Between the Catholic Church and the Mennonite World Conference, 1998–2003', nos. 198–206.

In the 1990s, several themes emerged. First, ecumenism is rooted in conversion. This is particularly poignant in the 1995 Apostolic Letter *Orientale Lumen* in which the pope discusses his own ministry of unity in relation to the Orthodox and other separated Christians. The pope noted that Christ gave to Peter the task of strengthening others in faith and unity precisely at the moment he was to betray him; thus, only in the awareness of his own failures and his continual conversion can Peter, and Peter's successors, engage in this task.[35]

Second, all are in need of forgiveness. At times, the effect of this statement is to call the Catholic side to greater self-examination and repentance.[36] But, it can also function to point accusingly to the (unacknowledged) guilt of others.[37] While the guilt of all is a reality of theological anthropology, its repeated invocation may in fact serve to undermine the discernment of particular kinds and degrees of historical responsibility. A blanket confession covers all. On the other hand, if convictions about the pervasiveness of sin leads to sincere attempts to discern its specific dimension, then historical particularity need not be obscured. The centrality of dialogue in the examination of conscience, as developed in *Ut Unum Sint*, is premised on the idea that one side may recognize its own failings only in light of how others see it. At the same time, an ecumenical dialogue is a dialogue with God before whom all stand in need of conversion. As both sides turn in repentance for the particular past that only dialogue could name, they grow in unity as they seek the forgiveness of Jesus Christ through the Holy Spirit.[38]

Third, as divisive memories are healed by repentance and purification, gifts from one particular tradition may circulate for the benefit of the whole. The pope acknowledged that Luther's call for the ongoing reform of the church is a gift to the entire church. As repentance creates conditions for overcoming past prejudices, the spirituality, theology and liturgy of Eastern Christianity may be received as treasures of all Christians.

Fourth, the priority the pope gave to the global nature of church, exemplified in his prodigious saint-making, required him

---

[35] Pope John Paul II, *Orientale Lumen: Apostolic Letter to Mark the Centenary of* Orientalium Dignitas *of Pope Leo XIII* (1995), no. 20.

[36] See Pope John Paul II, Ecumenical celebration, Synod of Europe, 7 December 1991.

[37] The emphasis on the guilt of all is noticeable in Pope John Paul II, Meeting with the Orthodox, Bialystok, Poland, 5 June 1991.

[38] Pope John Paul II, *Ut Unum Sint: Encyclical Letter on Commitment to Ecumenism* (1995), nos. 33–35.

to acknowledge the harmful effects of past Catholic actions in many places. Events held at locations of infamous acts of violence such as the execution of Jan Hus[39] or the St Bartholemew's Day Massacre[40] thus included at least implicit requests for pardon. At the 1995 canonization of Jan Sarkander, in the Czech Republic, the pope acknowledged that honouring a martyr who had been executed by Protestant authorities might exacerbate tensions. He said:

> This canonization must in no way reopen painful wounds, which in the past marked the Body of Christ in these lands. On the contrary, today I, the Pope of the Church of Rome, in the name of all Catholics, ask forgiveness for the wrongs inflicted on non-Catholics during the turbulent history of these peoples; at the same time, I pledge the Catholic Church's forgiveness for whatever harm her sons and daughters suffered.[41]

Finally, through cross-referencing past acts of repentance and anticipating future ones, there develops a tradition of ecclesial repentance. A declaration of the Italian Bishops to the Protestant Waldensians invoked Pope Paul's council speech, Pope John Paul's 1994 invitation for an examination of conscience in preparation for the Jubilee year, and *Ut Unum Sint*.[42] Even though the bishops only promised to reflect penitentially on the past, reference to a track record of repentance helps account for why this statement was interpreted as an important step towards reconciliation.[43]

Mending relationship with the Orthodox was at the top of Pope John Paul's ecumenical agenda. Repeated reference to the 1965 Joint Declaration shows how such an act of mutual pardon is seen to make dialogue possible. Yet, it is no guarantee of a warm reception. The pope's visits in 2001 to the Orthodox Churches in Greece and Ukraine, two places with marked Catholic–Orthodox tensions, proceeded quite differently. John Paul's repentance for sins of the past, including the sack of Constantinople, was well-received by the Greek Orthodox Primate, Archbishop Christodolous. The pope noted that 'models of reunion in the past no longer correspond to the impulse towards unity', presumably rejecting past Catholic practice of

---

[39] Pope John Paul II, Address to an International Symposium on John Hus, 17 December 1999.
[40] Pope John Paul II, Baptismal Vigil, World Youth Day, 23 August 1997.
[41] Pope John Paul II, Canonization of Jan Sarkander, 21 May 1995.
[42] Italian Catholic Bishops, 'We Can Heal the Wounds of Memory' (1997).
[43] As noted in Prescot Stephens, *The Waldensian Story: A Study in Faith, Intolerance, and Survival* (Lewes, UK: Book Guild, 1998), 344.

proselytizing Orthodox believers.[44] Despite some precedents against doing so, the two leaders said the Lord's Prayer, together, in private. By contrast, the pope was not well received by the Ukrainian Orthodox, despite making statements similar to those he had made in Greece.[45] His repeated praise of the faithfulness of the Ukrainian Catholic Church highlighted profound differences between the Roman Catholic view of jurisdiction and the Orthodox belief that all Christians in one place ought to be canonically united under a single bishop. The perception that the pope invoked repentance as a way of pushing the past aside without an honest engagement with the issues as the Orthodox defined them may have exacerbated the conflict.[46]

Over the centuries, strong views on church discipline and the relation between the church and the world have led to numerous divisions among the Mennonite churches. One modest attempt to use language of apology to heal a rift occurred in 1960 between two branches of the tradition that split in the nineteenth century over how to respond to the pietist revival. The General Conference Mennonite Church apologized for the negative feelings, words and actions of previous generations that were directed against the Mennonite Brethren church, the tradition that had embraced pietism. Yet, the statement acknowledged no responsibility for the fact of the split, and pleaded ignorance of its causes.[47] The Mennonite Brethren response asked forgiveness for times when it had not acted with respect, but implicitly affirmed the value of separate denominations.[48]

In contrast to this tentative exchange that refrained from engaging with historical particularity, an act of repentance and forgiveness for a very specific past occurred between the Canadian branches of these North American denominations. At the annual assembly of the Conference of Mennonites in Canada (CMC), the General Conference body, three leaders of the Mennonite Brethren conference expressed regret and asked forgiveness on behalf of their church for the actions of some Mennonite Brethren pastors who

[44] Pope John Paul II, Address to His Beatitude Christodoulos, Archbishop of Athens and Primate of Greece, 4 May 2001.

[45] Pope John Paul II, Address at the arrival in Kiev, 23 June 2001.

[46] Andrew Walsh, 'The Pope Among the Orthodox', *Religion in the News* 4, no. 2 (Summer 2001), 12–13.

[47] General Conference Mennonite Church, 'Centennial Study Conference Statement to Mennonite Brethren' (1960).

[48] General Conference of the Mennonite Brethren Church, Response to Greeting and Statement of Regret from the General Conference Mennonite Church (1960).

excommunicated their members who married members of a General Conference church. The statement notes that this was not a practice specifically authorized and was not widespread, but it did nonetheless occur.[49] The confession by the Mennonite Brethren seems to have been a surprise; most had been expecting routine fraternal greetings. The chairperson immediately accepted the apology on behalf of the CMC. Did he speak strictly for the church as a whole, or also in the name of those affected by the policy? While a hymn was being sung immediately following, a CMC minister 'came up and rather spontaneously embraced each person, a demonstration of love and forgiveness'.[50] The meaningfulness of the repentance was enhanced by the personal relationships of those involved. One of the Mennonite Brethren leaders who made the statement had personally excommunicated members for such inter-marriage. For many, the significance of this action resides in the concreteness of the history acknowledged as wrong and in the fact that the offence confessed was within living memory.[51]

Mennonites and others who trace their origin to the sixteenth-century Anabaptist movement have also been the subject of requests for forgiveness from those of other confessions. In 2002, Mennonites requested that a memorial plaque be placed in Zurich to commemorate the execution by drowning of the Anabaptist Felix Manz in 1525. Manz was executed under the authority of the Zurich town council, which had taken responsibility for instituting Zwinglian reforms. As a result of this request, the Evangelical–Reformed Church of Zurich reflected on their own past and invited representatives of Mennonite, Amish and Hutterite churches to a service of reconciliation in 2004. They confessed that, according to their present understanding, their forbears' persecution of Anabaptists was contrary to the gospel. They declared the condemnations against the Anabaptists no longer valid.

In response, the Swiss Mennonite Conference extended the requested forgiveness, and confessed that their tradition has also betrayed the gospel through withdrawal, conformism and pride. Both sides offered significant reflections about how the church's wrestling with its past might bear fruit in the present. The Reformed Church

---

[49] Canadian Conference of Mennonite Brethren Churches, Greetings to the Conference of Mennonites in Canada, 5 July 1986.

[50] *CMC Yearbook* (Winnipeg: Conference of Mennonites in Canada, 1986), 81.

[51] The CMC drafted a short written response, extending the requested forgiveness and acknowledging its own role in mutual misunderstandings, *Yearbook of the Canadian Conference of Mennonite Brethren Churches* (Winnipeg, 1986), 68.

confessed that despite having forgotten their role in the persecution of Anabaptists, they pledged to 'accept the history of the Anabaptist movement as part of our own . . . and to strengthen our mutual testimony through dialogue'.[52] Though the Mennonites noted their own embarrassment at being asked for forgiveness, since they no longer feel like victims, they stated that 'the fact that you recognize the difficult points of your history in relation to ours helps us to see ourselves and to meet you differently'. The end of confessional polemics does not lead to a lowest common denominator ecumenism, however. The Swiss Mennonites promised to commend their convictions about ecclesiology and ethics to the wider church. Renewed fellowship with the Reformed Church provides the condition in which such convictions might be truly presented as discernment *within* the body of Christ.[53]

The response to this event from the Old Order Amish churches is intriguing. They declined to participate as 'world travel is not in accordance with our culture'. They stated that they feel no hostility towards the Reformed churches, or to any other churches for that matter. 'We believe the descendants of the Reformed churches are not accountable for any actions their forefathers took against the Anabaptists. Far be it from us to request reconciliation.' And while they affirmed the existence of separate denominations ('the earth is a better place to live because of the various Christian churches and their principles'), they noted that the Amish churches were made stronger because of persecution. The blood of the martyrs is the seed of the church.[54]

Occasioned by its dialogue with Mennonite Church USA, the Evangelical Lutheran Church in America (ELCA) declared in 2006 that the condemnations of the Anabaptists in the *Augsburg Confession* did not apply today, nor did many of them apply to those who were the spiritual forbears of contemporary Mennonites. (However, the ELCA noted that the status of condemnations regarding baptismal practice and participation in the police power of the State are still outstanding questions.) They declared regret for the persecution they caused and repudiated the theological justification of such violence.[55] The LWF

---

[52] Evangelical–Reformed Church of Zurich, 'Statement of Regret' (2004).

[53] Swiss Mennonite Conference, Response (2004).

[54] Michael Baumann, ed., *Steps to Reconciliation: Reformed and Anabaptist Churches in Dialogue* (Zürich: Theologischer Verlag Zürich, 2007), 96–7.

[55] Evangelical Lutheran Church in America, 'Declaration on the Condemnation of Anabaptists' (2006). A letter of response from Mennonite Church USA received

Council authorized a statement (to be proposed to the LWF Assembly in 2010) that asked forgiveness for the persecution of Anabaptists and pledged 'to interpret the Lutheran Confessions in light of the jointly described history between Lutherans and Anabaptists'.[56] At a celebration in Schwarzenau, Germany, of the 300th anniversary of the Brethren movement, which identifies with both Anabaptism and Pietism, Ingo Stucke spoke for the Protestant Church of Westphalia to express regret for past persecutions and to ask the Brethren forgiveness. Stucke invited dialogue about whether the condemnations made against the Brethren, such as the one regarding the rejection of infant baptism, still apply today.[57]

The recent spate of asking forgiveness of the descendants of the Anabaptists is undoubtedly linked to the fact that they were persecuted and often executed. Given that contemporary sensibilities are scandalized less by divisions among Christians than the idea of killing others for their religious beliefs, these reconciling initiatives may be less about ecumenism than intolerance. Does attention to the sin of killing turn attention from the hard questions of divergent faith and practice? Does forgiveness offered and granted create a false sense that what is (or was) church-dividing has now been fully addressed?

Revisiting Reformation-era condemnations, which some present-day Reformed and Lutheran ministers are required to affirm, exemplifies the complexities of wrestling with church history. The basic formula by which the Zurich Reformed Church judged that past condemnations of Anabaptists no longer apply to *present* Mennonite churches was also used by the Presbyterian Church in Canada with respect to denunciations of the pope as the Antichrist[58] and most prominently applied to the mutual condemnations by the Catholic–Lutheran 'Joint Declaration on the Doctrine of Justification'. The formula refrains from a definitive judgement on the past, and thus whether the condemnations were warranted at the time. In this

---

the 'apology' (the word was not used in the Lutheran statement) with gratitude and forgiveness, and acknowledged 'errors of understanding, practice and attitude' on the Mennonite side, www.interchurchrelations.org/ELCAletter.pdf.

[56] Lutheran World Federation Council, Statement on Lutheran–Anabaptist Relationships, October 2009.

[57] Ingo Stucke, Greetings on behalf of the Protestant Church of Westphalia, 3 August 2008. This church is a member of the EKD.

[58] See Peter G. Bush, 'The Presbyterian Church in Canada and the Pope: One Denomination's Struggle with Its Confessional History', *Studies in Religion/Sciences Religieuses* 33 (2004), 105–15.

sense, it retains the possibility that there was a clash of incompatible positions; it does not chalk up divisions to strictly non-theological factors. However, it affirms that the present is where a new theological judgement is possible. The Reformed Church can now recognize true faith in the Anabaptist churches and as a result the present church adjusts its relationship with its own past confessions. The LWF's commitment to interpret past condemnations through the lens of a joint history provides the possibility that the condemnations need not be church-dividing. The basic orientation of the 2006 ELCA statement is similar with the added dimension of some historical evaluation of the context of the original condemnations. That dialogue used the framework of 'right remembering' as a mandate to pursue an accurate reading of the historical sources, to view history from the perspective of the other, and to do so for the sake of Christian discipleship. In light of either rhetorical excess or misinterpreting Anabaptist convictions, the ELCA thus judged that many of the condemnations ought not to have been applied in the first place. It also granted that some condemnations may accurately reflect the beliefs of Mennonites, in which case dialogue can determine whether they remain church-dividing. The Lutheran statements at both US and world levels therefore bear the tensions of both asking forgiveness for past enmity, while continuing to require Lutheran ministries to assent to confessional statements that condemn what may turn out to be beliefs that Mennonites hold.[59]

Repentance has continued as a theme in multilateral ecumenical contexts.[60] As stated in a 1980 Faith and Order paper:

> In our present divided state, in fact, visible unity cannot be restored unless, turning towards Christ, each Church takes the decision to repent in so far as it is a community of sinful Christians. Its repentance will be genuine only to the extent to which it implies a resolve to do what the complete reestablishment of communion demands of it: conversion through a constant return to the source which is Christ, a persevering effort of purification, a desire of authentic change. Such repentance will be truly constructive of unity only if it leads it to offer to others its own characteristic goods and to receive from others what it lacks itself. Now, at the heart of such repentance is the need to reach agreement

---

[59] See Jonathan Seiling, Letter to the editor, *Canadian Mennonite*, 8 March 2010, 10–11.

[60] Recently in the WCC's Canberra Statement: 'The Unity of the Church: Gift and Calling', *Signs of the Spirit: Official Report, Seventh Assembly*, ed. Micheal Kinnamon (Geneva: WCC, 1991), 172–4.

on a common profession of faith which, after centuries of mutual exclusion, will permit the churches to recognize each other as true brothers . . .[61]

Even as the shape and goals of ecumenism have changed throughout the past century, the theme of repentance points to the hope that churches will find their unity in radical *metanoia*, or turning, to Jesus Christ. Repentance is thus not merely an instrument for unity, but already an expression of unity in Christ. From both historical and theological perspectives, ecclesial repentance has its centre in repentance for the disunity of the church. Yet, there have been many more dialogues which have not been marked by statements of repentance than those that have. The WCC's current project on ecclesiology, *The Nature and Mission of the Church*, does not mention repentance.[62] Even the history I have recounted shows more calls for ecumenical repentance than instances of churches actually repenting. Is repentance implicit? Is any movement towards unity effectively penitential? Or has a loss of energy for the Faith and Order agenda of ecumenism[63] signified a decline in the sense of scandal and sin in the divisions among Christians?

OFFENCES AGAINST THE JEWISH PEOPLE

Repentance for offences in relation to the Jewish people and Judaism has followed a trajectory in the twentieth century. The horrors of the Holocaust[64] led many churches to examine their silence or complicity in Hitler's 'Final Solution', and also the anti-Judaism and anti-Semitism that was the context for such a programme. The amends that followed repentance frequently consisted of a reconsideration of anti-Jewish elements in Christian theology, particularly superses-sionism. Significant anniversaries of events such as *Kristallnacht* or the liberation of Auschwitz occasioned a series of statements in the

---

[61] Faith and Order Commission, 'Towards a Confession of the Common Faith, 1980', Faith and Order Paper no. 100 in *Documentary History of Faith and Order, 1963–1993*, ed. Günter Gassmann (Geneva: WCC Publications, 1993), 171.

[62] World Council of Churches, *The Nature and Mission of the Church: A Stage on the Way to a Common Statement*, revised Faith and Order Paper no. 198 (Geneva: WCC, 2005).

[63] As lamented in Carl E. Braaten and Robert W. Jenson, eds., *In One Body Through the Cross: The Princeton Proposal for Christian Unity* (Grand Rapids: Eerdmans, 2003).

[64] There is no settled consensus of how to best refer to the attempted extermination of the Jewish people by the German Third Reich. Common terms include Holocaust, which means 'burnt offering', and Shoah, which means 'disaster'. Repentance texts use both, a practice I will follow throughout this book.

1990s that reconsidered history itself, but with a deliberate intention to nurture Christian dialogue and relationship with Jews. Repentance is closely related to this experience of dialogue, in some cases preceding it and in others emerging from it. The documents in this section are particularly complex because many of them outline what a non-supersessionist theology might entail. They discuss biblical interpretation, guidelines for dialogue, the history of the Holocaust, and/or contemporary Israeli–Palestinian issues. My attention zeros in on beliefs and actions confessed as a wrong, and thus only touches on the manifold themes in the documents. To clarify terms, supersessionism is the belief that the church has replaced Israel in God's plan of salvation and thus that God's covenant with the Jews has ended. Anti-Judaism is the theologically argued marginalization of the Jewish religion, especially supersessionist arguments, attitudes and actions; anti-Semitism refers to racially based prejudice and hatred of Jews.

Six million Jewish people were killed by the German authorities in several European countries during World War II, together with Poles, Russians, Roma, communists, homosexuals, the mentally and physically handicapped, and others deemed incompatible with the 'new humanity' of the Third Reich. After the war, churches in Germany and others under German occupation were forced to reflect on their action and inaction during the war. The earliest statements (for example, two from the Evangelical Church in Germany, the 1945 Stuttgart Declaration of Guilt and the 1947 Darmstadt Statement; and the 1945 German Catholic Bishops Fulda Pastoral Letter) did not mention Jews or the Holocaust. As primarily concerned with their churches' support for the German government and the war in general, they will be examined in Chapter 3. However, in 1946 the Reformed Church in Hungary did say something. They passed a resolution instructing all congregations to hold penitential services for their failure to warn about a path that 'went against God's laws' and for their failure to defend the innocent. 'Under the responsibility resting on us because of the sins committed against the Jews, however late, we now ask the Hungarian Jews before God to forgive us.'[65]

The landmark 1947 document issued by the International Council of Christians and Jews[66] at Seelisberg, Switzerland, was the first

---

[65] Reformed Church in Hungary, 'Declaration on the Persecution of the Jews and the Mission to the Jews' (1946).

[66] This group consisted of its members. They did not have official sanction from religious bodies.

to suggest that Christian theology would be different after the Holocaust, especially with respect to how it spoke about 'the Jews.' The statement acknowledged that Christianity had failed to be vigilant against anti-Semitism, and that anti-Semitism led to the deaths of millions. Its 'Ten Points' exhorted Christians to remember the Jewishness of Jesus and the early church, and urged them to refrain from teaching that Jews are responsible for Jesus' death and thus cursed, or to misrepresent Jews as the enemies of Jesus.[67]

The First Assembly of the WCC called for penitence in light of the enormity of the Holocaust and the failure of Christians to fight anti-Semitism. It also acknowledged that church teaching about Jews as the enemies of Jesus contributed to secular anti-Semitism. Yet, in spite of recognizing Israel's 'unique position' in God's plan, the report calls for the continued evangelization of Jews.[68] The Second Assembly did not speak on this matter, though a minority group issued a statement which argued that the guilt for what Christians have done against the Jewish people ought to compel the church to continually seek the highest calling for them, which is conversion to the confession of Christ.[69] The Third Assembly did not mention guilt or confession, but condemned anti-Semitism as a sin.[70] These WCC statements exemplified the attitudes of many European and American churches. Jews were individuals whose rights and dignity, as individuals, had been unjustly violated. As individuals who were not Christian, they were proper subjects for conversion. These churches were not yet considering the *theological* significance of the Jewish people, nor God's continuing covenant with them.[71]

The terms of the debate within the Evangelical Church in Germany (*Evangeliche Kirche in Deutschland* [EKD]) about the church's relationship to Jews, past and present, are evident in the contrast between statements made in 1948 and 1950. In 1948, the Council

---

[67] International Council of Christians and Jews, 'The Ten Points of Seelisberg' (1947).

[68] World Council of Churches, 'The Christian Approach to the Jews', First Assembly (1948).

[69] World Council of Churches, *The Evanston Report: The Second Assembly of the World Council of Churches, 1954* (London: SCM Press, 1955), 327–28.

[70] W. A. Visser't Hooft, ed., *The New Delhi Report: The Third Assembly of the World Council of Churches 1961* (London: SCM Press, 1961), 48.

[71] Allan Brockway, 'Assemblies of the World Council of Churches', in *The Theology of the Churches and the Jewish People: Statements by the World Council of Churches and Its Member Churches* (Geneva: WCC Publications, 1988), 125.

of Brethren of the EKD issued a 'Message Concerning the Jewish Question' that confessed 'with shame and grief' that the church forgot about God's continued patience towards Israel and adopted the secular perspective of anti-Semitism. The statement rejected anti-Semitism, and warned that resentment toward the victorious allies might lead to its reemergence. But it affirmed a theological anti-Judaism. The church declared it should *not* teach that Jesus was a Jew or, indeed, a member of any nation or race. According to the statement, this meant that all humanity, not *just* Jews, are responsible for the death of Christ. Since Israel rejected its election, the church asserted that its efforts to convert Jews must continue.[72]

Increasing recognition of the scale of the Holocaust and the founding of the State of Israel stimulated further development of a theology of Judaism. The Berlin–Weissensee Statement, issued in 1950 by a synod much broader in representation than the council that spoke in 1948, not only denounced anti-Semitism but also rejected supersessionism, albeit with a caveat about a final Day of Fulfilment on which Jews would confess Jesus. It stated: 'We believe that God's covenant with his chosen people Israel also remains in effect after the crucifixion of Jesus Christ.' The synod confessed that the neglect of such a belief contributed to the 'crimes committed against the Jews by members of our people'. Finally, it called for a concrete action – the protection of Jewish cemeteries.[73] The statement reflects an emerging ambivalence about evangelizing Jews. It recognizes that history bears on what may or may not be affirmed theologically. The church remained silent, however, on the question of whether Jews were subject to God's judgement for rejecting Jesus as Messiah.[74]

Immediately after the war, the Catholic Church in Germany sought to comfort a defeated people. In the Fulda Pastoral Letter of 1945, the bishops presented the church primarily as a victim of the Nazis, praised individuals who opposed their crimes, and expressed gratitude for the loyalty of Catholics to their church. The bishops resisted pressure from occupying authorities to include some statement on collective guilt.[75] In the 1950s, a tone of triumphalism emerged

---

[72] Evangelical Church in Germany, 'Message Concerning the Jewish Question', (1948).

[73] Evangelical Church in Germany, Berlin–Weissensee Statement (1950).

[74] Matthew D. Hockenos, *A Church Divided: German Protestants Confront the Nazi Past* (Bloomington, IN: Indiana University Press, 2004), 168–9.

[75] Frank M. Buscher and Michael Phayer, 'German Catholic Bishops and the Holocaust, 1940–1953', *German Studies Review* 11 (1988), 472–3.

in the church which opposed reparations efforts and nurtured its connection with West German political leadership.[76] Little was said about Jews in official documents, save an acknowledgment in *Mainz Katholikentag* (1948) of German Catholic 'crimes against people of Jewish stock', and, in the shadow of the Adolf Eichmann trial, a 1961 instruction from the bishops that all churches pray for 'the murdered Jews and their persecutors'.[77] Only with the death of Pope Pius XII, the retirement or death of many of the bishops active during the war, the experience of dialogue with Jewish people, and the reorientation to Judaism articulated by Vatican II did official discourse broach the subject of what the church did or did not say and do during the Holocaust.

The Second Vatican Council marked an important development in Catholic thinking and acting towards Jews. In the conciliar debate, Bishop Léon-Arthur Elchinger of Strasbourg proposed incorporating a request for forgiveness for the many past injustices committed by Christians towards Jews, echoing a similar confession of offences against non-Catholic Christians.[78] Though this course of action was not taken, several significant affirmations were made in *Nostra Aetate: Declaration on the Relationship of the Church to Non-Christian Religions*.[79] The declaration is framed by the conviction that since God is the creator of all people and the source of all truth, the church is called to dialogue with other religions. Judaism is then distinguished from other world religions because of its intrinsic link with Christianity. The text affirms that though many Jews did not and do not recognize Jesus as Messiah, God 'does not repent of the gifts He makes nor of the calls He issues' (cf. Rom. 11.28–9). Drawing an implication from this repudiation of supersessionism, the declaration states that Jews 'should not be presented as repudiated or cursed by God'. Though some Jews did call for Jesus' death, there is no collective guilt for this crime. Anti-Semitism 'from any source' is deplored, though not

---

[76] Michael Phayer, 'The German Catholic Church After the Holocaust', *Holocaust and Genocide Studies* 10 (1996), 155–61.

[77] Cited in James Bernauer, 'The Holocaust and the Catholic Church's Search for Forgiveness', paper presented at Boisi Centre for Religion and American Public Life, Boston College (2002), www.bc.edu/research/cjl/meta-elements/texts/cjrelations/resources/articles/bernauer.htm.

[78] Richard Neudecker, 'The Catholic Church and the Jewish People', in *Vatican II: Assessment and Perspectives*, vol. 3, ed. René Latourelle (New York: Paulist Press, 1989), 288.

[79] Second Vatican Council, *Nostra Aetate* (1965), no. 3.

specifically named as a sin. While encouraging dialogue with Jews, *Nostra Aetate* counsels forgetting of the past as the way to mutual understanding, a position that would be dramatically reversed in later Vatican documents, most notably in *We Remember: Reflections on the Shoah*.

The first major declaration by the Catholic Bishops in West Germany occurred in 1975. They confessed that the church had largely ignored the plight of Jews, concentrating instead on its own fate. Christians persecuted Jews, though in some cases they did so out of fear for their own lives. The bishops emphasized that a 'new start' in relations with the Jewish people depended on making such a confession, learning from the guilt of the church and being vigilant against racism. The lesson of this history, they concluded, must be a redoubled commitment to the non-supersessionist tenor of *Nostra Aetate*:

> We Germans in particular are not permitted to deny or play down the connection between the salvation of God's people of the old and new covenants . . . [T]he credibility of our talk about the 'God of hope' rests upon the fact that there were countless people, Jews and Christians, who repeatedly named and called upon this God, even in such a hell.[80]

Though such a proposal could be criticized for implying that non-Germans might be permitted to deny the validity of the covenant with the Jewish people, it reflect an awareness that one's own history may illuminate the untenability of certain beliefs. The declaration ends by affirming that this history ought to become instructive for the entire Catholic Church.

The West German Bishops' next statement, in 1980, asked forgiveness both of God and of the Jewish people for the involvement of Catholics in the crimes of the Nazis. The bishops noted that the necessary establishment of relationships with Jewish communities and a renewed theology of Judaism, the concern of the overwhelming majority of the document, do not in themselves atone for the past. Only Christ's forgiveness atones. There are essentially two parallel tracks in the document – a confession of the guilt of some Christians for the Holocaust, and a recovery and elaboration of the common roots in both Christianity and Judaism.[81] The document issued by the German Bishops together with their Austrian counterparts in

---

[80] West German Catholic Bishops, 'A Change of Attitude Towards the Jewish People's History of Faith' (1975).

[81] West German Catholic Bishops, 'The Church and the Jews' (1980).

1988 begins to bring these two tracks together. Issued on the 50th anniversary of *Kristallnacht*, it not only acknowledges the silence of the church during the Holocaust and active complicity of individual Christians, but also considers some theological and institutional factors that may have contributed to this. It acknowledges that conversion and reconciliation are ultimately God's work, but the church is nevertheless required to learn from its history of both faithfulness and failures. 'For history is not something exterior, it is part of the particular identity of the Church and is able to remind us that the Church, which we proclaim as holy, and which we honour as a mystery, is also a sinful Church and in need of conversion [*eine sündige und der Umkehr bedürftige Kirche ist*].'[82]

On the Protestant side, the Lutheran World Federation initiated a number of studies broadly addressing questions of biblical interpretation, the meaning of Luther's writing on the Jews and missionary activity. The Løgumkloster Report (1964) and the Oslo Report (1975) are generally oriented by a replacement theology, whereas the Neuendettelsau Report (1973) and the 'Luther, Lutheranism, and the Jews' statement (1983), which emerged from a joint consultation with Jewish theologians, emphasize the continuing validity of the Jewish covenant, though all documents show traces of the tension between these positions. Three of these documents included statements of confession. The 1983 document deplored the 'sins of Luther's anti-Jewish remarks', which did lead, with other factors, to the 'failures which have been regretted and repeatedly confessed since 1945'.[83] The Løgumkloster Report confessed the guilt of Lutherans for anti-Semitism, and asked pardon of God and the Jewish people.[84] One German pastor warned that while he deplored Luther's writings on the Jews, any public denunciation of Luther's anti-Semitism would play in to the hands of the 'secular forces which are seeking to destroy the church' by linking Luther with Hitler.[85] The Oslo Report added a global dimension to repentance for anti-Semitism

---

[82] Catholic Bishops of West Germany, Austria and Berlin, 'Accepting the Burden of History' (1988).

[83] Lutheran World Federation and International Jewish Committee on Interreligious Consultations, 'Luther, Lutheranism, and the Jews', (1983).

[84] Lutheran World Federation, 'The Church and the Jewish People', [Løgumkloster Report] (1964).

[85] Harold H. Ditmanson, introduction to the Løgumkloster Report, in *Stepping-Stones to Further Jewish–Lutheran Relationships*, ed. Harold H. Ditmanson (Minneapolis: Augsburg Fortress, 1990), 21.

(which it linked to concrete action for peace, justice, and reconciliation). It acknowledged that Lutheran churches in Asia and Africa, for example, do not have the same history or responsibility regarding anti-Semitism, though these churches are encouraged to discern anti-Semitism in their own history and practice.[86] This distinction is rare in statements of ecclesial repentance, though deeply congruent with the logic of acknowledging a particular history. In so doing, the Oslo Report implicitly recognized a danger in the well-intentioned confessions of broad or global church communities – namely, that the sin of some churches is universalized and imputed to other churches whose agency is thereby silenced. At the same time, this caveat raises the question of whether and how a global church bears the burdens of its varied past. Might the spirit of communion among churches imply that African Lutheran and German Lutheran churches *together* bear the burdens of *both* European anti-Semitism and whatever the African church may discern as its own particular forms of sin, though in differentiated ways?

The American Lutheran Church, however, did choose to own some responsibility for the attempted destruction of European Jewry, given the Lutheran context in which Nazism flourished. Their 1974 statement also recognized that Judaism cannot be engaged as a 'denomination' since 'Jewishness is both a religious phenomenon and a cultural phenomenon which is exceedingly hard to define'. They also navigated a course between mission and dialogue with Jews, rejecting a simple exclusivity between them. They affirmed that while conversion is not the purpose of Jewish–Christian dialogue, this does not rule out mission more generally.[87] By contrast, the Lutheran Church–Missouri Synod was very clear about the permanent mandate to convert Jews who, like Gentiles, are sinners before God. While their 1977 resolution repents of anti-Semitism more generally, it declares that 'bypassing the Jewish people in missions and evangelism is one of the worst forms of . . . [anti-Semitism]'.[88] While repentance for most churches has marked some step in the journey away from supersessionism, and by extension from explicit evangelization, the

---

[86] Lutheran World Federation, 'The Oneness of God and the Uniqueness of Christ', [Oslo Report] (1975).

[87] American Lutheran Church, 'The American Lutheran Church and the Jewish Community' 1974).

[88] Lutheran Church–Missouri Synod, 'To Share Gospel with Jews' (1977).

Lutheran Church–Missouri Synod repented precisely of the temptation to move in that direction.

In the late 1970s, 80s and 90s, a series of statements by Protestant churches in Germany (and one in Hungary) named their replacement theologies a contributing cause of the Holocaust, and articulated varying degrees of non-supersessionist convictions.[89] The EKD confessed that only God can forgive its guilt for having remained largely silent regarding the plight of Jews. New life for the church is possible only in light of new beliefs with respect to Judaism.[90] The Evangelical Church of the Rhineland (1980) drew a direct line from its denial of the permanent election of the Jews to the attempt to eliminate them physically. It stated that repentance and conversion is the way to recognize the common witness of Christians and Jews.[91] The Reformed Church in Hungary built on its 1946 confession in a 1990 statement. Concerned by the reemergence of anti-Semitism, it asserted that its dialogue with Jews must be marked by 'responsibility and repentance'.[92] The Evangelical Church of Bavaria (1998) did not use the word 'repent' but rather declared that it 'knows itself to be co-responsible for anti-Jewish thoughts and actions that made possible or at least tolerated the crimes of the "Third Reich".' It identified the need for further work to be done on the anti-Jewish theology of Luther and Lutheranism, and committed itself to resisting intolerance within the church and beyond.[93] The Evangelical Church in Austria very clearly confessed a share of the guilt for the Holocaust. It said the 'anti-Jewish excesses' in its history demand a conversion in the church's interpretation of scripture and a rejection of mission to Jews.[94] On the 50th anniversary of its Berlin–Weissensee Declaration that rejected supersessionism, the Evangelical Church in

---

[89] For an overview, see Franklin Sherman, 'The Road to Reconciliation: Protestant Church Statements on Christian–Jewish Relations', in *Seeing Judaism Anew: Christianity's Sacred Obligation*, ed. Mary C. Boys (Lanham, MD: Sheed & Ward, 2005), 241–51. Several statements were made by regional church bodies of the Evangelical Church in Germany, especially marking the 40th, 50th and 60th anniversaries of *Kristallnacht* (1938).

[90] Evangelical Church in Germany, 'Declaration on the 40th Anniversary of the Jewish Pogrom of 9/10 November 1938' (1978).

[91] Evangelical Church of the Rhineland, 'Towards Renovation of the Relationship of Christians and Jews' (1980).

[92] Reformed Church in Hungary, 'Relations with the Jews' (1990).

[93] Evangelical Church in Bavaria, 'Christians and Jews' (1998).

[94] Evangelical Church in Austria (Augsburg and Helvetian Confessions), 'Time to Turn' (1998).

Germany admitted complicity in the Holocaust, and denied equivalency between the suffering of the Germans and that of the Jews. It rejected any notion of 'closing the book' on German history. Rather, it said the church must recognize that it was more than silently complicit but also deployed its theological tradition against Jews. Affirming God's continuing covenant with the Jewish people, the church stated that 'Jews are witnesses to us of God's faithfulness'.[95]

Mainline Protestant churches in North America initially issued guidelines for Jewish dialogue, which often included clarifications on theological and exegetical issues, and only subsequently made explicit statements of repentance. For example, the Episcopal Church rejected the charge of deicide against Jews and condemned anti-Semitism (1964), issued a statement on Jewish dialogue that emphasized shared spiritual links (1979) and elaborated further guidelines for dialogue (1988).[96] A brief resolution in 1997 confessed that 'moral blindness' by the church contributed to the mistreatment of Jews.[97] Whereas statements by German churches tended to repent for actions or silence related to the Holocaust, and then moved towards a condemnation of anti-Semitism and rethinking of anti-Judaism in theology, repentance by mainline churches in North America has been directed primarily at church teaching itself.

One of the most substantial of these statements, a 1987 report by the Presbyterian Church (USA), is framed by the agendas of local dialogue, religious pluralism, and conflict in the Middle East. It declared: 'We acknowledge in repentance the church's long and deep complicity in the proliferation of anti-Jewish attitudes and actions through its "teaching of contempt" for the Jews. Such teaching we now repudiate, together with the acts and attitudes it generates.'[98] The explication of this affirmation traces a long history of anti-Judaism, both its alleged root (the charge of being 'Christ-killers') and various consequences (Holy Week persecution of Jews, the ideological environment of the Holocaust). Constructively, it affirms that Christians continually find their identity in relation to the

---

[95] Evangelical Church in Germany, 'Christians and Jews: A Manifesto 50 Years After the Weissensee Declaration' (2000).

[96] The 1988 report, with 1964 and 1979 documents as appendices, is in *The Blue Book* (New York: Episcopal Church, 1988), 449–60.

[97] Episcopal Church, 'Reaffirm Interfaith Dialogue and Acknowledge Prejudice Against Jews' (1997).

[98] Presbyterian Church (USA), 'A Theological Understanding of the Relationship Between Christians and Jews' (1987), no. 5.

Jewish people, and invites further dialogue about the implications of God's covenant with both Christians and Jews.

In 1987, the United Church of Christ asked God's forgiveness and prayed for grace to 'turn from this path of rejection and persecution to affirm that Judaism has not been superseded by Christianity'.[99] It issued a confession of its own anti-Semitism in 2001.[100] The Evangelical Lutheran Church in America's 1994 declaration was formulated partly in response to some publicity around the anti-Semitic rhetoric of some of Luther's writing.[101] The church confessed complicity in the tradition of anti-Judaism and anti-Semitism which are contrary to the gospel.[102] The Alliance of Baptists (1995) confessed the sin of interpreting the Bible in ways that have made enemies of the Jewish people, and of 'indifference and inaction to the horrors of the Holocaust'.[103] In its 'Building New Bridges in Hope' document (1996), the United Methodist Church expressed repentance 'for the complicity of the church and the participation of many Christians in the long history of persecution of the Jewish people', followed by an account of how this history obligates the church to correct theological and historical misunderstandings.[104] Finally, in 2003 the United Church of Canada approved a resolution of repentance for anti-Judaism and anti-Semitism.[105] The accompanying study guide includes extensive discussion on the interpretation of biblical texts that have been frequently read in a supersessionist manner, and workshop outlines for congregational use. Among its appendices is a brief essay on a particular manifestation of supersessionist theology in which Christian feminism contrasts Judaism as the source of the sexism which the gospel overcomes.[106]

On the Catholic side, a series of public statements of repentance related to the Holocaust by national conferences of bishops appeared in the 1990s, in large part occasioned by Pope John Paul II's Jubilee

---

[99] United Church of Christ, 'Relationship Between the United Church of Christ and the Jewish Community' (1987).

[100] United Church of Christ, 'Resolution on Anti-Semitism' (2001).

[101] Sherman, 'Protestant Church Statements', 244.

[102] Evangelical Lutheran Church in America, 'Declaration of the Evangelical Lutheran Church in America to the Jewish Community' (1994).

[103] Alliance of Baptists, 'A Statement on Jewish–Christian Relations' (1995).

[104] United Methodist Church, 'Building New Bridges in Hope', (1996), no. 7.

[105] United Church of Canada, 'Bearing Faithful Witness: Statement on United Church–Jewish Relations Today' (2003).

[106] United Church of Canada, *Bearing Faithful Witness*, study guide (Toronto: Committee on Inter-Church Inter-Faith Relations, 1997), 87–8.

call for an examination of conscience, particular anniversaries, and by an increasing desire to reconcile Catholic–Jewish relationships. They formed a prelude to the Vatican's *We Remember* document, and the controversy it generated.

Each document reflected something of its nation's particular involvement in war. The Hungarian Bishops denounced the Holocaust as an 'unpardonable sin', and then asked God for forgiveness for those 'supposed Christians' who, 'through fear, cowardice, or opportunism, failed to raise their voices against the mass humiliation, deportation, and murder of their Jewish neighbours'.[107] The US Bishops celebrated the involvement of Americans in the fight against Hitler, but also expressed regret, though not repentance, at what was not done. However, the particular regrets – that the US did not bomb the rail lines to Auschwitz or that the refugee ship *The St Louis* was turned back – were failings of the government, not of the church or Christians per se. The bishops pledged a 'spirit of remembering' that must accompany the resolve to not let this happen again.[108] A statement by the Swiss Bishops wrestled with the role of Switzerland during the war, and the way in which centuries of anti-Jewish Christian teaching and practice contributed to the anti-Semitism of the period. Notably, the bishops asked forgiveness for the past teachings of the church not only of God, but of the heirs of the victims as well.[109] In their letter to the Jewish community in Italy, the Italian Bishops confessed the role of clergy in perpetuating incorrect anti-Jewish interpretation of scripture. They issued what they called a 'profound and conscientious *teshuvah* [repentance]' for this painful history.[110] The Slovak Bishops expressed regret for many aspects of their country's relationship with Jews. While they noted that the healing of memories requires that they ask forgiveness, it is unclear what they believe this forgiveness is for save the fact of a tragic history.[111]

German and Polish Bishops originally planned a joint statement on the 50th anniversary of the liberation of Auschwitz but issued

---

[107] Hungarian Catholic Bishops, and Ecumenical Council of Churches in Hungary, 'Joint Statement on the Occasion of the Fiftieth Anniversary of the Holocaust' (1994).

[108] National Conference of Catholic Bishops [U.S.], 'Commemorating the Liberation of Auschwitz' (1995).

[109] Swiss Catholic Bishops, 'Confronting the Debate About the Role of Switzerland During the Second World War' (1997).

[110] Italian Catholic Bishops, 'Letter to the Jewish Community of Italy' (1998).

[111] Slovak Catholic Bishops, 'Statement on the Vatican Document *We Remember: A Reflection on the Shoah*' (1998).

separate statements since they were unable to agree on one. Though this reflected an ongoing tension between these churches and nations regarding the war itself, it likely enabled each statement to be more historically specific. What distinguishes ecclesial repentance for historical wrongs from a general confession of human sinfulness is this engagement with actual history, from which follows resolution to mend particular relationships. The German text consists of a narrative account of Auschwitz as a symbol for the Holocaust, Jewish suffering, the complicity of Christians, and the heroic efforts of some to resist and oppose. The statement discusses the element of personal responsibility – the criminal involvement of 'not a few Catholics' – but it also recognizes an ecclesial dimension of guilt, part of which consists in the conditions that led to the Holocaust. Though the word 'repent' is not used, the statement is identified as a confession of guilt and a 'request [to] the Jewish people to hear this word of conversion and will of renewal'.[112] The Polish statement is clearly framed by the fact that Poland was under German occupation, a fact that elicits regret for the complicity of some Polish Christians in this, though not repentance. It notes that Auschwitz was set up on occupied Polish territory and held many Poles who were, like Jews, victims of German oppression. It concludes with a call to resist racism and anti-Semitism.[113]

Of all the statements by conferences of bishops, the one from France in 1997 was the most dramatic and the most significant. Henri Hajdenberg, the president of the Representative Council of Jewish Institutions, who participated in the service, said, 'Your request for forgiveness is so intense, so powerful, so poignant that it can't but be heard by the surviving victims and their children.'[114] Such a powerful effect is partly due to a simmering concern for repentance in the French Catholic Church. Calls for a penitent reflection on this past had been made by French bishops, including Bishop Elchinger's Vatican II intervention, Cardinal Roger Etchegaray's appeal at the Synod of Bishops on Reconciliation (1983) for a 'mission of penitence in relation to the Jews',[115] and the persistent advocacy of Cardinal

---

[112] German Catholic Bishops, 'Opportunity to Re-Examine Relationship with the Jews' (1995).

[113] Polish Catholic Bishops, 'The Victims of Nazi Ideology' (1995).

[114] Kevin Madigan, 'A Survey of Jewish Reaction to the Vatican Statement on the Holocaust', *CrossCurrents* 50 (2000–2001), 419.

[115] Helga Croner, comp. and ed., *More Stepping Stones to Jewish–Christian Relations* (Mahwah, NJ: Paulist Press, 1985), 62.

Jean-Marie Lustiger, a convert who was born Jewish and retained this double identity. At Auschwitz in 1986, the secretary of the Episcopal Committee for Jewish relations confessed the failures of Christians in light of Nazi crimes against Jews. Two years later, this committee convened a conference of theologians which considered, among other things, the kind of words that the church ought to speak to the Jewish people.[116]

The symbolic elements of the 'Declaration of Repentance' were carefully considered. The date, 30 September 1997, was selected to follow upon papal repentance for another element of French Catholic history (in August the pope spoke about the St Bartholomew's Day massacre of 1572), and to mark anniversaries of the Seelisberg Conference and the Vichy regime's statutes against Jews.[117] Though the declaration was on behalf of the French Bishops, those whose dioceses included internment camps were asked to reflect especially on the meaning of these camps in light of the church's mission.[118] The statement itself, often referred to as the Drancy Declaration, was delivered at the Drancy train station outside Paris, from which thousands of Jews were deported. Thus, careful attention was given to the many ways public repentance communicates, from the symbolisms of a public declaration to how its rootedness in time and place communicate that *this past*, not just general human failure and sin, is being addressed.

As with other similar statements, the judgement on the past is not entirely negative. There were Catholics who 'saved the honour of the church' by speaking out and by joining resistance movements. Yet, they were few, and ultimately 'indifference won the day'. On the one hand, the declaration echoes the traditional distinction between the sinful members and the holy church, which asks forgiveness on their behalf. Yet, this official view is immediately nuanced and a dimension of ecclesial sin is recognized. According to the text, anti-Jewish prejudices affected the theology, apologetics, preaching and liturgy of the church, leading to the church's failure to properly form the consciences of its members. Though the present church cannot judge the individual consciences of members, as the bishops noted, judgement is most properly made for the 'failing of the church of

---

[116] Thérèse Hebbelinck, 'Le 30 septembre 1997: L'église de France demande pardon aux juifs', *Revue d'histoire ecclésiastique* 103 (2008), 122–5.

[117] *Ibid.*, 129–30.

[118] *Ibid.*, 127.

France and of her responsibility toward the Jewish people'. They concluded: 'We confess this sin. We beg God's pardon, and we call upon the Jewish people to hear our words of repentance. This act of remembering calls us to an ever keener vigilance on behalf of humankind today and in the future.'[119]

The Drancy Declaration was generally well-received. A *New York Times* editorial described it as 'a full and anguished apology', which ought to be a model for a statement by the Vatican.[120] In contrast to widespread disappointment with the Vatican document *We Remember*, issued the following year, the Drancy Declaration was lauded for its ascription of some active guilt to the church, as well as to some members of the clergy.[121]

Controversy arose in the French context of a national debate about how to interpret the Vichy years. Since the bishops who spoke had not been personally involved in the acts and omissions they named, some questioned whether they could indeed repent on behalf of others, just as President Jacques Chirac was questioned for his recognition two years earlier of collective French faults during the war. How could the present generation pass judgement on a situation it did not have to face? While Chirac's distance enabled him to take a more critical view of the past, this distance also enabled him to more clearly speak for the nation without needing to delineate his voice as a mixture of the personal and the collective. Previous leaders had been too personally involved by wartime activities to lead in national repentance.[122] Likewise, the bishops' repentance had significance not because a present generation presumed to speak to the *personal* guilt of dead – indeed, they denied doing so – but because only in the present can the church say anything at all. Only the present church can exercise 'a permanent moral magisterium'.[123] That is, even if extenuating circumstances make the actions of a previous generation seem tragically understandable, the church must nevertheless name and denounce evil as it seeks to form moral consciences in the

---

[119] French Catholic Bishops, 'Declaration of Repentance [Drancy Declaration]', (1997).

[120] 'France's Bishops Apologize', editorial, *New York Times*, 12 October 1997, WK14.

[121] Patrick Henry, 'The French Catholic Church's Apology', *The French Review* 72 (1999), 1104.

[122] See Julie Fette, 'The Apology Moment: Vichy Memories in 1990s France', in *Taking Wrongs Seriously: Apologies and Reconciliation*, ed. Elazar Barkan and Alexander Karn (Stanford, CA: Stanford University Press, 2006), 259–85.

[123] Jean Duchesne, 'Letter from Paris', *First Things*, no. 80 (February 1988), 13.

present and future. Furthermore, church and state both rejected self-defining strategies of avoiding responsibility. Just as Chirac's recognition of collective French responsibility rejected the argument of his predecessors that Vichy was not 'true France', and therefore France had nothing to apologize for, so the bishops resisted defining the church as that which could not be complicit by definition.

In contrast to the Drancy Declaration, the long-anticipated Vatican document, *We Remember: A Reflection on the Shoah*, was widely criticized by Jewish leaders, editorialists and some Catholics.[124] While it rightly distinguishes anti-Semitism from anti-Judaism, it controversially denies any link between them. It claims that the cause of the Shoah was a 'neo-pagan' ideology that issued both in anti-Semitism and contempt for the church.[125] It thus positions the church as a victim and places significant emphasis on the exceptional individuals who saved Jews at great risk and sacrifice. While its claim that the Catholic Church in Germany condemned Nazi racism is true insofar as some individual bishops did so, it does not acknowledge that such denunciations were not made by the German Bishops Conference as a whole.[126] *We Remember* acknowledges only the guilt of some individual Christians, but not the church as such. It does not lament the roles played by top church leaders – the portrayal of the controversial role of Pope Pius XII is entirely positive[127] – nor church teachings. Finally, despite a statement of repentance (for the sins of the church's sons and daughters) and commitment to seek improved relationship with the Jewish people, the text somewhat puzzlingly pleads for an end to 'anti-Christian sentiment among Jews'.[128] Does the church regard Jewish anti-Christian sentiment as equivalent to Christian anti-Judaism in significance or historical effect? Does it seek an act of repentance in return? If so, does not at least the accusation of offence on the other side undermine the church's confession?

---

[124] See Madigan, 'A Survey of Jewish Reaction', and Judith H. Banki and John T. Pawlikowski, eds., *Ethics in the Shadow of the Holocaust: Christian and Jewish Perspectives* (Franklin, WI: Sheed & Ward, 2001).

[125] Commission for Religious Relations with the Jews, *We Remember: A Reflection on the Shoah* (1998), no. 4.

[126] Leon Klenicki, 'Commentary by Rabbi Leon Klenicki', in *The Holocaust, Never to be Forgotten: Reflections on the Holy See's Document* We Remember (New York: Paulist Press, 2001), 32.

[127] On the account of the role of Pope Pius XII, see Randolph L. Braham, 'Remembering and Forgetting: The Vatican, the German Catholic Hierarchy, and the Holocaust,' *Holocaust and Genocide Studies* 13 (1999), 222–51.

[128] *We Remember*, no. 5.

We Remember does develop a theology of history and memory that departs from the pleas to forget the past in *Nostra Aetate*. Because memory is one key to solidarity and identity among generations, it is also the basis for future relations between Christian and Jewish communities. The sins of past Christians must be remembered with repentance since 'we are linked to the sins as well as the merits of all her children'.[129] A common future demands that the church remember the horror of the Shoah, its own complicity in it, together with the church's covenantal connection with Jews.

The claim of *We Remember* that the horror and inhumanity of the Shoah may not be described by ordinary historical research is intended to point to the magnitude of evil. Yet, this claim seems to contradict the call elsewhere in the document that the fact that the Shoah occurred in 'supposedly Christian countries' demands a profound examination of conscience. How can the factors that misshaped consciences, or that led to some Christians becoming complicit despite their consciences, be identified without a close reassessment of the historical record and spiritual context? Does the warning about the limits of historical research function to deflect attention away from the (historically accessible) actions and inactions of church members and other moral agents? As *We Remember* acknowledges, the historical record shows that Christians have mistreated Jews, in part due to attitudes derived from 'erroneous and unjust interpretations of the New Testament' which have been explicitly rejected by Vatican II.[130] If historical research cannot account for the horror of the Shoah, why the certainty that its cause was 'neo-pagan' ideology and that Christian theology did not substantially contribute? The fact that the 'neo-pagan' ideology of the Nazis also denounced Christianity does not itself disprove that theological anti-Judaism may have been one of the many sources from which that ideology drew.

Though some Jewish responses were positive – the chief rabbi of Great Britain called it a 'step forward' – many Jewish commentators concluded it was 'so nebulous, so equivocal, so partial and so euphemistically formulated that it amounted to a lower-order sort of denial'.[131] In fact, the diplomatic caution in the document was reminiscent of precisely the posture during the war for which many believed the Vatican ought to apologize. One Catholic journalist

---

[129] *Ibid.*
[130] *Ibid.*, no. 3.
[131] Madigan, 'A Survey of Jewish Reaction', 494.

commented that it read as if it was written by lawyers 'whose job it was to protect Catholicism from the theological equivalent of civil suits'.[132]

In response to numerous criticisms, Cardinal Edward Cassidy, the president of the Commission for Religious Relations with the Jews, issued a clarification. He stressed the evil of anti-Judaism which 'stamped its mark in differing ways on Christian doctrine and teaching'.[133] While this implies that it was espoused by the church, at least in practice, he reasserted that the cause of the Shoah – racial anti-Semitism – had its roots outside of Christianity, decoupling any causal link between the church's anti-Judaism and the death camps.[134] Cassidy reiterated that since the Holy Spirit saves the church from fundamental error, the church repents strictly for the actions of its sinful children, which nevertheless includes not just laity but priests, bishops and popes.[135] Present members of the church are not responsible for what past members did, according to Cassidy, though repentance is made on the basis of the covenantal link between the merits and sins of the past community with the present. He cited Jewish philosopher David Novak to make his case that in Jewish or Christian communities one is 'existentially' responsible for the sins of others, even if not 'morally' responsible.[136]

Novak's own response to the largely negative Jewish reaction to *We Remember* takes issue with the way in which the mistaken assumption that the document was an 'apology' prevented many Jews from seeing it for what it was intended to be. For Novak, an apology is a non-religious act by which an offender simply tries to get over the past. Apologies are 'cheap'. An apology for the Holocaust is not possible because the victims are not alive to receive it or to forgive in return. Novak argues that Jews ought to agree that a religious tradition must act and change in ways consistent with that tradition, and not acquiesce to secular notions like apology. Thus, tradition-specific repentance (*teshuva*), which will look different when Catholics do it

---

[132] *Ibid.*, 500.

[133] Edward Idris Cassidy, 'The Vatican Document on the Holocaust: Reflections Toward a New Millennium', in *Ethics in the Shadow of the Holocaust: Christian and Jewish Perspectives*, ed. Judith H. Banki and John T. Pawlikowski (Franklin, WI: Sheed & Ward, 2001), 12.

[134] *Ibid.*, 10.

[135] *Ibid.*, 13.

[136] *Ibid.*, 8–9; citing David Novak, 'Jews and Catholics: Beyond Apologies', *First Things*, no. 89 (January 1999), 24.

than when Jews do it, is a highly appropriate ongoing *process* (unlike a singular apology) by which the Catholic Church, in this case, reforms its teaching and practices on the basis of a new assessment of its past and a return to its revealed authority. In this context, he argues that it is fitting for Catholics to make a distinction between a sinless church, a notion that has similarities in Jewish self-understanding, and the ethical responsibilities of individual members.[137]

Of course Jews will receive and interpret Christian acts of repentance or requests for forgiveness in their own religious framework. Collective apology or repentance highlights Jewish discomfort with the Christian assumption that God is able to forgive offences against Jewish people and with the fact that Christians seem assured of such forgiveness. Philosopher Solomon Shimmel argues that in the Jewish tradition, a third party may not forgive on behalf of someone else.[138] Though of course offences against Jews do offend God, and God may forgive that aspect of the offence, there is a remainder for which only the victims may forgive. But those now asking pardon were not the perpetrators, and so they cannot ask forgiveness of those Jews who, since they are dead, cannot offer it. Shimmel argues that the penitent who knows his guilt deeply throws himself utterly on God's mercy without any expectation of forgiveness, a posture he judges lacking in the Catholic Church's gestures towards Jews.[139]

The interpretation of church history in *We Remember* is challenged by Martin Rhonheimer, a Catholic priest. He objects to the way in which enmity between the Catholic Church and the Third Reich is taken as evidence that the church was actively defending Jews and opposing Nazi policies. The often-cited phrase of Pope Pius XI, that 'anti-Semitism is unacceptable . . . [for s]piritually, we are all Semites', does not prove that members of the hierarchy were not anti-Semitic, nor that anti-Semitism lay behind some of their responses. Ecclesial repentance should not be limited to only what individuals did contrary to church teaching, but also to what *functioned* as church teaching. In order to repent of the right thing, Rhonheimer argues the church must make historical and ethical distinctions more carefully. After having done this, repentance ought to be unconditional, sincere,

---

[137] David Noavk, 'Jews and Catholics', 20–5.

[138] This is a key premise in Simon Wiesenthal's classic work on forgiveness for Holocaust crimes, *The Sunflower* (New York: Schocken Books, 1976).

[139] Solomon Shimmel, *Wounds Not Healed by Time: The Power of Repentance and Forgiveness* (Oxford: Oxford University Press, 2002), 210–15.

and complete. If repentance itself is conditional or partial, then it will not only fail to repair relationships with Jewish people, it will lull the church into believing it is not as guilty as it may be.[140]

At the Day of Pardon service in 2000, Pope John Paul II made a confession for 'sins against the people of Israel', which was immediately followed by a 'pilgrimage' to Israel.[141] In perhaps the most dramatic gesture of that trip, the pope prayed quietly and alone at the Western Wall, inserting between its stones the words he had prayed at the Day of Pardon service:

> God of our fathers, you chose Abraham and his descendants to bring your Name to the Nations: we are deeply saddened by the behaviour of those who in the course of history have caused these children of yours to suffer, and asking your forgiveness we wish to commit ourselves to genuine brotherhood with the people of the Covenant. We ask this through Christ our Lord.[142]

Though the request for forgiveness is directed to God, its invocation at such a significant Jewish site suggests that the human audience does matter.

Despite hopes that he would issue a more specific apology for Catholic action and inaction during the Holocaust, the pope did not go further than the *We Remember* document. At the Yad Vashem Shoah memorial, in the presence of the Israeli prime minister and many Jewish leaders, the pope paid homage to the millions of Jews killed in the Shoah and pledged to remember this evil so that it would never be repeated. His 'deep sadness', at the persecution of Jews by Christians throughout history, together with his assertion that the church is opposed to such racism, evoked the disputed position that the church has always stood with Jews against those individual Christians who have harmed them.[143]

Ecclesial repentance for sins against the Jewish people is rooted in themes of memory and history. By the end of the twentieth

---

[140] Martin Rhonheimer, 'The Holocaust: What Was Not Said', *First Things*, no. 137 (November 2003), 18–27.

[141] In connection with the pope's pilgrimage, several individual bishops and episcopal conferences made statements of repentance to the Jewish people. For example, Archbishop Rembert Weakland of Milwaukee linked Catholic preaching about Jews as God-killers with the Holocaust, 'Asking the Jewish Community's Forgiveness', *Origins* 29, no. 54 (25 November 1999), 396–8. See also Polish Catholic Bishops, 'Letter on the Occasion of the Great Jubilee Year 2000' (2000).

[142] Pope John Paul II, Prayer of the Holy Father at the Western Wall, 26 March 2000.

[143] Pope John Paul II, 'The Depths of the Holocaust's Horror', speech at Yad Vashem, *Origins* 29, no. 42 (6 April 2000), 678–79.

century, the pledge to 'never forget' the Holocaust was regularly invoked as an ethical mandate. General consciousness about the horrors of the Shoah led churches to consider more specifically the dimensions of their complicity, including the role played by theological anti-Judaism. In many instances, this re-examination led to a repentance of the doctrine of supersession, a doctrine held and taught by the church for much of its history, and the initial sketches of a non-supersessionist theology.[144] While specific acts of anti-Semitic violence *may* be interpreted as the excessive actions of individuals and small groups acting contrary to church teaching, repentance for church theology presupposes the church as the agent whose sin is being confessed. Besides the challenge that this form of repentance makes to the holiness of the church, the substantive affirmation that God's covenant with the Jewish people is not rescinded also challenges narrow construals of the church's exclusive holiness.

As documented in Christian texts and statements on Judaism, the relationship is being reconfigured through repentance and memory. This memory consists both of a history of Christian persecution of Jews and also a common history of faith. The work of memory thus includes the naming of the sinful dimensions of the past and repenting of them in a way which points to what binds Jews and Christians together. Even the discussion between Christians and Jews over the possibility and conditions of forgiveness, and what each community interprets ecclesial repentance to mean, may be a hopeful sign of a truly *theological* conversation made possible by the people-forming activity of the electing God.

The acts of ecclesial repentance reviewed in this chapter share some important formal and theological similarities. In all cases, a church repents of some aspect of its relationship with a group which is currently external to it, a form made most visible when the statement is an explicit apology or request for forgiveness. It is quite unlike a church that addresses an internal constituency, for example, regarding racism. A Reformed church asks forgiveness from Mennonites; the Catholic Church repents for how it has treated the Jewish people. However, in the moment of repentance, the very structure of the communities involved is called into question. Ecumenically, the hope is for the repair of schism and separation; and a situation in which once divided Christians speak *within* the same

---

[144] For a constructive proposal, see R. Kendall Soulen, *The God of Israel and Christian Theology* (Minneapolis: Fortress Press, 1996), Chapters 5–8.

body. With respect to Jews, repentance moves toward a recognition of the manifold ways that God has initiated a saving relationship with Jews and Christians. The facts on the ground – the repentance of actual churches – challenge not only notions of the church's holiness, but the very boundaries of the penitent community. At the same time, the temporal boundaries of the church are called in to question. What can it mean for churches to ask pardon for acts against fellow Christians 500 or 1,000 years ago, or to repent of supersessionist theology that has held sway for nearly 2,000 years, or the inaction (and worse) during the Holocaust of a previous generation? Clearly, ecclesial repentance presupposes that the present church is linked with the sins of the past. But the practice raises questions not addressed in the statements themselves about the theological nature and implications of this connection to the past.

Chapter 2

WESTERN COLONIALISM AND ITS LEGACY

We failed you. We failed ourselves. We failed God. (Archbishop Michael Peers, Primate of the Anglican Church of Canada)[1]

In 1550, two learned clerics began a formal debate about the human nature of the Aboriginal people of the Americas. This theological disputation, held in Valladolid, Spain, makes plain the ugly face of the Western colonial project. On one side, Fr Juan Ginés de Sepúlveda argued that because of the low religious and intellectual capacity of the 'Indians', it was lawful for the Spaniards to wage war against them and subjugate them, prior to seeking their conversion to Christianity. He asserted that 'in prudence, talent, virtue, and humanity they are as inferior to the Spaniards as children to adults, women to men, as the wild and cruel to the most meek, as the prodigiously intemperate to the continent and temperate, that I have almost said, as monkeys to men'.[2] Their gross violation of natural law revealed them to be natural slaves, essentially less than fully human. Sepúlveda argued that enslavement would indeed be a fitting punishment for their sins.

On the other side, Bishop Bartolomé de Las Casas argued that Aboriginal people did have their own civilization. They were not natural slaves over which Europeans had either the right or the duty to exercise harsh dominion. The judges' agreement with Las Casas that the original people of the Americas were not natural slaves, and that their conversion and integration with the Western church should be sought only by peaceful means, have rendered

---

[1] 'A Message to the National Native Convocation' (1993).

[2] Lewis Hanke, *All Mankind is One: A Study of the Disputation Between Bartolomé de Las Casas and Juan Ginés de Sepúlveda in 1550 on the Intellectual and Religious Capacity of the American Indians* (DeKalb, IL: Northern Illinois University Press, 1974), 84.

him a hero, an early defender of human rights, even a precursor to anti-colonialism.

While Sepúlveda's odious views are a nadir in the church's theological justification of the subjugation of indigenous people in the Americas, and later of African slaves, the record of ecclesial repentance shows that churches are *also* confronting the legacy of Las Casas' position. Certainly churches have wrestled with the fact that slavery has, at various times, been advocated and justified theologically, and that churches have been directly complicit in slaveholding. But the more benevolent attitude which sought the conversion of Aboriginal people and their education in European civilization has left the church struggling with the more subtle ways it has equated Western culture with the gospel. Daniel Castro calls Sepúlveda and Las Casas 'two faces of the same empire'.[3] Not only did Las Casas' debating victory do little to change the practical treatment of indigenous people, but by limiting some naked aggression and conversion by overt violence, Las Casas provided the church (and the crown) with the illusion that their policies towards the Aboriginal people were truly in their spiritual best interest.

This chapter is about repentance for the part played by churches in European exploration, conquest, colonialization and settlement, especially in the Americas, Australia and South Africa, and the continuing legacy of that project. In 1992 Pope John Paul II acknowledged the need for the Catholic Church to make an act of atonement for the sin, injustice and violence done on the American continent and asked forgiveness first of Indians, then of black slaves.[4] Several years later, the Catholic Church in Brazil celebrated a mass of penitence in which it asked God's forgiveness 'for the sins and errors committed by the Roman Catholic clergy against the human rights and dignity of the Indians, the first inhabitants of this land, and the blacks who were brought here as slaves'.[5] Some indigenous groups refused to accept this apology because it was coupled with the defence by a Vatican representative of the overall legacy of the missionaries.[6] Indeed, contested interpretations of European

---

[3] Daniel Castro, *Another Face of Empire: Bartolomé de Las Casas, Indigenous Rights, and Ecclesiastical Imperialism* (Durham, NC: Duke University Press, 2007), 133.

[4] Pope John Paul II, General audience, 21 October 1992.

[5] 'Catholic Church in Brazil Apologizes for Sins Against Indians, Blacks', *National Post*, 27 April 2000, A15.

[6] Brief discussion in Joy Koesten and Robert C. Rowland, 'The Rhetoric of Atonement', *Communication Studies* 55 (2004), 75–6.

colonialism and settlement are central to many statements about this past. In this chapter, I treat separately what these two acts of repentance hold together: the legacy of the transatlantic African slave trade and the oppression of Aboriginal people. (I will primarily use the term 'Aboriginal'. However, if a particular statement uses a different term, such as 'Native', 'First Nations', or 'Indian', as in Indian Residential Schools, my discussion of that statement will follow that usage.) A third section examines the extension of colonialism in South Africa, particularly apartheid.

OFFENCES AGAINST ABORIGINAL PEOPLE

In 1986, Canada's largest Protestant church publicly recognized that it had been another face of empire. The United Church of Canada's (UCC) 'Apology to First Nations' was approved by the General Council and then delivered first by Moderator Robert Smith to a small group of Aboriginal elders gathered in a tepee outside the council meetings, then to the much larger group gathered around a fire in a gravel parking lot. The eight-sentence statement acknowledged cultural and religious imperialism:

> Long before my people journeyed to this land your people were here, and you received from your Elders an understanding of creation and of the Mystery that surrounds us all that was deep, and rich, and to be treasured. We did not hear you when you shared your vision. In our zeal to tell you of the good news of Jesus Christ we were closed to the value of your spirituality . . .

The church confessed that it 'confused Western ways and culture with . . . the gospel of Christ' and asked forgiveness.[7]

The All Native Circle Conference responded two years later by acknowledging the apology but not accepting it. Alf Dumont, an Aboriginal UCC minister, said that the verbal apology could not be accepted because it 'must be lived out if it's to be a real apology'.[8] Partly because of this response, the UCC was challenged to see an apology not primarily as 'closure,' but an ongoing task. The site of the 1986 apology, a gravel parking lot in Sudbury, Ontario, has become important. In August 2005, Aboriginal people of the UCC gathered there and erected a deliberately unfinished cairn as a sign of the work still required to live out the apology. A letter by Moderator

---

[7] United Church of Canada, 'Apology to First Nations' (1986).
[8] Quoted in Russell Daye, 'An Unresolved Dilemma: Canada's United Church Seeks Reconciliation with Native Peoples', *The Ecumenist* 36, no. 2 (May 1999), 11–15.

Peter Short on the twentieth anniversary of the apology reminded the church of the significant work yet to be done in achieving the right relationships envisioned by the statement.[9] While an apology claims to bind future generations to particular commitments, the challenge is whether and how this will be done.

Indian Residential Schools were mandated by the Canadian government but run by churches.[10] For over a century, tens of thousands of Aboriginal children were removed from their families and placed in these schools as part of the government's policy of cultural assimilation. A key objective, as infamously phrased, was 'to kill the Indian in the child'. This was achieved by forbidding traditional language, culture and spiritual practices. In addition, many students experienced emotional, physical and sexual abuse in the schools. The Canadian Government delivered a well-received apology on 11 June 2008 for its role in the schools.[11] This followed a settlement agreement that included compensation for former students, and the establishment of a Truth and Reconciliation Commission.

Beginning nearly two decades earlier, the four churches that ran the schools have all issued statements of apology, repentance or confession. The Catholic response is complicated by the question of which contemporary institutions, or individuals, can speak legitimately and authoritatively on behalf of past collective action. Catholic residential schools were run by dioceses and religious communities and not 'the Catholic Church as a whole', according to the Canadian Conference of Catholic Bishops.[12] Consequently, the Canadian Bishops have not apologized, despite a common perception that the Catholic Church in Canada, however this is understood legally or canonically, is ultimately responsible. (An ad hoc gathering of bishops and leaders of religious communities did issue a statement in their own names that expressed apology and regret for the pain and suffering many experienced at the schools.[13]) In 2009 Phil Fontaine,

---

[9] The Rt Rev Peter Short, United Church of Canada, 'A Letter on the 20th Anniversary of the Apology to First Nations' (2006).

[10] For an overview of this history, see J. R. Miller, *Shingwauk's Vision: A History of Native Residential Schools* (Toronto: University of Toronto Press, 1996).

[11] Canada, *House of Commons Debates*, Apology to Former Students of Indian Residential Schools (Rt Hon Stephen Harper), 11 June 2008. Prime Minister Harper's speech is available at www.pm.gc.ca/eng/media.asp?id=2149.

[12] Canadian Conference of Catholic Bishops, 'Apology on Residential Schools by the Catholic Church', (n.d.), www.cccb.ca/site/content/view/2630/1019/lang,eng/.

[13] Statement by the National (Canadian Catholic) Meeting on Indian Residential

the Grand Chief of the Assembly of First Nations, and himself a former student of residential schools, was granted a private audience with Pope Benedict XVI. The pope 'expressed his sorrow at the anguish caused by the deplorable conduct of some members of the Church' in the schools,[14] but did not use words such as apology, repentance or request for forgiveness. Yet, since Fontaine had publicly called for an apology, and declared the pope's response to be precisely what was needed for reconciliation, it is understandable why the media reported that the pope had apologized.

The leadership of the religious community which did issue an apology – the Missionary Oblates of Mary Immaculate – evidently did so without adequate consultation with the members of the community. As a result, they issued a completely unprecedented apology for an apology which acknowledged the flawed process by which the original statement was issued while reaffirming its substance.[15] This raised the question of whether an apology is collective because it speaks on behalf of a group by a duly authorized leader, or because it reflects convictions that are broadly shared by the community. In the first instance, an apology is partly an exhortation to begin a process to adopt certain attitudes and actions. In the second instance, an apology may be the result of the process by which these attitudes are already internalized to some degree.

The Oblates wrestled with the contentious issue of how the initial apology treated the many missionaries who served the schools in good faith. They apologized for the very existence of the schools, the ethnic and religious imperialism reflected in the denigration of Aboriginal religious traditions, and the fact that abuse happened at the schools. The apology acknowledged that the missionaries who ran the schools operated according to assumptions of cultural superiority but sincerely believed they were doing God's will and serving the interests of Aboriginal peoples.[16] Did this statement dishonour their memory? Did it explain their actions as those of sincere people in a bad system? Or, did this explanation minimize responsibility for the past?

As discussed in the Introduction, the Anglican Church of Canada's repentance for residential schools was delivered in a personal way

Schools (1991).

[14] Communiqué of the Holy See Press Office, 29 April 2009.

[15] Oblate Provincials, 'The Oblate Provincials Apologize' (1992).

[16] Missionary Oblates of Mary Immaculate, 'An Apology to the First Nations of Canada' (1991).

by the Primate, Archbishop Michael Peers, at a National Native Convocation. Peers spent several days listening to the stories of pain and suffering of those who lived in residential schools before making a statement on behalf of the church. In a series of direct 'I' statements, he acknowledged feelings of shame on behalf of the church, and a desire to proceed with steps of healing. He apologized for the church's participation in a system that separated families, denied language and culture, and in which many individuals were abused: 'We failed you. We failed ourselves. We failed God.' Acknowledging that some Anglicans would dispute that this apology was legitimately spoken in their name, Peers nevertheless attested that the residential schools had been run on their behalf.[17] The next day, on behalf of the elders and participants of the National Native Convocation, Vi Smith accepted the apology as sincere and compassionate, and prayed for God's continued reconciling power.[18]

The personal context of the Anglican apology contributed to its effectiveness. Though spoken with authority on behalf of the national church, it emerged from the particular relationships established over a week of hearing stories. Social ethicist Alain Durocher cites an interview with an Aboriginal person who witnessed genuine remorse and humiliation in the apology:

> We knew there were expectations of us for an apology, but we couldn't say where and when. . . Things needed to unfold, stories needed to unfold. Michael, our Primate, needed to hear them, and be present with us. We are so pleased he has given us his time, the whole week, at all the Indigenous gatherings. On the last day, he apologized and it was a very historical day in world history and our own church history as only the Spirit can bring it about. I can't say enough about Michael Peers.[19]

Yet, the intensely relational quality of the act may also mitigate the power of the moment for those who were not present to participate in it. Did Peers really speak for those not present at the gathering? And given that they had not heard the stories as he had, how would non-Aboriginal Anglicans share the primate's sense of pain at the past?

The next church to respond to the residential schools issue was the Presbyterian Church in Canada, which adopted a statement at

---

[17] Archbishop Michael Peers, Anglican Church of Canada, 'A Message to the National Native Convocation', (1993). The text is also available in Oji-Cree syllabics.

[18] Vi Smith, 'Response to the Primate', *The Anglican Journal*, September 1993, 6.

[19] Alain Paul Durocher, 'Between the Right to Forget and the Duty to Remember: The Politics of Memory in Canada's Public Church Apologies', Ph.D. dissertation (Graduate Theological Union, 2002), 167–8.

their 1994 General Assembly. A proposed text had been considered by the 1992 General Assembly, but it was referred back for a 'more balanced presentation of [the church's] mission and ministry to native people'.[20] This balance was essentially reflected in an extended document on the history and context of Presbyterian ministry with Aboriginal people.[21] Two dissenting objections to the 1994 statement were recorded in the minutes. One delegate raised the issue of the legal liability of both the church and individuals connected with the schools (an amendment to obtain legal opinion and cost analysis for the proposed confession had been defeated by the assembly). A second delegate argued that 'one generation cannot confess or apologize for the sins, failures, behaviour, mindset of another generation'.[22]

The approved text does not use the words 'repent', 'sorry' or 'apology'. It is a confession that addresses requests for forgiveness to Aboriginal people, to those whose prophetic voice the church ignored, and to God. The church stated that listening both to the Word of God and the stories of former residential school students led to a new understanding of its past. However, the new understanding did not mean the present church is morally superior to the church that ran the schools, nor that present members would have acted differently in that situation. The church acknowledged both that many good people worked in good faith in what is now recognized as a bad system, and that many lives have been scarred by the mission and ministry of the Presbyterian Church in Canada. As a result of linking the gospel with the dominant culture, the church 'misrepresented Jesus Christ'.[23]

The complexity of this past resides not only in the good intentions of many workers at the schools, but in the fact that many Aboriginal people reported good experiences. Not all were abused. Some former students have expressed gratitude for the education they received and appreciation for the positive influences their teachers had on them. While this mixed legacy is acknowledged in the assessment of many historians, others argue for a more wholesale revision.[24]

[20] *Acts and Proceedings of the General Assembly of the Presbyterian Church in Canada*, 118th General Assembly (1992), 52.
[21] *Acts and Proceedings of the General Assembly of the Presbyterian Church in Canada*, 120th General Assembly (1994), 365–76.
[22] *Ibid.*, 29.
[23] Presbyterian Church in Canada, 'Our Confession' (1994).
[24] Most recently Eric Bays, *Indian Residential Schools: Another Picture* (Ottawa: Baico, 2009).

Two further statements were made by the United Church of Canada: a resolution of repentance in 1997, and a specific apology for residential schools in 1998. The first one, a formal resolution by the General Council, spoke in the voice of the perpetrators of offences against First Nations people within a larger context of systemic racism. It resolved to advocate the Canadian government's involvement in the redress process.[25] A petition for an apology had been proposed but the approved resolution was of repentance. According to the denominational periodical, the advice of lawyers that an apology may increase exposure to legal liability (several cases were before the courts) carried the day,[26] though the official minutes report that apology was deemed 'inadequate theologically'.[27] The absence of the word 'apology', plus the use of the passive voice ('... the injustices that were done . . .') led to a perception within the church and beyond that a full and unconditional statement had not been made.[28] By contrast, the 1998 apology by Moderator Bill Phipps, delivered in the chapel of the national church offices directly to former students of residential schools, their families and communities, was made in spite of the potential legal implications of doing so.[29] He gave a clear and unequivocal apology for the suffering caused by UCC's involvement in residential schools, including the abuse that occurred in this system.[30]

These apologies triggered debates about the collective responsibility of the present church. Many in the UCC objected to the apology on the grounds that they were not personally responsible for the residential school policy or for what happened within them. Phipps addressed this by asserting that since the present church bears the blessings of ancestors, it must also bear the burdens. To

---

[25] United Church of Canada, 'Residential School Apology/Repentance' (1997).

[26] 'A Question of Repentance', *United Church Observer*, October 1997, 12.

[27] *Record of Proceedings* (United Church of Canada, General Council, 1997), 892.

[28] See, for example, 'Church's Courage Failed when Tested', editorial, *Toronto Star*, 25 August 1997, A12. Janet B. Bavelas analyses the various ways that the Canadian church apologies sought to avoid full acknowledgment through rhetorical tactics such as the passive voice. Recognizing the healing potential of apologies, she proposes that a collective apology should not be taken as an admission of legal liability. 'An Analysis of Formal Apologies by Canadian Churches to First Nations', Centre for Studies in Religion and Society, Occasional Paper (Victoria, BC: University of Victoria, 2004).

[29] Durocher, 'Between the Right to Forget and the Duty to Remember', 163.

[30] The Rt Rev Bill Phipps, United Church of Canada, 'Apology to Former Students of United Church Indian Residential Schools, and to their Families and Communities' (1998).

those who criticized these apologies as cheap attempts to score moral points at the expense of the dead, Terry Anderson responded with an argument about the continuous identity of the church over time.[31] To those who claimed that the criminal acts of abuse of some residential school workers ought not to stain the entire church, Keith Howard and Gaye Sharpe reflected on the experience of sitting through a trial of such an alleged abuser and feeling the pain and shame of being 'the church'. Whether or not they accepted it, they were in fact perceived by others as the church that had caused so much suffering. They concluded: 'If there are signs of hope emerging it remains with those individuals and congregations who are willing to bear the pain for the sake of relationships.'[32]

The idea that their apologies ought to be 'living apologies' have led churches to develop ongoing programme of healing and reconciliation in which apologies continue to play a central role. Healing funds were established to support grassroots initiatives of storytelling, support and reconciliation. In 2000, the UCC commissioned its past moderators to speak words of apology to individuals and communities with the full authority of the church.[33] At its 2008 General Assembly, the Presbyterian Church in Canada received reports about the money it has paid for legal settlements and its ongoing commitments to healing processes. A Cree Elder spoke to the assembly about her experiences at a residential school, to which the moderator responded by reiterating an apology. Leaders reflected on their participation in a 'Remembering the Children' tour across Canada. Lori Ransom wrote how one survivor explained 'the difference it makes to hear an apology or confession from another human being – how much more real and meaningful it is to be in the presence of someone apologizing to you, than it is to read an institution's apology or confession on a piece of paper'. Yet, she also warned the church to engage in listening and healing for the long haul: 'We need to be prepared to be exhausted by the process.'[34]

When a church apologizes to its own Aboriginal members, does it also speak on their behalf? In contrast to the church that addresses sins against the unity of Christians or against Jewish people, the

[31] Terry Anderson, 'Lessons from the Residential Schools: Some Beginning Reflections', *Touchstone* 16, no. 2 (May 1998), 22–8.

[32] Keith Howard and Gaye Sharpe, 'Were You There?' *Touchstone* 16, no. 2 (May 1998), 21.

[33] *Record of Proceedings* (United Church of Canada, General Council, 2000), 63–4.

[34] Lori Ranson, 'Remembering Forward,' *Presbyterian Record*, May 2008, 21.

church which addresses offences against Aboriginal people typically speaks in a collective voice which normally includes Aboriginal members of that church. Certainly ecumenical repentance laments precisely this absence of one collective voice, but when a Reformed church asks pardon of a Mennonite church, there is no overlap of membership. The 1986 apology was explicitly addressed to 'First Nations', yet as it was ritualized and later memorialized it is clear that it was most immediately addressed to Aboriginal people who were also members of the UCC. The apology was spoken by a majority group to a marginalized group within the same church. The collective apologetic 'we' implies that UCC members through time and space acknowledge responsibility for the past, yet it would be contrary to the spirit of the statement that Aboriginal members have the same responsibility. There is therefore an inherent tension in the use of voice, and whether one group can speak in the name of the denomination. If the UCC's collective 'we' does not include Aboriginal people, who were not responsible for their own oppression, does it also include very recent immigrants who are now UCC members? This form of collective apology may ironically reinforce the notion that the denomination's voice is a 'white' voice even as it seeks to undo the damage caused by such an assumption. However, if recognized, this tension may be a productive one. The church is forced to recognize that it is not a homogeneous corporate entity, but a differentiated, broken one in which certain voices have not been heard or represented. Even as the church attempts to confront this problem, it cannot do so from any perspective other than the reality of this brokenness.

The Anglican Church of Australia named this issue explicitly, and held a service in 1998 in which no one simply spoke for the whole church. Speaking 'on behalf of all the non-Aboriginal people of our Church', Archbishop John Grindrod, the primate, asked forgiveness from God and also from the Aboriginal Bishop, Arthur Malcolm, 'as a leader of your people' for the suffering caused by the church, which Bishop Malcolm granted, and asked forgiveness in return for any harm caused by his people.[35]

In its 1992 'Confession to Native Americans', the United Methodist Church (UMC) noted how its experience of ecumenical dialogue taught it that confession of guilt is crucial for wholeness and

---

[35] Anglican Church of Australia, *Standing Committee Report: General Synod 2007*, appendix E.

healing.³⁶ Its statement acknowledged sin, both past and present, intended and unintended against Native Americans, including 'the violent colonization of the land'. The UMC subsequently apologized for the 1864 Sand Creek (Colorado) Massacre of 200 Cheyenne persons at the hands of a militia led by a lay Methodist minister.³⁷ Ongoing discussion about a formal act of repentance regarding the church's treatment of Aboriginal people led to a 2008 resolution pledging such an act for the 2012 General Conference.³⁸

One Mennonite denomination held a 'Litany of Confession' back in 1970. It began: 'We have tried to be helpers without first becoming acquainted with you, the native people of Canada', and asked God's forgiveness for the many ways the church has failed to build truly mutual relationships.³⁹ Two statements by Mennonite entities coincided with the 500th anniversary of Columbus' 'discovery', including a litany of confession at a North American church assembly.⁴⁰ Mennonite Central Committee also asked forgiveness for the conquest of land, domination of Aboriginal people and denigration of their culture. It recognized with gratitude the contributions Aboriginal people have made to society and pledged to both hear and tell the true stories of their experience of the past 500 years.⁴¹ (Mennonite Central Committee is a relief, development and peace agency, not a church, but often speaks on behalf of the dozens of denominations it represents.)

One hundred years after US forces invaded and overthrew the Kingdom of Hawaii, the United Church of Christ apologized to Hawaii's indigenous people for the support it lent to that action. The church confessed its sins against those hearing the apology and their forebears. It acknowledged that well-meaning missionaries 'sometimes confused the ways of the West with the ways of the Christ'.⁴² When the US Congress passed a resolution apologizing for

---

[36] United Methodist Church, 'Confession to Native Americans' (1992).

[37] United Methodist Church, 'The Sand Creek Apology' (1996).

[38] United Methodist Church, 'Healing Relationship with Indigenous Persons' (2008).

[39] Conference of Mennonites in Canada, 'Litany of Confession' (1970).

[40] General Conference Mennonite Church, 'Statement of Confession' (1992).

[41] Mennonite Central Committee, 'Statement to the Aboriginal Peoples of the Americas in 1992: 500 Years After Columbus "Discovered" the Americas' (1992).

[42] Paul Sherry, president, United Church of Christ, 'An Apology to the Indigenous Hawaiian People' (1993).

the overthrow, the United Church of Christ apology was cited among its reasons for doing so.[43]

In 1997, the Episcopal Church (USA) authorized a 'Decade of Remembrance, Recognition, and Reconciliation', which was officially launched at a service in Jamestown, Virginia by Presiding Bishop Edmond Browning and numerous Aboriginal bishops, elders and members. These leaders signed 'A Covenant of Faith', sometimes called 'The New Jamestown Covenant'. Like the General Convention resolution establishing the Decade, the covenant does not dwell on the past but looks forward to the future.[44] Only in the address of House of Deputies President Pamela Chinnis during the service (the full text of which was not included in news releases or posted on the church's website) was the word 'sin' used to describe some of the church's past actions:

> The church of today must own up to the sins of yesterday... We apologize to the Indigenous Peoples of our own church, and of all communities who still bear the marks of the cross of colonialism. While recognizing the tragic history behind us, we resolve to change our present and hope for the history to come.[45]

Though neither the original resolution nor the New Covenant itself used words such as 'sin', 'repent', or 'apologize', all three have come to be associated with action the church took towards its Aboriginal members. In 2006, the Episcopal Church embarked on a second Decade, and referred to the 1997 Covenant as when the church 'apologized for centuries of abuse'.[46] This shows the fluidity, even interchangeability, of these terms in the minds of at least some church leaders. While precise word choice is important in crafting resolutions and official documents, collective memory may edit original intentions and commit to posterity an account of what was perceived to have happened.

The Government of Australia's report on the historic policy of removing Aboriginal children from their homes identified several

[43] United States Public Law 103–150, 103rd Congress Joint Resolution 19, 23 November 1993.

[44] Episcopal Church, 'A Covenant of Faith' (1997).

[45] Pamela P. Chinnis, Episcopal Church, 'Response to the New Jamestown Covenant', Office of the President of the House of Deputies (1997). The text of this statement provided by the Episcopal Church is not identical with the words she spoke at the event, as documented in Amy MacAusland and Steve MacAusland, prods., *The New Covenant at Jamestown: Launching the Decade of Remembrance, Recognition, and Reconciliation*, videocassette (New York: Native American Ministries, Episcopal Church Centre, 1997).

[46] 'From Columbus: 75th General Convention Charts Mission', *Episcopal News Service*, 23 June 2006.

specific ways in which apologies bring healing to an unjust past. The report specifically recommended that churches 'which played a role in the administration of the laws and policies [of removal] . . . make such formal apologies and participate in such commemorations as may be determined'.[47] Australia itself held a 'National Sorry Day' on 26 May 1998.[48] The Quakers issued a brief statement of regret and apology for their involvement in the dispossession and trauma of Aboriginal people, and made a commitment to reconciliation.[49] The General Synod of the Anglican Church of Australia approved a resolution of apology and request for forgiveness[50] a few days after the Primate and the Aboriginal Bishop exchanged words of forgiveness at a public service. The Australian Catholic Bishops requested forgiveness of indigenous families 'for any part the Church may have played in causing them harm and suffering'.[51] Notably, they did not take responsibility for harm, but merely granted the possibility that there may have been some. Their statement was not directed to the victims, but rather to the wider society ('. . . causing *them* harm . . .'). Two years later, following the pope's Jubilee Day of Pardon, the Australian Bishops confessed that their 'often misguided' efforts to assist Aboriginal Australians have had 'unintended but harmful long-term consequences'.[52] In 2001, the pope issued a letter noting that the Synod of Bishops for Oceania 'apologized unreservedly', to which he added a plea for forgiveness for times when the church's 'children have been or still are party to these wrongs' against indigenous people.[53]

Many of the statements discussed in this section are widely referred to as apologies, usually because the churches have presented them as

---

[47] Commonwealth of Australia, *Bringing Them Home: Report of the National Inquiry Into the Separation of Aboriginal and Torres Strait Islander Children from Their Families* (Sydney: Human Rights and Equal Opportunity Commission, 1997), 292.

[48] National Sorry Day included grassroots apologizing in the form of the many 'Sorry Books' that were signed by individuals throughout the country. However, the government of Prime Minister John Howard refused to apologize. Fulfiling an election promise, the new government of Prime Minister Kevin Rudd did issue an apology on 13 February 2008.

[49] Quakers in Australia, 'Sorry Statement to the Indigenous People of Australia' (1998).

[50] Anglican Church of Australia, 'Resolution Concerning the "Bringing Them Home" Report', (1998).

[51] Australian Catholic Bishops, 'Statement on National Sorry Day' (1998).

[52] Australian Catholic Bishops, 'Statement of Repentance' (2000).

[53] Pope John Paul II, *Ecclesia in Oceania: Post-Synodal Apostolic Exhortation* (2001), no. 28.

such. One reason for this may be the fact that Aboriginal groups have often called for apologies from both governments and churches. They have called for apology, rather than repentance, confession or forgiveness, because it is a form of speech recently associated with nations and have framed their expectations of the church similarly. However, it is also possible that the explicitly relational element of an apology makes it a particularly suitable rhetorical tool by which the churches and Aboriginal peoples renegotiate their social relations.[54] An apology acknowledges that those who were wrong possess a human dignity which was violated. The ways in which an apology is a risk to the apologizer – an apology could be refused or could lead to legal liability – shows that it can shift some of the power between unequal parties. Finally, in cases where living victims of a wrong are present (as opposed to representatives or heirs of those wronged in the distant past), an apology responds to the demand that a victim be faced, at least symbolically, and addressed by a person who is authorized to speak for what has happened.

Is an apology an act of repentance, or is it something else? David Novak draws a sharp distinction between them. He disparages the apology as secular, and as an attempt merely to get over the past.[55] Rowan Williams calls apology 'the world's currency',[56] (though he also intervened in a Church of England General Synod debate to advocate for a church apology for slavery[57]). One church study guide describes repentance as much more substantive than an apology, since the former includes a commitment to not repeat something in the future.[58] However, a church that apologizes believes such an act is consistent with its identity and mission and in that sense fully theological. Many churches presented their apologies not as a single act of closure, but as part of ongoing process of making right. In light of this, I propose that a church apology is an act of repentance that places particular emphasis on repairing human relationships. Recognizing that some churches or individuals may nevertheless draw

---

[54] Neil Funk-Unrau, 'Re-Negotiation of Social Relations Through Public Apologies to Canadian Aboriginal Peoples', *Research in Social Movements, Conflict and Change* 29 (2008), 1–19.

[55] David Novak, 'Jews and Catholics: Beyond Apologies', *First Things*, no. 89 (January 1999), 24.

[56] Archbishop Rowan Williams, Advent Pastoral Letter, 27 November 2004.

[57] Church of England General Synod, *Transcript of Proceedings*, February 2006.

[58] *Reparations: A Process for Repairing the Breach* (Cleveland, OH: Peace and Witness Ministries, United Church of Christ, 2003), 30.

sharp distinctions between terms, an apology may be understood to engage various dimensions of repentance – acknowledging a past wrong, accepting responsibility, expressing remorse and changing attitudes and behaviours – in relational terms. An apology may do much of what an act of repentance does, but it also symbolizes the need for new relationships between human communities and marks a step in that process. However, to repair the relationship with God, terms such as repentance, confession, forgiveness, are all used, but (with one exception[59]) not apology.

It is important to note that my while I focus primarily on acts of repentance or apology, such statements are just one element in a much larger process of reconciliation. My attention to these discrete actions and the questions they raise should not imply that they alone are sufficient for the work of reconciliation to which the church is called. Given that I do not examine instances where churches confront historic wrongs without explicit statements of repentance, I cannot even conclude that they are always necessary. A statement of repentance or apology may be fitting as the initiation of a process, or as the culmination of a process; but it may also be the case that authentic penitence and conversion are embodied in ways not explicitly expressed.

SLAVERY AND/OR RACISM

Ecclesial repentance has marked a change in how churches talk about racism. For example, a 1988 Vatican document on racism acknowledges that 'persons belonging to Christian nations' had participated in the slave trade but does not ascribe guilt for these actions to Christians as such, let alone church structures.[60] Rather, the document claims that the church has always combatted racism and defended oppressed minorities, or at least has always taught as much. However, the introductory note added to the revised text in 2001 grounds anti-racism in the concept of conversion at both the personal and institutional levels. Reviewing a series of requests for forgiveness made by the pope for the racism of Christians that has

---

[59] See discussion below on the Baptist Union of Great Britain, which apologized to God for slavery.

[60] Pontifical Council for Justice and Peace, *The Church and Racism: Towards a More Fraternal Society*, updated ed. (London: Catholic Truth Society, 2001), original text, no. 4.

marred the church's witness, it enjoins others to ask God's pardon and engage concretely in practices of reconciliation.[61] It was one thing for the church to condemn sin, call individuals to repentance, or advocate public policy changes. It is quite another for the church to acknowledge that before it speaks out, it must examine its own history and current practice. A milestone report in this regard was adopted by the WCC Assembly in 1975 that confessed the existence of racism in the churches, and identified its many forms, including apartheid.[62]

The Southern Baptist Convention's (SBC) decision to address the issues of slavery and racism at its 1995 meeting in Atlanta drew significant media attention, in part because the denomination had been founded by those who asserted that slaveholders could serve as missionaries. One magazine columnist charged that the resulting repentance/apology was insincere because it was too little too late and driven by a pragmatic desire to draw black congregations into the denominational fold,[63] while a key newspaper editorial welcomed it as a vital step towards racial reconciliation.[64] And despite being widely reported as a repentance for slavery,[65] it is not clear that this is what the SBC did.

The SBC drew a careful distinction between slavery, which it deplored as an historic evil but for which it neither apologized nor repented, and the conscious or unconscious racism of which *present* members are indeed guilty, for which it did repent and apologize to all African-Americans.[66] SBC leader Richard Land said, 'I can't change my great-great-great grandfather's standing before God . . . But I can apologize for the consequences of the man's ownership of slaves.'[67] While this was a unofficial comment, it reflects a key assumption of the resolution. Repentance is only for present sins. Actual slaveholding and its theological defence, which are fully in the past, cannot be addressed by the church's repentance.

---

[61] *Ibid.*, introductory update, nos. 6–12.

[62] World Council of Churches, 'Structures of Injustice and Structures for Liberation', Fifth Assembly (1975).

[63] Jack E. White, 'Forgive Us Our Sins', *Time* 146 (3 July 1995), 29.

[64] 'Baptists' Apology Helps Old Racial Wounds Heal', editorial, *The Atlanta Journal-Constitution*, 22 June 1995, A10.

[65] For example: Gustav Niebuhr, 'Baptist Group Votes to Repent Stand on Slaves', *New York Times*, 21 June 1995, A1, B7.

[66] Southern Baptist Convention, 'Resolution on Racial Reconciliation' (1995).

[67] Niebuhr, 'Baptist Group Votes to Repent Stand on Slaves'.

The statement thus raises several theological questions. Is the SBC's non-repentance for slavery ultimately because repentance cannot be on behalf of another and all actual slaveholders are dead? If so, does this imply that sins are strictly individual? Richard Land's comment linking repentance to 'standing before God' suggests this. The resolution does infer a structural dimension to racism, suggesting that the sin is not only individual. Can a structural sin be repented? Is the SBC's non-repentance for slavery because it denies ecclesial continuity over time, such that past sins of the church are not, in some way, the responsibility of the present church? The answer may lie partly in the SBC polity which strictly reserves the term 'church' to congregations (not the assembly that gathered in 1995 to pass the resolution) and Baptist theology that emphasizes personal responsibility.

By contrast, a number of moderate groupings of Southern Baptists – the Alliance of Baptists (1990) and the Cooperative Baptist Fellowship (1991) – passed resolutions that did plainly repent of having supported slavery, implying some temporal continuity of the church within which responsibility is conveyed. The Baptist Peace Fellowship, which consists of Baptists from several denominations, also addressed the failure of the SBC to speak out in 1963 against the racially motivated bombing of the Sixteenth Street Baptist Church in Birmingham, Alabama in which four children were killed. This 'Birmingham Confession' notes that at the time SBC refused even to pass a motion 'mourning [the] dead and lamenting the tragedy'.[68]

Decades later, the Baptist World Alliance held a Service of Memory and Reconciliation at the Cape Coast slave castle in Ghana which provided an opportunity for constituent groups to make public confessions. Some, such as the Dutch Baptist Union emphasized that it spoke strictly for the present generation. Others spoke of slaveholding as 'our sin'.[69] That same international gathering elected a Jamaican pastor and professor, the first non-white general secretary of the Baptist World Alliance.

One denomination that did not make a confession in Ghana, the Baptist Union of Great Britain, issued an apology later that year,

---

[68] These acts of repentance are discussed in E. Luther Copeland, *The Southern Baptist Convention and the Judgment of History*, rev. ed. (Lanham, MD: University of America Press, 2002), 30–1. Original documents, respectively: *Baptists Today* 9, no. 17 (1991), back page; *Baptists Today* 10, no. 10 (1992), back page; 'The Birmingham Confession', *Baptist Peacemaker* 13, no. 2 (Summer 2003), 1.

[69] Baptist World Alliance, 'Service of Memory and Reconciliation', Ghana, 5 July 2007.

and months later presented it to the Jamaican Baptist Union. They confessed their present sin of silence on racism, but also intimated responsibility extending back to the slave trade itself. They confessed benefiting from Britain's participation in the slave trade and offered an apology not only to those oppressed by this legacy and but also an apology to God, a formulation not encountered in any other statement I have found.[70]

European churches outside the UK have made few statements regarding prejudice or discrimination other than for anti-Semitism. An exception is a pair of statements by the Church of Norway (Lutheran) regarding the Roma people, the oppression of whom does not neatly fit the narrative of colonialism but who were subject to legal discrimination by state and church for hundreds of years. The 1998 Synod approved a resolution that included a plea for forgiveness from the Roma people. However, a proposal that this request be for sins that 'we [the church] carry', narrowly defeated in favour of sins 'our people carry', was perceived as an unwarranted attempt to portray the church as the defender of the Roma from prejudice they have experienced. Thus, a 2000 resolution asked forgiveness 'for the injustice and violations that have been done from the Church of Norway against the Roma people'.[71] This controversy indicates the possibility, especially for established state churches, to see their role as a priestly one, assuming and confessing the sins of wider society. The evident danger is that such a role may enable the church to avoid reflecting on its own specific culpability.

In the context of his many travels, Pope John Paul II made a series of statements about the legacy of colonialism. At a building in modern Senegal that housed captured people before they were shipped to the Americas as slaves, the pope confessed the 'weakness' and 'sin' of 'our civilization which called itself Christian' and yet engaged in slavery.[72] Several years later, the pope implored God's forgiveness for the slave trade, which he then specified as having always been opposed by the church. So why ask forgiveness? He acknowledged that papal bulls were insufficient to stop the slave trade but claimed that official teaching, and thus the church itself, was always clear on

---

[70] Baptist Union of Great Britain, 'An Apology for the Transatlantic Slave Trade' (2007).

[71] 'The Church of Norway and the Roma of Norway' (2002).

[72] Pope John Paul II, Visit to the House of Slaves, Goreé, Senegal, 22 February 1992. See also Message to Afro-Americans, Santo Domingo, 13 October 1992; General Audience, 21 October 1992.

the issue.⁷³ On the surface, this reflects a rather disembodied ecclesiology in which the church's position consists of its formal statements, though by seeking God's pardon implicitly acknowledges that the church did have an obligation to do more. However, the claim that even the church's official position was always clear is challenged by John T. Noonan, Jr's careful documentation of how the Catholic Church only recently 'discovered' the sin of slavery.⁷⁴

How does a church come to recognize complicity in a sin of which it has not always been conscious, such as racism? One answer is shown in the process by which the United Methodist Church (UMC) passed a resolution and then held a worship service repenting for racism (to be examined further in Chapter 7). The UMC explained that through ecumenical conversations with other, primarily black, Methodist denominations, their consciousness was raised about how racism divided the church, and continues to compromise the gospel. In addition to a service at the General Convention,⁷⁵ the resolution called for liturgical acts of repentance at local levels, to which most of the 64 regional conferences responded positively. A study guide for congregations delved into the history of how slavery and racism led to the proliferation of denominations. Discussion questions also prodded congregations to name specific ways that the rationalization of sin remains present in the church.⁷⁶

Like the UMC, several other US-based denominations have incorporated repentance for racism as part of an institutional commitment to anti-racism. A United Church of Christ service of repentance for slavery acknowledged the church's complicity, celebrated its role in abolition, and committed the church to becoming a more inclusive people.⁷⁷ In a lengthy document, the Presbyterian Church (USA) confessed its complicity in sinful racist structures and committed itself 'to confront spiritually the idolatry and ideology of white supremacy and white privilege'.⁷⁸ The Christian Church (Disciples of Christ)

---

[73] Pope John Paul II, Ad Limina visit of Brazilian Bishops, 1 April 1995.

[74] John T. Noonan, Jr., *A Church That Can and Cannot Change: The Development of Catholic Moral Teaching* (Notre Dame, IN: University of Notre Dame Press, 2005), 36–123.

[75] United Methodist Church, 'Act of Repentance for Racism', 4 May 2000.

[76] *Steps Towards Wholeness: Learning and Repentance*, study guide (United Methodist Church, n.d.).

[77] Gustav Niebuhr, 'Church to Repent Its Ties to Slavery', *New York Times*, 29 June 1999, A14.

[78] Presbyterian Church (USA), 'Facing Racism: In Search of the Beloved Community' (1999).

passed a resolution of repentance in 2001 confessing that the sin of racism is 'an historic and ongoing reality in the church'. It committed itself to becoming 'an anti-racist, pro-reconciling communion', and proposed several programmatic steps in that direction.[79] Two years later, the General Assembly repented of their church's 'wicked apathy' in the face of slavery.[80] Both the Southern Province and the Northern Province of the Moravian Church in America likewise adopted resolutions on racial reconciliation that apologized for their participation in slavery and committed themselves to the elimination of institutional racism in the church.[81]

In a reversal of the usual narrative, Catholic Bishop Charles Palmer-Buckle of Ghana apologized in 2002 for the role some of his ancestors played in selling other Africans into slavery. The bishop said he had become aware of the need for such a gesture years earlier when he was greeted by a black Caribbean priest who said: 'I am your brother, Joseph, whom you sold into slavery.' The day following the bishop's apology, Florida Bishop John Ricard accepted this apology on behalf of other African-American Catholics during a service of reconciliation.[82] Though Palmer-Buckle was not explicitly repenting for church actions, he evidently assumed a mandate to speak broadly on behalf of his people. Who can accept an apology for a historic wrong? Did Ricard accept the apology as a bishop speaking for his church, as an African-American descendent of slaves, or in virtue of some other identity? The Baptist World Alliance service of repentance included a statement by Ghanaian chiefs asking forgiveness for the role their forbears played in capturing and selling humans as slaves.[83] In that case, the mechanism by which responsibility for the past was carried to the present was more clearly delineated – the political institution of chiefs. Yet, given that some present chiefs may have been Christian, at least some of their forbears on whose behalf they spoke were not,

---

[79] Christian Church (Disciples of Christ), 'An Act of Repentance Calling the Christian Church (Disciples of Christ) to be an Anti-Racist, Pro-Reconciling Community' (2001).

[80] Christian Church (Disciples of Christ), 'An Apology for the Sin of Slavery' (2003).

[81] Moravian Church (Southern Province), 'Racial Reconciliation' (2006); Moravian Church (Northern Province), 'Racial Reconciliation' (2006).

[82] Tom Roberts, 'Ghanaian Bishop Offers Apology for Africans' Part in Slave Trade', *National Catholic Reporter*, 13 September 2002, 13.

[83] Baptist World Alliance, 'Service of Memory and Reconciliation', Ghana, 5 July 2007.

the meaning and implication of such a request in a Christian service, invoking Christian notions of forgiveness in Christ, is unclear.

In 2006, two provinces of the Anglican Communion repented of complicity in slavery and broached the question of church reparations for slavery. The House of Bishops of the Episcopal Church issued a pastoral letter on 'The Sin of Racism', which expressed repentance,[84] and the General Convention passed a formal resolution which led to a Service of Repentance in an historically black church in Philadelphia two years later. That service's Litany of Offence and Apology acknowledged that the church's 'record of racism, weakness, subjugation, neglect, complicity, arrogance and complacency in conforming to both slavery and associated evils is an affront to the teachings of Christ', and sought God's forgiveness for 'these sins and failings'.[85] One African-American Episcopalian leader, however, commented on the inappropriateness of the liturgy 'written by a white person who had no empathy for the pain that we went through', and planned without adequate consultation.[86]

With an eye towards possible monetary and non-monetary reparations, the original resolution initiated the collection of information about complicity in slavery at the diocesan level, and the ways in which the church in the south and the north benefited financially.[87] The Maryland diocese reported that in the eighteenth century, 'tobacco raised by slaves become the life-blood of the church', supporting its ministries, clergy and church buildings.[88] In her sermon at the Service of Repentance, Presiding Bishop Katharine Jefferts Schori noted that at the time of the Civil War, 80 per cent of Episcopalian clergy in Virginia were slaveowners. Slaves worked on the grounds of Virginia Theological Seminary. The Episcopal Clergy Pension Fund was founded with money from J. P. Morgan, whose U.S. Steel-owned mines in the south relied on convict-slave labour.[89]

---

[84] Episcopal Church, House of Bishops, 'The Sin of Racism: A Call to Covenant', 22 March 2006.

[85] Episcopal Church, 'Day of Repentance: Order of Service', 4 October 2008.

[86] Janet Kawamoto, 'Repentance for Slavery Has a Long Way to Go, Say Advocates', *Episcopal News Service*, 12 July 2009.

[87] Episcopal Church, 'Slavery and Racial Reconciliation' (2006). See also Jim DeLa, 'Church Acknowledges Role in Slavery, Plans Reparations Study', *Episcopal News Service*, 21 June 2006.

[88] Report of the dioceses of Maryland, Easton and Washington in response to resolutions A123 and A127 of the 75th General Convention, n.d., provided by the Office for Anti-Racism, Episcopal Church.

[89] The Most Rev Katharine Jefferts Schori, Homily at the Service of Repentance of the Episcopal Church, 4 October 2008.

What does this imply for reparations? The Diocese of New York has begun to examine its history in light of the following broad definition of reparation as 'a process to remember, repair, restore, reconcile and make amends for wrongs that can never be singularly reducible to monetary terms'. Reparation is 'an historical reckoning involving acknowledgment that an offence against humanity was committed and that the victims have not received justice'.[90] For the Episcopal Church, apology and repentance (often used interchangeably in this context), has meant a commitment to examine a history of injustice more closely, and reflect on what further response justice requires. A broad working definition of reparations has already resulted in historical research, the production of educational resources and local advocacy for government reparations. Does it also demand material reparations from the church? As the resolution is still being implemented, it remains to be seen what this church will decide.

The Church of England apologized for its role in the slave trade,[91] and subsequently led a public 'Walk of Witness' through London.[92] Though it was reported that the church was considering some form of at least symbolic material reparation – the church itself actually owned slaves[93] – the Archbishop of Canterbury clarified that monetary reparations would not be offered. He stated:

> Reparations as such offer too mechanical and calculating a model for making amends and there are seriously challenging questions to be asked about what, under such proposals should be paid and to whom. The point about moral responsibility is that the slave trade yielded considerable profit for institutions – but how that is dealt with now means asking the wider question about how that heritage is used to help most effectively those suffering because of the legacy of slavery.[94]

The Church of England's General Synod debate reflected differences of opinion about the relative significance of looking back versus looking forward. The original motion took the bicentenary of the abolition of the slave trade in England (2007) as an opportunity

---

[90] 'Update on Reparation Work in the Diocese of New York' (n.d.).

[91] Church of England, 'Bicentenary of the Act for the Abolition of the Slave Trade', (2006).

[92] *Walk of Witness: London.24.03.07*, programme book (2007).

[93] One of its missionary organizations, the Society for the Propagation of the Gospel in Foreign Parts, owned the Codrington Plantation in Barbados, which kept slaves until 1833.

[94] Archbishop Rowan Williams, press briefing from Lambeth Palace, 26 March 2007.

to celebrate the progress that has been made and to work against current forms of slave trafficking. Yet, discussion on the motion led to the inclusion of a more explicit acknowledgment of the church's complicity in the slave trade, and offered an apology to the heirs of those who were enslaved. Not only had the church owned slaves, but bishops in the House of Lords voted against the abolition of the slave trade and the church later paid compensation to bishops whose slaves were freed. Some synod members argued that church's social mission is best served not by talking about the past but by concrete commitments to action, such participating in an international coalition seeking an end to human trafficking. Others called for the recognition of *both* the church's complicity in the slave trade, and its efforts to end it. In the end, the Archbishop of Canterbury's intervention proved persuasive and the motion was amended. Rowan Williams spoke in favour of an apology as both 'necessary and costly', because the present body of Christ 'exists across history', and includes the sinfulness of its own past.[95]

Slavery is universally condemned. While slavery in North America and Europe has been abolished, racism remains insidious. Churches repenting of slavery are agreed that its legacy continues in the form of racism which affects church and society. They are repenting of a sin they and their members continue to commit. Racism consists not only of discrete acts, for which individuals are responsible, but it exists in the patterns, social norms, and institutions which produce people who may act in racist ways despite their best intentions. Racism may dwell in the 'ways of thinking and acting', for which Pope John Paul II called on the church to ask God's pardon.[96] The concept of structural or social sin, employed to describe this reality refers not primarily to the effect that an individual's sin has on others, but to the fact that there is a dimension of sin which is more than the sum of individual sins. This does not deny personal responsibility, but suggests that the personal is not the only dimension in need of conversion. If the church repents of racism, and pledges to undo the structures of racism with which it is infected, then racism is at least also a social or structural sin in addition to a personal one. Repentance for racism in and of the church thus entails not only wrestling with a past history, but a future commitment to avoid a sin that is often disguised in attitudes, patterns and institutions. Is social

---

[95] Church of England General Synod, *Transcript of Proceedings*, February 2006.
[96] Pope John Paul II, *Tertio Millennio Adveniente*, no. 33.

sin a legitimate theological category? If so, what are the implications of repenting of a social sin such a racism? And if so, how can the church commit to not repeating a sin which, as a social body, it has often been unable to see and to name?

Apartheid in South Africa

Dozens of church and other religious groups appeared before South Africa's Truth and Reconciliation Commission (TRC) in 1997. Their submissions, both written and oral, reflect the complex and even contradictory action and inaction of churches under apartheid. Some churches supported apartheid, others suffered as a consequence of active opposition to it and elements of both were present within many churches. Nearly all offered some kind of apology or confession, either for tacit support of apartheid, adopting an 'apolitical' stance which implicitly supported the status quo, or failing to oppose it more actively. In light of the literature on the church struggle with apartheid,[97] and its engagement with the TRC,[98] I will focus on instances of ecclesial repentance prior to the TRC, and then examine what the unique case of the TRC adds to our understanding of the repentance of churches.

As apartheid or 'separate development' came to be formulated and implemented in South Africa, a series of confessional statements, most notably the statement of the Cottesloe Consultation (1961), called on churches to declare their opposition to the policy. In 1982, the World Alliance of Reformed Churches (WARC) expelled from its memberships two churches that defended a theological basis for apartheid – the Dutch Reformed Church of South Africa (*Nederduitse Gereformeerde Kerk* [NGK]) and the *Nederduitsch Hervormde Kerk*. WARC declared that apartheid 'is a sin, and that the moral and theological justification of it is a travesty of the Gospel and, in its persistent disobedience to the Word of God, a theological heresy'. The WARC resolution acknowledged the pervasiveness of racism and called for 'repentance and concerted action' by all its member churches.[99] In effect they declared that while all are sinners, not all are heretics.

---

[97] See John W. de Gruchy, *The Church Struggle in South Africa*, 25th anniversary ed. (Minneapolis: Fortress Press, 2004).

[98] See James Cochrane, John de Gruchy and Stephen Martin, eds., *Facing the Truth: South African Faith Communities and the Truth & Reconciliation Commission* (Cape Town: David Philip, 1999).

[99] World Alliance of Reformed Churches, 'Apartheid and South Africa' (1982).

The sinful church at least grants the need to open its eyes to its faults and repent. The heretical church denies that the sin is a sin at all. The churches WARC expelled had no intention of turning from their position which they regarded it as biblically justified.

Calls for repentance from all churches continued through the years, including the *Kairos* document (1985), the National Initiative for Reconciliation (1985), the South African Council of Churches' Soweto Conference on Confessing Guilt (1989), the Rustenburg Conference (1990) and the Cape Town Consultation of WCC member churches (1991).[100] The ecumenical Rustenburg Conference issued is own declaration of repentance, in which parties acknowledged their church's complicity in the sin of apartheid. While the penitence is the consistent theme, the statement disavows a uniform guilt, rather acknowledging that different churches have very different histories and responsibilities with respect to apartheid.[101]

In February 1990, State President F. W. de Klerk announced the unbanning of the African National Congress and other opposition groups, and the freeing of prisoners including Nelson Mandela. In October, the NGK passed a resolution distancing itself from its past support for apartheid policy. Their resolution affirmed the 'honest and noble intentions' of apartheid – those of 'optimal development of all population groups within the framework of their own cultural traditions' – but confessed that in its implementation the policy became ethnocentric. The NGK said that because they had judged apartheid too abstractly and uncritically, they did not adequately perceive how it became *in practice* racist and oppressive. The statement concluded with a plea for the reconciliation of the entire nation.[102]

Was the statement sincere? Was it consistent to assert first of all, a distinction between a good policy in theory and its distortion in practice, while confessing that the theological defence of the policy had not only been practically misguided, but fully sinful? Given that political change was happening rapidly, the NGK faced a choice of, on the one hand, defending its past and meeting the pastoral needs of the Afrikaner community, or, on the other hand, seeking an active role in the emerging democratic South Africa, a role that would be

---

[100] This list is taken from James Cochrane, John de Gruchy and Stephen Martin, 'Faith, Struggle and Reconciliation', in *Facing the Truth*, 4.

[101] National Conference of Church Leaders in South Africa, 'Rustenburg Declaration' (1990).

[102] Dutch Reformed Church, 'Resolution on Apartheid', (1990).

possible only with a disavowal of apartheid. John de Gruchy notes that while the NGK leadership was inclined to the latter, it felt it needed to move slowly in order to bring its constituency along with it.[103]

An exchange at the Rustenburg Conference of South African church leaders held later that year illustrates the contested question of who is authorized to 'accept' a church's confession. NGK theologian Willie Jonker departed from his prepared remarks to deliver a personal confession of sin and responsibility for apartheid, and proposed that he might speak on behalf of the NGK and the Afrikaner people. In tone, his statement was notably contrite and did not invoke the theory/practice distinction that made the denominational resolution so problematic. An immediate response of forgiveness was offered by Anglican Archbishop Desmond Tutu, who in turn confessed the racism present in his and in every church. Yet, the delegates speaking for two Dutch Reformed churches that had opposed apartheid objected that Tutu's acceptance of Jonker's confession did not speak for them. Tutu later clarified that he spoke only for himself, as did Jonker, at least as first. The next day the president of the NGK said that his denomination 'fully identifies' with what Jonker had said.[104] So who was speaking, and who was responding? Was this exchange essentially a personal one between Jonker and Tutu, or did it somehow add to the NGK's self-reflection, repentance or even absolution?[105]

In its latter stages, the TRC asked the University of Cape Town's Research Institute on Christianity in South Africa (RICSA) to organize faith community hearings and draft a report on the results. Twenty-nine churches or ecumenical groups responded, nearly all with written and oral submissions. All but four made some kind of confession or apology. The church submissions to the TRC differ from other instances of ecclesial repentance in several respects. The churches were invited to respond, and specifically to consider several questions with respect to their past. This framework shaped what churches said and how they said it. In other contexts, it may seem inappropriate for a church to both confess complicity in racism,

---

[103] de Gruchy, *The Church Struggle in South Africa*, 209–11.

[104] Louw Alberts and Frank Chikane, eds., *Road to Rustenburg: The Church Looking Forward to a New South Africa* (Cape Town: Struik Christian Books, 1991), 100.

[105] See *ibid.*, 87–102, 261; and Desmond Tutu, *No Future Without Forgiveness* (New York: Doubleday, 1999), 275–7.

for example, and explain the many ways it sought to work against racism. Yet, in this case, churches were asked by RICSA to reflect on both, and they generally responded in kind. Second, churches addressed their submission to the government-mandated TRC for inclusion in a literal public record. The churches did not control the venue in which they made their statements. Nevertheless, some of the churches also addressed their repentance to God, and included explicitly Christian elements such as prayers. Third, analysis and interpretation of the submissions exists on public record in the form of a lengthy semi-official report by RICSA,[106] and a shorter one in the TRC's *Final Report*.[107]

Many churches expressed a deeply ambiguous relationship with apartheid – the same churches were often victims of oppression, opponents of oppression, and complicit in oppression. Direct support of apartheid could itself take several forms beyond the explicit theological justification given by the white Afrikaner Reformed churches. Even churches that opposed apartheid in principle often failed to create a context which effectively challenged their individual members who may have been active supporters or complicit in human rights abuses. Those that provided army chaplains acknowledged that this gave the actions of the armed forces implicit church sanction.

Churches confessed that their own structures often mirrored apartheid. Some were explicitly organized by race, while others were highly segregated in practice. Some churches ignored or suppressed the voices of their own members who opposed apartheid. Many lent tacit support to apartheid by their silence, inaction or by benefiting economically from the gross inequality of the system. The Church of the Province of Southern Africa (Anglican) noted its complicity in all of these dimensions. When apartheid laws benefited the church, the church often remained silent. The church confessed a sharp division between wealthy white parishes and poor black ones. They declared: '[O]ur chief expression of apology must be to our own black membership . . . Ours is primarily a black Church and it has been, and still is in many ways, a suffering Church: suffering at the hands of the Church itself.' Bishop Michael Nuttall apologized for

---

[106] Research Institute on Christianity in South Africa, 'TRC Faith Communities Report [RICSA Report]', in *Facing the Truth*, 15–80.

[107] 'Institutional Hearing: The Faith Community', Chapter 3 in *The Truth and Reconciliation Commission of South Africa Final Report*, vol. 4 (Cape Town: Juta, 1998), 59–92.

the many years that the church failed to heed the call of its then primate Archbishop Tutu for international economic sanctions. 'We took too long to come to a . . . clearer, uncompromising witness.' He asked forgiveness from Tutu, who was in the room as the chair of the TRC proceedings.[108]

The failure to do more was the refrain of many church statements. While its opposition to apartheid forms the majority of the Catholic Church's submission, it confessed to a sin of omission: 'Silence in the face of ongoing and systematic oppression at all levels of society is perhaps the church's greatest sin.'[109] Even the NGK confessed that while it had access to political leaders behind closed doors, it did not speak out strongly enough against abuses. Some churches confessed to having misunderstood their own traditions. The Salvation Army acknowledged that while its 'apolitical' stand enabled it to 'minister more freely', it thereby compromised its own tradition of serving the poor.[110] The Presbyterian Church of South Africa explained how its social history and doctrinal emphases shaped its initial unwillingness to speak on what was initially considered a 'political' issue.[111]

The church that most clearly supported apartheid policy, the NGK, did not write a document specifically for the TRC, but submitted a previously written history of its church which included various church statements, including the 1990 resolution. One scholar argues that its collaboration with the government was more active than it acknowledged in its de facto submission to the TRC.[112] Another contends that its insistence on being judged by its good intentions rather than actual results reveals that the church has not really faced its role in 'making the mind of the perpetrator, or even the inherent evil of apartheid'.[113] Moderator Freek Swanepoel testified to the TRC that 'the greater portion of the church' is committed to reconciliation – but he said with regret that he did not have the mandate to speak

---

[108] Church of the Province of Southern Africa (Anglican), 'Submission to the Truth and Reconciliation Commission' (1997).

[109] Catholic Church in South Africa, 'Submission to the Truth and Reconciliation Commission' (1997).

[110] RICSA Report, no. 3.2.1.2.5.

[111] Presbyterian Church of Southern Africa, 'Submission to the Truth and Reconciliation Commission' (1997).

[112] Tracy Kuperus, *State, Civil Society, and Apartheid in South Africa: An Examination of Dutch Reformed Church–State Relations* (Houndmills, UK: Macmillan, 1999).

[113] H. Russel Botman, 'The Offender and the Church', in *Facing the Truth*, ed. James Cochrane, John de Gruchy and Stephen Martin (Cape Town: David Philip, 1999), 130.

for the entire church.[114] TRC Commissioner Piet Meiring, himself a theologian of the NGK, wrote that it was one thing to pass resolutions repenting of the defence of apartheid, but that it may take generations to 'get it out of our hearts'.[115]

A truth and reconciliation commission, like the sacrament of penance (or reconciliation), is a truth-producing practice. What kind of truth does it produce? As with any confession, self-justification and self-deception remain possible. The RICSA Report stated that some churches with ambiguous pasts gave only general or vague accounts of themselves.[116] Recognizing that its raw material was not what the churches actually did but what the churches *said* they did, the final reports sifted the submissions with a critical eye and told a larger story about church complicity in apartheid. The result is a snapshot about how several churches at a particular time saw themselves in relation to issues of justice, truth and reconciliation in South Africa. In a particularly visible and explicit way this demonstrates how ecclesial repentance more generally serves to generate new (or perhaps reinforce old) narratives about the past, and aspires to do so for the sake of the future. The church submissions reflect the 'truth' aspiration of the TRC, though more ambiguously the 'reconciliation' element.[117]

How does truth reconcile? Repentance for the past not only presumes a truthful acknowledgement of what churches did, but particular attitudes towards that past and commitments for the future. In this sense, the truth of church statements exists in the present and the future. What does it mean for a church to truly regret what it has done? Does it imply the promise of reparations of some sort? How can a collective body like a church even have a disposition? Is the truth of a church's contrition, for example, related to its future actions and confirmed by these actions? Through the lens of the sacrament of reconciliation, these questions will be examined further in Chapter 7.

---

[114] RICSA Report, no. 3.1.

[115] Piet Meiring, 'The Dutch Reformed Church and the Truth and Reconciliation Commission', *Scriptura* 83 (2003), 254–5.

[116] RICSA Report, no. 3.1.

[117] On this distinction, see Megan Shore, *Religion and Conflict Resolution: Christianity and South Africa's Truth and Reconciliation Commission* (Farnham, UK: Ashgate, 2009), Chapters 5–6.

Chapter 3

SEXUAL ABUSE, VIOLENCE, INJUSTICE

The people expect their priests and bishops to be humble. (Fr Stephen Rosetti)[1]

This chapter deals with repentance for a variety of sins. Whereas the previous two chapters told the stories of how churches are wrestling with the scope of the people of God and the legacy of Western colonialism respectively, I do not presume that a single historical or theological framework encompasses the repentance statements that follow. While apologetic speech for clergy sexual abuse has been common and prominent, and thus the overall narrative remains a moving target, it is nevertheless an occasion to reflect on why apologies may 'fail'. Repentance in relation to issues of homosexuality is noteworthy for the way in which it functions in an ongoing debate. Other themes include war, crusades, women, science and the environment.

CLERGY SEXUAL ABUSE

Church apologies are frequently associated with clergy sexual abuse scandals. When I have explained my research to others, a common response assumes that these scandals would constitute the majority of the book. I initially excluded them though, on the grounds that I was interested in repentance for those things which were once church belief, policy or implicitly endorsed practice, not personal misconduct. Apologies by bishops and popes since the writing of this section may well require revision of the analysis. However, a book on ecclesial repentance would simply be incomplete without attention

---

[1] 'Renewal of the Priesthood in the Post-Dallas Era', *Origins* 33, no. 15 (18 September 2003), 245.

to sexual abuse by clergy. The relevant question is how churches have responded to situations in which leaders (often bishops) hid the abuse, quietly moved the abuser to another setting, or generally perpetuated a culture of secrecy and cover-up. I do not focus on apologies by actual abusers, but on church apologies for the way in which the church leadership tacitly enabled patterns of abuse or failed to protect victims. These patterns of cover-up attach to the church, and thus demand ecclesial repentance.

There are simply too many instances of church officials apologizing for past sexual abuse to make any claims to comprehensiveness, even of high profile instances. Though my focus is on the Roman Catholic Church, patterns of abuse and cover-up have been confessed in other churches. A recent study documented 191 reports of sexual abuse by 135 persons (clergy, pastoral staff, church volunteers) in the Anglican Church of Australia.[2] The Christian and Missionary Alliance made a statement of apology and asked forgiveness from those children of missionaries who were abused decades earlier by teachers in the Mamou Alliance Academy, a boarding school in Guinea. The church confessed that it failed to oversee the school, and responded too slowly to emerging reports of abuse.[3]

Sexual abuse by Catholic clergy and subsequent cover-up by some officials has been documented in Canada, the US, Ireland, Australia, Germany and other countries.[4] The most recent US crisis dates from the January 2002 publication in the *Boston Globe* of reports that priests who had abused children were quietly reassigned by bishops and their offences essentially covered up. These revelations, which some in the church have called 'our September 11', led to the resignation of Cardinal Bernard Law of Boston less than a year later and triggered other disclosures around the country. An independent study commissioned by the bishops concluded that there were almost 11,000 victims. Around 4,400 priests were accused, 150 of which had 10 or more victims. The peak of the abuse was the 1970s and 1980s.[5] The US Bishops held a crisis meeting in Dallas, June 2002, and

---

[2] Patrick Parkinson, Kim Oates and Amanda Jayakody, 'Breaking the Long Silence: Reports of Child Sexual Abuse in the Anglican Church of Australia', *Ecclesiology* 6 (2010), 183–200.

[3] Gayle White, 'Pain Relief', *Christianity Today*, 12 July 1999, 12–13.

[4] Reports from 23 countries are listed in Mary Gail Frawley-O'Dea, *Perversions of Power: Sexual Abuse in the Catholic Church* (Nashville: Vanderbilt University Press, 2007), 249–51, n. 74.

[5] Frawley-O'Dea, *Perversions of Power*, 173–9.

ultimately produced two documents, 'Charter for the Protection of Children and Young People' and 'Essential Norms' for dealing with allegations of abuse, revised with input from the Vatican later that year, that mandated a zero tolerance policy for any priest guilty of abusing a minor.

Dozens of US bishops made public statements in response to the scandal, often including an apology or request for forgiveness. *Origins*, the US Catholic News Service documentary service, published more than 20 apologies by bishops in 2002 and the years immediately following. One US prelate wrote that the bishops cannot apologize enough.[6] This comment may imply exasperation, but also a recognition that while an apology alone does not bring about healing or reconciliation, neither is an apology simply a licence to move on. Though there were apologies prior to 2002, the most recent wave began in the Boston Archdiocese. Cardinal Law issued an apology following news reports that he had reassigned former priest John Geoghan, whom he knew to have abused children.[7] While Law used the term 'apology' in several subsequent appearances and in his statement of resignation, his refrain that 'I wish we knew then what we know now' recasts the apology as sorrow for what happened, but also a mitigation of personal culpability.

In his remarks as president of the US Catholic Bishops meeting in Dallas, Bishop Wilton Gregory acknowledged that many faithful had lost confidence in episcopal leadership. Structuring his speech along the lines of the sacrament of penance, he specifically confessed the bishops' sins as lack of vigilance, lack of openness due to fear of scandal, and treating victims as adversaries. He expressed contrition by naming some of the effects of the abuse on victims, offering them 'a profound apology for the hurt and embarrassment you have suffered', and asking their forgiveness. Finally, he set forth the resolve of the bishops to address outstanding cases of abuse and ensure they do not happen again.[8] The preamble to the Charter the bishops adopted states, 'As bishops, we acknowledge our mistakes and our role in that suffering, and we apologize and take responsibility for too often failing victims and our people in the past'.[9]

---

[6] Cardinal Roger Mahony, 'My Hopes For Dallas', *America*, 27 May 2002, 7.

[7] Cardinal Bernard Law, 'Statement Apologizes for Clergy Sexual Abuse of Minors', 9 January 2002.

[8] Bishop Wilton Gregory, US Conference of Catholic Bishops, 'Presidential Address', 13 June 2002.

[9] US Conference of Catholic Bishops, 'Charter for the Protection of Children and Young People' (2002).

In spite of this and dozens of statements, there was widespread perception in the church, among the public and by groups of abuse survivors that these apologies were inadequate. Why?

Some statements appear apologetic, but fail to be full apologies. Cardinal Edward Egan of New York said he would be sorry 'if in hindsight we also discover that mistakes may have been made'.[10] Such a conditional statement fails to specify what those mistakes might be (and thus who might be responsible) but also raises the possibility that there were no mistakes. Other leaders declared forceful regret for what happened and outlined strategies to prevent abuse in the future, but without acknowledgment of a failure of oversight. Thus, Cardinal Anthony Bevilacqua of Philadelphia offered his 'deepest apologies and heartfelt sorrows' for what victims suffered, without assuming any responsibility himself or for predecessor bishops.[11] The 'empathic "I'm sorry"' is among the many ways ostensibly apologetic speech fails to be a full apology.[12] Was he simply expressing in the apologetic idiom regret that abuse happened? While there is no indication that the cardinal intended to speak on behalf of the abusers or for their personal sins, he left a merely vague impression that there *may* be responsibility at the higher levels of the church. When Cardinal Law apologized for 'the inadequacy of past policies and flaws in past decisions',[13] he implicitly suggested that procedures, rather than human agents, bore the responsibility. When he explained that he made the admittedly regrettable decision to reassign a known abuser to another parish (without telling anyone in the parish) on the advice of psychiatrists and in good faith,[14] he implicitly asserted that such good intentions mitigate his own responsibility.

Mindful of addressing many constituencies – the general public, Catholic laity, priests, as well as victims and their families, other bishops and the Vatican – many of the very true things included in apologies were received as qualifying their sincerity. Some observed that abuse is not unique to the church, or that abuse may be more infrequent in the church than in society as a whole. Bishops observed that the pathologies of abusive behaviour are better understood now

---

[10] Cited in Stephen Pope, 'Accountability and Sexual Abuse in the United States: Lessons for the Universal Church', *Irish Theological Quarterly* 69 (2004), 77.

[11] Cardinal Anthony Bevilacqua, 'Restoring Trust', *Origins* 31, no. 39 (14 March 2002), 659.

[12] Aaron Lazare, *On Apology* (Oxford: Oxford University Press, 2004), 86.

[13] Cardinal Bernard Law, 'Pentecost Letter', *Origins* 32, no. 3 (30 May 2002), 40.

[14] Law, 'Statement Apologizes for Clergy Sexual Abuse of Minors.'

then decades ago. Others complained about merciless treatment by media; accusations of an anti-Catholic agenda extended the claim that the church is the real victim here. Bishops rightly noted that the vast majority of priests were not abusers and some have indeed been falsely accused. And while bishops do indeed have a pastoral responsibility to priests guilty of abuse, the victims of that abuse are unlikely to welcome the reminder that even 'those who do have substantiated charges against them' have also done 'good work' as priests.[15]

Apologetic speech was undoubtedly affected by the reality of litigation and legal liability. Some bishops were advised by lawyers to avoid any statements that might imply institutional responsibility. In the name of protecting the assets of the church, others played 'legal hardball' by hiring private investigators to dig up compromising information on plaintiffs, or by subpoenaing therapists working with victims.[16] The financial stakes were high. By 2007, over US$2 billion had been paid in settlements to victims. Several dioceses had declared bankruptcy. Some bishops signed legal agreements with states' attorneys-general to manage liability or avoid criminal prosecution. For example, Arizona asserted that it had evidence that Bishop Thomas O'Brien of Phoenix was criminally negligent in his failure to protect children. However, 'in the public interest', the county prosecutor agreed to forgo charges if O'Brien surrendered some administrative responsibility and issued an apology. O'Brien signed a legal document acknowledging that 'he allowed Roman Catholic priests under his supervision to have contact with minors after becoming aware of allegations of criminal sexual misconduct' and promising to 'apologize and express contrition for any misconduct, hardship or harm cause to victims' by these priests, which he then did in a public speech.[17] (O'Brien resigned as bishop weeks later after being charged with a fatal hit-and-run for which he was ultimately found guilty.) Apologies given only when mandated, or when the legal risk to do so has been clarified, are of questionable sincerity and devalue apologies given under different circumstances.

The rhetoric of universal sinfulness also functions to minimize specific responsibility. Cardinal Justin Rigali of St Louis located the

---

[15] Cardinal Justin Rigali, 'Address to Priests on Sexual Abuse of Minors', *Origins* 31, no. 41 (28 March 2002), 679.

[16] Frawley-O'Dea, *Perversions of Power*, 135.

[17] 'Agreement with County Attorney Regarding Sexual Abuse of Minors', *Origins* 33, no. 5 (12 June 2003), 69–70.

sin committed by abusive priests within the sinfulness of all. The sexual abuse crisis 'is a moment for us truly to acknowledge all sin in our lives, to ask God's pardon and forgiveness', he said.[18] While this is true enough, victims do not want to hear that anyone could have abused them, or be reminded that, like their abusers, they too are sinful. At issue is this *particular* sin, and whether individual abusers and those who had oversight acknowledge particular responsibility and are held accountable. Moreover, victims are unlikely to see the primary problem in terms of the sinfulness of the priests, and what their acts might mean for their relationship with God. Theologian Norbert Rigali – a brother of Cardinal Rigali – argues that since many bishops framed the scandal in the terms of the pre-Vatican II moral theology in which they were trained, they failed to see that the issue was not primarily the 'fall' of individual priests. This sin-centred and confession-oriented moral theology attends to acts that priests did, the intentions underlying them, and the spiritual consequences for the offender, but not for the victim.[19] Moreover, Cardinal Rigali's definition of this fall as a 'violation of celibacy' – as if priests had *consensual* relations with *adults* over whom they were not in positions of *authority* – reflects a gross misunderstanding of abuse and its underlying inequality of power. This moral theology fails to take seriously the effect of sin on the abused victims and the social order more generally. Indeed, Cardinal Rigali has refused to meet with victims.[20]

Some victims reported that they sued the church only because officials refused to truly acknowledge their experience, apologize, and directly discuss with them ways to ensure it never happened again.[21] The accounts of the abuse itself reflect an enormous betrayal of trust, and legacies of broken relationships, isolation, self-loathing, addictions and suicide. But a second layer of victimization also occurred. For years, Peter Pollard was abused by Fr George Rosencrantz. Pollard recalls one instance in which a Monsignor McCarthy came upon Rosencrantz in the act of abusing him but rather than intervene he pretended not to see it, saying 'Could you put out the light when you are finished?' When Pollard reported the abuse to the

---

[18] Cardinal Justin Rigali, 'Address to Priests', 680.

[19] Norbert J. Rigali, 'Moral Theology and Church Responses to Sexual Abuse', *Horizons* 34 (2007), 190–4.

[20] Frawley-O'Dea, *Perversions of Power*, 132–3.

[21] *Boston Globe* Investigative Staff, *Betrayal: The Crisis in the Catholic Church* (Boston: Little, Brown, 2002), 81; Frawley-O'Dea, *Perversions of Power*, 133.

Boston Archdiocese years later, Cardinal Law's deputy, Fr John McCormack, responded with indifference. McCormack suggested that perhaps Pollard misinterpreted the past. McCormack said that since Rosencrantz had denied the charges, he was inclined to believe him. If there was anything to it, it was consensual, added McCormack. 'McCormack basically abused me again,' reflected Pollard. 'For me, the emotional and spiritual scarring came from the betrayal by Law and McCormack and was as damaging as what Rosencrantz did.'[22]

In 1989 Tom Blanchette attended the funeral of Fr Joseph Birmingham, a priest who had abused him but with whom he had a confrontation and some measure of reconciliation prior to his death. At the funeral reception, Blanchette approached Cardinal Law out of earshot of others and reported that Birmingham had abused him, his brothers, and many more. Asking to pray with him, Law placed his hands on Blanchette and intoned: 'I bind you by the power of the confessional never to speak about this to anyone else.' Blanchette said later, 'And that just burned me big time . . . I didn't ask him to hear my confession. I went there to inform him.'[23]

Some bishops did respond in ways that survivors reported to be genuine and pastoral. A few bishops attempted to apologize, in person, to every single victim in their diocese.[24] Oakland Bishop John Cummins held a service with victims in which he not only acknowledged the evil of abuse, but the failure of the church to be compassionate and pastoral in response. He named the insensitive ways that bishops have dealt with victims, often minimizing the issue, hoping the scandal will disappear, or treating victims as adversaries. Significantly, his apology and request for forgiveness were developed together with abuse survivors, who wrote the words they wanted to hear from the church. He pledged his successors to maintain an active dialogue with them.[25] Cummins held the service in a lodge rather than a church, given that many victims will not enter a church. As the apology became dialogical in these ways, it was an avenue through which survivors expressed moral agency. It was delivered in a way, and in a setting, in which those who needed to hear it most were

---

[22] *Boston Globe* Investigative Staff, *Betrayal*, 78–9.

[23] *Ibid.*, 96.

[24] Frawley-O'Dea, *Perversions of Power*, 137.

[25] Bishop John Cummins, 'Statement Apologizes for Past Treatment of Sexual-Abuse Victims', *Origins* 29, no. 44 (20 April 2000), 718–20.

able to do so. It began to undo the hurt caused by the failure of the church to truly hear stories of victims.

In both his address to the US cardinals who were summoned to Rome in 2002 to deal with the issue, and in his World Youth Day speech in Toronto of that year, Pope John Paul II framed the problem as a particularly American one of relativism and lax sexual morality. In Toronto he said that the actions of some priests 'fill us with sadness and shame', but as one spokesperson for clergy abuse victims noted, he did not apologize or say one word to victims or about victims.[26] The furthest John Paul went was to report and presumably concur with the decision of the Synod of Bishops for Oceania to 'apologize unreservedly to the victims [of clergy sexual abuse] for the pain and disillusionment caused to them'.[27]

There was great speculation about whether Pope Benedict would address the issue of clergy abuse during his 2008 visit to the US. In an interview on the plane, the pope expressed shame that this abuse happened and promised that paedophiles would not be admitted to the priesthood but did not identify responsibility at any level of the church beyond individual offenders. He was restrained and measured in his words at the public mass. He lamented the harm the abuse has caused to individuals – and to the reputation of the church.[28] He did meet with a small number of selected victims at an unannounced private meeting. Some victims described the meeting as very moving, but others remarked that, without concrete action and reform, words were insufficient.[29] The pope failed to recognize that, from the perspective of victims, their abusers were not just criminals, but priests who represented to church to them and for that very reason had the unqualified trust of vulnerable children. Regardless of the ecclesiological nuances, it was the church that failed them.

The pope did use the language of apology a few months later in Australia, where he also met privately with four victims. In a homily, Benedict said: 'I am deeply sorry for the pain and suffering the victims have endured and assure them that, as their pastor, I, too, share in

---

[26] Paul R. Dokecki, *The Clergy Sexual Abuse Crisis: Reform and Renewal in the Catholic Community* (Washington, DC: Georgetown University Press, 2004), 3.

[27] Pope John Paul II, *Post-Synodal Apostolic Exhortation Ecclesia in Oceania* (2001), no. 49.

[28] Homily of Pope Benedict XVI, Washington Nationals Stadium, Thursday, 17 April 2008.

[29] Ian Fisher and Laurie Goodstein, 'Benedict Meets with the Victims of Sexual Abuse', *New York Times*, 18 April 2008.

their suffering.'[30] While he recognized the necessity of speaking about the experience of victims, the apology remained regret that abuse happened and that it resulted in pain, but not for cover-up or any element of broader church responsibility.

The relationship between the Vatican and several national churches has been strained by the abuse scandals. Popes have routinely asserted that sexual abuse scandals are to be addressed at the local level, despite the widespread perception that given the pope's authority over local churches, especially with respect to the appointment of bishops, he must accept some responsibility for their failures. Indeed, calls for a papal apology are premised on the idea that only such an act reflects full acknowledgment by 'the church'.

In early 2010, Pope Benedict held an unprecedented summit with Irish Bishops to discuss the implications of a government report that documented decades of secrecy, silence, cover-up and collusion with police to protect abusive priests from punishment and the church from scandal in the Dublin Archdiocese. Despite the pope's unequivocal denunciation of the abuse, many victims groups remained unsatisfied that the pope did not acknowledge a cover-up, did not demand resignations and made no clear statement of apology.[31]

In his pastoral letter to the Irish Church, he apologized for the suffering of victims, though again the apology was for the fact that the abuse happened. The letter went further than previous statements by acknowledging the 'often inadequate response' by 'ecclesiastical authorities in your country' and by linking these failures with the language of sin (a clear predication, however, is not grammatically clear). Some criticism emerged because his letter did not demand resignations, establish new structures of accountability (other than the 'inspection' of some dioceses by the Vatican), or address abuse scandals in several other countries. Benedict did address the failures of the Irish Bishops (though often in the passive 'mistakes were made' voice) and exhorted them to set an example with their own lives by personal spiritual renewal, self-examination, honesty, transparency and 'accountability before God'.[32] Notably, he did not apply any of these exhortations to himself. Was there no need for a new tone to be set from the top? Does no responsibility whatsoever extend to the

---

[30] Homily of Pope Benedict XVI, Saint Mary's Cathedral, Sydney, 19 July 2008.

[31] David Quinn, 'Too Little, Too Late, Again', *The Tablet*, 27 February 2010, 8–9.

[32] Pope Benedict XVI, Pastoral Letter to the Catholics of Ireland, 19 March 2010.

Vatican and the pope? Benedict's most recent admission (at the time of writing) that he leads a 'wounded and sinful' church, may reflect a recognition that the crisis requires a deeper shift in perspective and language.[33]

A church that makes a statement about an aspect of its past ought to consider its history carefully and not apologize for that which it did not do. To apologize with reckless abandon for anything and everything does not reflect a serious look at the past and evinces no reason to think that appropriate reforms will follow. There are relevant 'conditions' to the apologies: most priests did not abuse, the pathologies of abuse were not as well-understood decades ago as they are today, bishops exercised varying degrees of inadvertent ignorance to wilful negligence. However, I do not believe that the suspicion by which many apologies have been received can be accounted for adequately by the inclusion of such qualifications. Even when episcopal responsibility for reassigning abusers is acknowledged, a larger issue has not been named. While there are many candidates for the 'real issue' both in terms of the abuse itself (moral relativism, selection and formation of priests, homosexuality, priestly celibacy), and the failure to intervene and protect children (misunderstanding the nature of abuse, the protection of church interests and assets, avoidance of scandal), the one that emerges most prominently with respect to the latter is clericalism.

R. Scott Appleby addressed the bishops in Dallas and warned them that their apologies will not be heard apart from a recognition that at the root of the protection of abusive priests is 'a sin born from the arrogance of power'.[34] Clericalism revels in the powers and privileges bestowed on clergy, especially bishops. Christopher Ruddy describes clericalism as a pattern of attitude and action 'that holds that clergy are a superior class and therefore virtually unanswerable to laity'.[35] This results in a secretive culture and a tendency to close ranks, disregard counsel from the outside, or project an external enemy (an anti-Catholic media or even a Jewish conspiracy[36]) when a threat appears. If docile loyalty to one's superior is the characteristic most evident in those 'promoted' within the hierarchy, as has often been

---

[33] 'The Comfort of Not Being Alone', *L'Osservatore Romano*, English edition, 28 April 2010, 2.

[34] Cited in Pope, 'Accountability and Sexual Abuse in the US', 83.

[35] Christopher Ruddy, 'Ecclesiological Issues Behind the Sexual Abuse Crisis', *Origins* 37, no. 8 (5 July 2007), 120.

[36] Frawley-O'Dea, *Perversions of Power*, 166.

alleged, then the system will remain insulated. Clericalism is a 'sin against baptism' because by equating the hierarchy with the church, it disregards the baptism of the laity as the basis for their active, not just passive, role in the mission of the church.[37] The issues that have most enraged those who were not directly abused themselves – the failure of bishops to be humble, to truly be open to the voices of the victims, and to respond in open and transparent ways – are all tied to clericalism. A dismantling of clericalism will not mean that no priest will ever abuse a child, but it will undo the structure that has enabled and protected abusers.

The meaning of any act of repentance cannot be analysed in isolation from the entire life of the church. The Catholic Church's ecumenical repentance is taken as sincere in part because the church has made an irrevocable commitment to ecumenism. Likewise, repentance for anti-Jewish theology, despite questions about whether the church has adequately acknowledged its role in relation to the Third Reich, is founded on an authoritative rejection of supersessionism. If a culture of clericalism is at the root of the church's failure to protect children from clergy sexual abuse, then unless quite profound reforms are implemented to address that culture, the perception will remain that the church hierarchy has failed to truly repent. (The very idea that the hierarchy speaks on behalf of the church need not be clericalist. In itself, it reflects a particular ecclesiological account of authority, which may be exercised in both faithful and unfaithful ways.) Unless there are concrete and systemic reasons to believe that any future allegations of abuse will be dealt with in a prompt, transparent way, with pastoral sensitivity for alleged victims as well as alleged abusers, the church's commitment to not repeat its past mistakes will be doubted.

Ruddy proposes reducing the size of dioceses so that bishops can be essentially pastors rather than CEOs. He argues that pastoral competence, and the ability to work collaboratively with laity and clergy alike to advance the mission of the church ought to be the primary factors in the selection of bishops. He recommends greater structures of episcopal accountability and even mechanisms for removal. Canon lawyer Sr Sharon Euart argues for greater participation of the laity in governance, greater transparency in decision-making, streamlined procedures for the removal of priests, and consultation with laity

---

[37] Ruddy, 'Ecclesiological Issues Behind the Sexual Abuse Crisis', 123.

and clergy alike in bishop selection.[38] In response to Pope Benedict's letter to Irish Catholics, Archbishop Diarmuid Martin responded that 'more participation of lay men and women is needed to avoid a false culture of clericalism'.[39] However, out of concern that laity not exercise authority over bishops, the lay review boards proposed by the US Bishops in 2002 were amended by the Vatican to serve a merely consultative role. Along similar lines, some Vatican officials initially said that bishops should not even be required to report abuse to civil authorities,[40] although approved norms do now require this. Whatever structural changes may be judged appropriate, there is no simple formula for reforming a mentality, though precisely at this point acts of profound repentance signal the need for such a shift.

War, Civil War, Crusades

Though a minor theme among some German church leaders during World War II, the discourse of church repentance gained momentum in Germany after the war. What follows concerns more general responsibility for war, whereas crimes against Jews and theological anti-Judaism have been discussed in Chapter 1. In 1945, the Evangelical Church in Germany (EKD) faced intense pressure from the allied countries and the ecumenical movement to acknowledge some share of war guilt. This external pressure combined with competing interpretations of how the Confessing Church acted during the war and competing visions for the future produced intense debates about whether to repent and what it would mean. Is repentance only individual or also corporate? Who could confess on behalf of the church? Ought the sins to be identified generally, or particularly? Ought forgiveness to be sought of victims, or of God alone? Could church leaders repent on behalf of the nation, or just the church?

At their 1945 Treysa conference, a reforming faction led by Martin Niemöller argued for an admission of the church's guilt in failing to hold to its own teachings and in supporting some policies of Hitler. He maintained that since the church ought to have recognized the

---

[38] Sharon Euart, 'A Canonical Perspective on the Sexual Abuse Crisis', *Origins* 37, no. 8 (5 July 2007), 113–19. Similarly Paul Lakeland, 'Roman Catholicism After the Sex Scandals', in *Faith in America: Changes, Challenges, New Directions*, vol. 1, ed. Charles H. Lippy (Westport, CT: Praeger, 2006), 45–61.

[39] Archbishop Diarmuid Martin, 'We Must Face the Truth of the Past', *Origins* 39, no. 42 (1 April 2010), 689.

[40] Frawley-O'Dea, *Perversions of Power*, 165.

wickedness of the path Germany was taking, it had a special duty to warn the nation. This faction proposed a 'Message to Pastors' that contained a confession of guilt and proposed that the church declare its distance from the state. Though its confession remained quite general, it was rejected for going too far.[41] The conservative majority of the EKD approved a 'Message to Congregations' that cannot be considered an act of repentance. It emphasized the faithfulness of those in the church who resisted and declared that *if* the church had been complicit with the Third Reich, it would have been involuntary. This statement interpreted the collapse of Germany as God's judgement, but for crimes named only in the passive voice: '. . . justice was thwarted . . . human beings had become mere numbers . . .' The overall tone was of comfort to the German people, encouraging them, as well as positioning the church as a key institution in the reconstruction of the nation.[42]

The landmark Stuttgart Declaration of Guilt was made in October 1945 by the EKD Leadership Council at the urging of WCC general secretary W. A. Visser't Hooft, who believed that only by some acknowledgment of guilt by the church could it participate in the ecumenical movement and play a constructive role in reconciliation between nations. The Declaration acknowledged that the church shared 'a great solidarity of guilt' with the German people, and as a result 'endless suffering has been brought to many peoples and countries'. While the church had struggled against tyranny, it was also guilty of 'not witnessing more courageously, not praying more faithfully, not believing more joyously, and not loving more ardently'. Finally, it prayed that the church may be a source of healing in the world.[43]

Church leaders interpreted this compromise statement in light of a spectrum of political and theological concerns. Niemöller saw it as a specific confession of the church's support of some egregious Third Reich policies. Conservative signatories such as Hans Asmussen believed that through the Declaration the church fulfilled its priestly role to accept responsibility on behalf of the German people. Thus, the church humbly and graciously accepted guilt which was not its own. Others believed that while the church might have a share in the universal sin of rebellion against God, such guilt ought to be confessed on the individual level, before God alone. In addition,

---

[41] Hockenos, *A Church Divided*, 180–2.
[42] *Ibid.*, 185–6.
[43] Evangelical Church in Germany, Stuttgart Declaration of Guilt (1945).

many were concerned about the political use the Allies would make of a statement of guilt.[44] Despite these variable interpretations and the fact that it did not mention the treatment of Jews, the Stuttgart Declaration was a landmark document that led to further self-reflection.

The Darmstadt Statement (1947) enumerated several ways in which the church 'went astray' through its support of nationalism and dictatorship. It thus confessed quite particularly that the church had aligned itself with a belief in 'a special German mission', supported particular political parties, and neglected its calling to promote reconciliation among nations and justice for the poor and marginalized. The statement then called the church to not be seduced by dreams of the past or the future, or by indifference, but to accept the responsibility to rebuild Germany and seek justice, peace and the reconciliation of nations. Its final claim, that in the act of confessing the church knows itself to be absolved, raises the question of whether the church is authorized to declare its own absolution. Though it did not mention Jews or anti-Judaism (statements in 1948 and 1950 would do so), it explicitly linked its confession of past sins to a renewed sense of call for the present. It affirmed that the church must bring gospel judgements to the political sphere, but not in a nationalistic or partisan way.[45]

It is notable that only churches in the defeated nations repented for their support of World War II, though Visser't Hooft did call upon allied and neutral countries to consider repentance.[46] Unlike Germany, the churches in Japan did not have even a minority opposed to the war policy. In a culture that placed a high value on public apologies, the repentance by the United Church of Christ in Japan in 1946 for failing to preserve the destiny of the nation, was really lament that Japan did not win the war.[47] By contrast, that church's advocacy of nuclear disarmament and opposition to the Vietnam War two decades later led it to examine its own history of militarism and issue a completely different statement of repentance.[48] In 1967 it

---

[44] Hockenos, *A Church Divided*, 81.

[45] Evangelical Church in Germany, Darmstadt Statement (1947).

[46] John S. Conway, 'How Shall the Nations Repent? The Stuttgart Declaration of Guilt, October 1945', *Journal of Ecclesiastical Studies* 38 (1987), 607.

[47] Iwao Morioka, 'Japanese Churches and World War II', trans. Akira Demura, *Japan Christian Quarterly* 34 (1968), 81.

[48] Shishido Yutaka, 'The Peace Movement of Postwar Japanese Christians', *Japan Christian Quarterly* 51 (1985), 219.

confessed that it was sinful to have aligned itself with the militaristic aim of the government, supported the war and prayed for victory. The church ought to have criticized official policies, and served as the 'watchman' of the nation.[49] This statement was an important one for the renewal of the United Church of Christ in Japan's sense of mission and purpose. Decades earlier the government had pressed for the union of Protestant denominations in order to marshal their support for war. With its 'Confession of Responsibility', this church sought to ground its future existence, integrity and mission in discontinuity from its origin.[50]

The Anglican Communion in Japan admitted responsibility and confessed its sin in 1996 for having supported Japanese aggression and colonial rule, and for not apologizing much earlier. (In 1945, a single bishop did repent for the church's complicity in government war policy.) The church acknowledged that it had compromised with the government, considered obedience to the emperor to be the will of God and supported Japanese rule over others. But the church recognized that without church-wide repentance, its mission would continue to be corrupted by ethnocentrism and a focus on institutional survival.[51] Significantly, for both the Anglican and the United churches in Japan, new understandings of mission – whether advocating nuclear disarmament, an ethnically inclusive church or a witness to the state – propelled a reexamination and judgement on the past.

The Catholic Church in Germany did not make a statement along the lines of the Protestant Stuttgart Declaration. The bishops' 1945 Fulda Pastoral Letter, noted in Chapter 1, granted that even some Catholics were persuaded by Nazi rhetoric and abetted their crimes. Years later, on 11 June 1961, a prayer was offered in all German churches on the instruction of the bishops that contained an implicit recognition of sins of omission by Christians during the war. From the 1970s through the present, German Catholic Church statements have attended more specifically to their role in the Holocaust, rather than support for the war itself.

Pope John Paul II has acknowledged the complicity of Christians in the mentality of war, as well as World War II in particular. His state-

---

[49] United Church of Christ in Japan, 'Confession on the Responsibility During World War II' (1967).
[50] Morioka, 'Japanese Churches and World War II', 84–5.
[51] Anglican Communion in Japan (*Nippon Sei Ko Kai*), 'Statement on War Responsibility' (1996).

ments have emphasized the failure of individuals and their need for repentance, though perhaps by implication this includes church's failure to pursue peace more actively. At the first Day of Prayer for Peace in the World, held in at Assisi in 1986 together with other religious leaders, he confessed that Catholics have not always been faithful to Jesus' way of peace, and thus could regard the Assisi event as an act of penance.[52]

The relationship between the Catholic hierarchies and Latin American dictatorships in the 1960s, 70s and 80s is a complicated one.[53] The Argentine Bishops Conference made a somewhat tentative statement in 1996 that acknowledged that Catholics were on both sides of the 'Dirty War'; some advocated violent revolution and others supported government repression of such revolution. While the church asked for pardon for such crimes 'in solidarity with our people and the sins of all', the relative silence of the church was essentially defended on the grounds that the bishops attempted to find practical ways to minimize suffering in the face of 'intransigence'.[54] They rejected a stronger statement that acknowledged and asked God's forgiveness for those times when the church was silent, guilty of 'indecision, weakness or erroneous judgment', or acted in a 'lukewarm or unworthy manner'.[55]

A resolution of repentance regarding the Vietnam war was approved by the (North American) General Conference Mennonite Church in 1971. Consistent with its pacifist convictions, the church had already spoken out against the war, and some members refused to pay that portion of federal taxes used to support the military. The statement confessed guilt 'of injury to our Asian brothers by virtue of our participation in the economic system which finances the American position'.[56] The resolution thus addressed the complicity of citizens who were also church members, rather than a specific act or omission by the church itself. It enlisted ecclesial repentance as a basis on which to speak prophetically about the war in Vietnam.

In 1994 and 1995 Archbishop of Canterbury George Carey and Cardinal Cahal Daly of Northern Ireland made a series of confes-

---

[52] Pope John Paul II, Day of Prayer for Peace in the World, Assisi (1986).

[53] A detailed discussion of the role of the Catholic Church in Chile under Pinochet is found in William T. Cavanaugh, *Torture and Eucharist: Theology, Politics and the Body of Christ* (Oxford: Blackwell, 1998).

[54] Argentine Catholic Bishops, Statement on National History (1996).

[55] Luigi Accattoli, *When a Pope Asks Forgiveness: The Mea Culpa's of John Paul II*, trans. Jordan Aumann (Boston: Daughters of St Paul, 1998), 92–3.

[56] General Conference Mennonite Church, 'Resolution of Repentance' (1971).

sions and requests for forgiveness. Archbishop Carey asked that the English be forgiven 'for our often brutal domination and crass insensitivity in the eight hundred years of history of our relationship with Ireland',[57] while Cardinal Daly asked forgiveness for the 'wrongs and hurts inflicted by Irish people . . . particularly in the past 25 years'.[58] Was this ecclesial repentance? Both spoke on behalf of their 'people' rather than their churches.

The legacy of the crusades has been addressed by the Catholic Church in a number a statements to various Orthodox Churches, discussed in Chapter 1. A unique grassroots initiative by American evangelicals to address the history of crusades warrants discussion, even though the acts of repentance considered in this book are primarily those on behalf of churches. In 1996, a group of Christians departed from Cologne by foot and headed for the Balkans, Turkey, and Jerusalem. Along this 'Reconciliation Walk', they apologized to Muslims and Jews, as well as ordinary citizens on the streets, for the crusades carried out by their Christian forebears. Their prepared apology text included the following:

> We wish to retrace the footsteps of the Crusaders in apology for their deeds and in demonstration of the true meaning of the cross. We deeply regret the atrocities committed in the name of Christ by our predecessors. We renounce greed, hatred and fear, and condemn all violence done in the name of Christ . . . Forgive us for allowing His name to be associated with death.[59]

Reconciliation Walkers described their journey as following Jesus' example of crossing social boundaries in order to be signs of peace. They spoke about humbling themselves as individuals and listening to the stories of those they encountered. They explained the importance of simply being faces of a non-imperialist Western Christianity and hearing from local people that present day fears about cultural, economic or political invasions from the West evoke the pain of the crusades.[60] About 450 Christians arrived in Jerusalem in 1999. On 15 July, the 900th anniversary of the Crusaders' capture of Jerusalem, they delivered apologies to the Chief Rabbi, Greek Orthodox Patriarch and Grand Mufti of Jerusalem. Though they did not speak as representatives of a particular church, their assumption

---

[57] Archbishop George Carey, Sermon in Christ Church Cathedral, Dublin, 18 November 1994.

[58] Cardinal Cahal Daly, 'Forgiveness: Necessary Condition for Peace' (1995).

[59] Reconciliation Walk, 'Statement of Apology' (1996–1999).

[60] C. Lynn Green, prod., *The Reconciliation Walk: From Europe to Jerusalem*, videocassette (A Reconciliation Walk and JEMS/Skunkworks Production, 1999).

that as (primarily) Protestants they could apologize for what Catholic Christians had done a millennium earlier points to a remarkably generous ecumenical identity, and challenge to fellow Protestants to regard their history (and responsibility) as extending to the time before the Reformation.

Highly critical of this endeavour, historian of the crusades Jonathan Riley-Smith argues that the Reconciliation Walkers failed to interpret history correctly – the crusades were as much against other Christians as against Muslims. Given the theological justifications of violence at the time, past Christians participated in crusades in good faith.[61] While crusaders undoubtedly sinned as individuals, Riley-Smith maintains that an apology for a policy of the church is impossible. It would imply that 'either the Church can no longer be regarded as a reliable moral teacher or ethics are relative'.[62]

Though this was not a stated intention of the organizers, the Reconciliation Walk has been appropriated by several writers on Christian evangelism among Muslims, a controversial connection given historical links between conquest and conversion. One book frames the apology as a way to overcome a Muslim barrier to embracing Christianity.[63] Another presents it as evidence that not only is true Christianity antithetical to the crusades, but the fact that the apology was a *Christian* confession shows that only the blood of Christ can forgive the brutality of the crusades and end the spiral of violence they represent.[64]

Women

Two notable Catholic statements of confession regarding the dignity of women preceded the pope's inclusion of offences against the dignity of women in the 2000 Day of Pardon. In 1995, a decree of the General Congregation of the Society of Jesus acknowledged that the oppression of women has damaged the mission of the church.

---

[61] Jonathan Riley-Smith, 'Rethinking the Crusades', *First Things*, no. 101 (March 2000), 20–3.

[62] Jonathan Riley-Smith, letter to the editor, *First Things*, no. 105 (September 2000), 6.

[63] Keith E. Swartley, ed., *Encountering the World of Islam* (Atlanta: Authentic Media, 2005), 239–40.

[64] Ergun Mehmet Caner and Emir Fethi Caner, *Christian Jihad: Two Former Muslims Look at the Crusades and Killing in the Name of Christ* (Grand Rapids: Kregel, 2004), 209–12.

The Jesuits confessed their need of conversion as a part of a church tradition 'that has offended against women'. They recognized that they have 'unwittingly. . . often contributed to a form of clericalism which has reinforced male domination with an ostensibly divine sanction' and pledged to listen to the experiences of women in order to make appropriate personal and corporate changes.[65]

Pope John Paul II addressed a 'Letter to Women' on the occasion of the UN Conference on Women. The letter has a patronizing tone at points – 'Thank you, *every woman*, for the simple fact of being *a woman!*' – and praises the 'feminine genius' of women, especially in familial and social roles. It acknowledges that the dignity of women has often been relegated to the margins, especially in particular (though unnamed) contexts. For this, a conditional apology – *if* blame belongs to 'not just a few members of the church' – is given. The pope wrote that if the church recalls how Jesus treated women, then it will renew its commitment to the dignity of women. However, the letter regards the 'historical conditioning' that led to these injustices as essentially alien to the church and somehow smuggled in. While the pope called for a courageous examination of the past, he placed a much greater emphasis on telling previously silenced stories of women's achievements in history than on identifying the mechanisms and agents of sexism and exclusion.[66]

Repentance for a very specific policy, the 'Disjoining Rule', was made by the United Church of Canada in 2006. The rule, abolished in 1957, required women clergy or deacons to relinquish their ministry if they married. Moderator Peter Short wrote a letter to each woman known to have been effected, and the General Council Executive held a Service of Apology. Participants in the service were invited to place a stone in a pottery bowl to symbolize the many gifts of women and as a sign of the church 'coming round' to affirm these gifts. In her meditation, the Rev Elizabeth Eberhart-Moffat told the stories of several women affected by the rule. She also warned, 'But lest we become known only as the church of the next apology, let us also remind ourselves of the temptations of cheap grace, which revels in drama and false pride.' Referring to her own 'kaleidoscope of emotions', Wilma Cade responded that she could not speak for others who had been required to relinquish their formal ministry

---

[65] Society of Jesus, 'Jesuits and the Situation of Women in Church and Civil Society' (1995).

[66] Pope John Paul II, 'Letter to Women' (1995), italics in original.

under the rule, and thus she could not accept the church's apology on their behalf. 'However, I will say that I forgave the United Church this Disjoining many years ago.'[67]

The UCC's action was strikingly specific. It apologized for one policy, but not for having denied ordered ministry to women in the past. Neither have other mainline churches that have changed their position on women's ordination.[68] For example, the UMC passed a resolution condemning sexism in the church but did not repent, apologize or ask forgiveness for any of its policies or practices, past or present, despite having done so with respect to other sins in the church.[69] Why?

Throughout the church's history, changes and reforms have been introduced without specific repudiation of the past. One may infer that churches hold that it was not unfaithful to restrict ordination to men, but given new spiritual insights, it is now apparent that gender should not be a barrier to ordered ministry. Those pushing for change may have been satisfied by a change in policy and practice and regarded efforts to seek an apology for the past an unnecessary battle. A lack of internal consensus may account for the absence of such repentance in denominations such as the Church of England in which women may be admitted to the priesthood but not the episcopacy. Nevertheless, it is very difficult to even speculate on the reason for an absence of repentance in progressive churches. It may point to a conviction that solemn ecclesial repentance is not the way to address every past injustice, or there may be no discernible reason at all.

Homosexual Persons

One striking exception to the general rule that repentance is made only on issues where there is a broad church-wide consensus, either within a denomination or ecumenically, is in regard to homosexual persons. Perhaps because of a dramatic increase in apologies by

---

[67] Documents from the 2006 Service of Apology were provided by the Office of Faith Formation and Education, United Church of Canada.

[68] See J. Gordon Melton, *The Churches Speak on – Women's Ordination: Official Statements from Religious Bodies and Ecumenical Organizations* (Detroit: Gale Research, 1991).

[69] United Methodist Church, 'Eradication of Sexism in the Church', adopted 1996, amended and readopted 2004, in *Book of Resolutions of the United Methodist Church 2008* (Nashville: Abingdon Press, 2008), 525–6.

churches in the late 1990s, this form of speech has become entangled in the debate about homosexuality in the church. Particularly within the Anglican Communion, a range of positions have been staked out by means of repentance and calls for repentance.

The Synod of the Church of the Province of Southern Africa (Anglican) acknowledged their role in perpetuating an attitude of 'harshness and hostility' towards homosexual people. The church repented of this prejudice and asked forgiveness of those hurt by it. Its statement affirms that sexual intercourse is reserved for people in opposite sex marriages, but acknowledges the need for appropriate pastoral responses to people in a wide variety of relationships.[70] The Episcopal Church apologized 'to its members who are gay or lesbian, and to lesbians and gay men outside the Church, for years of rejection and maltreatment by the Church', while proposing to continue to dialogue on the issue.[71] Though the Anglican Church of Canada General Synod rejected, in 1995, an amended motion to repent for bigotry towards homosexual persons, Bishop Michael Ingham of New Westminster, BC, has apologized to gays and lesbians 'for the slowness of the process of your full inclusion in the Body of Christ'.[72]

The Anglican Communion's *Windsor Report* invited the Episcopal Church to express regret for its consent to the episcopal consecration of Gene Robinson, a man in a committed same-sex relationship, which was widely reported as a call for repentance. The sentence preceding the invitation to express regret identified repentance as one of the 'imperatives of communion'.[73] The Anglican Churches in Canada and the US were also invited to express regret for authorizing rites of blessing for same-sex unions,[74] while those bishops (but not the churches per se) who intervened in other jurisdictions to give oversight to more conservative dissenting groups were invited to express regret for the consequences of their actions.[75] A more explicit

---

[70] Noel Bruyns, 'Southern Africa's Anglican Bishops Apologise to Homosexual People', *Ecumenical News International* bulletin 97–0123 (1997).

[71] Episcopal Church, 'Apologize for the Church's Rejection of Gays and Lesbians' (1997).

[72] Solange de Santis, 'Ingham Apologizes to Gays for Church Slowness', *Anglican Journal*, General Synod Supplement, September 2001, 4.

[73] Lambeth Commission on Communion, *The Windsor Report* (London: Anglican Consultative Council, 2004), no. 134.

[74] *Ibid.*, no. 144.

[75] *Ibid.*, no. 155.

call for the repentance of the Episcopal Church came from a meeting of Anglican Primates in the South.[76] In response, the Episcopal Church General Convention did apologize for its 'failure to accord sufficient importance to the impact of our actions on our church and other parts of the Communion'. It requested a generalized forgiveness from the wider Communion but rejected an apology for the action in question – the consecration of Bishop Robinson.[77]

The 2008 Lambeth Conference called bishops to repentance more generally: 'As Bishops we need to repent of the ways in which our hardness of heart toward each other may have contributed to the brokenness of our Communion at this present time. We need to repent of statements and actions that have further damaged the dignity of homosexual persons.'[78] As the rift in the Anglican Communion deepens, it appears that the discourse of ecclesial repentance will continue to be invoked to solemnize positions on all sides, as well as seek a middle ground.[79]

RELATION TO SCIENCE/SCIENTISTS

Lament for having embraced the spirit of an age is a theme that runs through a range of ecclesial repentance statements. However, the specifically scientific spirit of the age has rarely been addressed. The Catholic Church's Day of Pardon included a reference to those who abuse biotechnology and distort the aims of science.[80] The only other similar kind of statement appears to be the United Methodist Church's resolution repenting for support of eugenics. That resolution incorporates an extensive history of how Methodist churches gave theological support to the science of eugenics. Churches supported 'Race Betterment Conferences', encouraged the 'strongest and best' to have large families and advocated forced sterilization laws, all of which are now condemned for their overt racism. The resolution also

---

[76] 'Anglicans in Global South Urge Repentance for U.S. Gay Bishop Consecration', *Ecumenical News International* bulletin 05–0057 (2005).

[77] Episcopal Church, 'Express Regret for Straining the Bonds of the Church' (2006).

[78] Lambeth Conference of Anglican Bishops, 'Lambeth Indaba: Capturing Conversations and Reflections from the Lambeth Conference' (2008), no. 107.

[79] The theme of repentance recurs throughout Ephraim Radner and Philip Turner, *The Fate of Communion: The Agony of Anglicanism and the Future of the Global Church* (Grand Rapids: Eerdmans, 2006).

[80] Pope John Paul II, Universal Prayer, Day of Pardon, 12 March 2000.

warned that contemporary practices such as Preimplantation Genetic Diagnosis connected with *in vitro* fertilization are a slippery slope to a 'new eugenics'. However, little theological rationale is provided for this apart from the statement that: 'As Christians, we are not called because of our genetic identities; we are not called to reengineer our bodies or those of our children . . . but rather to follow Christ.' The resolution concludes without any programmatic implications or provisions for further action.[81]

The more common narrative of the church and science is that the former suppressed the latter. Galileo is widely regarded as a persecuted hero in the conflict between church and science, even though the emergence of science cannot be understood as simply emancipation from the rigid control of church, nor can the relation of church and science be reduced to 'conflict'. Nevertheless, the Catholic Church condemned his views in 1633, forced him to recant and placed him under house arrest. In 1992, Pope John Paul II made a significant speech about this case which has been interpreted as an apology. The case is complex because it involves precise points of disciplinary procedure and canon law. Galileo was found guilty of 'vehement suspicion of heresy' (a declaration more akin to a charge than a verdict) for holding the heliocentric thesis contrary to scripture and for the belief that a thesis could be defended if contrary to scripture.[82] Whether this is how Galileo would have defined the matter is partly the issue here.

In 1979, Pope John Paul II acknowledged that Galileo suffered a great deal 'at the hands men and organs of the Church', and asserted that a true examination of the case would show the harmony of faith and science.[83] However, according to one of the members of the commission he established to review the case, the commission was essentially inactive, uncoordinated. It failed to gain access to key Vatican archives and did not deliberate on the final report issued in its name.[84] Nevertheless, in that final statement, the commission's president, Cardinal Paul Poupard, acknowledged the inability of Galileo's judges to dissociate 'faith from an age-old cosmology' as a

---

[81] United Methodist Church, 'Repentance for Support of Eugenics' (2008).

[82] Maurice A. Finocchiaro, *Retrying Galileo, 1633–1992* (Berkeley, CA: University of California Press, 2005), 11–12.

[83] Accattoli, *When a Pope Asks Forgiveness*, 126.

[84] George V. Coyne, 'The Church's Most Recent Attempt to Dispel the Galileo Myth', in *The Church and Galileo*, ed. Ernan McMullin (Notre Dame, IN: University of Notre Dame Press, 2005), 350–4.

mistake.[85] (The use of the phrase 'Galileo's judges' obscures the fact that these judges consisted of members of the Holy Office and the pope, acting as the highest possible church court.[86]) According to Poupard, Galileo's mistake was scientific, not theological; he failed to recognize the *hypothetical* nature of the Copernican thesis, which was irrefutably proven only 150 years later. Given the available facts and conditions, the members of the Holy Office were subjectively correct and believed themselves duty-bound to find Galileo guilty of claiming unwarranted certainty.

In response the report, the pope characterized the case as one of tragic mutual incomprehension.[87] The pope acknowledged error, but, according to Poupard, he did not apologize.[88] Since Galileo's judges were sincere though ill-informed, they cannot be considered guilty. The pope noted that Galileo perceived better than the theologians of his day that scientific discovery demands a reassessment, not of the truth of scripture, but of the methods used by its interpreters. On the other hand, the church's judgement on Galileo shows its high regard for the scientific method. In claiming objective certainty for what he should have regarded as a hypothesis, said the pope, Galileo did not adhere to those standards of science for which he is often regarded as a martyr.

Sometimes an act of ecclesial repentance is 'produced' by the fact that it matches a particular narrative all too well. In 2008, London's *Daily Mail* reported:

> The Church of England will tomorrow officially apologise to Charles Darwin for misunderstanding his theory of evolution. In a bizarre step, the Church will address its contrition directly to the Victorian scientist himself, even though he died 126 years ago. But the move was greeted with derision last night, with Darwin's great-great-great-grandson dismissing it as 'pointless' and other critics branding it 'ludicrous'. Church officials compared the apology to the late Pope John Paul II's decision to say sorry for the Vatican's 1633 trial of Galileo.[89]

However, the Church of England issued no such apology, and never had any intention of doing so. On its website commemorating the 150th anniversary of Charles Darwin's *On the Origin of Species*, the

---

[85] Accattoli, *When a Pope Asks Forgiveness*, 132.

[86] *Ibid.*, 127.

[87] Pope John Paul II, 'Address to the Pontifical Academy of Sciences' (1992).

[88] William R. Shea and Mariano Artigas, *Galileo Observed: Science and the Politics of Belief* (Sagamore Beach, MA: Science History Publications, 2006), 184.

[89] Jonathan Petre, 'Church Makes "Ludicrous" Apology to Charles Darwin – 126 Years After his Death', *Daily Mail*, 13 September 2008.

church's Director of Mission and Public Affairs, the Rev Malcolm Brown, wrote that the church initially misunderstood him but has come to realize that nothing in Darwin's work contradicts Christian teaching. He concluded his essay with a rhetorical flourish, addressed the Darwin:

> 200 years from your birth, the Church of England owes you an apology for misunderstanding you and, by getting our first reaction wrong, encouraging others to misunderstand you still . . . Good religion needs to work constructively with good science – and I dare to suggest that the opposite may be true as well.[90]

Despite a failure of fact-checking, the story confirmed a narrative about a bumbling church that got it wrong then, and still gets it wrong now. It reflected a deep ambivalence about the general trend of apologies – one MP who left the Church of England for the Catholic Church was quoted as saying 'Why don't we have the Italians apologising for Pontius Pilate?' – and revelled in the bizarre prospect of church prelates solemnly addressing a corpse. Ironically, according to this narrative, the church in Darwin's era was irrelevant due to ignorance, while the church today is irrelevant because it has succumbed completely to political correctness run amok. Though there was no apology, a public perception that ecclesial repentance for the past is absurd and irrelevant was nevertheless reinforced.

Environmental Destruction

Ecumenical Patriarch Bartholomew I of Constantinople has often been called the 'Green Patriarch' for his persistent call for human care of creation. His many statements call Christians individually and collectively to repentance for past and present treatment of the environment. Because selfishness and self-centredness are at the centre of how humans have related to the earth, he claims that only a dramatic *metanoia* will turn humans from 'environmental sin' to God and responsible relations with the earth.[91]

The patriarch issued a joint declaration with Pope John Paul II in which they delved more deeply into what environmental repentance would entail. Repentance will affirm that the problems are not

---

[90] Malcolm Brown, 'Good Religion Needs Good Science', *The Church of England* (2008), www.cofe.anglican.org/darwin/malcolmbrown.html.
[91] John Chryssavgis, ed., *Cosmic Grace, Humble Prayer: The Ecological Vision of the Green Patriarch Bartholomew I* (Grand Rapids: Eerdmans, 2003), 220.

primarily technological, but moral and spiritual. Repentance ought to lead to humility, and a recognition of the limits of human power and knowledge. An inner conversion is the only sustainable basis for changing unsustainable patterns of consumption and production. The centrality of human beings within creation must be seen in light of God's interdependent and life-giving plan for all of creation.[92] While the patriarch has not called on the *church* to repent, let alone repented on behalf of the church – Orthodox ecclesiology affirms that though members may sin corporately, the church as a divine/human reality is sinless – Metropolitan John (Zizioulas) of the Ecumenical Patriarchate does claim that Christian theology and the pastoral teaching of the church must undergo a 'profound *metanoia*' in order to confront its responsibility for the ecological crisis.[93]

In 2004, a 15-year process culminated in 'The Accra Confession' of the World Alliance of Reformed Churches. Though not a doctrinal confession, it reflects a consensus among WARC member churches that economic injustice and environmental destruction are matters central to the gospel. Impetus for this statement came largely from churches in the global South, who pointed out the link between economic inequality and environmental degradation. The majority of the document addresses economic issues. It rejects 'any ideology or economic regime that puts profit before people, does not care for all creation and privatizes those gifts of God meant for all'.[94] Within the commitment to seek justice, the statement confesses that both churches and members are complicit in unjust economic structures, even by simply benefiting from them, and calls for a confession of sin. The document itself makes two such confessions: for 'our sin in misusing creation and failing to play our role as stewards and companions of nature', and for Christian disunity that has impaired the church's ability to respond to God's mission.[95]

As recognition of the magnitude of the environmental crisis and climate change increases, ecclesial repentance may be one of the many ways by which churches clarify their own positions and move towards greater engagement. Engagement by no means assumes repentance, but the documents above indicate some movement in

---

[92] Pope John Paul II and Ecumenical Patriarch Bartholomew I, 'Common Declaration on Environmental Ethics, 2002', in *Growth in Agreement III*, ed. Jeffrey Gros, Thomas F. Best and Lorelei F. Fuchs (Geneva: WCC, 2007), 184–6.

[93] Metropolitan John (Zizioulas), preface to *Cosmic Grace, Humble Prayer*, vii.

[94] World Alliance of Reformed Churches, 'The Accra Confession' (2004), no. 25.

[95] *Ibid.*, no. 34.

that direction in the Catholic, Orthodox, and Reformed traditions. The complication with respect to repentance for climate change is that the worst consequences remain in the future. By contrast, the worst of the transatlantic slave trade is over, though of course a legacy of racism and inequality remains. The role of the churches in slavery may be debated, but it is a history that can be studied. However, the direct consequences of human complicity in climate change remain in the future, though many regions especially in the global South are already dramatically effected. Even if churches confess responsibility, the consequences of this sin are not yet available for reflection. Moreover, any request for forgiveness would presumably be made of *future* generations, rather than asking forgiveness in the present for what past generations had done, as in the case of slavery. Theologian Ernst Conradie asks, 'How could my grandchildren (who may be born only in 25 years time) forgive me for something that they have not yet experienced? . . . Why, they would ask us, if you heard what the scientists were telling you, did you not change before it was too late?'[96] Indeed, the sincerity and meaning of any ecclesial repentance for climate change will be judged by the reality that future generations inherit.

The breadth of the histories for which churches have repented, as recounted in the chapters so far, signal a reassessment by these churches of their faithfulness through time. The churches implicitly claim, counterintuitively on the surface, that future mission can, and must, be built on the acknowledgment of failed past mission. At the same time, the recognition of their sinful pasts tempers any certainty that an act of repentance is itself unambiguously faithful. It may be 'just words'. It may miss the point. It may betray the church's past, compromise the church's future or reflect its captivity to political correctness. However, as I will show in Chapters 5 to 7, ecclesial repentance draws on the richness of the Christian doctrinal tradition, and as such may be a faithful occasion for the ongoing reform and development of that tradition. The close examination in the following chapter of one particular act of ecclesial repentance, the Catholic Church's Day of Pardon, will already indicate ways that this practice reflects the development and reframing of doctrine.

The narration of actual repentance of churches does not prove that the Holy Spirit has been at work through this practice. Yet,

---

[96] Ernst M. Conradie, *The Church and Climate Change* (Pietermaritzburg, South Africa: Cluster Publications, 2008), 90.

churches claim that the Spirit has been leading them to repentance, and thus that the Spirit has *also* been at work in spite of the unfaithfulness they confess. Thus, I will proceed as if it is indeed *possible* that through ecclesial repentance, the Spirit is loosing the church from the sins that have marred its mission, and binding its future to conformity with Christ as the witness for which it is called and sent.

Chapter 4

DAY OF PARDON

This is an entirely new thing. . . I think it will take years for the Church to absorb it.
(Joachim Navarro-Valls, papal spokesperson)[1]

More remarkable than the actual novelty of the Day of Pardon was the Catholic Church's explicit *acknowledgement* of its novelty. Change in Catholic practice or belief is typically framed as extending or deepening existing tradition. Yet, the International Theological Commission asserted: '[I]n the entire history of the Church there are no precedents for requests for forgiveness by the Magisterium for past wrongs.'[2] In spite of references to Pope Adrian VI's acknowledgment in 1522 of abuses in the Roman court, Pope Paul VI's request for forgiveness during the Second Vatican Council and John Paul's many prior statements, there was something qualitatively different and new about this event. This novelty actually reinforces the intention of the action; it signals a break with aspects of the past and a renewed commitment to the future. The image of the aging Pope John Paul II on his knees in St Peter's Basilica, asking God's forgiveness for a multitude of sins committed in the name of the church, remains perhaps the most widely received instance of ecclesial repentance to date. In this chapter, I will examine and analyse the Roman Catholic Church's Day of Pardon, some historical and theological context, its primary texts, and the debate surrounding its meaning and implication. Delving more deeply into this one case will reveal some tensions and inconsistencies, as well as some significant theological developments.

---

[1] Cited in Alessandra Stanley, 'Pope Asks Forgiveness for Errors of the Church Over 2,000 Years', *New York Times*, 13 March 2000, A10.
[2] International Theological Commission, *Memory and Reconciliation: The Church and the Faults of the Past* (2000), no. 1.1.

Preparation for the 2000 Year of Jubilee formally began in 1994 with the publication of *Tertio Millennio Adveniente: Apostolic Letter on Preparation for the Jubilee of the Year 2000* which, together with *Incarnationis Mysterium: Bull of Indiction of the Great Jubilee of the Year 2000* (published in 1998), developed the core themes of conversion, purification and forgiveness, and set in motion various planning commissions and events. *Tertio Millennio Adveniente* was preceded by a confidential (and still unpublished) memo in the spring of that year in which the pope signalled to the cardinals his intention to lead the church in an examination of its history with a view to confessing publicly those sins which have compromised the witness of the church.[3] The Jubilee Year itself began on Christmas Eve in 1999 with the opening of the holy door in the Basilica of St John Lateran. On Ash Wednesday, four days before the Day of Pardon, the International Theological Committee, working under the oversight of the Congregation for the Doctrine of the Faith (CDF), held a news conference to release its extensive study *Memory and Reconciliation: The Church and the Faults of the Past* (hereafter *MR*). The Day of Pardon itself, on the First Sunday of Lent, 12 March 2000, consisted of a papal mass concelebrated in Italian with 30 cardinals and bishops. A 'Universal Prayer', in which invitatories read by seven cardinals or archbishops for seven kinds of sin were followed each time with a prayer by the pope, constituted the core act of asking God's forgiveness. The service concluded with a series of promises by the pope on behalf of the church to never again commit certain offences. Within days, John Paul left for a pilgrimage to the Holy Land which included further penitential acts aimed at reconciliation particularly with Jews, but also Muslims and Eastern Christians.

PREPARATION

As the preparatory documents explain, celebration of the 2,000th anniversary of the incarnation witnesses to God's redemption of humanity by dwelling in history and, in turn, sanctifies human history by setting aside specific periods of thanksgiving and renewal. Attention to the triune persons shaped the development of Jubilee themes of conversion and reconciliation, introspection and public witness. The year of Jesus Christ (1997) focused on catechesis and

---

[3] Luigi Accattoli, *When a Pope Asks Forgiveness: The Mea Culpa's of John Paul II*, trans. Jordan Aumann (Boston: Daughters of St Paul, 1998), 55–60.

baptism, the basis of Christian life and witness. The second year (1998), dedicated to the Holy Spirit, attended to growth in faith, hope and church unity. The pope explained that through dialogue and increased understanding, the Spirit becomes the author of 'the new evangelization' and of 'reconciliation and solidarity' among people.[4] He described the journey towards God the Father, the theme of the third year (1999), as the journey of conversion marked especially by the sacrament of penance and the virtue of charity.

Different ecclesiological images have different implications for the relation of sin and repentance in the church. The image of the mystical body of Christ emphasizes the fact that all Christians bear the burden of the sins of others, though a distinction is made between burden and responsibility. (The writings of Hans Urs von Balthasar were significant in shaping the pope's thinking of the church and 'the burdens of the dead'.[5]) As new creation, the church embodies God's forgiveness of sins sincerely repented, and the fruits of faith, hope and charity which this multiplies. As the bride of Christ, the church is distinguished from its members who have hindered her 'from shining forth in all humanity'. The forgiveness which the bride receives from her bridegroom causes her to radiate beauty and holiness.[6] Finally, sinless mother church implores God's forgiveness for her sinful children.[7]

In Jubilee years past, many pilgrims travelled to new lands, especially Rome or other holy sites, for the sake of penance and forgiveness. *Lumen Gentium*'s account of the church as pilgrim applies to the church approaching the new millennium, its history an 'unfinished pilgrimage'.[8] Because this pilgrim church 'embraces sinners in its bosom, is holy and always in need of being purified', it, like the individual pilgrim on the way to Rome during a Jubilee year, must follow the 'path of penance and renewal'.[9]

A link between pilgrimage and the church's repentance also emerged from the pope's ambitious programme of beatification and canonization, especially of individuals whose lives were geographically removed from the historic centres of Catholicism. These

[4] *Tertio Millennio Adveniente*, no. 45.
[5] Accattoli, *When a Pope Asks Forgiveness*, 3–5.
[6] *Incarnationis Mysterium*, nos. 10–11.
[7] *Tertio Millennio Adveniente*, no. 33.
[8] *Incarnationis Mysterium*, no. 7.
[9] Second Vatican Council, *Lumen Gentium: Dogmatic Constitution on the Church* (1964), no. 6, cited in *Tertio Millennio Adveniente*, no. 34.

'pilgrimages' brought the pope to many new lands where he both affirmed local expressions of authentic faith by creating saints, but also reflected on how many such expressions had been denied or marginalized in the past. Thus, John Paul's extensive travels may be one reason why he has initiated so many requests for pardon.[10] Pilgrimage may itself be an act of penance, but is also an occasion by which the church ventures into 'new territory' to become more fully aware of its failure to point to Christ.

The core of the pope's proposal for reflection on the faults of the past is framed in terms of repentance and purification:

> Hence it is appropriate that, as the Second Millennium of Christianity draws to a close, the Church should become more fully conscious of the sinfulness of her children, recalling all those times in history when they departed from the spirit of Christ and his Gospel and, instead of offering to the world the witness of a life inspired by the values of faith, indulged in ways of thinking and acting which were truly forms of counter-witness and scandal . . . It is fitting that the Church should make this passage with a clear awareness of what has happened to her during the last ten centuries. She cannot cross the threshold of the new millennium without encouraging her children to purify themselves, through repentance, of past errors and instances of infidelity, inconsistency, and slowness to act. Acknowledging the weaknesses of the past is an act of honesty and courage which helps us to strengthen our faith, which alerts us to face today's temptations and challenges and prepares us to meet them.[11]

The strong distinction in this passage between the church and its members will be taken up at several points in this book. It is noteworthy that purification is undertaken both by individual members (through repentance) and the church (by leading its sinful children to repentance and by purifying the memories of those things that impede the its witness). These official documents clearly deny that the church is an agent of sin, and yet the church does do penance. That the church thus proposes to do penance for a past not fully its own (but rather its members) raises questions about which histories and which memories the church will indeed examine in order to discern the pardon to be sought from God. Nevertheless, the fact that the sins of Christians have prevented the church from 'fully mirroring' Christ,[12] and even 'impeded the Spirit's workings

---

[10] See Michael R. Marrus, 'Papal Apologies of Pope John Paul II', in *The Age of Apology: Facing up to the Past*, ed. Mark Gibney, Rhoda Howard-Hassman, Jean-Marc Coicaud and Niklaus Steiner (Philadelphia: University of Pennsylvania Press, 2008), 264.

[11] *Tertio Millennio Adveniente*, no. 33.

[12] *Ibid.*, no. 35.

in the hearts of many people',[13] provide language for thinking how individual sins may in some way become the church's sins, despite assertions to the contrary.

Several commissions were established in 1995 to oversee Jubilee preparations, including a Historical-Theological Commission headed by Fr Georges Cottier, divided into subcommissions for History and Theology. The Historical Subcommission was charged specifically with examining elements in the church's past for which pardon ought to be requested. Other bodies such as the Ecumenical Commission, the Interreligious Dialogue Commission and the Social Commission were also mandated to examine the past. Allaying the fears of some, the commissions clarified that their task was to gather and interpret the data but reserve judgement of past error to the pope alone. At a plenary meeting of the Jubilee Central Committee, the Historical-Theological Commission received suggestions to work in areas such as the church and slavery or the relations between Catholics and Orthodox, but also received expressions of concern that its work on the shortcomings of the past might gloss over the wrongs done to Catholics through the centuries.[14]

The Historical Subcommission convened a closed symposium in October 1997 on 'The Roots of Anti-Judaism in the Christian Environment'. About 60 Christian theologians were invited to participate, including some Orthodox and Protestant scholars, though the agenda of the meeting was not made public. The pope delivered a keynote address in which he explained how anti-Jewish sentiments contributed to mistaken interpretations of the Bible 'in the Christian world', though not by the church as such. These extra-ecclesial misinterpretations created conditions in which some Christian consciences were 'lulled' by anti-Semitic ideas and practices.[15] Thus, the church must repent for ideas and influences that have touched it from the outside. Most of the short papers published in the official Jubilee journal do not address the specific theme but rather make general remarks on the theological links between Christianity and Judaism, recent advances in dialogue and John Paul II's personal role in forging better relationships.[16] Though many of the papers from the

---

[13] *Incarnationis Mysterium*, no. 11.

[14] 'Summary of Debate in the Assembly', *Tertium Millennium* (June–September 1996), 26.

[15] Pope John Paul II, 'The Roots of Anti-Judaism', *Origins* 27, no. 22 (13 November 1997), 365–7.

[16] *Tertium Millennium* (November 1997).

symposium have not be published, for thematic reasons it is plausible to assume that they formed the basis for 1998 document *We Remember: Reflections on the Shoah*, including its widely criticized emphases on the sacrifices some Christians made to save Jews and denial that anti-Semitism has any roots in the church or church teaching.

A symposium on the Inquisition(s) was held in 1998, the proceedings of which were published several years later.[17] Authors typically analysed the circumstances, procedures, results and implications of the various local inquisitions. For example, William Monter assigns direct responsibility for some 150 executions to the Inquisition run directly by the Church of Rome, while reckoning that effective responsibility for the much bloodier Spanish Inquisition belongs to the rulers of Spain rather than the church. Though he argues that even a single such execution by Rome was immoral, Rome's concern for the offender's soul resulted in more moderate judicial procedures in contrast with the more harsh procedures that resulted elsewhere in Europe where political authorities' concerns about public order trumped spiritual ones.[18]

In his letter marking publication of the proceedings four years after the Day of Pardon, the pope noted that 'exact knowledge of the facts' is required before asking forgiveness.[19] However, the papers were qualified as strictly the opinions of their authors and no final report was written. It is thus unclear whether this exact knowledge was generated and whether it meaningfully contributed to the very general request for pardon which did not even use the word 'inquisition'. Rather than a strict sequence of research followed by repentance, the self-examination stimulated by the Jubilee may be better understood as an ongoing process of repentance, renewed ecclesial self-awareness, and the promise of further research into the church's past. This is even consistent with the official description of the Day of Pardon as '*inaugurat*[ing] a journey of conversion and change vis-à-vis the past'.[20] One specific action of the Roman Inquisition was addressed in a letter from the Vatican's Secretary

---

[17] Agostino Borromeo, ed., *L'Inquisizione: atti del simposio internazionale* (Vatican City: Biblioteca Apostolica Vaticana, 2003).

[18] William Monter, 'The Roman Inquisition and Protestant Heresy Executions in 16th Century Europe', in *L'Inquisizione*, 547–8.

[19] Pope John Paul II, 'Letter to Cardinal Roger Etchegaray on the Occasion of the Presentation of the Volume *L'Inquisizione*', 15 June 2004.

[20] Office of Papal Liturgical Celebrations, 'Presentation: Day of Pardon', 12 March 2002, italics added.

of State, Cardinal Angelo Sodano. Sodano expressed regret for the execution in 1600 of philosopher Giordano Bruno, and encouraged a rereading of that particular history from the perspective of 'the healing of memories'. While Sodano warned we are not in a position to judge the consciences of Bruno's judges, the link he made between the Day of Pardon and the need to reexamine this particular episode led many to report the statement as an apology.[21]

The objections of some cardinals to the pope's programme of Jubilee repentance were registered back when he first raised the issue in a 1994 closed meeting.[22] Journalist Luigi Accattoli wrote that the pope proceeded despite 'pointed opposition' from the curia and strong support from perhaps just two cardinals (Roger Etchegaray and Edward Cassidy).[23] Objections were vocalized by Cardinal Giocomo Biffi, while the defence of the papal programme was assigned to Fr Georges Cottier, president of the Historical-Theological Commission and Theologian of the Papal Household (and made a cardinal in 2003).

In spite of their differences on the advisability of the pope's intended action, Biffi and Cottier agreed on several key assumptions. Both agreed that the church's holiness is rooted entirely in its relationship to Christ. Both agreed that sin is a personal reality, and that any action by the pope would be for the actions of individuals, not the church itself. Both denied that the church is a sinner. They emphasized that the history confessed must be a true account of the past, not a biased history projected by the church's critics. Cottier even quotes Biffi's writings specifically and approvingly.

Yet, they differed in their assessment of whether the mission of the church, both in terms of the message presented to non-Christians and the ongoing formation of members, is served by a papal request for pardon. Biffi worried that the 'ordinary faithful who, since they do not know how to make theological distinctions, may find that their serene adhesion to the mystery of the Church has been shaken by these self-accusations'[24] with the result that these simple believers will be denied the 'joy, the gratitude, the pride of belonging to the

---

[21] Cardinal Angelo Sodano, Letter to the Dean of the Pontifical Theological Faculty, 14 February 2000.

[22] Accattoli, *When a Pope Asks Forgiveness*, 60–6.

[23] Luigi Accattoli, 'A Pope Who Begs Forgiveness: John Paul II and His "Mea Culpa" at the Turn of the New Millennium', in *John Paul II: A Pope for the People* (New York: Abrams, 2004), 93, 107.

[24] Accattoli, *When a Pope Asks Forgiveness*, 64.

Church; and without this it becomes very difficult for all, except perhaps for intellectuals, to live the life of faith'.[25] He asked, for example, why the church should apologize for its role in the Galileo case when current university rectors are not asked to apologize for the roles their institutions played in the proceedings. For Biffi, the church's rush to apology is ill-advised because it confirms the prejudices many people have against it. Furthermore, given the cultural currency of apology, such an action might teach Christians that principles such as peace and solidarity are derived from a cultural consensus rather than from following Christ.

By contrast, Cottier argued that the church's credibility in the world is increased by repenting for the sins of her members. Since scandal is already present, it is lessened, not exacerbated, by acknowledgment.[26] If the church is to avoid repeating past errors in the future, which is more likely if consciences are formed in full knowledge of the past, then its holiness will be more visible to the world.[27] In addition, Cottier argued that the church provides an example to other institutions who may be inspired to examine their consciences, ask forgiveness and resolve to act differently.[28]

The basic theological difference underlying these assessments is Biffi's construal of sin as by definition external to the church. He acknowledges that all members are sinners, but following Charles Journet, he argues that the boundary of the church runs through each individual such that only what is holy and without sin may be considered truly in the church. Those who call the church a sinner (Biffi names Hans Küng), misconstrue Ambrose's description of the church as a *casta meretrix*, or 'chaste harlot'. Ambrose interprets the shelter offered by the prostitute Rahab to Joshua's spies as a type of the church. For Biffi, Rahab's 'promiscuity' prefigures the way the church welcomes all who seek shelter, but it does not indicate the sin of the church. As *casta*, the church is the pure bride of Christ; as *meretrix*, the church is the mother of all. While the church provides an indiscriminate refuge to sinners, they are spiritually reborn by their

---

[25] Desmond O'Grady, 'Cancel the Mea Culpa?' *Inside the Vatican*, May 1996, 15.

[26] Georges Cottier, *Mémoire et repentance: pourquoi l'Église demande pardon* (Saint-Maur: Parole et Silence, 1998), 48.

[27] *Ibid.*, 28.

[28] Georges Cottier, 'Repentance in an Ecumenical Context', *Theology Digest* 47 (2000), 108.

incorporation into the church. Because their mother the church is the very source of forgiveness, sin is excluded from the church.[29]

Like the moon, the church's external appearance may change while remaining identical in essence.[30] Like the moon, its light is always reflected from an outside source: Christ. The church appears to be a sinner, but this is only so if viewed without the eyes of faith that distinguish essence from appearance. Thus, Biffi worries that the ordinary faithful will be confused or manipulated into seeing the church as the world sees it. They might be misled to think that the church is a source of evil and flee from it, rather than be assured that evil and sin do not invade the refuge of the church.

For Cottier, sin *in* the church is plain for all to see, though the eyes of faith recognize this sin as that of members, not the church itself. Cottier's argument for why asking pardon advances the church's mission is not simply a pragmatic calculation or an accommodation to what society expects of a good corporate citizen. Rather, because sin truly *is* in the church – specifically in its members – it compromises the visible witness of the church. The same church is both invisible in its theological constitution and visible as a historical institution publicly perceived.[31] By making judgements on those things which have obscured its mission and its nature, the church seeks to make its holy constitution truly visible to the world.[32]

In light of issues such as those raised by Biffi and Cottier, and possible misunderstandings of the papal intention to repent, the International Theological Commission was charged to provide a substantial theological framework and clarification.

THEOLOGICAL REFLECTION: *MEMORY AND RECONCILIATION*

Memory and Reconciliation: The Church and the Faults of the Past is a significant document on the issues underlying the Day of Pardon, though its status is difficult to delineate. On the one hand, the International Theological Commission serves in a merely advisory capacity to the CDF. Its members cannot be bishops and its documents are not an exercise of the magisterial charism. On the other hand, its publication

---

[29] Giocomo Biffi, *Casta Meretrix: 'The Chaste Whore': An Essay on the Ecclesiology of St Ambrose*, trans. Richard J. S. Brown (London: Saint Austin Press, 2000), 19–23.

[30] *Ibid.*, 42–3.

[31] Cottier, *Mémoire et repentance*, 32.

[32] Cottier, 'Repentance in an Ecumenical Context', 106–7.

was introduced at a press conference by Cardinal Joseph Ratzinger, CDF Prefect, and later referred to by the pope as 'very useful for correctly understanding' the church's request for forgiveness.[33]

The document itself consists of an introduction and six chapters. The first chapter examines the historical context for the proposed ecclesial repentance in light of past precedent, the teaching of Vatican II, and Pope John Paul II's other requests for forgiveness. Chapters 2 and 3 consider respectively the biblical and the ecclesiological issues raised, while Chapter 4 proposes hermeneutical guidelines for the work of judgement of past wrongs by both historians and theologians. Chapter 5 develops the theme of ethical discernment in general, intergenerational ethical responsibility and some particular wrongs confessed. The final chapter identifies the pastoral and missionary risks, hopes and implications of the papal request for pardon.

The public perception of the Day of Pardon is clearly important to the authors of *MR* on several levels. The tenor of *MR* reflects an awareness that it may be misunderstood theologically, or interpreted to confirm prejudices of those outside of it and to undermine its authority among its members. Yet, the text asserts that as the church deals with its past the credibility of the gospel increases. In addition, the church may inspire other religious groups, civil institutions or nations, to seek forgiveness and reconciliation through an examination of their past.[34]

In spite of the confidence about the understanding and reconciliation this initiative may promote, the potential of the church's action to stimulate other requests for pardon and statements about the opportune timing of this initiative, there is a note of caution about expectation of 'results'. Bruno Forte, chair of the subcommission that drafted *MR*, argues that a papal request for forgiveness must be judged by whether it is consistent with God's Word, and not whether it is effective.[35] Indeed, the church's primary obligation to the truth means both that it is obedient to God's will that it repent and, moreover, that it provides a truthful account of the past for which it repents.[36] Practical reconciliation, it is hoped, will be the fruit of such obedience to truth.[37]

---

[33] Pope John Paul II, Homily, Day of Pardon, 12 March 2000.

[34] *MR*, no. 6.3.

[35] Bruno Forte, 'The Church Confronts the Faults of the Past', trans. Adrian Walker, *Communio: International Catholic Review* 27 (2000), 679.

[36] *MR*, introduction; no. 5.3.

[37] *Ibid.*, no. 6.3.

A hierarchy of truth over reconciliation, however, in which the latter is desirable but not essential, produces a problematic account of both. If it is the case that the church must first get its facts straight, and then act on the implications of these facts to seek reconciliation, then truth is essentially propositional rather than embodied. An embodied account of the truth that reconciles will take seriously the perspective on the past that can only be given by those who have been hurt by it. If the church confesses sin in its past, it must recognize that this sin may also obscure the account that may be given of that sin. But the propositional account of truth assumes that the perspective of those (non-Catholic Christians, Jews, Aboriginal people) sinned against is not essential for arriving at the truth. Once this truth is determined, only then is reconciliation sought. By contrast, engaging dialogically with their interpretations of the past would not only provide a more comprehensive picture of what 'really happened', the process of jointly owning a new account of the past and the mutuality and respect presupposed by it, will already contribute to a healing of those relationships.

Despite the fact that the papal liturgy ultimately asked forgiveness from God alone and was criticized for not simultaneously asking forgiveness from persons, *MR* does envision the latter possibility. God's forgiveness 'opens the way for mutual reconciliation'.[38] Any human recipients of a request for forgiveness (again not necessary, but possible) must be identified with 'appropriate historical and theological discernment', in part to engage in suitable acts of reparation. It is as this point in the process that dialogue is envisioned.[39] Whereas Pope Paul VI's declaration that 'men on both sides' were at fault for church divisions and schisms was a landmark confession of guilt on the Catholic side, such a mixture of confession and accusation would be heard at the beginning of the third millennium more as a position in a negotiation, and less as sincere repentance. *MR*'s reference to 'dialogue and reciprocity' among human recipients of forgiveness is difficult to interpret on this score. While it may be read as an openness by the church to make a request for human forgiveness, 'the gratuity of love [that] often expresses itself in unilateral initiatives' more likely shifts to the emphasis to the possibility that the Catholic Church will grant forgiveness for wrongs

---

[38] *Ibid.*, no. 5.5.
[39] *Ibid.*, no. 6.2.

done to it even when 'the religious convictions of the dialogue partner' inhibit a reciprocal offer.[40]

MR contains an extensive discussion of the biblical precedents for ecclesial repentance. It organizes dozens of Old Testament examples in which the past or present sins of a community are confessed by the people or by leaders on their behalf. Of particular note are the texts in which leaders confessed the sins of forebears that are linked to present sins (for example, the penitential prayer in Ezra 9.7.[41]) Though *MR* clarifies that these are not an 'exact parallel' with the pope's present action, the nature of the dissimilarity is not named.[42] Discussion of the New Testament emphasizes the radical newness which the disciples and early Christian communities experienced through the forgiveness of sins. Because of this orientation to the future, 'there is no indication that the early Church turned her attention to sins of the past in order to ask forgiveness'.[43] Thus, the letters to the churches in Revelation 2–3 are interpreted not as a call for the present churches to consider repentance, but for individual Christians to be continually mindful of how their lives do not reflect their new life in Christ.

Whose guilt does the church confess? Its own, or that of its members? If it confesses the sins of its members, is it their personal guilt in relation to God or the guilt of actions taken in the name of the church?

The Christology of *MR* presents a strong analogy between the incarnation and the church. Just as Christ assumes the sins of the world, so mother church 'make[s] herself responsible for the sin of her children' on the basis of the communion of the human and divine proper to her.[44] Certainly, a dissimilarity exists insofar as Christ is sinless and the members of the church are sinful. Yet, it is unclear whether the church becomes responsible for these sins by freely assuming them or whether there is a more objective responsibility which the church is called to continually *acknowledge*. Standing behind these questions is that of the relationship between Christ and the church. What does it mean for the church to 'take in sinners'? Could mother church choose to accept no children? While such a

---

[40] *Ibid.*
[41] *Ibid.*, no. 2.1.
[42] *Ibid.*, no. 2.4.
[43] *Ibid.*, 2.2.
[44] *Ibid.*, no. 3.4.

choice would keep sin from the church, a church with no members is not the church; its *raison d'être* can no longer be salvation.

MR asserts that sin is always personal. Responsibility for a sin belongs to the one who committed it, or consented to it voluntarily or by omission.[45] The text denies the concept of collective guilt, which has been especially pernicious when applied to the Jews for the death of Jesus.[46] Sin is *in* the church, in its members, but this is not the sin *of* the church. Except that it becomes the responsibility of the church for the sake of confession and forgiveness.

On an ethical level, *MR* distinguishes between the subjective responsibility, which depends on an individual's awareness of wrongdoing and which thus ends with death and the objective responsibility for a sinful act. The church is not judging individual consciences.[47] Repentance is not for this subjective responsibility. Objective responsibility may extend across time because the consequences of past actions create burdens, obstacles and memories that endure. The objectively sinful exists in the present in the form of memories and consequences. In some Catholic statements it thus appears that the church is repenting for the past itself, without specifying agency. When a living generation recognizes past sin, it may assume subjective responsibility for it in order to purify the memory.[48] Thus, it seems that the church is repenting for sin that is not its own but for the sins of 'others' it makes its own, as does Christ.[49]

However, the text also asserts that no one can repent for the sin of another.[50] While this claim is intended to reinforce the personal nature of sin and counter any account of 'social sin' that minimizes personal responsibility, it raises a question about whether the sin for which the church repents is in the past or the present. For example, while *MR* denies that guilt for past separations from the Catholic Church can be objectively imputed to those born into such communities after the fact,[51] because this past has negative consequences in the present, those Catholics indifferent to the fact of separation, or who do not strive to remove barriers to unity, are guilty of a 'solidarity

---

[45] *Ibid.*, no. 1.3.
[46] *Ibid.*, no. 1.2.
[47] Pope John Paul II, Angelus, 12 March 2000.
[48] *MR*, no. 5.1.
[49] *Ibid.*, nos. 3.4, 6.2.
[50] *Ibid.*, no. 1.3.
[51] *Ibid.*, no. 1.2, citing *Unitatis Redintegratio*, no. 3.

in the sin of division'.[52] Does this limit the church's repentance to that of present sin? Such a limitation seems inconsistent with the general orientation towards the history of the church. However, while an obligation is placed on the church to address a burden of the past (to do so is an 'objective common responsibility'[53]), the past is a burden precisely because sin was *there*. It is important to distinguish between the way in which the past is mediated to the present (through memories and consequences, for example) and the sin itself. The memory of a sin is not the sin. If sin is tied with responsibility and repentance is tied to both, then repentance is at least also for what was done in the past, even the distant past. But if one cannot repent for the personal subjective sin of another, let alone a person who has died, then the question is how exactly personal sins in the past become the responsibility of the whole church in the present. In light of this, repentance by the pope in the name of the church is coherent only if there exists an essential theological link by which the individual sins become in some sense that of the church. And indeed, ecclesial repentance is rooted in the communion of the human and the divine that binds the baptized over time and space.[54]

Ratzinger argues that the church's confession is not an alienated act, but the speech of the church as a single theological subject. In and through the pope, the church makes a first-person confession. 'The entire living Church, in her living members, is saying this: "I have sinned."'[55] Ratzinger denies that the church is an agent of sin, but he contends that the church confesses sin that has become its own. The church, made into a single subject by the Holy Spirit, reflects this divine communion by confessing the sin of its members as its own. And herein lies some ambiguity that *MR* does not entirely resolve. On what basis does (personal) sin become the church's to confess? On the basis of Christ's free assumption of sin of others? Or by fact that individual wrongdoing accrues to the church some (objective) diminution of the gospel's light? Put differently, does the church *choose* to make itself responsible for the sins of its members? Or does it already *find* itself with that responsibility?

---

[52] *MR*, no. 5.2.
[53] *Ibid.*, no. 5.1.
[54] *Ibid.*, no. 3.1.
[55] Joseph Ratzinger, 'The Church's Guilt', in *Pilgrim Fellowship of Faith: The Church as Communion*, trans. Henry Taylor (San Francisco: Ignatius Press, 2005), 276. This is also linked to Ratzinger's view of the ontological priority of the universal church over the local churches.

However the church comes to have responsibility for the sins it confesses, it repents in part in order to purify its memory. This purification refers to,

> eliminating from personal and collective conscience all forms of resentment or violence left by the inheritance of the past, on the basis of a new and rigorous historical-theological judgment, which becomes the foundation for a renewed moral way of acting. This occurs whenever it becomes possible to attribute to past historical deeds a different quality, having a new and different effect on the present, in view of progress in reconciliation in truth, justice, and charity among human beings and, in particular, between the Church and the different religious, cultural, and civil communities with whom she is related. Emblematic models of such an effect, which a later authoritative interpretative judgment may have for the entire life of the Church, are the reception of the Councils or acts like the abolition of mutual anathemas. These express a new assessment of past history, which is capable of producing a different characterization of the relationships lived in the present. The memory of division and opposition is purified and substituted by a reconciled memory, to which everyone in the Church is invited to be open and to become educated.[56]

Though the text cites the agreement of Pope Paul VI and Ecumenical Patriarch Athenagoras I to *remove* from memory certain aspects of the past, purification is not here described in a way that might evoke images of the deletion of undesirable comrades from group photographs. While *Nostra Aetate* rather ominously advocates simply forgetting the history of Christian–Muslim hostility,[57] for example, such is not the perspective of *MR*. Past deeds are not forgotten, but rather remembered in a new way grounded in mutual love. The 'reconciled memory' has a positive function for the present church. The process of purification is closely identified with repentance and its interrelated processes of naming the past, taking responsibility for it, asking forgiveness and pledging to act differently in the future. While the work of purification is a divine task, grounded in the work of Christ, the church is called to actively cooperate in substituting reconciled memories for harmful ones.

The past asserts its influence on the present in the form of memory, especially the 'common memory' that carries the burdens of conscience.[58] Because these scandals are remembered, their negative effects continue in the present. Since the church examines its conscience prior to ecclesial repentance, the actual focus of this introspection will be the church's collective memory. This means

---

[56] *Ibid.*, no. 5.1.
[57] *Nostra Aetate*, no. 3.
[58] *MR*, nos. 5.1–5.2.

that the church as a single subject carries not only the goodness of tradition that it ought to, but also the negative experiences of the past. While this does not necessarily prove that sin accrues to the church as a subject, it does affirm that the church as such carries through time not only the positive elements of tradition, but also the consequences of sin.

Is it only the *memory* of scandals that harms the present or might those scandals themselves have an effect on the present in ways that may not be consciously borne in memory? Put differently, is the past only mediated in memory? For example, the legacy of slavery persists in structures of racism that have social forms that are often hidden from the conscious memory of the dominant community. Yet, throughout *MR*, the memory that is examined and then purified seems to be that of the church, or of church members. While the mystical solidarity of the body of Christ functions to link Christians over time and space,[59] an expression of which is a common ecclesial memory, there is no account given of how common memory links those who have offended and those offended against when some of these are outside the church. Given that the church's reflection on its own memory is not a wholly sufficient source for identifying the burdens of the past, the process of the examination of conscience may require dialogue with those outside of the church, just as an individual penitent may require a dialogue with a confessor in order to bring to mind the nature and scope of sins to be named.

The claim that the purification of memory is primarily rooted in a truthful account of the past, especially one provided by the church's own account of itself, raises numerous issues of historical hermeneutics. *MR* envisions a process in which the historian, sensitive to the past's otherness as well as its connections to the present, produces what will essentially serve as a new reconciled memory of the past.[60] However, memory and history are not identical. The memory that a particular group has – for example, that of Jews regarding the role of Pope Pius XII during the Holocaust – is not only about the past per se, but about the matrix of present perceptions about the past and their lingering effects. Thus, subjective interpretations of the past, or even misinterpretation depending on perspective, are highly relevant if the aim is a purified and reconciled memory. While the text does recognize the subjective element in how the motives of the *historian*

---

[59] *Ibid.*, no. 3.1.
[60] *Ibid.*, no. 4.1.

affect the account of history produced, there is no reflection on the need to take seriously that the memory of groups outside the church may not be 'purified' by a unilateral, if well-intentioned, historical account the church gives of itself. Were the definitive archival file to be discovered that cleared Pius XII of any responsibility, this would not in itself address the effect that a particular collective memory of his role has played in the relationship between Catholics and Jews.

MR commends close attention to the context – events, customs, mentalities – in which past sins were committed, rather than generalized or stereotyped accounts of the past. It rightly calls for careful work to be done to determine which actions, by which actors, are in need of pardon. The past ought to be considered in its otherness, and not as a projection of contemporary concerns.[61] The text thus aims to allay the concerns that ecclesial repentance will take as fact what are mere prejudices about the past. Yet, there are significant contradictions in the tasks assigned to historians.

The first concerns the proper subject of study: individual Christians or the church as such. If the historian cannot consider the corporate acts and customs of the church as church, then neither can historical work be a basis for ongoing reforms in the church.[62] According to Christopher Bellitto, the historian is better equipped to 'establish the objective failings of the corporate church' than 'the subjective culpability' of members, but the former is excluded a priori on the theological grounds of the indefectible holiness of the church.[63] It is one thing to understand the mentality of a culture, even to establish whether it might have been *possible* for a historical actor to know that his action was wrong, but it is an 'impossibly high standard' to judge objectively an individual's *subjective* moral state.[64] Even if such judgements could be made, their usefulness is unclear given that repentance is not for that subjective responsibility which in any case ends with the death of the individual. Repentance is for what was objectively sinful and persists in the form of consequences and memories.

It is furthermore unclear how historians are to reconcile *MR*'s insistence that judgements proper to the present not be erroneously

---

[61] *Ibid.*, no. 4.2.

[62] Christopher M. Bellitto, 'Teaching the Church's Mistakes: Historical Hermeneutics in *Memory and Reconciliation: The Church and the Faults of the Past*', *Horizons* 32 (2005), 131.

[63] *Ibid.*, 134.

[64] *Ibid.*, 129–30.

applied to the past[65] with the requirement that this 'not justify in any way a relativistic idea of moral principles'.[66] Does not the requirement to identify objective responsibility demand a judgement about a situation in which part of the problem may have been the failure to recognize a sin as such? A case in point is the distinction between 'authority', which *MR* asserts bishops and popes may exercise erroneously, and the 'magisterial charism', which does not admit of fault.[67] Bernard Prusak argues that Pope Urban II would not have acknowledged such a distinction. By all accounts, Urban believed he was exercising his magisterial charism when he called for a crusade in 1095.[68] Given that it is the contemporary legacy, memory and moral implications of this action that makes this event the subject of reflection in the first place, Urban's self-understanding is not particularly relevant if the church is not presuming to speak to Urban's subjective responsibility or his personal standing before God. The question remains, was there something objectively sinful about Urban's action? Neither Prusak nor Bellitto are objecting to the fact that the church must make theological judgements about the past that historians, strictly speaking, cannot make. However, they urge the church to be more forthcoming about how contemporary moral and ecclesial commitments do, in fact, shape the church's penitential engagement with its history.

In his press conference, Cardinal Ratzinger made a telling remark about how apologetic agendas have often negatively shaped the church's interpretation of its the past. Following the Reformation, both Protestant and Enlightenment historiography aimed to demonstrate the thorough corruption and ruin of the Catholic Church, and Catholic leadership responded by framing its history as that of a holy church of holy saints. In such an apologetic context, no side saw a benefit in ecclesial confession and repentance. Only with the recent failure of secular ideologies, and (though Ratzinger does not mention it) dialogue with Protestants in part furthered by common repentance for sins against Christian unity, has there been created a 'new situation, in which the Church can with greater freedom, invite

---

[65] *MR*, no. 4.2.

[66] *Ibid.*, no. 5.1.

[67] *Ibid.*, 6.2.

[68] Bernard P. Prusak, 'Theological Considerations – Hermeneutical, Ecclesiological, Eschatological Regarding *Memory and Reconciliation: The Church and the Faults of the Past*', *Horizons* 32 (2005), 147–9.

us to return to the confession of sins'.[69] In this new situation, the truth and power of the Christian faith is advanced not by claims of perfection but by a historiography of humility.

FIRST SUNDAY OF LENT, 12 MARCH 2000

The service began with the pope, wearing penitential purple, praying before Michaelangelo's *Pietà*. According to the official description, this meant that 'the Church, like Mary, wishes to embrace the crucified Saviour, to take responsibility for the past of her children and to implore the Father's forgiveness'.[70] The pope then led a penitential procession during which the Litany of Saints was sung, signifying their intercession for pilgrim Christians.[71]

In his homily, the pope reflected on the sinlessness of Christ even in the face of Satan's temptation, juxtaposed with Christ's assumption of humanity's sin and guilt (2 Cor. 5.21) for the sake of redemption. The proper response to this act of love is an examination of conscience. By recognizing the faults of the past, consciences become trained to see the many present evils and temptations. The pope then linked the father's welcome of his prodigal son (Lk. 15.13–17) to God's promise of forgiveness for all who return to him. Christ's assumption of sins makes this forgiveness possible; it reconciles human beings with God. Though he made no mention of seeking forgiveness from those offended by the children of the church, the pope exhorted that a people forgiven by God must in turn forgive others.[72]

The request for pardon itself consisted of a Universal Prayer, ordered in seven categories. For each one, a member of the curia read the intention, after which followed silence, a prayer by the pope to God the Father through Jesus Christ and the simultaneous lighting of a candle with the singing of *Kyrie Eleison*. Placed in front of a fifteenth-century wooden cross venerated during past holy years, the seven-branched candlestick signified the shining of light on points of darkness in the church's past. The active involvement of curial officials signified the collegial nature of the service, as well as

---

[69] Ratzinger, 'The Church's Guilt', 281.

[70] Office of Papal Liturgical Celebrations, 'Presentation: "Day of Pardon"', sect. II, no. 1.

[71] A DVD of the service is available from CTV Centro Televisivo Vaticano.

[72] Pope John Paul II, Homily, Day of Pardon, 12 March 2000.

dialogue between specific elements of the church's ministry past and present, and the pope in his capacity as primate.

The pope began by petitioning God to 'accept the repentance of his people' and 'grant them mercy'. Even though not every subsequent prayer segment used the words repentance or forgiveness, they may all be taken as constituting acts of repentance requesting God's pardon. The first category of sin, 'sins in general' was introduced by Cardinal Bernadin Gantin, dean of the College of Cardinals. He prayed that the Holy Spirit would inspire deep sorrow and lead to 'true conversion' through a 'purification of memory'. After a time of prayerful silence, the pope acknowledged that the disobedience of Christians contradicts the gospel, and asked God for forgiveness. Then followed Cardinal Joseph Ratzinger, CDF prefect, who confessed that 'men of the Church' have used methods contrary to the gospel 'in the service of truth'. In his prayer, John Paul identified this as 'intolerance' that violated the command to love. He implored mercy for the Church's 'sinful children' and resolved to 'promote truth in the gentleness of charity'.

Cardinal Roger Etchegaray, president of the Central Committee for the Jubilee, invited prayer for 'the sins which have rent the unity of the Body of Christ'. The pope responded in prayer, that indeed the disunity of Christians is disobedience to Christ. He prayed for a penitent heart and 'urgently implored' God's forgiveness so that all Christians may be reconciled to full communion with each other in Christ. The president of the Commission for Religious Relations with the Jews, Cardinal Edward Cassidy, prayed that 'in recalling the sufferings endured by the people of Israel throughout history, Christians will acknowledge the sins committed by not a few of their number against the people of the Covenant and the blessings'. John Paul then prayed the same words he would deposit a few weeks later between stones of the Western wall, asking God's forgiveness for those who caused suffering to 'the people of Covenant' and committing to a spirit of brotherhood with them.

Archbishop Stephen Fumio Hamao, president of the Pontifical Council for Migrants and Itinerant Peoples, prayed for the strength to repent of the ways that 'the weakest groups in society, such as immigrants and itinerants' have been harmed by hatred and the 'desire to dominate others'. The pope's prayer asked forgiveness for those who 'have violated the rights of ethnic groups and peoples, and shown contempt for their cultures and religious traditions'. Sins against human dignity and particularly against women, to which

Christians have 'acquiesced', were named by Cardinal Francis Arrinze, president of the Pontifical Council for Interreligious Dialogue. Evoking the image of God, which the pope confessed Christians have violated by acts of discrimination, Arrinze asked God for healing so that all people know themselves as God's sons and daughters. Finally, sins against the rights of the person – victims of abuse, the poor, those killed by abortion and those 'exploited for experimental purposes by those who ... distort the aims of science' – were named by Archbishop François Xavier Nguyên Van Thuân, president of the Pontifical Council for Justice and Peace. With reference to recognizing Christ in the hungry and imprisoned (Mt. 25), John Paul prayed that God grant forgiveness and accept the repentance of those who have committed injustice against 'the "little ones"'. Before embracing the crucifix as a sign of penance, the pope prayed a final time that God 'Grant that our forbears, our brothers and sisters, and we, your servants, who by the grace of the Holy Spirit turn back to you in whole-hearted repentance, may experience your mercy and receive the forgiveness of our sins.'[73]

At the end of the service, the church was sent forth with the following blessing and resolve:

> Dear brothers and sisters, may this liturgy which has celebrated the Lord's mercy and has sought to purify the memory of the journey made by Christians over the centuries, awaken in the whole Church and in each of us renewed fidelity to the perennial message of the Gospel: never again actions opposed to charity in the service of truth, never again actions against the communion of the Church, never again offences against any people, never again recourse to the logic of violence, never again acts of discrimination, exclusion, oppression, contempt for the poor and the defenceless. And may the Lord by his grace bring our resolve to fulfilment and lead us together to eternal life. Amen.[74]

In the Angelus delivered later that day in St Peter's Square, the pope affirmed that the action of the church was not to judge the subjective responsibility of Christians who have died – that judgement belongs to God – but that by asking God's forgiveness for, presumably, the objective immorality of their actions, the church seeks to 'reawaken consciences', and pursue love, reconciliation and peace.[75]

Given the controversy following *We Remember* over whether the church's confession of the sins of its members included those of bishops and popes, and the church's insistence that it did, it is surprising that the grammar of the pope's prayer created a rhetorical distance

---

[73] Pope John Paul II, Universal Prayer, Day of Pardon, 12 March 2000.
[74] Pope John Paul II, Benediction, Day of Pardon, 12 March 2000.
[75] Pope John Paul II, Angelus, 12 March 2000.

between himself and the sinners in the church. He prayed for 'them', 'those' and 'their' sin. Rather than praying for the behaviour of 'those' who offended against the Jews, he could have with consistency prayed for the behaviour of 'those *of us*' who caused offence. This would not have *necessarily* included the pope as an individual let alone in his primatial role, but it would signify the solidarity in sin that touches all members. If indeed the temptations of power, discrimination and exclusion are pervasive, it would neither imperil the papacy nor the infallibility of the church for the pope to have included himself as an individual Christian who faces these specific temptations and fails. Though he did include himself in some categories of sin, it is more likely that this was due to an inconsistency in editing the final text rather a signal of his personal culpability for some sins and not others.

RESPONSE, DEBATE, RECEPTION

The service must not be understood as an isolated event that definitively laid to rest elements of the past but as a touchstone in the church's continuing purification, penance and renewal. The prayers themselves invoked the Holy Spirit's help to recognize further sins and to repent of them. Though prayers were addressed to God, the entire service was conceived with additional audiences in mind: local churches, those who have suffered on account of the sins named, the watching world, and future generations. The way in which the events of the first Sunday of Lent were interpreted in the secular and religious media, by Catholics lay and cleric, and by other interested groups, shapes the context in which the meaning of the event is made. After an initial discussion of responses and emerging themes, I will conclude this chapter with an examination of how the Day of Pardon is being received into Roman Catholic tradition.

News reports portrayed the unprecedented request for forgiveness by a pope as very significant. They typically framed its meaning in terms of the arrival of the third millennium as an occasion for 'moving on' from a harmful past. Some print media reports heightened the drama of the event by portraying it as a personal triumph of the pope in the face of opposition within the hierarchy, and in light of his age and advancing Parkinson's disease.[76] The *Toronto Star* cited

---

[76] For example, Rory Carroll, 'Pope Says Sorry for Sins of Church: Apology for Attacks on Jews, Women and Minorities Defies Theologians' Warnings', *The Guardian*, 13 March 2000.

Catholic theologian John Pawlikowski's view that it 'could change the entire culture of the church's tradition-bound institutions'.[77] Whereas church documents gave priority to the church's relationship with God, media reports emphasized the potential for the Day of Pardon to promote social reconciliation, especially among religions, though some observed that its flaws might be a detriment to such a goal.[78] The influential editorial in the *New York Times* was representative in its assessment. It celebrated the Day of Pardon as genuine progress, evidence of the pope's moral influence on history, and hope for the reconciliation of communities. It was a good start, but did not go far enough.[79]

The daily press overwhelming located the pope's action within a narrative of Catholic–Jewish relations, and particularly the expectation of an apology for silence and complicity during the Holocaust and the role of Pope Pius XII. The reactions of Jewish leaders were sought and cited (besides Catholic bishops and theologians, the responses of other groups were generally unreported). Rabbi Marvin Hier of the Simon Wiesenthal Center praised the gesture as an important step forward, but regretted that the Holocaust was not explicitly identified.[80] Israel's Chief Rabbi Meir Lau was widely quoted criticizing the omission of the Holocaust: 'To mention the Inquisition from the year 1492 and to exclude the Wannsee conference from 1942 demonstrates a severely warped view of history.' But he expressed hope that such a statement may be coming when the pope would visit Yad Vashem a few weeks later.[81]

The use of the term 'apology' to refer to the pope's action was widespread. Even Catholic bishops and theologians, who must have known of the Vatican's deliberate avoidance of the word, were quoted interpreting the pope's 'apology'.[82] An implication of this shift in nomenclature may be found in one columnist's contention that, by

---

[77] Steve Kloen, 'Pope Repents, Seeks Forgiveness: Sweeping Apology Marks a First in Christianity', *Toronto Star*, 13 March 2000, 1.

[78] Simon Heffer, 'This Pathetic Urge to Keep Saying Sorry', *Daily Mail*, 14 March 2000, 12.

[79] 'The Pope's Apology', editorial, *New York Times*, 14 March 2000, A22.

[80] Stanley, 'Pope Asks Forgiveness', A10.

[81] Ron Kampeas and John M. Hubbell, 'Some Were Moved; Some Wanted More: Church's Failure to Mention Holocaust Upsets Israel's Chief Rabbi', *Ottawa Citizen*, 13 March 2000, A7.

[82] James Beverley, 'Mea Culpa: What Comes Next?' *Toronto Star*, 18 March 2000, 1, quoting Cardinal Aloysius Ambrozic of Toronto.

the standards of an apology, the pope's action was deficient. Unlike a true apology, it was not directly to the persons offended, it was insufficiently specific and it was not followed by some form of reparations.[83]

The criticism that emerged in response to the Day of Pardon may be grouped into four themes: the distinction between church and members; the general character of the confessions; the problem of judging the past by the standards of the present; and the charge that the church was insincere or hypocritical.

The press quoted theologian Hans Küng's complaint that the confession was not for the actions of the church, nor leaders who acted in the church's name, but only for its members.[84] The Catholic periodical *America* applauded the request for pardon but took issue with this distinction: 'If we [popes, bishops, members in the pews] are the church, then the church has sinned.'[85] By contrast, one commentator argued that by confessing sin in its human dimension, the church draws attention to the sinless perfection of the church's divine dimension.[86]

One nuance on this debate is the question of whether the wrongs confessed reflect the failure in practice to live up to the church's teachings, or actual error in the teachings themselves. Since the church is frequently called a teacher, the stakes in the debate may entail the ascription of sin to the church. Avery Dulles argues that repentance is strictly for failures to follow teachings, contending that unless this distinction is clearly drawn, the faithful will be unsure that present teaching is reliable.[87] According to this view, the church is understood theologically as a body that cannot teach falsely, thus any false teaching by definition was not the position of the church. Francis A. Sullivan counters that some of the Christians who failed in their callings were also members of the hierarchy, with a teaching charism, acting in the name of the church. Teachings and teachers are not so easily separated. Neither is a sharp distinction between

---

[83] Nicolaus Mills, 'The Modern Notion of a Public Apology', *Los Angeles Times*, 19 March 2000, 3.

[84] Richard Bourdreaux, 'Pope Apologizes for Catholic Sins Past and Present', *Los Angeles Times*, 13 March 2000, 1.

[85] 'Asking Forgiveness', editorial, *America*, 25 March 2000, 3.

[86] Robert A. Sirico, 'The Pope's Nostra Culpa', *Wall Street Journal*, 15 March 2000, A26.

[87] Avery Dulles, 'Should the Church Repent?' *First Things*, no. 88 (December 1998), 40.

teaching and action tenable; teachings are actions.[88] Even if the term sin is ascribed only to individuals, sins committed by members of the hierarchy issued in church policies and practices that 'have been objectively in contradiction to the Gospel and have caused harm to many people'. The abiding presence of the Holy Spirit in the church is not a promise that it will never take a wrong turn, says Sullivan, but that any such turn will not ultimately compromise the eschatological destiny of the church.[89]

Second, many commentators identified as problematic the general nature of the confessions, and particular omissions. No specific individuals or groups were identified by the pope as bearing particular responsibility for the sins named. The confessions identified attitudes and habits of sin, such as intolerance, disobedience, pride, and hatred, which are potentially applicable to all Christians. It was left for others to detect whether the sin of intolerance, for example, is specific enough to constitute an acknowledgment of a root of the suffering of the Roma people, for example, or an awareness of their story.

Two groups which had asked for acknowledgment interpreted the actual confessions quite differently. A coalition of Pagans sent a letter to the pope requesting that the Day of Pardon mention that many witches and pagans were forcibly converted to the church, or killed. Though neither witches nor pagans were named in the liturgy, they interpreted the pope's prayers as broad enough to 'encompass the ethnic, ancestral traditions of Paganism and Witchcraft'.[90] An Italian gay rights group had implored the pope to address the treatment of homosexuals, but they did not regard themselves among those the pope named as suffering at the hands of the church. Their spokesperson noted that the Vatican did not ask forgiveness from homosexuals, 'who are among the most numerous victims of the theocratic violence of yesterday and today'.[91]

The general nature of what was confessed, together with the emphasis on the culpability of individuals as opposed to the church, has led some to conclude that a key aim was for the church to

---

[88] Joseph E. Capizzi, 'For What Shall We Repent? Reflections on the American Bishops, Their Teaching, and Slavery in the United States, 1939–1961', *Theological Studies* 65 (2004), 774.

[89] Francis A. Sullivan, 'The Papal Apology', *America*, 8 April 2000, 22.

[90] 'The Pagans' Letter to the Pope', *The Oaks*, no. 2 (Summer 2000), *World Congress of Ethnic Religions*, www.wcer.org/newsletter/oaks2/oaks2_09.html.

[91] Paul Tuns, 'Problems with Papal Apologies', *Ottawa Citizen*, 15 March 2000, A17.

reaffirm the stainless character of itself as an institution.[92] Gerard Mannion identifies the 'nagging doubt' that this was the reason that some histories were not addressed more specifically.[93] One professor of Jewish history argued that the pope will not advance the healing of memories without understanding and addressing the central role that the Holocaust plays in collective Jewish memory, and in particular the role of Pope Pius XII.[94] The International Council of Christians and Jews, along with others, expressed hope that the self-reflective attitude of the Catholic Church would extend to its relations with Muslims, who had not been named.[95]

The third general criticism was that the Day of Pardon gave undue priority to present moral convictions and thus interpreted the past anachronistically. One columnist wrote that given that the crusades and inquisitions were conducted in accord with the standards of the day, the pope essentially apologized for the fact that past ages 'had different ideas of right and wrong than our age'.[96] Despite the fact that the pope was a frequent critic of the spirit of the present age, some columnists accused him of naively succumbing to the modern penchant for overwrought apologies.[97] Another pointed out that so many apologies may give liberals inside and outside the church unrealistic expectations that the church will change its position on issues such as birth control or women's ordination.[98] One ultra-conservative schismatic[99] leader, Bishop Richard Williamson, charged that '[i]nstead of thinking like a child of the Church, proud of her incomparable glory, the pope is seeking to adapt to the mentality of the world which perversely blames the Church for all sorts of fabricated but fashionable sins, like anti-Semitism, racism, sexism,

---

[92] Lance Morrow, 'Is It Enough to Be Sorry?' *Time*, 27 March 2000, 28.

[93] Gerard Mannion, *Ecclesiology and Postmodernity: Questions for the Church in Our Time* (Collegeville, MN: Liturgical Press, 2007), 144.

[94] David Cesarani, 'Unfinished Business', *The Tablet*, 1 April 2000, 443.

[95] 'Statement in Response to Papal Apology', 15 March 2000, www.iccj.org/en/index.php?item=112.

[96] George Jonas, 'Why Seek Forgiveness for Others' Past Sins?' *National Post*, 13 March 2000, A16.

[97] Heffer, 'This Pathetic Urge to Keep Saying Sorry'.

[98] Tom Bethell, 'Is the Pope Overdoing the Apologies?' *Beliefnet* (2000), www.beliefnet.com/story/14/story_1458_1.html.

[99] He was excommunicated in 1988 after being consecrated by Archbishop Marcel Lefebvre without papal authorization. The controversial lifting of the excommunication in 2009 was followed by public attention on his Holocaust denial.

etc.'[100] This will only erode the church's moral authority internally and reinforce external anti-Catholic prejudice, he said.

Fourth, respondents charged the church with insincerity or hypocrisy. A *New York Times* editorial accused the church of hypocrisy for confessing discrimination against women while continuing to oppose birth control, abortion, and the ordination of women.[101] Sr Carmel McEnroy challenged the church to review the role of women in the church as a sign of sincere contrition.[102] (McEnroy had been dismissed from her seminary faculty position for publicly opposing the church's teaching on the ordination of women.) Others argued that without a promise to not repeat the offences,[103] or some form of symbolic reparations,[104] the exercise was 'just words'.

A controversial book by former Harvard professor Daniel Jonah Goldhagen shows how the Day of Pardon does indeed expose the Catholic Church to various expectations and assumptions about the meaning and consequences of its action. Goldhagen argues that a truly penitent Catholic Church owes not only political and monetary reparations, but moral reparations which entail greater public disclosure about the church's involvement in the Holocaust and an acknowledgment of a link between church doctrine and gas chambers. Some of his suggestions, such as asking victims directly for forgiveness, a dedicated program to combat anti-Semitism, and an end of the Holy See's status as a sovereign nation, are indeed constructive.[105] However, Goldhagen's list of institutional reforms required as evidence of sincerity are grounded in a 'universal moral duty' which he claims trumps the church's self-understanding,

---

[100] Richard Williamson, 'The Pope's Millennial Apology: Deeply Confused, Deeply Confusing', *Society of St. Pius X* (2000), www.sspx.ca/Documents/Bishop-Williamson/April2–2000.htm.

[101] 'The Pope's Apology', A22

[102] Carmel McEnroy, 'Papal Apology a First Step', *National Catholic Reporter*, 24 March 2000, 7.

[103] Kay Carmichael, *Sin and Forgiveness: New Responses in a Changing World* (Aldershot, UK: Ashgate, 2003), xiii.

[104] Zenon Szablowinski, 'Apology Without Compensation, Compensation with Apology', *Pacifica* 18 (2005), 336–48.

[105] Daniel Jonah Goldhagen, *A Moral Reckoning: The Role of the Catholic Church in the Holocaust and Its Unfulfilled Duty of Repair* (New York: Knopf, 2002), 221–53. His argument against the sovereign status of the Vatican is premised on a general claim that a state must be protected from religion, an analysis which he does not apply to Israel whose existence as a nation for Jews he argues the Catholic Church is obliged to support.

tradition and practices. For example, he contends that the church must give up its claim to be the only way to salvation, since such a belief is inevitably imperialistic.[106] Without considering the nuanced and limited senses in which the Catholic Church understands papal infallibility, and the church's infallibility as a whole, Goldhagen argues that only by renouncing any and all claims to infallibility would the church demonstrate its intention to never again become complicit in mass murder.[107] Acknowledging that laudable church statements have failed to curb apparent widespread anti-Semitism and supersessionism among Catholics, he holds that what will change their minds is the removal of 450 specific verses in the New Testament that he deems anti-Semitic. Ironically, he appeals to the sheer authoritarian power of the church that he elsewhere denounces as the means by which the church could excise these texts from the Bible.[108]

How the church could simply alter the Bible by ordering its adherents to do so when it is apparently unable to order the implementation of Vatican II's view of Judaism is among the many inconsistencies in Goldhagen's approach. Criticized for ignoring primary sources and relying on selected, hostile secondary sources,[109] his work does not betray an understanding of the Catholic Church's doctrine, practices or self-understanding. The obligation to do this does not belong to every critic but does belong to one whose argument partly depends on what he claims the church ought to recognize as consistent with its Day of Pardon action. Though Goldhagen may have written *A Moral Reckoning* even if the church had not held a Day of Pardon, some of his demands create the impression that the church cannot repent without consenting to impossible demands made on it in the public square, or by essentially ceasing to be the church. If this is what repentance means, then the church cannot really do so and ought not to try.

The Day of Pardon was an act of the pope, in his role as universal pastor, on behalf of the entire church. How has it been received? How has it become integrated into the life and tradition of the church? First, to the extent that the event was intrinsic to the church's faith and witness, yet novel in expression, it contributes to the devel-

---

[106] *Ibid.*, 253–4.
[107] *Ibid.*, 255–6.
[108] *Ibid.*, 262–74.
[109] Vincent A. Lapomarda, 'Reckoning with Daniel J. Goldhagen's Views of the Roman Catholic Church, the Holocaust, and Pope Pius XII', *The Journal of the Historical Society* 3 (2003), 493–502.

opment of doctrine. William McDonough and Catherine Michaud argue that papal repentance functions as authoritative teaching on topics such as ecumenism, Judaism, and religious liberty. They link the six specific requests for pardon with precedents in Vatican II documents, though the references to actual history add a depth to the teaching. For example, repentance for sins committed in the service of truth may be understood as a development of the acknowledgment in *Gaudium et Spes* that some of the conflict between science and religion resulted from 'a short-sighted view of the rightful autonomy of science'.[110] The pope's repentance in relation to sins against the people of Israel deepens *Nostra Aetate*'s denunciation of anti-Semitism by acknowledging that Christians have been also guilty of that sin.[111] Repentance does not signify an aberration of the tradition, but marks its dynamic and true progress.

Second, repentance is linked with ongoing reform in the church.[112] One canon lawyer argues that, in light of the pope's request for pardon for sins committed in the service of truth and assertion that the Inquisition has been abolished, he ought to abolish existing forms of extrajudicial punishment still in canon law.[113] A broad range of reforms may indeed be understood as a kind of penance for the sins confessed. Bradford Hinze contends the church must foster dialogue on many levels in order to determine the nature of the failures and the reparative steps required to address them, including specific reforms of teachings or practices. Dialogue is essential for reform because it adds the perspective of the previously marginalized or excluded. For example, past Jewish–Catholic dialogue led the church to revise its Holy Week liturgy, removing reference to 'the perfidious Jews'.[114] Hinze argues that greater openness to dialogue, and the humility and polyphony presupposed by it, is itself a substantial reform required. Dialogue ought to engage with and learn from the

---

[110] William McDonough and Catherine Michaud, 'Papal Apologies Embody and Advance Vatican II on the "Tradition Poured Out in the Church"', in *Revelation and the Church: Vatican II in the Twenty-First Century*, ed. Raymond A. Lucker and William McDonough (Maryknoll, NY: Orbis Books, 2003), 108, citing *Gaudium et Spes*, no. 36.

[111] McDonough and Michaud, 'Papal Apologies and Vatican II', 110–11, citing *Nostra Aetate*, no. 4.

[112] As noted in *MR*, no. 6.1.

[113] Ruud G. W. Huysmans, 'The Inquisition for Which the Pope Did Not Ask Forgiveness', *The Jurist* 66 (2006), 469–82.

[114] Bradford E. Hinze, 'Ecclesial Repentance and the Demands of Dialogue', *Theological Studies* 61 (2000), 237.

Bible as well as 'the history of the Church, those marginalized voices within the community, those silenced in our midst and at the borders, especially the poor, but also neighbors and those from alien lands with different beliefs and practices'.[115]

Despite the way in which ecclesial repentance may mark the development of doctrine or lead to church reforms, it ought not to denote present moral superiority. While the development of doctrine clearly depends on an organic connection of past and present, there is a danger that ecclesial repentance effectively severs the connection rather than develops it. To the extent that contemporary Christians do not imagine how they could sanction torture in the name of an inquisition, for example, they vilify the past. To shudder at the horrors of what 'others' have done may create a disjunction with the past that impedes the vision needed to continuously name wrongdoing. There is the further possibility that addressing the sins of the past may be a way to avoid dealing with the sins of the present. However, John Paul repeatedly described his action as one that ought to lead individuals, as well as local churches, to examine their own consciences and seek God's forgiveness. To the extent that the Day of Pardon promotes this type of reflection on the past, it will shape a historically attuned people who vigilantly identify new and recurring sins, and seek ongoing conversion.

Indeed, many individual bishops and episcopal conferences took up the pope's call for examination of conscience and repentance at the local level, a third type of reception into tradition.[116] The Australian Bishops addressed their history of relations with Aboriginal people, while the Swiss and Polish Bishops made separate statements about the church's relation to Jewish people during the Holocaust. In addition to the themes addressed by the pope, Archbishop Michael Sheehan of Santa Fe addressed the retributive justice and prison system, and asked pardon for those Catholics who have failed to apply the principle of forgiveness in such systems. His statement, and that of Bishop Robert Morlino of Helena, Montana, actually identify 'the church' rather than Christians or even individual pastors, as responsible for the wrongs identified.[117] In spite of *MR*'s careful ruling of

---

[115] *Ibid.*, 213.

[116] Several are discussed in 'Asking Pardon Worldwide', *National Catholic Reporter*, 24 March 2000, 7 and documented in *Origins* throughout the following year.

[117] Archbishop Michael Sheehan, '"Mea Culpas" for Service of Reconciliation', *Origins* 29, no. 40 (23 March 2000), 654–5; Bishop Robert Morlino, 'Service for the Healing of Memories', *Origins* 31, no. 23 (15 November 2001), 381, 383–5.

such admissions as doctrinally inadmissible, the call for corporate penitence has been received by numerous bishops as stating plainly that in systematic ways the church itself has been at fault and, implicitly, in sin. Years later Cardinal Marc Ouellet invoked the Day of Pardon as the basis for an open letter to Quebec Catholics which addressed similar themes, but also asked God's forgiveness for ones particular to his context, such as the Quebec Bishops' opposition in the 1920s and 30s to universal women's suffrage.[118]

In the service of repentance he led, Cardinal Roger Mahony of Los Angeles correlated specific sins with concrete archdiocesan commitments to address them. After naming the effects of racial and economic discrimination, he noted the failure of the church to support a particular civic housing policy and pointed to church initiatives to provide affordable housing. He asked pardon from gays and lesbians for times when the church was not supportive of their struggles or was guilty of homophobia. He highlighted outreach ministries to homosexual persons and pledged to help protect their civil rights. Mahony's repentance for stereotyping other faiths had a distinct local adaptation. He explained that the Los Angeles Archdiocese must be careful when it criticizes the negative impact of movies and television to not assign blame to the involvement of Jews in their production.[119]

Rather than keeping the discourse about past faults behind closed doors, these local services show how the pope's confession is being built upon and extended, and how not only statements of repentance but also the histories they name are becoming part of the church's authorized identity. This local reception will likely lead to repentance for histories that are only now being reexamined. Catholic ethicist Joseph Capizzi's case for the Catholic Church in the US to repent of its nineteenth-century teaching about slavery, which 'misled Catholics of goodwill', is an example of what may be to come.[120]

The reception of John Paul's initiative at the local level addresses some of the criticism that the pope's confession was far too general. According to Joseph Komonchak, only if and where local churches review their past and make specific promises for the future is the

---

[118] Archbishop Marc Ouellet, 'Open Letter to the Catholics of Quebec', *Le Devoir*, 21 November 2007, A9.

[119] Cardinal Roger Mahony, 'Mapping the Road to Reconciliation: Message of Apology', *Origins* 29, no. 40 (23 March 2000), 652–3.

[120] Capizzi, 'For What Shall we Repent?' 790.

universal church responding to the pope's call.[121] In this perspective, the pope's Universal Prayer may be viewed primarily as the authorization and invitation for the examination of consciences in particular contexts, rather than the final and definitive request for pardon. As some sins committed 'locally' have harmed the witness of the universal church, so confession and reconciliation at local levels reflect the church's universal mission. Without entering into the complicated debate about whether the local or universal church has theological priority,[122] the Day of Pardon may nevertheless be assessed in terms of the different ways that the universal church enables local churches to turn attention to their historical particularity, and *vice-versa*.

The calls to repentance addressed to the angels of some of the seven churches in Revelation 2–3 are differentiated in an instructive way. Some angels are both commended for their faith and called to repent of particular sins (Ephesus, Pergamum, Thyatira); others are not called to repent at all (Smyrna, Philadelphia). Little positive is said about church at Sardis, though some individuals are faithful. The lukewarm faith of Laodicea may be reason why they are blind to even their need to repent. No church is called to repent simply because it consists of human members who sin. If this were the case, all churches would be addressed in the same way. The messages to the churches reflect a differentiated judgement about their faithfulness in their particular places. John of Patmos records what the Spirit is saying to *local* churches.

The prominence of the Catholic Church's public action led to a response by the United Methodist Church which held its General Conference just weeks after the Day of Pardon. They approved a letter to the pope accepting his 'apologia' for the use of coercion in the service of truth against their Protestant forebears, and in turn asked forgiveness for their actions and inactions that have harmed the Catholic Church. The United Methodists also confessed their 'shared culpability in wrongs of both thought and action' with Catholics towards 'the multitudes of persons living in poverty, in illness, without education and under the scourges of racism; indigenous peoples of the world; women; Jews, Muslims; and peoples of

---

[121] Joseph A. Komonchak, 'Preparing for the New Millennium', *Logos: A Journal of Catholic Thought* 1, no. 2 (1997), 52.

[122] For an overview, see Kilian McDonnell, 'The Ratzinger/Kasper Debate: The Universal Church and Local Churches', *Theological Studies* 63 (2002), 227–50.

other living faiths'.¹²³ The development of tradition here may be seen both in the way Methodists joined their view of the past with the Catholic account in order to create a shared narrative requiring repentance, but also in how they nudged the Catholic Church to extend the meaning of the Day of Pardon by including within its scope the history of the relationship with Muslims. This contribution to an emerging ecumenical tradition of ecclesial repentance constitutes a fourth mode of reception. By contrast, various Orthodox authorities explained that no mea culpa by the Orthodox Churches would be forthcoming since they had nothing for which to ask forgiveness, a specific disavowal that may make it more difficult for the Orthodox to hold anything like a Day of Pardon in the future.¹²⁴

Fifth, the Day of Pardon has become an authoritative point of reference for subsequent Catholic discourse on particular issues of justice and reconciliation. As discussed in Chapter 2, the introductory note added in 2001 to the text *The Church and Racism* shows how the Day of Pardon reorients the entire approach of the document from the prophetic critique of others to penitent self-examination of a church seeking to embody its calling.¹²⁵ The 'purification of memories' language in post–2000 statements to the Orthodox invoke the pope's Jubilee confession for sins against the unity of the church. In dialogue with Mennonites, the Catholic delegation applied the general Day of Pardon statements to the particular case of relations with Mennonites 'asking forgiveness for any sins which were committed against Mennonites, asking God's mercy for that, and God's blessing for a new relationship with Mennonites today'.¹²⁶ In a dialogue with the United Church of Canada, the Day of Pardon and especially *MR* served as authoritative sources for clarifying convergences on issues of sin and reconciliation.¹²⁷

---

¹²³ United Methodist Church, Letter to Pope John Paul II (2000).

¹²⁴ Authorized statements were made by bishops of the Greek Orthodox Church and the Russian Orthodox Church, Robert F. Taft, 'The Problem of "Uniatism" and the "Healing of Memories"', *Logos: A Journal of Eastern Christian Studies* 41–2 (2000–2001), 182–3. Taft proceeds to discuss a range of past actions for which Orthodox Churches ought to examine their consciences and ask pardon: forced conversion of Jews, persecution of Roman Catholics, sanction of mob violence, violations of ecclesiastic jurisdictions, and complicity in political repression.

¹²⁵ Pontifical Council for Justice and Peace, *The Church and Racism: Towards a More Fraternal Society*, updated ed. (London: Catholic Truth Society, 2001).

¹²⁶ Roman Catholic Church and Mennonite World Conference, 'Called Together to be Peacemakers', no. 202.

¹²⁷ Canadian Roman Catholic/United Church of Canada Dialogue, 'Sin, Reconciliation, and Ecclesial Identity' (2004), www.united-church.ca/files/partners/relations/ecumenical/report_rc_02.pdf.

Sixth, the Day of Pardon has occasioned some development of the doctrine of the church, particularly around sin, holiness and images of the church. Several introductory texts treat it as the point of departure for explaining how the church is both indefectibly holy and, as a church of sinners, always in need in purification.[128] Furthermore, several Catholic theologians have indeed pointed to the Day of Pardon, and other similar acts by the pope, as implicit recognition of social sin in the church and, by extension, that the church itself has sinned (examined in Chapter 6). Archbishop Rembert Weakland correlates the church's self-examination with the rise of images of church as pilgrim and as people of God, both of which were expressed at Vatican II.[129] Of course, the influence is mutual. Images that highlight the church 'on the way' will stimulate reflection on the course that way has taken, but so does the fact that sins that have marred the church's witness shape the way that certain images resonate as descriptive of the church. Since one of the functions of the image of church as mother is to assert the controversial distinction of sinless mother church and sinful members, the image does not help the church communicate its contrition before a watching world. Yet, if the church decides that penitence necessitates a reassertion of the distinction between the church and its members, the image of church as mother may be deployed even more often.

Seventh, the historical past identified by the prayer of repentance has formed something of a research agenda for church historians. The stated openness of the church to reconsider controversial elements in its past may well lead to more specific acknowledgments put on record and a closer consideration of how the past continues to shape the church's mission today. Alternately, historical accounts may become more defensive, limiting to scope of wrongdoing to what has already been admitted and showing how particular individuals corrupted the true intentions of the church. A mixture of these elements is evident in Keith D. Lewis' recent work, which examines

---

[128] This formulation is from *Lumen Gentium*, no. 8. For examples, see Gerald O'Collins and Mario Farrugia, *Catholicism: The Story of Catholic Christianity* (Oxford: Oxford University Press, 2003), 329; and Thomas P. Rausch, *Towards a Truly Catholic Church: An Ecclesiology for the Third Millennium* (Collegeville, MN: Liturgical Press, 2005), 137–8.

[129] Rembert G. Weakland, 'Images of the Church: From "Perfect Society" to "God's People on Pilgrimage"', in *Unfinished Journey: The Church 40 Years After Vatican II*, ed. Austen Ivereigh (New York: Continuum, 2003), 78–90.

historical episodes correlated to the pope's request for pardon.[130] His historical accounts narrate the affect of political and personal factors, and generally downplay the agency of the church per se. Is this because the possibility has been excluded on theological grounds, or because the evidence warrants it? He assigns the excesses of the Spanish Inquisition to the political aims of the monarchy, not the church, though oddly he does not refer to any of the research on the inquisitions generated by the Jubilee Historical Subcommission. In any case, he shows how a hermeneutic shaped by papal actions is being received and implemented.

An eighth and final way of gauging reception is certainly the most important, but most difficult to substantiate. Is the Catholic Church now more faithful in its calling to reflect Christ's grace and truth in the world? Has Pope John Paul II's intention been realized for the church to enter the third millennium strengthened in faith, more alert to temptations and challenges and better prepared to meet them?[131] Has the church kept its pledge to never again commit 'acts of discrimination, exclusion, oppression, contempt for the poor and the defenceless',[132] and if not, how ought this to be addressed? By what signs may these questions be answered?

The chapters in Part 1 have presented an overview of ecclesial repentance in the twentieth and early twenty-first centuries, and a close examination of one complex instance. My working assumption is that as church practices, these acts may reflect the work of the trinitarian God, but just so may require Christian theology to speak a bit differently about God, and particularly about the role of the church in the mission of this God. In Part 2, I will move from doctrine to practice to show how the Christian tradition helps us to understand this relatively new practice, and to address some of the questions and tensions raised by it. But ecclesial repentance is not only about continuity but also, in the church's disavowal of some aspect of its past, about discontinuity. Therefore, I also move from practice back to doctrine to suggest how the very fact of church apologies as they have emerged necessitates a revision and a reshaping of some theological concepts.

---

[130] Keith D. Lewis, *The Catholic Church in History: Legends and Reality* (New York: Crossroad, 2006). A similar approach is taken by the Indian Catholic journal *Jeevadhara* 36, no. 241 (2006).

[131] *Tertio Millennio Adveniente*, no. 33.

[132] Pope John Paul II, Benediction, Day of Pardon, 12 March 2000.

Issues and constructive possibilities in the preceding chapters constellate around three themes. First, there are questions of history, memory and the temporal nature of the church. In what way does the church's penitential engagement with specific elements of its history take this history up into its own identity? What assumptions about the temporal continuity of the church are made by the fact that the church speaks in the present to something done centuries earlier? The doctrine of the communion of saints will be the focal point for these reflections. Second, there is a cluster of concerns about the nature and meaning of sin in the church. While many of these centre around the Catholic distinction between a sinless church (which nevertheless repents) and sinful members, actual practice ought to prod both Catholic and Protestant theology to rethink what it means to say that the church is holy. Third, what is the nature of forgiveness and reconciliation implied by ecclesial repentance? How does the deep logic of church confessions of past wrongs configure the relationship between divine and human forgiveness? Attention to the sacrament of penance and reflection about other instances of collective apology in the public sphere will prove instructive for how ecclesial repentance might further the church's mission of reconciliation.

Part 2

DOCTRINE AND PRACTICE: FRAMEWORKS AND IMPLICATIONS

Chapter 5

THE COMMUNION OF SAINTS

> *But the truth is, we are the bearers of many blessings from our ancestors, and therefore, we must also bear their burdens.* (The Right Reverend Bill Phipps, Moderator of the United Church of Canada)[1]

Pope John Paul II's visit to Greece in 2001 was very controversial. Reflecting the ongoing tensions between the Roman Catholic and the Greek Orthodox traditions, the Orthodox Primate, Archbishop Christodoulos, had for years resisted inviting the pope. He agreed to meet with the pope only because John Paul was coming anyway, on the invitation of the Greek President. Some Orthodox monks took to the streets in protest to express their sense of being wronged and offended by, among other things, the sack of Constantinople by Roman Catholic crusaders in 1204. In a scripted interchange between the two religious leaders, Archbishop Christodoulos explained that many Orthodox opposed the pope's presence because he had not asked them for forgiveness for what he called the 'maniacal' actions of the crusaders in the thirteenth century.[2] The pope replied with a request to God for forgiveness for those 'occasions past and present, when sons and daughters of the Catholic Church have sinned by action or omission against their Orthodox brothers and sisters ...'. The pope singled out, with regret, the 'deep wound' of the sack of Constantinople. He said: 'To God alone belongs judgement, and therefore we entrust the heavy burden of the past to his endless mercy, imploring him to heal the wounds which still cause suffering

---

[1] The Rt Rev Bill Phipps, United Church of Canada, 'Apology to Former Students of United Church Indian Residential Schools, and to their Families and Communities' (1998).

[2] Andrew Walsh, 'The Pope Among the Orthodox', *Religion in the News* 4, no. 2 (Summer 2001), 12.

to the spirit of the Greek people'.³ Christodoulos received this gesture as the required request for pardon.

The pope made a similar statement of regret and repentance for the sack of Constantinople to Ecumenical Patriarch Bartholomew I a few years later. There, the pope prayed that 'the Lord of history will purify our memory of all prejudice and resentment and obtain for us that we may advance in freedom on the path to unity'.⁴

But is it possible to repent of such a distant past? In a magazine column in 1997, British historian Paul Johnson chastised church leaders such as the pope for jumping on the bandwagon of public apology. He wrote:

> These are bogus apologies by people who had nothing to do with the events deplored and lose nothing by saying they were wrong. They are an attempt to gain moral kudos at the expense of the long dead ... The truth is, historical apologising is an absurdity. Are we to say sorry for destroying the Spanish Armada, or should the Spanish apologise for sending it in the first place? Before we know where we are, the sodomites will be demanding that God apologise for destroying the Cities of the Plain.⁵

Besides the implication that there will be no end to apologies for the past, the essence of Johnson's *reductio ad absurdum* is that it is wrong for the present to judge the past. Though Christians centuries ago may have acted in good faith based on the cultural and moral frameworks available to them, this fact may be lost when their actions are compared to present understandings. Johnson's charge raises a key question that will be examined in this chapter. Given that churches are repenting of the actions of generations long past, even for events in the thirteenth century, in what ways, if any, are such actions meaningful? In what sense is a penitent twenty-first-century Catholic Church the same church as the thirteenth-century one? The issue is more complex for the churches emerging from the Reformation, whose objections to some of the elements of the Catholic Church led to schisms and new church structures. Does whatever ties the present Catholic Church with the crusades also tie the present day Mennonite churches, for example, with the crusades?

My argument is that the continuity of the church ought to be

---

³ Pope John Paul II, Address to His Beatitude Christodoulos, Archbishop of Athens and Primate of Greece, 4 May 2001.

⁴ Pope John Paul II, Welcome Address to the Ecumenical Patriarch Bartholomew I, 29 June 2004.

⁵ Paul Johnson, 'When is God Going to Apologise for Raining Fire and Brimstone on Sodom?' *The Spectator*, 8 November 1997, 28.

understood within the doctrinal locus of the communion of saints, the doctrine that explains how the long dead remain bound with the living, under Christ, the living head. In this chapter, I argue that the doctrine of the communion of saints helps to illuminate what ecclesial repentance is, how it is possible, how it might actually contribute to the reconciliation among churches for wrongs that extend for generations, and that the practice itself provides an occasion for some constructive rethinking of the doctrine itself. Furthermore, the often invoked aim of healing or purifying memories through public repentance may best be understood through the interplay of past, present and future that is opened up by attention to the communion of saints. Though churches have recently repented of myriad sins, my focus will be particularly on ecclesial repentance for sins against the unity of the church, a theme with obvious implications for the communion of saints. I will consider first Robert Jenson's account of how the temporality of the church is rooted in the act and being of the triune God. In the second section, I examine the doctrine of the communion of saints and, in the third, the concept of the healing of memories in dialogue with Miroslav Volf.

THE CHURCH IN TIME: ROBERT JENSON ON THE TRINITY

Robert Jenson posits a strong account of the continuity of the church rooted in a temporal conception of the triune God. At first glance, his high ecclesiology renders him a unlikely resource. One might assume that a theologian who has been criticized for collapsing Christ and the church[6] would refuse to recognize sin in the church's life or argue against a penitent church. The context of my constructive appropriation of Jenson is important. I am not proposing a wholesale Jensonian account of ecclesial repentance,[7] let alone a full assessment of his theology, though the coherence of his thought requires that I start with what he says about the Trinity in order to explain his view of the church. Rather, I am proposing that his systematic framework, especially his doctrine of God, helps us to account for this particular

---

[6] Colin Gunton, '"Until He Comes": Towards an Eschatology of Church Membership', *International Journal of Systematic Theology* 3 (2001), 190; George Hunsinger, 'Robert Jenson's *Systematic Theology*: A Review Essay', *Scottish Journal of Theology* 55 (2002), 194–5; Ian A. McFarland, 'The Body of Christ: Rethinking a Classic Ecclesiological Model', *International Journal of Systematic Theology* 7 (2005), 232–7.

[7] I have not found any published source in which Jenson directly engages the actual practice of ecclesial repentance as I am using the term.

practice in the life of the church, specifically as it relates to the church's temporal nature. An underlying theme throughout this book is that ecclesial repentance is a consistent, and even necessary, element of a robust ecclesiology, though one must not be evasive about the seriousness of the judgement this represents. Thus, in this chapter, I make use of Jenson's thoroughly trinitarian future-oriented doctrine of church as a way of articulating the church's continuity over time and of locating ecclesial repentance within the trinitarian story of God that comprises that continuity. My contention is that the theological structure of ecclesial repentance requires theology to venture out into some of the daring directions that Jenson has charted. Given that ecclesial repentance is happening, I aim to provide a theological account for what it would mean for this practice to be the work of the Spirit in the church. Mapping ecclesial repentance on to Jenson's thought in turn highlights a distinction of Christ and church, and thus bolsters the theological viability of Jenson's project.

Jenson is illuminating because his theology is fiercely attentive to the particularity of the church. He boldly remarks that God the Father intends that there be a church, and 'that this church be exactly the one that exists'.[8] That the actual church is the intention of God the Father challenges the function that the concept of the invisible church typically plays in ecclesiology and moreover undercuts any 'blueprint ecclesiology' approach to the church.[9] There is no ideal church, only the one that exists. This is not to say that Jenson simply endorses the church as it is. Indeed, he often vehemently criticizes much actual church practice as captive to the politically correct spirit of the age. Rather, Jenson shows how the church's particularity is not accidental or alienated from its essence, but is 'played out' through the mutual interaction of God's intention, God's presently risen Son, and God's future, which is the Holy Spirit. The church's temporal character matters because the dynamic relationship of Father, Son and Holy Spirit is temporal. Time, for Jenson, is not an extrinsic category, but is enclosed by the perichoretic life of the triune God.

---

[8] Robert W. Jenson, *Systematic Theology: The Works of God*, vol. 2 (Oxford: Oxford University Press, 1999), 173.

[9] The logic of 'blueprint ecclesiologies' is identified and critiqued in Nicholas M. Healy, *Church, World and the Christian Life: Practical–Prophetic Ecclesiology* (Cambridge: Cambridge University Press, 2000), Chapter 2.

God and Time

Jenson argues that the elusiveness of substantial progress by Catholics and Protestants towards the visible unity of a shared table is rooted not in some basic difference but in shared flaws. They both presuppose the Greek philosophical notions of time as external to God and of God's infinity as immunity to time. Christian theology has thus been unable to comprehend that 'time and personal being are not mutually exclusive'.[10] When Catholics and Protestants disagree about what the church mediates, and how, their disagreement reflects a shared inability to think of the church's temporal continuity in terms of institution *and* event. The Catholic perspective emphasizes that being in time perdures in the form of institutions. Though some events do remain discrete and past, Catholics maintain that significant saving events may be carried forward by an institution, the church. The church's institutional dimension is thus a part of the gospel, making Christ's work present and active.[11] By this reasoning, sinful (non-saving) events in the past cannot be carried forward by an institution the purpose of which is divine mediation. Since nothing sinful is carried forward, what sense is there in repenting for an act in the distant past? For Protestants, 'when the Lord acts the church occurs, and when the same Lord acts again the same church occurs again'. Events and institutions are exclusive.[12] Thus, there is little cost associated with granting sin and corruption to an institutional dimension of the church and repenting since that dimension is incidental to the work of Christ and even to the church as such. In both cases, it is difficult to maintain that the church is truly penitent, *and* that it is so as truly church. Any yet, churches Catholic and Protestant are actually repenting.

Jenson argues that time is not a condition to which God must adjust, or rise above. 'Time, in both the Hebrew Scriptures and the New Testament, is itself a sort of event; it is what happens when the Spirit "comes".... Nor then can time and events be mutually external'.[13] Time is the consequence of God being God. Time is the space in which Father, Son and Holy Spirit are the persons they are, which is to say perichoretic expressions of perfect love, drawing

---

[10] Robert W. Jenson, *Unbaptized God: The Basic Flaw in Ecumenical Theology* (Minneapolis: Fortress Press, 1992), 111.
[11] *Ibid.*, 110.
[12] *Ibid.*
[13] *Ibid.*, 111.

creatures into that love. God's actions (which are identical with God's being) create time as the sphere of their existence. God's eternity is not timelessness or immunity to change, but the dramatic unity of personal relations with God. Because of who God is, eternity is not 'immunity to change, but ... *faithfulness* in action'. Being is not 'persistence in what is but ... *anticipation* of what is not yet'.[14]

Narrative is a fitting way to render the temporal identity of this God. God is a story whose narrative poles, or *persona dramatis*, are Father, Son and Holy Spirit, in subsistent relation to each other and in relation to creation. Jenson writes provocatively of God as 'a *going-on*, a sequentially palpable event, like a kiss or a train wreck'.[15] The story of the Bible, a story of promise and anticipation, points to precisely this 'going-on'. God the Father predestines and intends, while God the Holy Spirit is the promise of God's own future and thus of ours. The Father is the whence of God, the Spirit the whither and the Son the 'specious present' that reconciles past and future by defeating death, 'time's ultimate act'.[16] The oneness of God refers to the single perichoretic life – the mutual action and dramatic interplay of Father, Son, and Holy Spirit.[17] Though one critic has charged that for Jenson the threeness in God is merely derivative of the three tenses,[18] such a claim presupposes the mistake Jenson is trying to correct. The charge assumes a view of time as external, independent, or even prior to God, which subsequently constrains God. Of course we cannot imagine anything other than three tenses, but this is so because we live in the creation, and thus in the temporal structure that the biblical God created (and is creating, and will create). The dramatic interplay of God's identities narrated in scripture and centred in Jesus Christ provides the context for thinking about time, and for thinking about how events at different points in time might be related.

That the three 'identities' (the term Jenson prefers to 'persons') in God relate to past, present and future raises the spectre of modalism, of which Jenson is well aware. Furthermore, Jenson's panentheism, by which history is within God though not plainly identical with God,

---

[14] *Ibid.*, 138. In notes, I follow Jenson's use of italics.

[15] Robert W. Jenson, *Systematic Theology: The Triune God*, vol. 1 (Oxford: Oxford University Press, 1997), 214.

[16] *Ibid.*, 219.

[17] *Ibid.*, 214.

[18] Andrew Burgess, 'A Community of Love? Jesus as the Body of God in Robert Jenson's Trinitarian Thought', *International Journal of Systematic Theology* 6 (2004), 296.

does indeed raise the possibility that the distinction of creator and creation ultimately collapses.[19] In response, it should be noted that Jenson defends a strong identification of the immanent Trinity and the economic Trinity. The dramatic coherence of God's personal identity is located in the history told in the Bible, the specious present of the risen Christ and the end to come. Following the Cappadocians but in contrast to Gregory Palamas' interpretation of them, Jenson maintains that there is no God that stands above these activities.[20] At the centre of this trinitarian argument stands a rejection of Western Leonine and Nestorian Christology, which respectively distinguishes and outrightly separates Christ's human nature from his divine nature to protect the divine from contamination by time and contingency. Jenson advocates a Cyrillian emphasis on the single personal identity of Jesus Christ. In Jesus Christ, God has made time and contingency the sphere of his activity, and thus an element of his identity. While this move helps to dispel the risk of modalism – the Second Person is no mere mask if he is unequivocally Jesus of Nazareth – it heightens the risk of blurring the creator/creation distinction insofar as God appears to be dependent on the unfolding of creation to be God.

Pneumatology is an answer to this charge. The Holy Spirit is the mystery of God's personal love that comes from God's future and is oriented by the anticipation of this future. The Spirit is the promise of God by which the past and present are held together by the anticipation of the future. But the Spirit is not just an abstract promise or 'power' of a functionally binaritarian God, the Spirit is a *person* whose being makes possible divine community. The Spirit gives a gift which is himself. To give himself means to be a 'bond' between Father and Son such that each are truly available to the others in love and freedom. By contrast, a binitarian ontology leads to a dyadic struggle in which freedom and personhood cannot be maintained. For Jenson, the Spirit is thus the liberator by which Father and Son are freed from any determination in order to be both subject and object to the other. To be this bond means to actually *be* the Love of Father and Son, so that in freedom this love is the end of God's ways. By thereby freeing Father and Son to be persons for each other, the Spirit *is* the divine future, 'the Love into which all things will at the

---

[19] A concern developed by Douglas Farrow in Douglas Farrow, David Demson and J. Augustine Di Noia, 'Robert Jenson's *Systematic Theology*: Three Responses', *International Journal of Systematic Theology* 1 (1999), 89–91.

[20] Jenson, *Systematic Theology* 1, 153.

last be brought'.[21] In a community of Love, it is possible for the Father and Son to be truly one, and truly persons.

This divine love is the same love that circulates between human beings and between creation and creator. For Jenson, this move is crucial and is predicated on taking the particular personhood of the Spirit with utmost seriousness. The love that binds the church into a communion is the very love which will be perfected eschatologically. Among creatures, this love will not be perfectly realized but will still be the Spirit among us. At this point, it is possible to see how a high ecclesiology is possible with still-to-be-perfected love in history. 'Gifts of love can genuinely belong to the recipient, without transforming the recipient into the giver ... And yet the gifts are nothing but the giver, who in his identity with them gives precisely him*self* to me'.[22] Forgiveness of sins will thus feature prominently as the Spirit continually comes to the church to free it from those things that inhibit its availability to others, or bind it to mere historical determination. Forgiveness is a love which frees the church for its future as a communion of love. This love is not a trace of the Spirit or an attribute of the Spirit, it is the Spirit.

It is helpful to observe a key divergence of Jenson with Karl Barth at this point. Jenson agrees with Barth's revolutionary relocation of the doctrine of election in the doctrine of God, but disagrees with the way in which Barth makes God's decisive act the *primordial* decision to be the God of Jesus Christ. For Jenson, the narrative 'centre' of God's action – that by which God is God – is God's *future*, not God's origin. History is not the unfolding of a prior decision, but the drama (freedom, love, decision) that is yet to be, but since it is promised by God, is already present and past. 'It is in that the Spirit is God as the Power of God's *own* and our future and, that is to say, the Power of a future that also for God is not bound by the predictabilities, that the Spirit is a distinct identity of and in God. The Spirit is God as his and our future rushing upon him and us[.]'[23] The unity of God is not the persistence of an original condition, but rather the continuity of promise and faithfulness oriented by anticipation of the end.

The way in which the Holy Spirit exercises a transcendence over the entire story helps to maintain a distinction between creator

[21] *Ibid.*, 157.
[22] *Ibid.*, 149.
[23] *Ibid.*, 160.

and creation. The end of a story may be conceived of as the cause of the story, though how this is the case may be seen only from the perspective of the end. Jenson points to Aristotle's concept of a good story as one in which twists of plot cannot be predicted in advance, but can be seen as consistent and necessary in light of the end.[24] Thus, while in the middle of the story we cannot always ascertain where and how the Spirit comes, our inability to perceive does not minimize God's work in our midst, often in spite of ourselves. The church's practice of discerning the Spirit will be distorted if it thinks of it as unfolding something laid out in advance. As Jenson puts it,

> The church can and must discover and practice her temporal continuity as *dramatic* continuity, the kind of continuity that constitutes Aristotle's good stories. Looking forward at any time of historical challenge, the church cannot decide in advance what she must become; she cannot manipulate the Spirit's daily advent. She can neither faithfully wish thus to bind the future, nor hope to succeed if she attempts it. Yet after every large or small or partial step of change or resistance to change, she can look back and recognize that given the whole history of the church to this moment, this was what had to happen. Or she can look back and recognize that this is what had not to happen and must be repented.[25]

How ecclesial repentance can be a moment of the church's narrative coherence and dramatic resolution depends on the ecclesiology that follows from this account of God and time.

Ecclesiology

This account of the dramatic continuity within God's own life thus has ecclesiological implications for how the church exists in time. There can be no sense in which the church somehow accidentally or imperfectly exists historically. The temporal integrity of the church is not rooted in mere institutional continuity the way Ford's business charter makes it the same corporation in 2008 as it was in 1958, but in the fact that the church is constituted within the intention of the Father, the presence of the Son, and the anticipation of the Holy Spirit. This 'positioning' of the church only heightens the significance of the church's historical character, especially since the coming of the Spirit constitutes the future of the church, and thus places its past in light of that future.

To anticipate my argument below: if ecclesial repentance is the work of the Spirit, then ecclesial repentance provides for its own possibility

---

[24] Jenson, *Unbaptized God*, 141.
[25] *Ibid.*, 145.

in history. My appropriation of Jenson is predicated on the possibility that acts of ecclesial repentance are plot twists, perhaps unexpected and perhaps insufficient, but nevertheless within the story of God and the church. It is not as if we must first establish continuity between the thirteenth-century church and the twenty-first-century church on non-theological grounds in order for John Paul's act of repentance to meaningfully address sins of the past. Rather, ecclesial repentance as the 'resolution' (I use this term cautiously) of an episode in the church's life is what gives the past coherence and thus continuity with the present. In repentance, the Spirit frees the Son – more specifically the *totus Christus*, Christ together with his church – from determination by a history of sin.

The analogy of God as a conversation enables Jenson to explain how God is both consistent with his identity but as such not strictly determined. A conversation is an event that takes time – and because the words exchanged are those of God, they are immediately the cause of what is real. Yet, a true conversation is not scripted. If the participants are truly persons and thus free, a conversation will move in genuinely unexpected directions, yet in ways that ultimately accord with the community of persons represented. This divine conversation, as it is revealed to us, is expressed most paradigmatically in the prayer of the Son to the Father in Gethsemane. The prayer of the Son, fully divine and fully human, also reflects the way that all of creation is ultimately taken up into the divine conversation. Jenson writes that 'unabashed petitionary prayer is the one decisively appropriate creaturely act over against the true God'.[26] In such prayer the Spirit draws the human creature into God's own life, joining these prayers with the cry of the Son to the Father. Prayer is the work of the Spirit because it shows a faith in the future; God's answer is God's future made present. It is prayer because it is the cry of the creature to God, for forgiveness and for wholeness. As repentance is essentially prayer, it is thus also a very human word, one that presupposes that it takes time to come to conviction of sin and repent. As prayer, it is taken up into the conversation that is God, wherein the Spirit convicts of sin and converts the penitent to Christ. God does not refuse the contamination of history nor of the church that anticipates its future as the Spirit speaks together with the church the words of repentance.

In repentance the church seeks the coming of the Holy Spirit in the midst of its entire history to make things new, and bring the Body

---

[26] Jenson, *Systematic Theology* 1, 222.

of Christ to the end the Father has always intended. This future is not a clean slate, but faithful change in time, and thus cannot circumvent repentance, forgiveness and reconciliation. God listens, responds and acts on this prayer, and as such this prayer becomes a part of the conversation that God is. A notion of God 'changing His mind' as the result of prayer presupposes the problematic Greek view of time as external to God, though God as an agent powerful enough to alter what was to be. Rather, by acting into a new future, God is faithful with himself, the Holy Spirit and the church upon which the Holy Spirit descends to unite it with Christ. This enables us to take a long view of the church, yet one still bound to historical particularity. It is possible that when the Church of England defended slavery it was still the church, though deeply mired in sin. And it is possible that this Church acted and spoke in a way consistent with its mission when in 2007 it acknowledged this past and repented. That the Church of England did not cease to be the church when it taught that humans could be owned as chattel can be seen in light of the fact that – as we know how the story goes – the church would *repent* of this, or rather that the Spirit would make its future possible by converting it from such darkness. In repentance, this entire history is taken fully into the divine conversation, and the church is thereby freed for its future. This is what it means for the church to 'know herself as the temporal mission not of resistance to time but of faithful change in time, and know her own continuity in that mission not as hanging on to what is already there but rather as receiving what must come'.[27] This recognition and reception must not be confused with progress or moral improvement.

As noted above, God the Father intends that there be a church, 'and that this church be exactly the one that exists'.[28] Just as there is no God that hovers above God's activities, neither is there a church that hovers above the one that exists. The church itself came about as a plot development that was not predicted but in light of its occurrence is profoundly consistent. Jenson explains that the church is instituted as God decides that Jesus' resurrection is not the end.[29] This opens up a temporal delay in God's own life that he describes as 'roominess in God', in which the Spirit 'unites each moment of the church's life with the one person of the risen Son, and so mediates

---

[27] Jenson, *Unbaptized God*, 138.
[28] Jenson, *Systematic Theology* 2, 173.
[29] *Ibid.*, 170.

every churchly "now" with every churchly "then".'[30] Not only is the church part of God's own life, but also it is the church in its actuality, the one that historically exists with its life of hopeful prayer, ambivalent past, and open future, that precisely as such constitutes the church's continuity within the relation of the persons of the Trinity.

That the church is Christ's body is, for Jenson, not an analogy but a reality. To be a body is to be available to others. God is available to the world through Jesus Christ, whose present body is the church. Specifically, the risen Christ is available to the world as Christ the head is united by the Spirit with his members as the *totus Christus* – the total Christ. As a 'body', the *totus Christus* is the availability of the church as an object, most notably as the way God has himself for an object.[31] This kind of objective availability is crucial for how Jenson wants to construe the freedom of the church within God's freedom. The Spirit, who liberates the Son and Father to be persons for each other, and thus to be a triune communion, likewise liberates the church from 'merely historical determination' towards its eschatological goal. The church anticipates this goal by itself being a communion of persons, available to each other and the world through time and space.

Jenson denies that his account of the church as the body of Christ renders Christ and church in a simple relation of identity: '[A]s the individual Christ, the *totus Christus* is sinless; as the community related to the one Christ, the *totus Christus* is sinful'.[32] The sin thereby taken into the life of the *totus Christus* and thus of God, is not overcome by the church's effort strictly speaking. Christ must discipline his body, denoting a close relationship that maintains a distinction. The reform of the church is not the work of its members in merely human association (*Gesellschaft*) with one another. Yet, insofar as Christ is the person who makes his body into a community whose spirit is the Holy Spirit (*Gemeinschaft*), then Christ reforms his body with and through the church. If it is what it the church claims it be, then ecclesial repentance is the work of the Spirit in the general sense of being God's work, and in the particular sense of the mission of the Spirit to liberate the Son, the *totus Christus*, to be the body he is.

A pneumatic deficit in ecclesiology obtains when institutions are extrapolated directly from the historical career of Jesus, unliberated

---

[30] Jenson, *Unbaptized God*, 136.
[31] Jenson, *Systematic Theology* 2, 215.
[32] *Ibid.*, 1, 85.

as it were by the newness of the Spirit's intervention to free the church for God's future (the inclination of Catholicism),[33] or alternately in the spiritual ecclesiology of Protestantism that ultimately affirms Christ's divinity but obscures Christ's humanity in the church, and consequently the irreducibly historical dimension of Christian existence.[34] In the present age, what does it mean for the Spirit to liberate the *totus Christus* to be truly available to the world? Surely ecclesial repentance is one answer. A penitent church acknowledges that in its failures, it has pointed to something other than the gospel. The gift of confessing this sin, as a step towards making way for the gospel's proclamation and embodiment, is the work of the Spirit as God's future and thus as the church's. In light of the fact that Catholic offences against the Orthodox during the crusades have had the effect of fostering resentment, the Spirit may act to bring the church to a confession of its past, and to pray for freedom from a future limited by that history. In light of the Church of England's past support of slavery, the Spirit may liberate the body of Christ by identifying the defence of slavery as a wound it bears.

Jenson's portrayal of the church as the availability of the body of Christ draws attention to the essential missionary dimension of the church. The church cannot be what it is unless it is self-conscious of its outwardly turned face. This does not mean that the church must uncritically adopt the beliefs and practices of the world in order to be received by the world. Such logic is backwards, according to Jenson, because the church is the standard for historical existence. Rather, Christ's judgement and discipline of his body must be understood as a correction of the church's failure to fully be the risen Christ to the world. By joining the penitent prayer of the church to the prayer of the Son to the Father, the Holy Spirit frees the church to truly be the availability of Christ's body in the world.

Jenson's conception of the continuity of the church, and the mutual involvement of divine and human agency in the church, is helpful for understanding the deep structure of the new practice of ecclesial repentance. He helps us to consider more carefully how the twists and turns, failures and sins, confessions and repentance of the actual church might now be understood as a part of the church's

---

[33] *Ibid.*, 2, 179.

[34] Jenson follows Luther on this point: 'It is God's hiding in human embodiment that is our salvation; Christ's naked deity – were there in actuality such a thing – would be "nothing to do with us" and just so destruction for us'. *Systematic Theology* 2, 214.

identity, and thus of the Holy Spirit's identity. The relative novelty of these acts of repentance is not in itself a problem. Though claims to knowing what new thing the Spirit is doing must be made cautiously and provisionally, it is indeed possible that the Spirit stands behind the requests of churches for forgiveness: '[D]ramatic necessity can be perceived only when the event is there'.[35] Indeed, whether ecclesial repentance may be acquired by the church as a practice of faithfulness may only be judged in terms of the dramatic coherence realized after the fact. 'But by the character of the gospel's promise we *can* judge after the fact between historical turnings dramatically appropriate to the church's fulfillment and others inappropriate to it and so discern when the Spirit can or cannot have been leading'.[36] A judgement that the Church of England is faithful now, in repentance for slavery, whereas it was faithless to support it, might strike a reader of Jenson as hubris of the present moment, or misplaced faith in progress. However, merely granting that it is *possible* that the Spirit was not leading the Church of England in its slaveholding (though it was still the church that owned slaves), but led an appropriately penitent church to change its ways, is already significant. It posits a distinction between Christ and the church of variable faithfulness just so in the eschatological tension between them. Here 'the church is what she is as anticipation of her transformation into God'[37] precisely in its contingent freedom and actual decisions.

As in the case of the Catholic Church repenting for the actions of thirteenth-century Catholic crusaders, the integrity of such an action with respect to the past is usually framed in terms of first determining if the present church bears some kind of responsibility for these actions. Such responsibility might reside in legal institutional continuity, or through some lingering benefit that the present church received (for instance, if the loot from Constantinople was still providing material benefit to the Catholic Church). It is evident that the past is present in the sense of injustice and violation still felt by the Greek Orthodox, and from the fact that these actions are barriers to the unity of the church. While these concerns are valid and ought to be treated with utmost seriousness, they are not the basis for the

---

[35] *Ibid.*, 2, 239.

[36] *Ibid.*, 240. These quotations are drawn from Jenson's argument about how a historically contingent institution such as the episcopacy can be seen to be the work of the Spirit; I argue that an application to a practice such as ecclesial repentance is analogous.

[37] *Ibid.*, 2, 239.

ecclesial continuity by which the pope may meaningfully repent for the sack of Constantinople. In pneumatological perspective, it is the action of ecclesial repentance itself that is a basis for the continuity of the church through time.

Repentance is a plot twist in a story that encompasses the crusades which have come to be seen as sinful. The crusades are integrated into the church's story as primarily a forgiven past (for which penance may be required, as examined in Chapter 7). Through repentance this history is fully taken into the church's own. In retrospect it is recognized that this history has always belonged to the church; what was needed, and what is provided by repentance, is the proper posture towards this history. The church of the present is in continuity with the past in part because repentance tends towards the resolution of historical drama by which the actual church is freed to be the church that bears a true witness. The church's continuity is in its reception of what must come (and, we may venture provisionally, what partially has already come). The binding of past to present is seen most clearly in the action of the Spirit to pronounce a word of judgement on the crusades and lead into forgiveness and reconciliation. In this drama, the church participates by repenting of a past it now sees as having compromised its mission of pointing to Christ, and by so doing finds itself pointing to the forgiveness of Christ.

That the triune life of God is unified not so much by the persistence of an origin but by anticipation of the End has profound implications for ecclesiology and for the church's repentance. If the church's continuity is conceived as the persistence in time of its founding as an institution, then ecclesial sin anywhere in its past will fatally disrupt this continuity and thus its mediatorial capacity. But if the church's continuity is conceived in terms of anticipation of its End, then forgiveness and reconciliation will have the final word. Such an event, always a gift of the Spirit given in history, is as such also the intention of God by which the church lives, moves and has its being.

The mutual repentance of the Catholic and Orthodox churches in the Joint Declaration of Pope Paul VI and Ecumenical Patriarch Athenagoras I is particularly helpful for displaying the power of a present word to objectively change the relationship of the past with the present. Coming just after the close of the Second Vatican Council, this joint action recognized that the mutual excommunications of 1054 were ongoing barriers to fraternal relations. Pope and patriarch solemnly declared regret for this past and removed 'from memory and from the midst of the Church the sentences of excommunication which followed these events, the memory of which has influenced actions up to our day and has hindered closer relations in charity; and they commit these excommunications to oblivion'. Each side claimed God's promise that in their mutual pardon they are in fact pardoned.[38]

The objectivity of this action is especially visible given that it had canonical implications: sentences of excommunication were nullified. The excommunications as both cause and consequence of schism were removed. However, attention to the canonical effects of this action only highlights what is the case in all actions of ecclesial repentance prompted by the Holy Spirit. In retrospect, the word of the present church became what the past church *anticipated* as the overcoming of the enmity it was fostering. Joseph Ratzinger writes that '[T]he new evaluation of history that leads to a new evaluation of the present has taken place here with full binding power ... [The reciprocal anathema of 1054] has been nullified by the act of forgiveness'.[39] To the extent that this action leads to greater communion between Catholic and Orthodox churches, and helped make possible the 2001 exchange between Pope John Paul II and Archbishop Christodoulas, the synchronic unity of the church will have been enhanced by diachronic continuity.

That a present word has a binding effect on the past helpfully captures the way in which the past does remain past, even though transformed. That the offence ever occurred is not negated. If this was the effect of repentance, then the moment repentance was uttered it would cease to have meaning because its referent would disappear. Though the 1965 declaration claims to 'remove from memory', it is the excommunications rather than the memories of them that are truly consigned to oblivion. The pope and patriarch were not denying that the excommunications of 1054 were made, but they made a solemn judgement that these excommunications ought not to have been made. To apply Jenson's language to this case, the church(es) decided something in 1965, which as the word of the *totus Christus*, came to be decided by the Holy Spirit,

---

[38] Pope Paul VI and Ecumenical Patriarch Athenagoras I, 'Joint Catholic–Orthodox Declaration' (1965).

[39] Joseph Ratzinger, *Principles of Catholic Theology: Building Stones for a Fundamental Theology*, trans. Mary Frances McCarthy (San Francisco: Ignatius Press, 1987), 212.

and had been decided as the antecedent intention of the Father.[40] The actions of the church in 1054 and 1965 are held together by the dramatic intervention of the Holy Spirit. In this view, the church of 1054 is in continuity with the church of 1965 because the latter repented of its past, resolving the story (admittedly only to a degree – a great deal of reconciliation remains to be realized).

Likewise, the slaveholding Church of England is in continuity with its repentance for such a past, embracing a mission to undo racism in the present. As Rowan Williams wrote (before he became Archbishop of Canterbury), 'We can only be grateful that even a slave-owning Church had just enough sensitivity to the challenge of the gospel for a protest to be generated (however slowly) ... '[41] We may not often be able to see the church's dramatic unity amidst its twists and turns, or how apparent discontinuities may be transformed by the Spirit. The point is that the future is not bound to the past but is genuinely new. In fact, it is this future, brought into focus by the Holy Spirit, which ultimately binds the past to the present as the dramatic interplay of Father, Son and Holy Spirit.

Jenson also helps the church to think about the problem of historical distance in specifically ecclesiological ways. An illustrative example is that of Mennonite Brethren pastor Isaac Thiessen, who was the animator behind the 1986 act of apology by the Mennonite Brethren church in Canada to the Conference of Mennonites in Canada. The apology was made for occasions when Mennonite Brethren pastors excommunicated their members for marrying members of the other Mennonite denomination. The actions confessed had occurred as recently as a few decades earlier, and there were those in the audience who had been directly affected. Thiessen himself had excommunicated perhaps 20 members and always felt uneasy about it. After what he described as an 'intense spiritual battle', he vowed to seek the forgiveness of those individuals, and urged his denomination to apologize more formally.[42]

---

[40] This dynamic is analogous to Jenson's discussion of the election of the individual: '[T]o the penitent's question, "But how do I know that I am among the elect?" the confessor's right answer must be, "You know because I am about to absolve you, and my doing that *is* God's eternal act of decision about you".' *Systematic Theology* 2, 177.

[41] Rowan Williams, *Resurrection: Interpreting the Easter Gospel*, rev. ed. (Cleveland: Pilgrim Press, 2002), 58–9.

[42] Conrad Stoesz, 'Undoing a Long-Standing Practice', *Mennonite Brethren Herald*, 29 April 2005, 11.

Many Mennonites regarded this instance of ecclesial repentance as particularly meaningful and sincere because Thiessen himself, personally guilty of the sin confessed, was involved in the apology process. One commentator wrote: 'Here was had a specific person, a specific sin confessed and we, by the grace of God, have the opportunity to forgive'.[43] Without denying the significance of this healing for Thiessen or for those with whom he reconciled, it would be a mistake to conclude that the historical distance between the excommunications and the church apology was bridged primarily by the personal agency of those involved. The sin Thiessen confessed was that he excommunicated members for marrying outside the denomination, and that this action purported to be the action of the church. It is not ultimately the case that the Mennonite Brethren church's repentance was possible because of the minimal temporal distance involved or the fact that Thiessen as a person was involved (though these added layers of meaning). Rather, simply because the church repented of this aspect of its past, it claimed this history as its own. In this sense, repentance itself (with its Christological and pneumatological presuppositions) became a basis for the continuity of past and present.

Nor does the continuity of the church have a biological or ancestral dimension. A common objection to apology or reparations, made frequently in the discussions about the history of slavery, is that 'my ancestors did not own slaves', and therefore responsibility does not fall to me. Whether or not this is the case for individuals, let along for nations, is a separate question. Indeed, the fact that some Southern Baptist Convention leaders were descended from slaveowners was noted as part of that denomination's 1995 apology. But the church is not constituted in familial terms, and responsibility for the actions of the church does not descend through bloodlines. At the 2009 Mennonite World Conference assembly in Paraguay, the general secretary of the Lutheran World Federation, Ishmael Noko, gave greetings in which he indicated that his communion intended to ask forgiveness of the Mennonites for past persecution. This overture was warmly received by the Mennonite World Conference president, Danisa Ndlovu. Neither Noko nor Ndlovu, both of whom are from Zimbabwe, have any strictly ancestral connections to the sixteenth-century European

---

[43] William Klassen, 'Seeing Jesus in a M[Ennonite] B[Rethren] Penitent', *Mennonite Reporter*, 28 July 1986, 5.

history being acknowledged.[44] Yet, as the authorized leaders of their respective communions, they represent and embody reconciliation for the actions of their churches more than an individual Lutheran and an individual Mennonite who might happen to claim a familial connection to events in Europe centuries ago.

The amenability of ecclesial repentance within Jenson's system highlights the way in which his thought does maintain a distinction of Christ and church. The distinction is located within the eschatological tension of the Holy Spirit leading the church into God's future by binding it together with its head. To the extent that the Holy Spirit is God's future, the church is presently not the simple union of Christ and church. This is reinforced at an intuitive level: the church of the crusades or of slave ownership is not simply identical with the risen Christ. To Jenson's many critics, the rhetorical effect of such a reminder is important. And while it does not thereby cease to be church, as church it cannot simply remain in contradiction to the gospel, but prayerfully anticipates the future which the Holy Spirit is, a future it may discern in the practice of ecclesial repentance.

Rowan Williams writes that the practice of church history is the difficult task of finding God's coherence in the midst of human failures, and the wonder of God's hiddenness in and through such a history.[45] '[T]he very difficulty of making sense, making a tidy and edifying story, becomes part of the theological point of the whole enterprise; the actuality of failure reinforces what is being said about God'.[46] I conclude this section with a reminder that the fact that God is the basis for the continuity of the church does not thereby make the past familiar nor wrestling with the past straightforward. Even as the faithfulness of God is contrasted with the plot twists of the human story, it is not a simple matter to discern which is which. The fact that it often takes the church decades or centuries to make a solemn judgement about a particular sin in its past may be due to the church's wilful blindness, or also due to the fact that discerning just where the church pointed to Christ and where it did not is a spiritual process that takes time. It takes prayer. It takes ears to hear and eyes to see. My portrayal of the dramatic coherence of God,

---

[44] Paul Schrag, 'The Global Church Unites', *Courier* 24, nos. 3–4 (2009), 4. The request is scheduled to occur at the LWF Assembly in Stuttgart, July 2010.

[45] Rowan Williams, *Why Study the Past? The Quest for the Historical Church* (Grand Rapids: Eerdmans, 2005), 9.

[46] *Ibid.*, 10.

which embraces the church and all of creation, does not imply that wherever drama is, there is God. It ought not imply that in its acts of ecclesial repentance, the church has finally got it right, nor that repentance is the only thing the church should do with respect to what it has done as an agent in history. Rather, my more modest point is that *if* ecclesial repentance is the work of the Spirit, and there are reasons for believing it might be, then through repentance the church may be granted a share of its own continuity in God's triune life.

COMMUNION, FORGIVENESS, INTERCESSION

With Jenson's trinitarian framework in mind for understanding how the dramatic unity of God relates to the unity of the church through time, I turn to an explicit consideration of the doctrine of the communion of saints. In the Apostles' Creed, this phrase follows belief in the holy catholic church and precedes the forgiveness of sins. In the communion of saints, Christians are linked with all other Christians, through time and space. As I shall develop further, this connection is premised on Christ's forgiveness. According to a recent German Catholic–Lutheran dialogue, 'because the communion of saints is communion with the Risen One, it transcends all boundaries and limitations of time and space'.[47] Christ stands at the centre, making this communion possible. The cloud of witnesses in Hebrews 11–12 show the relationship of the past, present and future, bound together in faith. The patriarchs, prophets and judges are commended as exemplars of faith, but they 'did not receive what was promised, since God had provided something better so that they would not, apart from us, be made perfect' (Heb. 11.39b–40). These past saints lived in anticipation of a reality which the writer of Hebrews argues is present in Jesus, not only the pioneer but also the perfecter of faith (Heb. 12.2). Furthermore, the fulfilment of the promises made to saints past is embodied not only in Jesus but in the 'us' of Hebrews 11.40. In Jesus, saints of the past and saints in the present are bound in some way, and together anticipate the fullness of faith to come.

In the Greek-speaking early church, the creedal confession of

---

[47] *Communio Sanctorum: The Church as the Communion of Saints*, Official German Catholic–Lutheran Dialogue, trans. Mark W. Jeske, Michael Root and Daniel R. Smith (Collegeville, MN: Liturgical Press, 2004), no. 5.

the communion of saints primarily referred to communion in holy things, particularly the eucharist. In the Latin-speaking West, the more personal fellowship of holy persons was intended.[48] Of course, a eucharist implies the collegial ties among the bishops through space, their links through apostolic succession over time, and the direct personal connections with the congregants who received the elements from their hands. The fellowship of holy persons sometimes refers to the more restricted sense of designated (later: canonized) holy people who may be venerated and whose intercession may be sought. It may also refer to the congregation of those

> patriarchs, prophets, martyrs, and all other righteous men who have lived or are now alive, or shall live in time to come ... since they have been sanctified by one faith and manner of life, and sealed by one Spirit and so made one body, of which Christ is declared to be the head, as the Scripture says.[49]

This latter sense will be the primary concern in this section, though the practice of some Christians who invoke the prayers of these saints will also prove to be instructive.

Both the communion in holy things and in holy persons are received as gifts of the Holy Spirit. The Spirit who descends on the eucharistic elements or the baptismal waters is the same Spirit that thereby binds Christians to the body of Christ. The communion of saints is thus a community sanctified by the work of the Holy Spirit. Fellowship in the Spirit implies the essential unity of the church (see Eph. 2.16–18 and 1 Cor. 3.16). Through Christ's victory on the cross, relationships within this fellowship are constrained not even by death (Rom. 8.38–9).

The grounding of the communion of saints in the sole mediatorship of Christ is a point of ecumenical consensus.[50] Christ binds together human beings and human action through time. According to Pierre-Yves Emery: 'To become one with Christ is necessarily, and at one and the same time, to acknowledge oneself bound to one's brethren in the faith by the similar bond of unity'.[51] Christ mediates all relationships, both the ones in which the lives of exemplary Christians encourage others in faith and life, but also those

[48] J. N. D. Kelly, *Early Christian Creeds*, 3d ed. (London: Longman, 1972), 389–91.

[49] *Ibid.*, 391, citing Nicetas of Remesiana.

[50] H. George Anderson, J. Francis Stafford and Joseph A. Burgess, eds., *The One Mediator, the Saints, and Mary: Lutherans and Catholics in Dialogue VIII* (Minneapolis: Augsburg Fortress Press, 1992) and *Communio Sanctorum*.

[51] Pierre-Yves Emery, *The Communion of Saints*, trans. D. J. Watson and M. Watson (London: Faith Press, 1966), 8.

characterized by sin and pain. The fact that the church is linked to not only to the merits of past Christians (the more common implication of the communion of saints, especially regarding veneration and intercession of canonized saints in the Catholic tradition) but also to their sins, is explicitly noted in several repentance texts.[52] The connection to these 'saints', who are also sinners, tellingly displays the way in which Christ's forgiveness is the basis for any communion in the first place.

In his encyclical *Ut Unum Sint*, Pope John Paul II notes that all 'horizontal' dialogue between separated Christians rests on a foundation of 'vertical' dialogue which consists of 'our acknowledgment, jointly and to each other, that we are men and women who have sinned'. This may be general sin, but in the context of the encyclical, it also refers specifically to sins against the unity of the church. This acknowledgement, and the repentance that logically follows, 'creates in brothers and sisters living in Communities not in full communion with one another that interior space where Christ, the source of the Church's unity, can effectively act, with all the power of his Spirit, the Paraclete'.[53] Yes, there is a solidarity in sin, but true communion is founded on God's forgiveness in Christ. As the pope contends, repentance opens separated Christians to a communion which is realized first in God's forgiveness of the sin of separation. This communion extends not only to those presently separated, but through the invocation of repentance for the past, those who are separated in time as well.

The pope's apostolic letter *Orientale Lumen* explains that Christ's promise of forgiveness binds human action through time. In that letter, he sought to improve relationships with the Orthodox Churches by noting that the Apostle Peter showed human weakness in his denial of Christ. He linked the petrine ministry of unity, a point of contention between the Roman Catholic and the Orthodox, with the ongoing need for the church to repent of the sins of its members, and seek forgiveness. The capacity of Peter to strengthen others in faith, and therefore in Christian unity, is premised on Peter's recognition of his need for conversion and on the source of his hope.[54]

---

[52] For example, Commission for Religious Relations with the Jews, *We Remember: A Reflection on the Shoah* (1998), no. 5, and The Rt Rev Bill Phipps, United Church of Canada, 'Apology to Former Students of United Church Indian Residential Schools, and to their Families and Communities' (1998).

[53] Pope John Paul II, *Ut Unum Sint*, no. 35.

[54] Pope John Paul II, *Orientale Lumen*, no. 20.

Unity is not based on Peter's achievement, but on the one who loves and forgives him.

As the successor of Peter, Pope John Paul implicitly invoked the communion of saints by repenting for the actions and attitudes, past and present, that have harmed the church's unity and thereby diminished its witness. Peter repented, so the church repents. In *Orientale Lumen*, the pope acknowledged fault on the Catholic side for division and enmity, and prayed for God's mercy and reconciliation.[55] The plea for this reconciliation is a recognition that the unity of the church is rooted in its witness to the single source of its forgiveness and reconciliation. The pope exercises a ministry of primacy precisely in the repentance that points to the true source of unity.

Though repentance is a human action, it is also a gift of the Spirit that turns the church to the forgiveness of Christ. The premise of ecclesial repentance is connected to its substance: it is *possible* for the church to repent of actions long past because the living Christ mediates the communion of the saints then and now. Because he is the same one, yesterday, today and tomorrow, the forgiveness Christ offers is ordered to the realization of the communion of saints, which is to say the reconciliation and unity of the church.

The organic unity between Christ and his church, often expressed by the phrase *totus Christus*, has sometimes been taken to mean that there is no sin *of* the church, or even no sin *in* the church, since Christ himself is sinless. A more thorough examination of the question of the sin of and in the church is found in the following chapter. Here I argue, with reference to recent work by Michael McCarthy on Augustine that the Christological mediation of the communion of saints provides a nuanced way of thinking about sin in the church.

McCarthy's particular concern is to show that Augustine's exegesis and preaching of the Psalms reflects a concrete, rather than merely spiritual, ecclesiology. McCarthy argues that in Augustine's sermons, the Psalms are heard as the voice of the *totus Christus*. Traditional exegesis sought to distinguish where the Psalms spoke in the voice of Christ, and where they spoke in the voice of the church, a practice Augustine occasionally employs. But more often, and here I am mindful of McCarthy's warning to not turn Augustine's exegesis into a systematic method or principle, Augustine interprets the Psalms as the words of Christ together with his church. When Augustine preached the words of Psalm 51, 'Have mercy on me, O God,

---

[55] *Ibid.*, no. 21.

according to your steadfast love; according to your abundant mercy blot out my transgressions', this preaching was at the same time the ongoing repentance of the church, and the groaning of Christ who assumes the transgressions of the church so that they may be blotted out. Augustine 'actively appropriates for the Church the groans which resound throughout the Psalter and indicates that, by lamenting with the psalmist and reflecting deeply and continually on that affect, the Church comes to learn what it is, and to be what it is'.[56]

Augustine's preaching of Psalms reflects his belief that human and divine are joined in the church so that human sin may be assumed and overcome. Thus, in the *totus Christus* the sin to be assumed by the head is mixed among the members, and together they all bear its burden. In Psalms of confession and lament, voiced by each congregation in its place, Jesus Christ and all saints are joined together in the mire of present scandal and in prayerful anticipation of healing. When a church repents for sins of the past, even for faults of the thirteenth century, the present generation bears the burdens of the past, because the *totus Christus* bears the burdens. An important distinction must be noted. As head, the sinless Christ assumes the sins of others. And since Christ is bound to his body, these sins are assumed by the entire church, across space and time. However, this does not mean that these sins are not truly the church's own. Sin also belongs to the church not only through Christ's assumption and forgiveness of them, but through the church's own disobedience and transgressions. Yet, because the church is the communion it is because of Christ's forgiveness of sin, this sin of the church does not mean that the church has ceased to be the church. Rather, it is the church in virtue of its connection to Jesus Christ, and its consequent continual reception of his forgiveness.

This brief excursus on Augustine and the Psalms illustrates one way in which church tradition has imagined the nature of the bonds between Christ and Christians over time and space. It also shows how a practice of the church, whether preaching the Psalms in the congregation, or repenting of particular sins against the unity of the church, invoke these bonds and the forgiveness that constitutes them. When a church repents for sins of the past, even for the sack of Constantinople, the connection of the past to the present need not be tied to controversial theories of collective guilt or more cynically,

---

[56] Michael C. McCarthy, 'An Ecclesiology of Groaning: Augustine, the Psalms and the Making of Church', *Theological Studies* 66 (2005), 27.

to politically correct sentiment at the expense of the dead. Rather, the present bears the burdens of the past in the church, because Christ's forgiveness stands at the centre of the communion of saints. Though neither the present pope nor the saints currently living are personally responsible for the sack of Constantinople, the pope's fellowship with them renders his confession a first-person confession.[57] The nature of this communion only magnifies the tragedy of the actual division of the church. The very logic by which the church repents of anything presupposes the communion of saints, and ought to redouble the church's sorrow for the actual division that stands in place of its true unity.

Since the relatively new practice of ecclesial repentance is just being integrated into various theological categories, I suggest that the practice has several constructive implications for how we understand the doctrine of the communion of saints. I will reflect first on how we might rethink the nature of intercessory prayer within and among the saints, and then how the boundaries of the communion of saints might be conceived beyond those of the church. In turn, I consider implications for the nature of the judgement on the past that is rendered through acts of ecclesial repentance.

Among the more controversial implications of the doctrine of the communion of saints are the practices of venerating and invoking the intercession of specific saints, and praying for the dead. These have been points of disagreement between Catholics and Protestants, especially Lutherans, but for that reason have also been the subject of several bilateral dialogues. Protestants have expressed concern that asking saints in heaven to intercede compromises the sole mediation of Christ, while praying for the souls of the dead appears to suggest that Christ's death is not wholly sufficient.[58] The Second Vatican Council acknowledged that various 'abuses, excesses or defects' were present regarding the intercession of the saints and praying for the dead.[59] It nevertheless affirmed that such practices were appropriate, though not required, given the active love obtaining between the earthly church, the purifying church and the heavenly church, a communion rooted in the unity of Christ.[60] Recent Lutheran–

---

[57] Joseph Ratzinger, 'The Church's Guilt', in *Pilgrim Fellowship of Faith: The Church as Communion*, trans. Henry Taylor (San Francisco: Ignatius Press, 2005), 277.
[58] *Communio Sanctorum*, no. 231.
[59] *Lumen Gentium*, no. 61.
[60] *Ibid.*, no. 49.

Catholic dialogues in the US and in Germany have affirmed all such spiritual traffic remains mediated by Christ alone and conclude that differences in practice need not be church dividing. In what follows, I propose that the practice of invoking the intercession of the saints may provide one helpful way of creatively understanding how ecclesial repentance might work (I do not propose it as a definitive or exclusive meaning), and that this might cause us to adjust or expand the scope of what we understand the communion of saints to be.

In the first instance, ecclesial repentance may be conceived as the earthly church asking for the penitential intercession by the saints in heaven. In terms of the case discussed at the beginning of this chapter, it would be that the repentance by the pope for the actions of Catholic crusaders was effectively imploring those thirteenth-century Christians to repent of their actions. Though this proposal exceeds the current expression of official Catholic theology,[61] it could be theologically warranted by the practice of ecclesial repentance itself.

Death ends the immediate moral responsibility of each individual. But the premise of my proposal is the belief that the departed and living alike await what Miroslav Volf calls the 'eschatological transition' for the final judgement and the world to come.[62] The heavenly church is bound in solidarity to the earthly church, under the present and anticipated judgement of Christ. Thus, the heavenly church ought to be concerned for the character of the earthly church's witness. Christians are called to pray for each other, and to thereby build up the church. It is an extension of this imperative that is the basis for such prayer to cross even the threshold of death, and time, rooted solely in God's mercy and grace.[63] But the earthly church's witness to Christ is compromised by the sins of the past, by the lack of charity in the church: schisms, condemnations and violence, for example. Thus, ecclesial repentance could be conceived of as a request to the departed faithful to strengthen the witness of the church by offering prayerful repentance for their own past failures.

Are the departed 'aware' of earthly concerns? That a Catholic may

---

[61] Thus Christoph Schönborn denies that any spiritual goods travel from those on earth to the 'glorified disciples', 'The "Communion of Saints" as Three States of the Church: Pilgrimage, Purification, and Glory', trans. Walter Jüptner, *Communio: International Catholic Review* 15 (1988): 177.

[62] Miroslav Volf, 'The Final Reconciliation: Reflections on a Social Dimension of the Eschatological Transition', *Modern Theology* 16 (2000), 91–113.

[63] *Communio Sanctorum*, no. 240.

invoke St Francis to intercede with God on her behalf suggests that St Francis cares for the present church on earth. On the Lutheran side, the *Augsburg Confession* affirms that saints in heaven do pray for the earthly church,[64] though the US Lutherans assert that there is no basis on which to know the content of such prayers and by extension whether they are affected by petitions by the living.[65] Yet, if the saints are moved by a loving concern for the well-being of the church, this presupposes some specific knowledge of the church's condition.[66] Jenson reminds us that communication with the saints must never be conceived as our way to God, rather God is the way to the saints.[67] It is enough to say therefore that, in the power of the Spirit, the church prays to Jesus Christ for forgiveness, and he in turn mediates the response of the saints, the 'cloud of witnesses', so that the church may continue running its race.

The Catholic practice of invocation calls on the prayers of those officially canonized – that is, asserted in faith to truly be in the presence of God – whereas my proposal invokes the prayers of those believed to have sinned in a way that stained the witness of the entire church. Thus, I am pushing the boundaries of even Roman Catholic liturgical practice. However, though the canonized are regarded as exemplary and holy, sinlessness cannot be predicated of them. Thus, St Bernard of Clairvaux whose preaching gave inspiration and theological rationale to the crusades, might be implored to offer a penitential prayer. Augustine wrote that even the blessed in heaven will have a memory of the sin they committed, but as healed sin without the pain or sorrow that once accompanied them.[68] If their remembered *forgiven* sins provide a basis for their knowledge of what these sins were, could it not be imagined that they might grasp how their lingering effects continues to mar the church's witness? Even here, the emphasis ought to be on the ecclesial essence of repentance, rather than the individual dimension. We cannot fathom the mercy of God, and it is not for us to judge the status or destiny of individuals who sacked Constantinople. All, some, or none, may be in the presence of God in heaven. And churches often clarify that their repentance is not intended to address the personal sin of those

---

[64] Jenson, *Systematic Theology* 2, 268.
[65] *The One Mediator*, no. 79.
[66] Emery, *The Communion of Saints*, 118.
[67] Jenson, *Systematic Theology* 2, 368.
[68] Augustine, *City of God*, trans. Henry Bettenson (London: Penguin, 1984), 20.30.

who have died. Yet, as these sins have hindered the church shinning forth, Christ's forgiveness is sought. The church of the thirteenth century, of whom a more direct responsibility for the crimes of Constantinople may be imputed, is called upon to acknowledge its guilt as a way of participating in Christ's active reconciliation of this past and its consequences.

I have noted that not only is the unity of the church strengthened through repentance for divisive actions in the past, but that the premise for such repentance is the unity in Christ of the communion of saints. However, churches have recently repented for sins against those who may not currently identify themselves with the church, such as Jews, for example, or the Aboriginal people of North America, many of whom are also in the church. In these cases, Christ's forgiveness may be mediated through those outside the church, and thus create a shared memory of healing that extends beyond the traditional boundaries of the communion of saints. Whomever becomes an agent of forgiveness for the faults of the church thereby mediates Christ's forgiveness and may be understood in some sense as part of the communion of saints. The church must think beyond itself, not only as it does mission, but as it encounters the Spirit coming to it from outside of itself. Ecclesial repentance may push the church to think of the communion of saints as a reality that is greater than the church as we know it.

Numerous individual statements have explicitly requested the forgiveness of groups that are somewhat or entirely outside the church. While the role of the human forgiveness of offended groups will be examined further in Chapter 7, I note two examples here in order to specify how the boundaries of the communion of saints may be blurred or extended by these practices. The first case is that of the Southern Baptist Convention which repented of its support of slavery and racism more generally. Their formal statement of repentance does include several references to the racial discrimination experienced by African-Americans in their churches. Yet, they apologized to 'all African-Americans for condoning and/or perpetrating individual and systemic racism' and requested forgiveness from them, 'acknowledging that our own healing is at stake'. This apology appears to be extended to those who are not Christian. They explicitly tied the reception of such forgiveness and the resulting reconciliation to the mission of the church to be light to others, thereby glorifying God. In this sense, even African-Americans who are not Christian become part of the communion of saints through which the church undertakes its ministry, a ministry aimed towards a future in which, according to the resolution, 'redeemed persons will stand together in restored family union as joint-heirs with Christ (Rom. 8.17)'.[69]

A second instance may be seen in the confession made by the Presbyterian Church in Canada regarding Indian Residential Schools.[70] Among others, they addressed their request for forgiveness to Aboriginal people, not just those who were/are Presbyterian. A few months after approving the resolution, Moderator George Vais presented it to Aboriginal leaders, including Phil Fontaine, Grand Chief of the Assembly of First Nations, at a ceremony in Winnipeg, Manitoba. Fontaine received this 'apology' (as he described it, though the document does not use that word) as a crucial step in the healing process.[71] The significance is that the church sought an installment of forgiveness, which it would understand as ultimately rooted in Christ, mediated through the non-Christian political entity representing many Aboriginal people in Canada. Does this somehow extend the communion of saints to embrace both Aboriginal peoples and the Presbyterian Church? As stated in the preamble to the text, the Presbyterian church understands its 'mission and ministry in new ways, in part because of the testimony of Aboriginal peoples'. If the integrity of its mission is inseparable from its being as church, then, at least given its historical past, the Presbyterian Church in Canada finds its ecclesial identity in part through its relationship with Aboriginal people, whether Christian or not.

I do not want to suggest that particular Aboriginal persons ought to locate their identity in the fact that they were offended by the church, nor am I suggesting that they are in some way co-opted into being 'anonymous Christians'. However, the risen Christ stands at the centre of history, and is the condition by which history is possible. It is an implication of the ecclesiology developed in this chapter to conclude that the historic continuity of all communities finds decisive points of reference in relation to the living presence of Christ and in anticipation of the Spirit. At the same time, ecclesial repentance ought to engender in the church a deep humility with respect to

---

[69] Southern Baptist Convention, 'Resolution on Racial Reconciliation' (1995).
[70] Presbyterian Church in Canada, 'Our Confession' (1994).
[71] Michael Farris, 'Moderator Presents Confession', *Presbyterian Record*, November 1994, 20.

groups it has offended, and not turn out to be a sleight of hand concealing ecclesial triumphalism.

The intensity of communion within the church and between the church and Christ ought to temper human judgement on the past. The church ought not to adopt an attitude of moral superiority in relation to the past, nor presume a trajectory of progress. The judge of the church's sin is not the present church, but rather Christ whose judgement over his temporally extended body is one of its very bonds. Rowan Williams warns that mere ecclesial self-critique reflects the tyranny of the church's present understanding. By contrast, a penitential perspective on the church's past recognizes Christ as judge of the church, yet also the basis for its forgiveness.[72] Like Williams, H. Richard Niebuhr claims that the church's self-criticism is false faith in the church's human capacity, whereas true repentance points to faith in God.[73] Because repentance turns to God, and submits to God's judgement (wherein it finds its future in the Spirit), the church can do so hopefully and in faith that sins will be healed. Even by its own repentance, the church will not finally get it right, but rather participates faithfully in light of the promise of the Spirit's transforming power.

This ought to engender fear and trembling as any church considers repenting for sins in its past, because in presuming to speak penitentially for the past, the church is presuming to reflect Christ's judgement on the past. It may be presuming to implore the simultaneous repentance of the saints in heaven. In her statement on behalf of the Episcopal Church to Aboriginal people, House of Deputies President Pamela Chinnis said: 'We must repent on behalf of those who went before us, shedding the tears of remorse they would shed if they saw their actions from our perspective'.[74] This bold statement does indeed presume to speak for the dead, and moreover suggests not only that they ought to be judged by the perspective of today, but that they themselves would wish this to be so. I have been arguing that this is indeed possible, but the Christological premise that makes it possible also necessitates prayerful prudence prior to any act of ecclesial repentance. The church is indeed called to be

---

[72] Williams, *Resurrection*, 58–59.

[73] H. Richard Niebuhr, 'The Disorder of Man in the Church of God', in *Man's Disorder and God's Design: The Amsterdam Assembly Series*, vol. 1, World Council of Churches (New York: Harper & Brothers, 1949), 78.

[74] Pamela P. Chinnis, Episcopal Church, 'Response to the New Jamestown Covenant' (1997).

prophetic, but it must not repent with careless abandon, nor merely with the trends of the time. Indeed, what churches are naming sinful are those instances when they truly believed to know what Christ's judgement on the church and on the world required of them: persecution of supposedly schismatic or heretical Christians, persecution or proselytization of the Jews, structuring human relationships based on hierarchies of race or gender. In retrospect, such judgements which were held to be Christ's own were recognized to have been wrong and sinful. The penitent church must recognize, in humility, that Christ will exercise judgement over the present church through the repentance of its spiritual great-grandchildren. What that future church will repent of may be not only what the present church knows to be sinful, but what the present church sincerely believes are actions consistent with the gospel.

HEALING OF MEMORIES

Having already considered the communion of saints as a framework within which Christ's mediation connects Christians through space, and especially through time, it is fitting to consider how these connections are mediated in memory. Though Christ is always present as head of his body and the Spirit acts to bind the church to its future, at a human level the church has access to the past only in memory, a complex reality that includes texts, practices, dispositions and testimonies. A church reflective on its past is engaged in a process of memory formation and reformation. Its historical identity is intimately bound up with what it remembers, how it remembers, who remembers and what ends its memories serve. As narrated in Part 1, churches search their collective memories to discover past fault, or listen to the collective memories of others who ascribe their pain to the church's action. Ecclesial repentance often serves as a milestone in this process of remembering. Besides occasioning repentance, memories may be reshaped and healed, in turn prompting further reparative action.

After analysing some explicit and implicit claims about the healing or purification of memory in repentance statements, I engage with Miroslav Volf's constructive proposal in *The End of Memory: Remembering Rightly in a Violent World*. I will show how the doctrine of the communion of saints, as I have been arguing is implied by the practice of ecclesial repentance, has particular bearing on the healing of memories.

The healing of memories is a phrase commonly associated with ecumenical dialogue and the Jubilee programme of Pope John Paul II. However, it has been employed in recent decades with several distinct nuances. First, a pledge to remove something from memory – the reciprocal excommunications of 1054 – was made by the Joint Declaration of Pope Paul VI and Ecumenical Patriarch Athenagoras I who referred to Phil. 3.13 as the biblical mandate to forget something for the sake of the gospel.[75] Though Vatican II also makes a plea to forget (the history of Christian–Muslim hostility[76]), this theme is not found in later statements, most likely because of the post-Holocaust discourse on the obligation to remember the past.

Given the frequency with which the 1965 act of removal from memory is cited in subsequent Catholic–Orthodox exchanges, it is evident that 1054 is not forgotten but rather remembered in a different way. This second meaning, a purification of memory, refers to the removal of resentment attached to particular memories. The pledge of two communities to purify their memories in this way is both a concrete means towards a restored relationship and a sign of a significant realization of reconciliation.

A third meaning implies a return to historical sources to establish an accurate account of the past. Since resentment and enmity have undoubtedly shaped the perception of the past, careful research may clear away misunderstandings or prejudices.[77] Careful historical and theological research was reflected in the acknowledgment by the 'Joint Declaration on the Doctrine of Justification' that sixteenth-century Lutherans and Catholics traded polemics rooted in different conceptual frameworks and starting points. Preceding dialogues and repentance statements, for example the pope's recognition that Martin Luther's intentions were faithful and sincere,[78] show how a healing of memories may facilitate deeper ecumenical reconciliation.

A return to the sources with respect to relations with Aboriginal people has shown the pervasive cultural assumptions of superiority that churches have since repudiated as sinful. Yet, such delineations may minimize the responsibility taken by the church. If church actions simply reflected the cultural context, so the reasoning goes, then what the church said or did may be regrettable but hardly culpable.

---

[75] See also Ps. 25.7 and Jer. 31.34.
[76] *Nostra Aetate*, no. 3.
[77] Pope John Paul II, *Ut Unum Sint*, no. 2.
[78] Pope John Paul II, Ecumenical celebration, Paderborn, 22 June 1996.

However, in the present era of heightened historical consciousness in which we know that perspective matters, the challenge for a penitent church is to not allow the strangeness of another time and place to preclude the present church making a judgement about sin, which precisely as sin will be strange as well.

The US Lutheran–Mennonite dialogue embraced the concept of 'right remembering', suggesting it was preferable to 'healing of memories' in part because there is no visceral memory of animosity in need of healing. Rather, there is a history to be interpreted with new eyes.[79] This approach emphasizes the objectivity of what is remembered, even as an ecumenical spirit oversees the historical study. It also suggests, or at least implies, that getting the past right will have a positive effect on present relationship. But if the investigation is truly an open process, this cannot be assumed. The church must be prepared to recognize that any particular past event or practice may have in fact been more horrific than previously assumed.

Though related, collective memory and 'what happened' as determined by historical methods are not identical. As discussed in Chapters 2 and 4, some Roman Catholic efforts to delineate the nature of Catholic complicity in the Holocaust have not always considered the nature and power of a collective memory held by another community. A unilateral account of what the historical sources mean is not enough. Addressing the collective Jewish memories of twentieth-century anti-Semitism and the Holocaust is ultimately a matter of relationship rather than a strictly archival one.

Fourth, the healing of memories may consist of a particular result of historical research: the discovery that convictions that once appeared incompatible are not really so. In the 'Joint Declaration on the Doctrine of Justification', Catholics and Lutherans agreed that mutual condemnations emerged from different philosophical premises, and thus led to misinterpretations of the other position.[80] The past is not disavowed: the condemnations continue to condemn specific teachings. In this respect, the crucible of history has providentially provided abiding warnings to the church about specific theological errors. What has changed is the conclusion that since neither the present Lutheran or Catholic churches hold such

---

[79] John D. Roth, 'Forgiveness and the Healing of Memories: An Anabaptist–Mennonite Perspective', *Journal of Ecumenical Studies* 42 (2007), 582–7.

[80] Lutheran World Federation and Roman Catholic Church, 'Joint Declaration on the Doctrine of Justification, 1999', nos. 41–2.

teachings, then the condemnations do not apply to these churches. In this sense, memories are healed to the extent that past enmity does not have a contemporary referent.

Reading history together, a strategy in which mutual accountability seeks to avoid reproducing old prejudices is a fifth sense of the healing of memory. The international Catholic–Reformed dialogue identified a need 'to share one sense of the past rather than two'.[81] The international Mennonite–Roman Catholic dialogue engaged in what it called 'an exercise of penitential history', recognizing that for each side, negative views of the other have shaped their interpretation of history.[82] Though an accurate account of the past is sought, this quest is undertaken in light of the shared conviction that 'both sides continue to hold in common much of the Christian faith'.[83] A common penitential reading of history may also entail both reconsidering one's own deeply held views, and regarding as complementary theological positions once held as contradictory. Viewing the past from the perspective of the other has a proximate goal of creating a new framework of self-understanding that encompasses both traditions. From the Mennonite–Catholic dialogue: 'Our common re-reading of the history of the church will hopefully contribute to the development of a common interpretation of the past. This can lead to a shared new memory and understanding. In turn, a shared new memory can free us from the prison of the past'.[84]

A shared memory is not only a goal (certainly realized together with the visible unity of the one Church of Christ), but also a way to get there. The LWF Council pledged to use 'the jointly described history between Lutherans and Anabaptists' as the lens through which current Lutheran condemnations are interpreted, presumably to render their effect non-church-dividing.[85] In their confession to the heirs of the Anabaptists, the Reformed Church of Zurich stated: 'It is time to accept the history of the Anabaptist movement as part of our own, to learn from the Anabaptist tradition and to

---

[81] Reformed–Roman Catholic Dialogue, 'Towards a Common Understanding of the Church' (1990), no. 17.

[82] Roman Catholic Church and Mennonite World Conference, 'Called Together to be Peacemakers' (2003), no. 24.

[83] *Ibid.*, no. 191.

[84] *Ibid.*, no. 27.

[85] Lutheran World Federation Council, Statement on Lutheran–Anabaptist Relationships (2009).

strengthen our mutual testimony through dialogue'. The basis for such remarkable willingness to accept as their own an expression of faith they once persecuted as heretical is Christological: 'We do not belong to ourselves. We belong to Jesus Christ who calls us to follow him and to be reconciled with those brothers and sisters who have any just reasons to reproach us'.[86] That this occurred within the body of Christ both magnifies the tragedy but also constitutes the ground for reconciliation. The Mennonite delegation explained that integrating a painful past into a shared memory serves the future witness of the church. It provides the basis for Mennonite convictions about the church and ethics to be commended to the wider church, and a commitment to debate them as plausible expressions of faithfulness.[87]

I have argued elsewhere that in relation to Catholics who once put Anabaptists to death, Mennonites as heirs of the Anabaptists ought to regard these martyr memories within a common, though still differentiated, Christian memory.[88] Can Anabaptist martyrs be regarded as witnesses to Christ not only by Anabaptists, but by the wider church that includes the heirs of those who put them to death? Can Mennonites recognize their sixteenth-century Catholic persecutors as one with them in the body of Christ, confessing also Mennonite capacity for violence and unfaithfulness? If so, then these communities will be on the way to a significant healing of memories. The healing on both sides contributes to a single ecclesial memory with Christ at the centre. Fundamentally, ecclesial repentance helps to bind divided churches together in their realization that their common hope is God's forgiveness in Christ.

Sixth, the pledge to remember may itself be considered an act of penance, intimately connected with the resolve to not repeat the offence. The Catholic Bishops of West Germany, Austria and Berlin spoke about accepting the full burden of their history as something *owed* to the victims. They described the duty to remember and to oppose all attempts to misrepresent this history as an ongoing one, the purpose of which is to transform attitudes and actions towards

---

[86] Evangelical-Reformed Church of Zurich, 'Statement of Regret', (2004).

[87] Swiss Mennonite Conference, Response (2004).

[88] Jeremy M. Bergen, 'Problem or Promise? Confessional Martyrs and Mennonite–Roman Catholic Relations', *Journal of Ecumenical Studies* 41 (2004), 367–88.

Jews and the Jewish faith.[89] Holding a particular memory may be healing to the extent that it strengthens the relationship with the Jewish community. A healed memory is still remembered, and that memory exercises a critical 'never again' function in the life of the church.[90] The French Bishops spoke about the way in which 'conscience is formed in remembering'.[91] The duty to remember is served by public commemoration, physical monuments and anniversaries, which become occasions for further reflection.

Ecclesial repentance thus points to several ways in which the healing of memories may be a condition or a goal. Painful, violent or sinful pasts ought to be remembered, since 'what is forgotten cannot be healed, and that which cannot be healed easily becomes the source of greater evil'.[92] What is not assumed is not healed – this ancient formula about the soteriological significance of Jesus Christ's full humanity is analogously applied to the church's memory. The church's memory is not fully its own, but Christ's who through memory disciplines, reforms, reconciles and heals his own body.

Remembering, Forgetting, Final Reconciliation

This overview gives a glimpse at several of the ways the churches believe that their repentance contributes to the healing of memories. Many of the theological presuppositions of the healing of memories are hinted at in the documents, though their implications undeveloped. I turn now to a theology of memory that helps us probe more deeply the relationship between memory, forgetting, healing and the work of Christ. Miroslav Volf engages both the theological tradition and concrete situations of injustice in *The End of Memory: Remembering Rightly in a Violent World*. The book is framed by very personal meditations on Volf's experience of being imprisoned in the former Yugoslavia, interrogated, threatened and psychologically abused by 'Capt G.'. The personal dynamic of perpetrator and victim in a situation of political repression does not exactly parallel that of which churches are repenting (that is, collective identities of offender and

---

[89] Catholic Bishops of West Germany, Austria, and Berlin, 'Accepting the Burden of History' (1988), no. 2.

[90] This theme is prominent in Pope John Paul II, 'The Depths of the Holocaust's Horror', speech at Yad Vashem, *Origins* 29, no. 42 (6 April 2000), 678–9.

[91] French Catholic Bishops, Drancy Declaration (1997).

[92] Lionel Chircop, 'Remembering the Future', in *Reconciling Memories*, enlarged ed., ed. Alan D. Falconer and Joseph Liechty (Dublin: Columba Press, 1998), 20.

offended, for sins often described more in terms of patterns rather than discrete episodes). This is not to minimize the complicity of the churches, but rather to suggest that some degree of translation will be required from his framework to the somewhat different situations in which churches find themselves. In what follows, I will seek to make a distinction between Volf's arguments as they might apply to the specific situation of individuals in relation to state-violence and consider how they might relate to the less immediately visceral *collective* memories referred to in the contexts of ecumenical reconciliation.

Volf begins with a helpful discussion of memory as both a sword and shield. Respectfully engaging the work of Elie Wiesel, he complicates Wiesel's assertion that memory itself is necessarily saving and redeeming. A memory of pain makes pain present; it preserves the festering of past wounds.[93] Memories function as a sword if preserved in ways that provoke revenge, violence, or despair. The possibility that memory serve as a shield, that is, to promote well-being, depends 'on how we see ourselves in the present and how we project ourselves into the future'.[94] Memory may function to create solidarity among victims, and foment strategies for resisting the further perpetration of injustices. Yet, this shield may turn into a sword. The formation of an identity of victimhood may perpetuate cycles of revenge.[95]

Memory and identity are intimately linked, Augustine has argued, and both are grounded in God. Augustine writes of memory as a 'vast hall' of sensations, images and ideas, in which 'I meet myself and recall what I am, what I have done, and when and where and how I was affected when I did it, ... and on this basis I reason about future actions and events and hopes'.[96] Augustine confesses that God knows him better than he knows himself, therefore the search for God must also be a search in memory.[97] Yet, one also exists in the memories of others, for better or worse. Complex collective memories constellate into complex collective identities. And memories obviously also transmit failure, pain, and resentment. In terms of Volf's concern for reconciliation, the question is whether one's identity is formed

---

[93] Miroslav Volf, *The End of Memory: Remembering Rightly in a Violent World* (Grand Rapids: Eerdmans, 2006), 21–2.

[94] *Ibid.*, 26.

[95] *Ibid.*, 33.

[96] Augustine, *Confessions*, trans. Henry Chadwick (Oxford: Oxford University Press, 1991), 10.14.

[97] *Ibid.*, 10.26.

by truthful memories, and ultimately *how* memory and identity are grounded in God, and taken up specifically by Jesus Christ.

Truthful memories are a condition for the redemption of memory and reconciliation. Remembering falsely denies justice to the victims, in the first case, but for this reason also mitigates the possibility of a future reconciliation with perpetrators. Truthful memories must name the wrong done, and name the wrongdoers. Though the dynamics of selective or false memories at the psychological level are quite different from those at the collective or historical level, any temporal gap nevertheless opens the possibility of falsehood. There are two dimensions in need of healing: the past itself, and the memories of the past. To simply forget the past posits a false happiness, the denial of justice to the victims, and the constant threat of memories will return in destructive ways.[98] Christian salvation entails a redemption of the past, but 'only *truthful* memories give access to the events with which peace needs to be made'.[99]

Though Volf does not develop the concept of truthful memories in this way, it counters the idea reflected in some of the ecclesial repentance statements that what the church must do to reckon with its past is primarily a unilateral exercise of determining the objective past. The requirements of truthfulness point to the importance of using historical research where this is helpful, but such results will only contribute partially to the memory of the past. What must be truthful is a *memory*, which is to say a perception of the past that is genuinely held and embodied. If Roman Catholics and Mennonites seek to establish truthful memories about Anabaptist martyrs killed by Catholics, the work does not end with the writings of professional historians, though such work will be a crucial foundation.[100] If historical work complicates current confessionally oriented perceptions of this past, these will become truthful memories only if they are received widely, and in fact reshape the meaning that is drawn from the past.

Volf proposes remembering as primarily a kind of practice, rather than simply a mode of knowledge.[101] As a practice, remembering is embedded in a context of actions and meanings that make it

---

[98] Volf, *The End of Memory*, 73.

[99] *Ibid.*, 75.

[100] These are precisely the commitments underlying the work collected in Peter C. Erb, ed., *Martyrdom in an Ecumenical Perspective: A Mennonite–Catholic Conversation* (Kitchener, ON: Pandora Press, 2007).

[101] Volf, *The End of Memory*, 67.

imaginable or desirable in the first place. Remembering expresses an identity and embodies particular hopes, or lack thereof. Those who have experienced tremendous suffering may find themselves defined and thus imprisoned by such an identity. Redemption in Christ may be imagined as being given a new identity, one which opens to a new future of justice, healing and hope. A past evil or a history of suffering is removed as a basis for identity and replaced by a memory of God's deliverance of captives and God's decisive overcoming of alienation in the passion of Christ. The memories of past suffering become ever more *past* as they move to the periphery of identity, and are integrated into a memory of healing as the fulfilment of God's promise. As Christians engage in the range of communal practices of remembering the exodus and especially the passion, they remember their future as God's future.

The truth of memory is not determined only by whether it justly and accurately mediates the past to the present, but also by whether the memory acknowledges what is ultimately most truthful about the persons and communities divided by pain, which is that God intends the future to be a world of perfect love. As an expression of love, a truthful memory will bring an offender or offending community to repentance and ultimately toward reconciliation. A truthful memory in this sense already points to the healing of memories. '[T]he proper goal of the memory of wrongs suffered – its appropriate end – is the formation of the communion of love between all people, including victims and perpetrators'.[102] Repentance, in turn, creates the possibility that a truthful memory can be released, even recede in memory, because its truth remains embodied in reconciled relationships.[103] In a sense, memory is like a ladder which can be kicked away once the summit is reached, but it is crucial that the ladder not be kicked away too soon, or by the wrong person.

The most creative element of Volf's proposal is his understanding of the relationships among memory, final reconciliation and forgetting. Memory presupposes forgetting, for if everything were remembered, the entire past would be fully present at every moment and as such completely unusable and paralyzing. Identity is formed through selective remembering and selective forgetting. Critical of the extent to which the social dimension has been neglected in treatments of 'heaven' – the world to come, or the consummation – Volf proposes

[102] *Ibid.*, 232.
[103] *Ibid.*, 65.

that, given that those who die may not be fully reconciled with other human beings, there must be something that happens in the 'eschatological transition' to achieve such reconciliation. Only then can heaven be a true world of perfect love not only between God and creatures, but among creatures themselves.[104] From the perspective of the offended, final blessedness must entail forgetting, or rather 'not-coming-to-mind',[105] lest the pain of the past remain present through memory. Ultimately, the memory of sin and suffering is incompatible with perfect love and joy. Given that many people die before there is any measure of justice with those who have offended against them, the process of social reconciliation must extend eschatologically. Social reconciliation is therefore not only social, for its orientation towards perfect love presupposes the trinitarian economy of God whose being *is* this love.

If victims will ultimately be released from painful memories so that they will not come to mind, what does this mean for the memories of those who committed the offences? After all, ecclesial repentance concerns those situations in which the church is the offender. Volf's primary interest is in the memory of suffering, and thus he does not focus on the implications for the offenders or, as is more likely the case in situations of ecumenical healing of memories, degrees of guilt on both sides. Yet, it is clear that he would not grant that these may be unilaterally forgotten, apart from social reconciliation which may be initiated in this world, and completed in the next. In anticipation of the eschatological transition, sins are visible for the sake of reconciliation and final non-remembrance. As the church encounters the painful memories it has caused, it confronts God's judgement on the church. This occasions repentance, justice for victims and the possibility of forgiveness.[106] This does not mean that the ultimate fate of offenders is solely in the hands of victims, but rather that God's gifts of non-remembrance are mediated by those victims who receive the promise of such non-remembrance of their suffering as a gift of a new identity in Christ. The gift of 'non-remembrance' is not a direct gift of God, but rather an implication of the promised gift of the world

---

[104] Volf, 'The Final Reconciliation'.

[105] Volf's prefers 'not-coming-to-mind' or 'non-remembrance' to 'forgetting'. The latter suggests either an erasure which negates the past, or an act of will to 'get over' the past. The other terms evoke the 'passivity of the agent ... [as] a consequence of God's gift to the transformed self enjoying reconciled relationships with the world'. *The End of Memory*, 147.

[106] *Ibid.*, 211.

of perfect love.[107] For ecclesial repentance this calls into question the belief that, with respect to its past, the church is accountable to God alone. The healing of memories cannot bypass those who have suffered.

The creativity of Volf's work lies in his willingness, on the one hand, to question the post-Holocaust consensus that the obligation to remember is eternal and, on the other hand, to argue that justice for victims may be served by an obligation to remember indefinitely in *historical* time. Holding these together through a concept of social reconciliation beyond death in an 'eschatological transition' accords with my earlier proposal that ecclesial repentance may be understood, in part, as intercessory prayer within the communion of saints. It allows us to see how historic wrongs of the church can be genuinely acknowledged and confessed. There, the key was the mediation of Christ, and so too Christ acts on human memories to redeem them by substituting them for a different memory. Victims are given a new identity in which God's love in Christ, not past oppression, is decisive. Wrongdoers 'are remembered as forgiven and freed from the hold of evil on their lives'.[108]

It is noteworthy that Volf makes the Augustinian distinction between a final reconciliation that entails, for victims, the gift of past offences not coming to mind, and wrongdoers retaining a trace of their sins, albeit as fully forgiven sin. If this is the case, then the adaptation of Volf's proposal for ecclesial repentance implies that while those who suffered injustice at the hands of the church will finally be granted a release from that memory, the church will retain a memory of that past, though completely healed. The heavenly church is not an ideal church or a pristine church, but in the first place a church that has been somewhere – on a pilgrimage – and has arrived at a world of perfect love. But the church does not lose its irreducibly historical character, nor the healed marks of its sins.

Though Volf did not set out to write a book about the church, ecclesiological themes are underdeveloped even when they may have been instructive. His choice to focus on individual perpetrators and victims is rightly driven by the tragic familiarity such suffering has in the world, but as these particular relationships are translated eschatologically, Volf gives the impression that heaven is primarily about the

---

[107] *Ibid.*, 146.
[108] *Ibid.*, 118.

status and reconciliation of individuals. There is no significant role for the church as such, either in its earthly state or in the world to come. While Volf's account of memory and the final transition points to some eschatological assumptions about repentance of churches, mapping this back on to Volf's proposal supplements its ecclesiological deficit.

The eucharist is absent in Volf's account, which is surprising considering its themes of memory, forgiveness and eschatology, and therefore its capacity to shape Christian practice even if the perpetrator and victim are not both within the church. The eucharist is a constant reminder to the church of its capacity for betrayal, a betrayal which belongs not just to Judas but to all the disciples who denied Jesus and fled, and thus also to the church. The church which continues to celebrate the eucharist is the community that remembers its own failures when it remembers Christ. It is the community of the guilty and restored. The church recognizes that its identity is always dependent on Christ's forgiveness, a forgiveness that unites disparate persons with Christ to form the *totus Christus*. The healing of memories is not simply a programme the church pursues, but a promise the church receives as it gives itself over to being shaped by the singular memory of Christ's death and resurrection. The church obedient to Christ's command to take and eat in remembrance of his death is the church located in history, and complicit in its ambiguities. Penitence is thus the rightful posture of the church until the eschatological moment when the church's history becomes identical with the memory that Christ gives to it, a memory of sins fully judged, forgiven, and healed.

Robert Jenson's trinitarian and ecclesiological account of the past's salutary presence in memory is particularly helpful in light of my argument that the Spirit's bringing the church to repentance binds the church's past to its present in a way that frees it for the future. The key is the concept of eucharist as *anamnesis*, or memorial, in which the eucharist is the event by which Christ's singular and effective past action is made present and effective.[109] This is usually taken to mean that the memorial reminds the church of Christ's work, making it effective in the church's life. Jenson goes further to suggest that the eucharist also reminds God of Jesus. That *God* remembers something makes whatever past event is remembered thereby present. 'We may generalize: anamnetic being is present reality created by a word of

---

[109] Jenson, *Unbaptized God*, 35.

God that simultaneously evokes a past event and opens its future, to make it live in the present'.[110]

What may be seen paradigmatically in the eucharist is the case wherever the church offers a prayer of thanksgiving, intercession or confession. To pray to God for the healing of memories, especially in the context of the eucharist, is to ask that God answer this prayer by making a particular past present to the church in a way delineated by the particular relations of Father, Son and Holy Spirit. The sack of Constantinople, the violence of Reformation-era persecutions – these are made present in *God's* memory and, in this way, they are made present to the church, precisely as judged, forgiven and healed by Jesus Christ. A healing of memories thus envelops a temporally extended community of offenders and victims (both personally and as communities) in such a way that enmity is taken up decisively by the power of the cross and overcome in the resurrection. Healing of memories is not primarily a human task, but God's gift.

The penitent church that seeks a healing of memories does so 'eucharistically', a claim I advance without sorting out the disagreements among churches over precisely what eucharist or sacrament means. The church must find itself fully dependent on – that is, in the real presence of – the forgiveness that Christ makes possible through his death and resurrection; in repentance the church declares its intention to do so. However, to the extent that divisions exist at the Lord's Table, the church is not yet in the presence of the forgiveness it needs. It does not manifest the unity proper to it, and its memories have not be healed and reconciled. The need for the 'death and rebirth of many forms of church life as we have known them', as stated by the New Delhi Assembly,[111] must be understood as a plea for churches to find their memories healed on the other side of resurrection. Until that time, sin and death fracture the church, manifesting in divided denominations and in other ways, inhibiting its full availability to the world as the body of Christ. The atomization caused by sin and death is a reality that infects all communities, though the church has as its mission to point to the true source of unity and wholeness. Thus, as the church seeks to witness to the world, it 'must recognize constantly its failure *as* a community to *be*

---

[110] Jenson, *Systematic Theology* 2, 258, citing scriptural warrant in Exod. 2.24 and Ps. 25.5.

[111] World Council of Churches, 'Report of the Section on Unity', Third Assembly (1961), 117.

a community of gift and mutuality, and warn itself of the possibility of failure'.[112] In repentance for its failure in the distant past and in the present to be the unity it has been given, the church turns to the source of that unity – forgiveness in Christ – as its hope for the future.

As the church delves into its own memory, it finds that a 'healed memory' is both its own and not its own. The church's memory reflects its own particular sojourn of faithfulness and unfaithfulness. The histories that churches are recounting about themselves are an essential part of this practice. Christ forgives actual sins. But in the eschatological transition, the church confronts those who have experienced from the church not healing but pain. Through the strangeness and otherness of these memories, the church confronts God's judgement. By asking forgiveness, the church submits to judgement for these transgressions and prays that these memories of resentment can be incorporated as reconciled with its own. But there is another sense in which the memories are not the church's own. Through this eschatological transition whereby the church finds its identity entirely in Christ, its memory becomes Christ's memory. That memory will be centred on the passion and resurrection, and by extension, all things which are reconciled by that event. All history will be healed history; all history will turn on Jesus Christ. As Volf contends, Christ grants to victims the gift of their suffering 'not-coming-to-mind', while for those who caused this suffering, he replaces a memory of sins committed with that of sins forgiven. The saints will remember their forgiven sins because precisely these bind them to Christ.[113] Communities of Christians – presently divided as Catholic, Orthodox, Lutheran, Mennonite and so on – will remember their share in division as entirely healed. Within this healed memory, therefore, there will effectively be no community of victims, just the church as a forgiven sinner whose everlasting joy will be to give thanksgiving and sing praise to God.

In this chapter I have argued that the temporal continuity of the church is rooted in God's triune life. This assertion does not lessen the historical character of the church, but affirms history as precisely where God has placed the church. I have proposed that, as the action of the Spirit, an act of ecclesial repentance becomes the very basis for the present church's continuity with its sinful past. This makes the church's penitent communication with respect to its sins in its past

---

[112] Williams, *Resurrection*, 48–9, italics in original.

[113] Jenson, *Systematic Theology* 2, 333.

possible, meaningful and necessary. As a communion of saints whose communion is mediated by Christ's forgiveness of sins, the church rightly repents of its failure to be this communion in history and it is granted the possibility of ecumenical repentance. Finally, Christ's mediation of the church's continuity in time takes the form of the church's memory, in which the past is made present to God and thus in God. As God thereby acts to reconcile all things in Christ, ecclesial repentance expresses the irreducibly historical and eschatological character of the church.

Chapter 6

SIN AND THE HOLINESS OF THE CHURCH

Humanly speaking, holiness is always like this:
God's endurance in the middle of our refusal of him,
his capacity to meet every refusal with the gift of himself. (Rowan Williams)[1]

On the night of 9 November 1938, a pogrom was unleashed in Germany and Austria. The smashing of windows in Jewish homes, businesses and synagogues gave this event its name – *Kristallnacht*. As a premeditated outburst of violence in which Jewish people were beaten and killed, it was an ominous precursor to the even more lethal elements of the 'Final Solution'. Just over a month after *Kristallnacht*, Cardinal Michael von Faulhaber spoke from his pulpit about '... one advantage in our time; in the highest position of the Reich we have the example of a simple and modest alcohol and nicotine-free way of life'.[2] Undoubtedly, individual Christians were involved in the pogrom. But how did churches gave tacit or explicit sanction to this event? What message was sent by their failure to denounce it? What role was played by church teachings about the Jewish suffering being a deserved consequence of their rejection of Christ?

The Catholic Bishops of West Germany, Austria and Berlin, marked the 50th anniversary of *Kristallnacht* with a recognition of the failures of the church under the Third Reich. In reflecting on this history, the bishops acknowledged that there was sin *in* the church: 'Among us Catholics, too, there has been failure and guilt' in both remaining silent – no bishop denounced *Kristallnacht* from his pulpit – but also for actively participating in the killing of Jews. Yet, they went a step further

---

[1] Rowan Williams, *A Ray of Darkness: Sermons and Reflections* (Cambridge, MA: Cowley Publications, 1995), 115.

[2] Quoted in Ernst Christian Helmreich, *The German Churches Under Hitler: Background, Struggle, and Epilogue* (Detroit: Wayne State University Press, 1979), 294.

by acknowledging that the silence of the church and 'traditional prejudices' against Jews in Catholic theology also constituted a failure *of* the church. The church accepted a 'co-responsibility' for what was done in the name of the German people, from *Kristallnacht* to the death camps. While the document also notes several ways that the church was a victim alongside the Jews, and points to the efforts of some Catholic leaders to condemn the violence and anti-Semitism, it describes the identity of the church as inseparable from its history both good and bad. While the church is honoured as a mystery, it is also 'a sinful Church and in need of conversion'.[3] In this chapter, I examine what it means for a church to confess that it *sinned*, in its silence and complicity in *Kristallnacht* for example, and what it means for a church to *confess* that it sinned.

Holiness is a surprisingly elusive mark of the church. At a popular level, holiness is related to manifest purity, moral perfection and set-apartness. Holiness may be connected with the otherness of religion in a 'pure' sense: Otto's *mysterium tremendum et fascinans*. Or, holiness is linked to the absence of taint, doubt and malice – the (non-existent) perfect saint. Since such ideal perfection is true neither of individuals nor communities, the church's claim to be holy in light of its actual history seems blatantly hypocritical. The controversial theology that arose after the Reformation endeavoured to interpret the marks of the church as signs by which the true church may be discerned. This contributed to the expectation that the church must be visibly holy. The Catholic Church claimed holiness because it possessed the true sacraments, a celibate clergy or produced those holy lives it canonized as saints, while various Protestants located holiness in conversion experiences, the moral lives of members, or the truth of their doctrine. The apologetic demand for holiness to be empirically obvious has contributed to some of the confusion about what it can possibly mean for the church to holy.

There is ecumenical consensus that God alone is truly holy and the source of all holiness. The holiness of individuals, and of the church, is the consequence of their being drawn into the economy of salvation. The church is holy because it is the subject of God's action. Paul writes to Christians in Corinth that they are holy because God's Spirit dwells in them (1 Cor. 3.16–17), but elsewhere notes that sanctification ought to be demonstrated by following Christ's instructions (1 Thess. 4.3–8). The WCC's *The Nature and Mission of the Church*

---

[3] Catholic Bishops of West Germany, Austria, and Berlin, 'Accepting the Burden of History', (1988).

document explains that 'the essential holiness of the Church stands in contrast to sin, individual as well as communal'. So even if the church responds to the call for 'repentance, renewal and reform', thereby recognizing that the power to defeat sin comes from God alone, there lingers the sense that holiness must be manifest for all to see, and in this sense a visible mark by which the church may be identified. The problem is that the church has been identified with its ambiguous and often oppressive history; in repentance, it self-identifies with that history. How then can a holy church at the same time be a sinful church? Are sin and holiness in a zero-sum relationship?

The link between holiness and sin is assumed in a key passage from *The Nature and Mission of the Church*. However, the text also identifies this as a theme on which there remains significant disagreement among churches.

> All the Churches agree that there is sin, corporate and individual, in the Church's history (cf. Rev. 2.2). Yet they differ as to how this reality should be understood and expressed.
>
> For some, it is impossible to say 'the Church sins' because they see the Church as a gift of God, sharing in God's holiness. The Church is the spotless bride of Christ (cf. Eph. 5.25–7); it is a communion in the Holy Spirit, the holy people of God, justified by grace through faith in Christ (cf. Rom. 3.22; Eph. 2.8–9). As such, the Church cannot sin. The gift is lived out in fragile human beings who are liable to sin, but the sins of the members of the Church are not the sins of the Church. The Church is rather the locus of salvation and healing (cf. Isa. 53; Lk. 4.16–19). According to this perspective one can and must only speak of the sin of the members of the Church and of groups within the Church, a situation described by the parable of the wheat and the chaff (cf. Mt. 13.24–30), and by the Augustinian formula of *corpus permixtum*.
>
> Others while they too state that the Church as the creature of God's Word and Spirit, the body of Christ, is holy and without sin, at the same time say that it does sin, because they define the Church as the communion of its members who although they are justified believers brought to birth by the Spirit, and Christ's own body, in this world are still sinful human beings (cf. 1 Jn. 1.8–10).
>
> Yet others believe that while one cannot speak of the sins of the Church, sin in the Church may become systemic and also affect the institution.
>
> While there are these different understandings concerning the Church and sin, we ask whether all churches might not be able to agree on the following proposition:
>
> The relationship between sin and holiness in the Church is not a relationship of two equal realities, for sin and holiness essentially do not exist on the same level. Rather, holiness denotes the Church's nature and God's will for it, while sinfulness is contrary to both (cf. 1 Cor. 15.21–6).[4]

---

[4] World Council of Churches, *The Nature and Mission of the Church: A Stage on the Way to a Common Statement*, revised Faith and Order Paper no. 198 (Geneva: WCC, 2005), no. 56.

It is clear from this passage that the holiness of the church is entirely derived from God's holiness. The church's holiness is not its own, but Christ's whose body the church is and the Spirit's who indwells. There is an eschatological tension between the holiness of the church's nature and the holiness to which it is called. The church's holiness is thus confronted by the problem of sin, which is a contradiction to what the church really is.

In this chapter, I propose that the recent practice of ecclesial repentance reorients the conversation about the holiness of the church, especially as it relates to sin. It is thus necessary to sketch the basic terms of this conversation in both Protestant and Catholic theology. I argue that these sketches of the church's holiness are, in different ways, inadequately equipped to account for what ecclesial repentance implies about the historically located sin that is contrary to God's will. Despite differences of ecclesiology, it is a given fact that both Catholic and Protestant churches are repenting. This fact provides some new vocabulary for Protestant and Catholic ecclesiology to find common ground. I will focus on repentance for sins against Jews and Judaism in order to pursue an instructive connection between the form of ecclesial repentance and this particular content. The Gentile church's forgetfulness of God's ongoing covenant with the Jews has contributed to the forgetfulness that the church's holiness is rooted in God's promises to it. Constructively, my argument is that ecclesial repentance requires an account of the church's holiness as the action of the Holy Spirit to conform the penitent church into the body of Christ.

Discourses of Sin and Holiness

In this section, I survey the starting points and presuppositions of key representatives of each side in order explain how, in different ways, there are impediments in both traditions to recognizing the irreducibly historical character of the church, and consequently the church's holiness under the historical conditions it finds itself. Protestant theology begins by contrasting the pervasive sinfulness of humanity to the holiness of God. The danger is that the historically specific character of what is being confessed will be obscured by the church's mandated confession that as a human community it is *always* sinful. In the Catholic construal of ecclesial repentance, the church purifies itself by confessing the sins of its members. While in theory this preserves the possibility that there will be greater attention to particular sins confessed, it reflects an ultimately inadequate ecclesiology which posits an abstract church over against its members.

The Holy Church in Protestant Theology

As a historical movement, Protestantism was premised on the belief that the church succumbed to some basic error(s) and was thus in need of decisive reform. However, Reformation leaders frequently argued that the Catholic Church was not a sinful *church* but rather that its sins rendered it the whore of Babylon – no church at all. They maintained that a recognition of the pervasiveness and universality of sin, in the church as elsewhere, is a condition for the absolutely crucial confession of *sola gratia*. Commenting on the Westminster Confession, Michael S. Horton writes, 'A church that is not sinful and does not sin is not a church at all, but a religious society that stands in defiance of grace and forgiveness'.[5] In contrast to Catholicism's ostensible denial, a Protestant church's confession of its sinfulness, and consequent ongoing reform, are embraced as signs that it recognizes that its holiness is rooted in God, not itself.

The church's holiness is never its own holiness, but is given to it as a gift. The church's holiness thus delineates a distance between human beings and God, and God's promise to traverse that distance. The church's sinfulness is an expression of the fact that its members are sinners, and it is these sinners who populate the church and act on its behalf. '[T]he full horror of the sin of the Christian can be seen only as it is recognized that he sins as one who has been made a member of Christ and therefore involves the whole church in his sin'.[6] Like the individual, the church is always becoming what it is called to be, but is at the same time sinful. Church and Christian alike die and are reborn to new life in Christ. Reformed theologian G. C. Berkouwer expresses these convictions in terms of the church as *simul justus et peccator*. He argues that the *simul* must not be understood as a mechanism of balance, as if the church is a settled mixture of good and bad. The sin of the church ought not to be regarded as inevitable or as part of its mystery. Yet, given the universality of human

---

[5] Michael S. Horton, *People and Place: A Covenant Ecclesiology* (Louisville: Westminster John Knox Press, 2008), 195–96. Similarly Eberhard Jüngel, 'The Church as Sacrament?' in *Theological Essays*, ed. and trans. John B. Webster (Edinburgh: T & T Clark, 1989), 191–213.

[6] Claude Welch, *The Reality of the Church* (New York: Scribner's, 1958), 130.

sin, the church is in fact always a sinful body, contrary to its calling.[7] Jürgen Moltmann puts it this way: 'In the confession of sin and faith in justification the church is simultaneously *communio peccatorum* and *communio sanctorum*. It is in this very thing that its sanctification, and consequently its holiness, consists'.[8]

The formula *simul justus et peccator* is a statement not only about justification but about the profundity of sin as the denial of God's grace. In calling the church the 'greatest sinner', Martin Luther points to the fact that the church's confession of itself as a sinner is an affirmation of faith. For Luther, being a 'true sinner' depends on acknowledging, repenting and being healed of sin. Thus, the holiness of the church consists, in part, of the church's awareness of the magnitude of its sin, but just so, in penitence, of its being redeemed by the cross. David Yeago explains that for Luther, 'precisely *in* its prayer for forgiveness, and therefore in its admission of sin, the church is disclosed as something *more* than a crowd of sinners, for "no one says this except someone who is holy".'[9] Protestant worship often includes a corporate confession of sin, though significantly the emphasis in such repetition is the fact of sinfulness, rather than discernment of particular sins.

Luther initially retained private confession in part because he believed one should confess the sins that burdened one's conscience – the good news consisting of being forgiven those *particular* sins. However, the general confession in public worship tends to not be the result of the searching of conscience or a communal process of discerning which particular relationships present or past have been ruptured by the church's action.[10] In fact, the differentiated judgement that may emerge from a close examination of history, in terms of greater or lesser sins, mitigating circumstances, and the like, mixed as these are with the perennial possibility of self-justification, may be perceived to be a threat to the church's vocation to always confess its sinfulness.

---

[7] G. C. Berkouwer, *The Church*, trans. James E. Davison (Grand Rapids: Eerdmans, 1976), 334–57.

[8] Jürgen Moltmann, *The Church in the Power of the Spirit*, trans. Margaret Kohl (Minneapolis: Fortress Press, 1993), 353.

[9] David S. Yeago, '*Ecclesia Sancta, Ecclesia Peccatrix*: The Holiness of the Church in Martin Luther's Theology', *Pro Ecclesia* 9 (2000), 346.

[10] For an overview of the historical background and present practice, see Frank Senn, 'Confession of Sins in the Reformation Churches', in *The Fate of Confession*, ed. Mary Collins and David Power (Edinburgh: T & T Clark, 1987), 105–16.

A strict deduction from the fact that all members are sinners, or that recognizing the sinfulness of the community as a whole denotes openness to God's grace, cannot account of the twentieth-century *emergence* of ecclesial repentance for historical wrongs. What is new is the recognition that there are *kairos* moments in which a particular history is must be examined and a particular sin confessed.

Like the individual, the church knows itself a sinner only because it knows the grace of its forgiveness. Sin is clarified in light of Christ's victory over it; it is not a simple reality to be read off of history. The complication is that it took the church a long time to realize that its rebellion against God took the particular *forms* of racism, slavery, anti-Semitism or supporting wars of aggression. Even if the church knows itself to be the greatest sinner, it has not always known itself to be the greatest racist, and therein lies the irreducibly historical dimension of ecclesial repentance and the challenge it represents to a Protestant account of the church's holiness.

Moltmann points to the danger that a doctrine of universal sin and justification can make people blind to 'specific, practical guilt'.[11] In response, he highlights the justice and righteousness of God as the overarching context within which sin is recognized and confessed. Since God's justice and righteousness is concerned also for those victims of sin who have been denied justice, it cannot be separated from the tangible new life of faith. '[B]ecause God has mercy on all sinners generally, he quite specifically brings justice to people who have been deprived of it, and leads the unjust to repentance'.[12]

It is this attention to the victims of injustice that brings a concreteness to both how the church confesses its past, and the reforms it implements to prevent repetition. Though sinful as a historical institution, the church differs from the world in its knowledge of the depths of its sin and thus its dependence on justification. But this justification has meaning in history precisely through the liberating forms its sanctification takes. Moltmann cites the examples of repentance by German and Japanese churches in relation to World War II and by American churches for slavery as signs of the church's concrete sanctification that make possible a different future.[13] Though holiness always has it source in God, the church's holiness may be reflected in a particular

---

[11] Jürgen Moltmann, *The Spirit of Life: A Universal Affirmation*, trans. Margaret Kohl (Minneapolis: Fortress Press, 1992), 126.

[12] *Ibid.*, 128.

[13] Moltmann, *The Church in the Power of the Spirit*, 352–7.

response to God. Moltmann emphasizes that church's holiness is not primarily seen in what it does, but in what it suffers, and whether what it undergoes is expressed in true and genuine fellowship with the poor and the humiliated.[14]

Dietrich Bonhoeffer's grounding of the church's holiness in Christ both magnifies the church's sin as offence against God and calls it to embody a Christological character and mission. Yet, a logic of abstraction appears here too, in a different form than discussed above, despite Bonhoeffer's emphasis on the concrete call of Christians and the church to discipleship and his own engagement on behalf of the Confessing Church. Thus, attending to the actual practice of ecclesial repentance can serve to supplement his theology.

In his early writings, Bonhoeffer describes sin as the breaking down of humanity's true sociality into a mere amalgam of selfish individuals whose end is death.[15] Taking cues from personalism and idealism, he describes the church in formal terms as a collective person constituted by Christ's vicarious representative action. Christ renders the church a person, a centre of activity and ethical responsibility, by being in himself true social existence characterized by the mutual love and service for which human beings were created but cannot achieve on their own.[16] The holiness of the church is therefore linked with the formal way by which the church becomes one person, the principal sign of which is the announcement of forgiveness. Sin remains, even as the new humanity is being realized in the church.

In *Ethics*, Bonhoeffer is concerned less with the church's formal constitution than with how Christ's work of assuming the sins of the world is reflected in the church's mission in the world. Essentially, the church is the medium through which Christ assumes these sins in order to forgive them. Because the church is 'Christ existing as community', the church takes on this guilt, and confesses the world's sins as its own. Bonhoeffer suggests that the ten commandments provide the template for the sins the church confesses. These are individual sins which come to infect the corporate personality of the church and other institutions in society. The church must truly bear the sins of the world, because uniquely in the world only the church

---

[14] *Ibid.*, 355–6.

[15] Dietrich Bonhoeffer, *Sanctorum Communio: A Theological Study of the Sociology of the Church*, trans. Reinhold Krauss and Nancy Lukens (Minneapolis: Fortress Press, 1998), 107–18.

[16] *Ibid.*, 145–57.

knows the depths of all sin as offence against Christ. Through this vicarious action, the church witnesses to Christ, whose forgiveness and call to discipleship is the world's hope. Aware that the church might think that this guilt is not 'really' its own, Bonhoeffer exhorts the church to penitence 'without any sidelong glances' at fellow offenders or calculation of degrees of guilt.[17]

However, this account of a penitential church actually minimizes the particular shape of this or that sin in history and especially those of which the church is culpable in favour of a generalized assumption of sin. Without a 'sidelong glance' will the church be able to distinguish between the sins for which it is directly responsible and those it has 'truly assumed' for the sake of the world? If not, how can it reform or make appropriate amends? Moreover, if the church is truly sinful and not identical with Christ himself, exhortations to take no sidelong glances will be transgressed, and the *vicarious* nature of the church's guilt remembered. Given an ecclesiology of accepting the guilt of others, the danger is that the 'guiltiest' church will regard itself as the most faithful church, that whatever it has suffered it has suffered for Christ. This may only compound the church's delusion about itself.

The warning against distinguishing degrees of guilt reveals the central concern to be the *fact* of human sinfulness before God, and the church's exhortation to recognize this fact. The church's confession of sin depends not primarily on an examination of conscience or historical past, nor on a specific examination of the world's sins which it vicariously assumes, but is at bottom a confession of faith in Christ. Bonhoeffer's point is that only the church knows that whatever these sins are, they are ultimately against God and redeemed only in Christ. The church's confession of sin is necessarily repetitive and continuous but as such is only tenuously grounded in history. What is acknowledged about the church's action in history – and the world's for that matter – is ultimately the *fact* that history is not yet conformed to God's intended purposes. The warning against sidelong glances is also warning against the church minimizing its guilt with self-justification. Thus, from the perspective of the church's penitential vocation, its mission is fulfilled by engaging less profoundly with its context rather than more so.

An abstract repentance is clearly contrary to what Bonhoeffer

---

[17] Dietrich Bonhoeffer, *Ethics*, trans. Neville Horton Smith (New York: Macmillan, 1955), 111.

intended. On an ethical rather than ecclesiological level, the concept of accepting guilt is intended to call Christians to concrete action even if all options reflect some complicity in sin. A theme of *The Cost of Discipleship* is that the preaching of forgiveness is cheap if it is not accompanied by repentance and amendment of life. It is not enough for the church 'simply to deplore in general terms that the sinfulness of man infects even his good works. It is necessary to point out concrete sins, and to punish and condemn them'.[18] It is noteworthy, however, that this call for repentance of concrete sins is directed to the individual. The church's role is to preach repentance to individuals and exercise the power of the keys. When the church confesses its corporate sins, the focus shifts to the Christologically grounded mechanism of vicariety and the danger of abstraction returns. The holiness Bonhoeffer identifies with the church's confession of sin is ultimately unable to account for the way in which ecclesial repentance names particular sins as its own and makes the discriminations of guilt necessary, even by 'sidelong glances', in order to amend its common life appropriately and undertake faithful social action. Ecclesial repentance helps to point to the particular character of sin, the specification of God's judgement and the spiritual vision required to discern. The indiscriminate acceptance of guilt hinders what I am taking to be a legitimate purpose of the church's task of repentance. If the church is the 'sorriest' institution around, it may come to take this state of affairs for granted and ignore particular sins for which it is directly responsible. Though this in itself would be an additional sin, the church will have lost the habits by which to identify this pattern, and turn in another direction.

Since World War II, statements of confession by the Evangelical Church in Germany gradually recognized greater degrees of responsibility for its action and inaction. Some initial statements that described the church's sinfulness as a strict consequence of universal sinfulness thereby minimized what had just happened. The 'Message to Congregations' approved at Treysa in 1945 made the general confession of the church's not being Christian enough, but did not touch concretely on things that were done or not done. One conservative church leader advocated keeping discussion of the church's guilt on a 'religious' level – as 'guilt from another world' – because

---

[18] Dietrich Bonhoeffer, *The Cost of Discipleship*, trans. R. H. Fuller (New York: Macmillan, 1963), 324.

in this way the church confessed that its sin was before God alone.[19] Since such a confession was universally true and a matter of faith, it did not necessarily point to any particular failure of its mission in history.

Gradually, the unique character of the church's action and inaction during the war was acknowledged. The trajectory I traced in Chapter 1 moved from recognition of how the church participated in secular anti-Semitism, to an examination of the roots of this anti-Semitism in the church's theology of Judaism. The Evangelical Church in Germany confessed in 2000 that the church's guilt was not limited to inaction and silence, or even just a failure to live out its convictions. It named the theological tradition of enmity towards Jews as having contributed to the church's complicity in the killing of Jews and as inhibiting a genuinely new relationship between church and the Jewish people.[20] Not only is the church's sinfulness an implication of the universal sinfulness of its members, but also it is bound to the church's responsibility for a historically specifiable failure to embody truthfully God's covenant with the Jewish people. Repentance requires a conversion in the church's theology – an epochal change in the church's self-identity. This is true because the church is actually rethinking its teaching about Judaism. While it might appear tautological to say that the church's attention to its historical past shows that it ought to give such attention to its past, it significant to say that the church's sinfulness cannot be considered apart from the concrete way the church has been an agent in history.

If indeed the action of the Holy Spirit to lead the church into truth may be seen through the church's repentance, then the church's holiness is manifest, at least in part, in the course of confession and repentance as it actually unfolds. In this way, the practice of ecclesial repentance reflects a shift in the terms of Protestant thinking about how the sinful church as it exists in history is also the holy church.

The Holy Church in Roman Catholic Theology

Incapable of sin, the holy church repents for the sins of its members. This succinct statement of official Catholic teaching is authoritatively expressed in various documents, including *Lumen Gentium*'s

---

[19] Matthew D. Hockenos, *A Church Divided: German Protestants Confront the Nazi Past* (Bloomington, IN: Indiana University Press, 2004), 71.

[20] Evangelical Church in Germany, 'Christians and Jews: A Manifesto 50 Years After the Weissensee Declaration' (2000).

reminder that 'the Church, embracing sinners in her bosom, is at the same time holy and always in need of purified',[21] and *Unitatis Redintegratio*'s qualification that on earth, the church is liable to sin 'in its members'.[22] It is clear from these phrases that Catholic ecclesiology negotiates the issue of sin and the holiness of the church in terms of a particular relationship between individual members and the church as a whole. Within these terms, the twentieth-century debate has moved from whether or how sinners are members of the church, to whether the church itself is sinful. The holy church clearly repents, but of whose sin? From the numerous studies on this issue,[23] it is evident that three authors loom large as influential and representative figures: Charles Journet, Yves Congar and Karl Rahner, as well as the conciliar documents already noted. The Day of Pardon service in particular, and Pope John Paul II's programme of ecclesial repentance more generally, have provided new points of reference for the ongoing debate.

Writing in the decades before Vatican II, Journet acknowledges that sinners are in the church, but defines the church such that sin itself is outside of it. For him, the church is as person whose soul is the Holy Spirit and whose formal cause is charity. The church is by definition sinless in virtue of the formal cause of its personhood. As the material cause of the church, members are members only in virtue of what is holy in them. The result is that the boundary of the church runs through each individual. What is sinful in each member is, necessarily, outside the church. In this way, the unblemished holiness of the church in Eph. 5.27 does refer to the Catholic Church in history, though its boundary can be seen only in faith. Because the formal cause of the church, charity, leads individuals to

---

[21] *Lumen Gentium*, no. 8.

[22] *Unitatis Redintegratio*, no. 3.

[23] The most comprehensive overview of these debates is found in the unpublished dissertation by Bernard E. Yetzer, whose analysis has helped me structure this section, 'Holiness and Sin in the Church: An Examination of *Lumen Gentium* and *Unitatis Redintegratio* of the Second Vatican Council', unpublished STD dissertation (Catholic University of America, 1988). See also Patrick McGoldrick, 'Sin and the Holy Church', *Irish Theological Quarterly* 32 (1965), 3–27; Avery Dulles, 'A Half Century of Ecclesiology', *Theological Studies* 50 (1989), 419–42; Herwi Rikhof, 'The Holiness of the Church', in *A Holy People: Jewish and Christian Perspectives on Religious Communal Identity*, ed. Marcel Poorthuis and Joshua Schwartz (Leiden: Brill, 2006), 321–35; Francis A. Sullivan, 'Do the Sins of Its Members Affect the Holiness of the Church?' in *In God's Hands: Essays on the Church & Ecumenism in Honour of Michael A. Fahey, S.J.*, ed. Michael S. Attridge and Jaroslav Z. Skira (Leuven: Peeters, 2006), 247–68.

repentance, there is a sense in which the church takes responsibility for repentance precisely to preserve its members in holiness while excluding their sin from the church as such.[24]

Though Congar agrees that the church does not sin, he criticizes Journet's formal conception of the church as not fully human. A church that contains only a part of each member cannot adequately identify the visible and historical institution that Catholic theology must affirm is truly the church. For Congar, the entire individual sinner is inside the church. In this sense, there is sin in the church though it does not become the sin *of* the church. The key for Congar is to view the one historical church from two different perspectives. The church in its members or human element, is sinful, though in its divine element remains the pure bride of Christ. He thus prodded Catholic theology towards a greater distinction between Christ and the pilgrim church, whose holiness is truly in Christ, but in history also imperfect and in need of purification and reform. Congar's historical sensibility is reflected in the acknowledgment that like other institutions, the church is liable to historical faults and misunderstandings resulting from inattention to context. Yet, he asserts that these faults are not sin. Historical faults point to the necessity of church reform, while the underlying sin is ascribed solely to individuals.[25]

Though some council fathers argued for a clear statement that the church is sinful, and others that it is sinless, Vatican II did not make a definitive judgement. One forceful intervention in the deliberation on *Lumen Gentium* was made by Bishop Stephen Laszlo who argued that in the presentation of the union between Christ and church, the distance between the penitent pilgrim church and Christ must be adequately drawn. On its eschatological journey, the people of God are a sinful people who constantly depend on the reception of God's grace.[26] Pope Paul VI's last minute intervention in another text (*Unitatis Redintegratio*), qualifying the sinfulness of the church as 'in its members', may be interpreted as keeping open the debate about whether the church itself is sinful, rather than closing debate.[27] Bernard Yetzer classifies the diverse interpretations of whether the

---

[24] Yetzer, 'Holiness and Sin in the Church', 12–29.

[25] *Ibid.*, 30–44.

[26] Stephen Laszlo, 'Sin in the Holy Church of God', in *Council Speeches of Vatican II*, ed. Hans Küng, Yves Congar, and Daniel O'Hanlon (Glen Rock, NJ: Paulist Press, 1964), 44–8.

[27] Thus Johannes Feiner, quoted in Robert Kress, '*Simul Justus et Peccator*: Ecclesiological and Ecumenical Perspectives', *Horizons* 11 (1984), 263.

logic of Vatican II implies a sinful church: some argued that it did (Rahner, Hans Küng, Heribert Mühlen, Gustave Martelet as well as Joseph Ratzinger and Avery Dulles immediately after the council), others that it did not (Journet, Congar and Gérard Philips, a primary drafter of *Lumen Gentium*), while a third group held a middle ground somewhere inbetween (Louis Bouyer, René Latourelle).[28]

In any case, the essentialist and triumphalist ecclesiology reflected in the 1943 encyclical *Mystici Corporis* and the construal of the church virtually over against its members was rejected in favour of portraying a more humble church in history. The vision of Vatican II places the church in the hands of Christ and Holy Spirit, who through it bring to completion the saving plan of the Father. The Spirit's work is primarily ecclesiological. By the Spirit the church grows towards its proper end on the basis of its true nature. This growth is realized by the Spirit's purifying of individuals and binding them ever closer to Christ.

The key concept of the 'genuine though imperfect holiness' of the pilgrim church is intended to capture this eschatological tension.[29] Whereas Journet wrestled with the problem of how sinners can be in the church, *Lumen Gentium* assumes that it is the church's mission precisely to incorporate sinners in order that they may be sanctified by the Spirit.[30] Thus, an 'imperfection' is proper to the pilgrim church on account of the sin of her members. Growth in holiness requires, among other things, that the members continually seek God's forgiveness for their sins.[31] Since the church's sanctifying mission is located in 'this passing world', it takes on the appearance of this world 'in its sacraments and institutions'. Even though the church will be perfect only 'in the glory of heaven', the pilgrim church is where the Holy Spirit continues the mission of Christ.[32]

The historical nature of the pilgrim church consists in the fact that it undergoes 'afflictions and hardships' in time. That the sins of its members truly wound the church,[33] rendering its temporal holiness 'imperfect', is intended to affirm that the subject of the Spirit's promise of indefectibility is the entire visible church. By God's grace,

---

[28] Yetzer, 'Holiness and Sin in the Church', 257–314.
[29] *Lumen Gentium*, no. 48.
[30] *Ibid.*, no. 8.
[31] *Ibid.*, no. 40.
[32] *Ibid.*, no. 48.
[33] *Ibid.*, no. 11.

the church will be preserved from the path that leads away from salvation.[34]

The decree *Unitatis Redintegratio* speaks most concretely to the collective dimension of personal sin, and its effect on the church's mission. Because its subject matter is a fact of historical circumstance – the divided churches – it is less concerned with the essence of the church than its historical shape. The 'sin of separation' is a reality, for which 'men of both sides were to blame'.[35] Though neither inevitable nor ingredient to the church's mystery, divisiveness has been present in the church from the beginning as seen, for example, in 1 Cor. 11.18–19. Furthermore, as a result of what is specified as the failures of members, 'the radiance of the Church's face shines less brightly'.[36]

The call for a 'change of heart' to be at the core of the renewal of the church, especially in ecumenism, is made particularly concrete in the following statement: '[I]n humble prayer, we beg pardon of God and of our separated brethren, just as we forgive those who trespass against us'.[37] It permanently placed repentance at the centre of ecumenical practice, a process by which the Spirit leads the church into unity, and thus into holiness. It is clear that the subject that asks pardon – the 'we' – is not the church but its mass of members. The preceding statement cites 1 Jn. 1.10 about the sinfulness of all. Yet, Karl Rahner argues that the overall logic of these conciliar documents is that the church which is always purifying itself, as in this request for pardon, must be purifying itself of the *church*'s sin: '[T]he Church cannot be the *subject* of her *own* renewal and purification if she was or is not also in the first place and in a certain sense the subject of sin and guilt'.[38]

In an article written prior to the council, Rahner rejects as 'ecclesiological Nestorianism' a view of the church that regards its institutional and visible dimension as merely human in contrast to a

---

[34] See *ibid.*, no. 12, and Richard R. Gaillardetz, *Teaching with Authority: A Theology of the Magisterium in the Church* (Collegeville, MN: Liturgical Press, 1997), 150.

[35] *Unitatis Redintegratio*, no. 3.

[36] *Ibid.*, no. 4.

[37] *Ibid.*, no. 7.

[38] Karl Rahner, 'The Sinful Church in the Decrees of Vatican II', in *Theological Investigations*, vol. 6, trans. Karl-H. Kruger and Boniface Kruger (Baltimore: Helicon Press, 1967), 285, italics in original.

true, spiritual, dimension (a danger in Congar's position).[39] To affirm the visible church as truly the church requires the recognition that even a sinner 'wandering far from God' is a member of the church, 'a part of the visible presence of God's grace in the world, a member of the Body of Christ!'[40] The logic of a sinful church follows: if the church's members 'are sinners and as sinners remain members, then [the church] herself is sinful'.[41] Though disavowing an illegitimate separation of the human and divine in the church, the two remain conceptually distinguished – in Christological terms Rahner's ecclesiology is more Leonine than Cyrillian – for the sake of relating them by means of the concept of sacrament.

As sacrament, the church signifies the visible and effective presence of God's grace in the world. As in the case of individual sacraments, which can be valid though unfruitful if not received in faith and charity, so a sinful member may be visibly part of the church but fail to display the fruits of the Spirit.[42] Since membership in the church cannot be separated from the visible and historical institution, a member of the institution is a member of the church. Yet, a sinful member undermines the sacramental purpose of the church, which is to concretely signify the grace of Christ to the world. As the church fails to be a fully effective signification of Christ in the world, through its members or activities, the church fails Christ, and yet is still the church through which God works. Rahner writes:

> But once we have honestly wept over the sins of the Church and our own sin, if in this confession of our fault it has dawned on us that all true holiness is a miracle of God and a grace and not something to be presumptuously taken for granted, then after being washed clean in the tears of repentance our eye may be capable of seeing clearly the sacred miracle which God daily renews in his Church: ... that the Spirit of God continually wakens men to holiness within her, ... that in her the Lord's act of redemption continually takes place to the end of time.[43]

Rahner's contribution is important because he starts from the traditional problem of how the individual sinner is in the church, and proceeds to make an argument which also addresses the fact that, as some perceived in 1947, the church itself had failed. Rahner affirms

---

[39] Karl Rahner, 'The Church of Sinners', in *Theological Investigations*, vol. 6, trans. Karl-H. Kruger and Boniface Kruger (Baltimore: Helicon Press, 1969), 258.
[40] *Ibid.*, 257.
[41] *Ibid.*, 260.
[42] *Ibid.*, 259. A similar distinction is made in *Lumen Gentium*, no. 14.
[43] Rahner, 'The Church of Sinners', 268.

that the church can be sinful as a historical actor in its specific actions, though he makes this argument primarily on the grounds of the sinfulness of individual members. Most visibly, the church is sinful when members of the hierarchy act sinfully in the name of the church.[44]

However, Johann-Baptist Metz famously noted that nowhere in Rahner's theology is Auschwitz mentioned.[45] Something in his theology is deficiently historical. Rahner wrestles with how the church can contain *some* sinners, especially those who are 'devoid of God's grace' and may be destined to eternal damnation.[46] It is not the church's actual corporate history, but rather a general theological anthropology, that provides for Rahner the decisive tension in the church's historical character. What is 'historical' about the sinful church is that it contains a succession of sinful members, who in time and space partially obscure the church's mediation of Christ to the world, while others in the church, assisted by grace, indeed reflect Christ's light to the world. In turn, the church is holy as it brings these sinners to repentance. With history as the sphere of the relation between individuals and the church, the church's history is conceived in terms of that basic relation, rather than as a story whose plot cannot be known in advance. What matters is the category of history, rather than the particular history in which the church acted as an agent in the torture of other Christians in sixteenth-century Europe, in the teaching of contempt for the Jews or in providing theological justifications for the enslavement of Africans. Yet, these all belong to the permanent history of the church, which at various times held these teachings and practices to be consistent with its call to holiness. Such a historical identity of the church, which admits the genuine mutations and epochal shifts characteristic of institutions in history, is not exhausted by the claim that the church at various times in the past, as now, contains sinners.

While Rahner is insufficiently concrete with respect to sin in the church, such concreteness is exhibited in his approach to saints in the church. He explains that faith in the holiness of the church affirms the actual and realized activity of the Spirit in history. The

---

[44] *Ibid.*, 261.

[45] Johann-Baptist Metz, 'Facing the Jews: Christian Theology After Auschwitz', in *Faith and the Future: Essays on Theology, Solidarity, and Modernity*, Johann-Baptist Metz and Jürgen Moltmann (Maryknoll, NY: Orbis, 1995), 40.

[46] Rahner, 'The Church of Sinners', 257.

canonization of saints reflects the church's belief that the Holy Spirit's presence is visible in the church, and as such can be pointed to from time to time with the certainty of faith. For Rahner, the life of a saint does not follow a rule laid out in advance; it is more akin to an adventure. While the existence of such saints is a corollary of the church's holiness, the form this takes is part of the church's 'genuine history ... of salvation and hence also of holiness'.[47] Holiness is not lessened by the surprising and unexpected forms of life and witness taken by saints – Rahner's examples include the unecclesiastical desert hermit and the daring scholar[48] – but truly expressed through them. It is only in retrospect that the church judges that a personally embodied adventure was truly holy living in that particular context, and as such is a permanent, public witness to the Holy Spirit in the church.[49]

In canonization, the church makes a definitive judgement about its actual history, and here the parallel with ecclesial repentance comes into focus. The holiness of the church is expressed not only in the fact that the church forms exemplary individuals, but in the judgements it makes through canonization that display its ability to discern the specific activity of the Spirit and its openness to being instructed by that activity. No saint is formally recognized as such during his or her lifetime; the church awaits signs from the Spirit of posthumous confirmation. Likewise, ecclesial repentance is premised on present judgements about which actions of the church were *not* Spirit-led and an openness to being instructed by this failure. The calling of the church to make such judgements, about saints as well as sin, suggests greater attention to how the Spirit sustains the church precisely through these judgements. When the church makes a judgement, expressed in a solemn statement of repentance, about how its witness was obscured in the past, it is making a judgement about an ecclesial dimension of its past as church, not just about individual members. Just as the meaning of a saint's life is recognized posthumously through canonization, so the meaning of anti-Jewish theology is recognized through repentance as having truly ecclesial dimensions, even though individuals in the past may not have recognized their subjective complicity in it. The

---

[47] Karl Rahner, 'The Church of the Saints', in *Theological Investigations*, vol. 3, trans. Karl-H. Kruger and Boniface Kruger (Baltimore: Helicon Press, 1967), 99.
[48] *Ibid.*, 100.
[49] *Ibid.*, 103.

relation of the individual to the church is thus not the only way that sin harms the church.

A (Catholic) Theology of a Sinful Church

Assuming that Vatican II and Pope Paul VI intended to leave open the question of whether the church sins, then even despite the fact that many of Pope John Paul II's statements have advanced one side of this debate, there is room within even a Roman Catholic framework to argue that actual acts of ecclesial repentance are evidence for the position that the church is indeed sinful. Before briefly examining some Catholic theologians' arguments to this effect, I examine how actual repentance texts, especially the 1997 Drancy Declaration of the French Bishops, add to the debate.

There have been various instances of the term 'sinful church' in official discourse, including one by Pope John Paul II.[50] In the flurry of responses to the clergy sexual abuse scandal, Pope Benedict XVI referred to the church as 'wounded and sinful'.[51] The West German Bishops' 1988 statement about the 'sinful Church in need of conversion', was repeated in the German Bishops' 1995 document, dispelling the possibility that the initial expression was unintentional.[52] In an earlier statement, they spoke about 'our church's guilt'.[53] The Swiss Bishops confessed culpability and asked pardon for what churches did during the war. The Catholic Church's submission to South Africa's TRC identified silence as the 'church's greatest sin'.[54] In the Drancy Declaration, the French Bishops referred to the failing of the church – a concept Congar insisted did not imply ecclesial sin – as 'this sin'.[55]

---

[50] In a speech at Fatima, Portugal on 12 May 1982, he referred to 'the living, holy and sinful church'. Cited in Joseph A. Komonchak, 'Preparing for the New Millennium', *Logos: A Journal of Catholic Thought* 1, no. 2 (1997), 44.

[51] 'The Comfort of Not Being Alone', *L'Osservatore Romano*, English edition, 28 April 2010, 2.

[52] Catholic Bishops of West Germany, Austria, and Berlin, 'Accepting the Burden of History' (1988); German Catholic Bishops, 'Opportunity to Re-Examine Relationships with the Jews' (1995).

[53] West German Catholic Bishops, 'A Change of Attitude Towards the Jewish People's History of Faith' (1975).

[54] Catholic Church in South Africa, 'Submission to the Truth and Reconciliation Commission' (1997).

[55] French Catholic Bishops, Drancy Declaration, (1997). Sin appears to be ascribed to the church in the following statements as well: Archbishop Michael Sheehan, ' "Mea Culpas" for Service of Reconciliation', *Origins* 29, no. 40 (23 March 2000), 654–5;

In its most explicit statements, Drancy assigns sin to individuals, even as it cautions against simple judgement of individuals who at the time did not know what we now know. Yet, a sinful church is implicitly affirmed. In accounting for the inadequacy of the church's response during the Holocaust, Drancy identified the 'ecclesiastical interests' that 'took priority over the demands of conscience', and the 'conformity, prudence and abstention' motivated by 'fear of reprisals against the church's activities'.[56] While these failures may be accorded to the fears, interests and sins of individuals, the effect of 'ecclesiastical interests' also shows that institutional structures perpetuate their own logic. An inadequate ecclesiology may lie at the root of an inordinate love for the church as institution, one that equates its visible holiness with institutional preservation. This suggests a failure in the church's teaching, particularly about itself.

In various Catholic documents repenting for offences against the Jewish people, and especially Drancy, the authors search for reasons why the church was blind to the plight of the Jews. Here too, the church's actual teaching is faulted. The bishops declared that the anti-Jewish prejudice of Christians has its source not only in secular anti-Semitism but in the 'anti-Jewish tradition [which] stamped its mark in differing ways on Christian doctrine and teaching, in theology, apologetics, preaching and in the liturgy'.[57] Preaching and teaching, though done by individuals, become as such the action of the church. Church teaching is not limited to solemn statements by the highest authority, but includes what is actually taught and received as teaching. The confession that the church's failures are linked to inadequacies in its liturgical life, in which is manifest 'the real nature of the true Church'[58] is a remarkable acknowledgement that, as it examines its history, the church finds the roots of sin even in its practice of worship.

Drancy is concerned not only with the problem of sinners in the church, but the way in which the church was unable to name its own sin and consequently how the church itself aided and abetted personal sin. Drancy confesses that pastors must bear a particular

---

Cardinal Roger Mahony, 'Mapping the Road to Reconciliation: Message of Apology', *Origins* 29, no. 40 (23 March 2000), 652–3; Bishop Robert Morlino, 'Service for the Healing of Memories', *Origins* 31, no. 23 (15 November 2001), 381, 383–5.

[56] French Catholic Bishops, Drancy Declaration (1997).

[57] *Ibid.*

[58] Second Vatican Council, *Sacrosanctum Concilium: Constitution on the Sacred Liturgy*, no. 2 (1963).

responsibility for letting prejudice and indifference go unchallenged, even though some spoke up. If the church promoted a since-repudiated anti-Judaism, then the sin of these individual pastors was partly in their failure to be prophetic voices *to* the church; that is, to name, confess, and correct the actions of a sinful church. That the church 'failed in her mission as teacher of consciences' names the degenerative dimension of ecclesial sin.[59] The church ought to be a school of holiness, or to switch metaphors, a fertile mother generating children in the Spirit. Instead, the church failed to nurture the consciences of its members by which they might have resisted participating in evil. To be a cause of the sin of another is to be guilty of a sin. In repenting for these personal sins, the church is separated by one degree from its own.

A (partial) failure of the mission of the church is a serious state of affairs, especially within a sacramental ecclesiology. To be sure, the promise of the Holy Spirit to abide ensures that the church will not fail entirely and cease to be the path of salvation, yet ecclesial repentance points to the ways in which the church has partially obscured the light of Christ's face to the world. In the Day of Pardon litany, the pope confessed that particular acts and attitudes of Christians sullied the very face of Christ.[60] Drancy declared that church leaders

> failed to realize that the church, called at that moment to play the role of defender within a social body that was falling apart, did in fact have considerable power and influence, and that in the face of the silence of other institutions, its voice could have echoed loudly by taking a definitive stand against the irreparable.[61]

If personal sin is, at its core, disobedience to what God has called humans to be, then the church's disobedience to its calling is ecclesial sin. Yet, as the Drancy text shows, the particular form of disobedience, and consequently how it might be avoided in the future, matters profoundly.

Bradford Hinze highlights what he sees as the problematic tension between ecclesial repentance and the assertion that only individuals sin. He recognizes the magisterium's concern that ascribing sin to structures may give individuals excuse to deny personal responsibility. Nevertheless, he believes social sin is a useful category, and names what in fact many churches are repenting of, even if only

---

[59] French Catholic Bishops, Drancy Declaration (1997).
[60] Pope John Paul II, Universal Prayer, Day of Pardon, 12 March 2000.
[61] French Catholic Bishops, Drancy Declaration (1997).

implicitly. For Hinze, social sin functions as ideology and blindness, and exists in the church as well as society. This idea that there are not only social effects of personal sin, but institutionalized patterns or structures that produce the fruits of sin, will be examined more closely in the next chapter. What matters here is the situation the French Bishops identified in which the church need not have been aware it was sinning. At one time the church was largely blind to those things for which it has since repented. Where the sin of the church is concerned, a network of influential leaders, teachings and practices, may all constellate to legitimate silence in the face of Jewish persecution, for example, such that many Christians will believe it is compatible with Christian faith. The church need not be collectively guilty in a 'fully volitional' sense to be collectively responsible and accountable, and to repent.[62] Hinze argues that dialogue, especially with marginalized groups, in necessary if the church is to identify its false consciousness and institute reforms. The obligation to dialogue falls to a sinful church.

Francis Sullivan and Joseph Komonchak rely heavily on Rahner's account of how the church has sullied its face to press their argument for speaking of a sinful church. With Rahner, they warn against a hypostasized or reified church standing over against the church in history. Sullivan concludes that it is fitting that 'the pilgrim people of God should confess its faults'[63] – 'its faults' as a single subject rather than just those of individual members. According to Komonchak, the mystery of the church is 'God's holy presence in the imperfect human community'. The 'concrete community of believers' is both blessed by God and in need of repentance.[64]

In Chapter 4, I identified a significant ambiguity in *Memory and Reconciliation* about who is the agent of the sin of which the church is repenting. That document, together with most authoritative reflections on acts of ecclesial repentance by the Catholic Church, insists that the church is not repenting for the subjective guilt of individuals who have died. Rather, the church addresses the objective dimension of what its members have done, and the memories and consequences that render this past present. The danger is that moral agency will drop out of view entirely. If the church repents for consequences, obstacles, burdens or

---

[62] Bradford E. Hinze, 'Ecclesial Repentance and the Demands of Dialogue', *Theological Studies* 61 (2000), 229–31.

[63] Sullivan, 'Sins of Its Members', 286.

[64] Komonchak, 'Preparing for the New Millennium', 50.

memories, then repentance is for a state of affairs but not for sin, because there are no agents who properly bear the guilt and responsibility that attaches to this sin. That would be regret but not repentance. When this is considered in light of the concern of the Catholic magisterium that the concept of social sin not serve to eliminate responsibility for sin, that is, at the personal level,[65] then the problem with insisting that only individuals sin and that the church does not judge or repent for what those individuals would have known to be sin, becomes apparent. The irony is that the insistence that sin is only personal appears to render an act like the Day of Pardon to be repentance for sins without agents who committed them. If there is no guilty agent, who is in need of forgiveness?

Official Catholic documents respond that the church acts as a single theological subject, and as such nevertheless repents for the sins of its members, including deceased members. It appears that the church's subjective assumption of the sins of others (its members), for the sake of repentance, follows the analogy with Christ's assumption of human sin. But this contributes to the problematic ecclesiology of a church over and above its members. The church which voluntarily assumes these alien sins is thus not really an agent guilty for the consequences, obstacles, burdens, or memories of which it repents. However, I believe it possible for even Catholic theology to say that the church finds itself with the objective responsibility to repent. The church is rendered a single theological subject by the Holy Spirit for the sake of its mission, and disobedience to that mission is sin for which the church repents. In the previous chapter, I argued that it is repentance itself, as a work of the Holy Spirit premised on the communion-constituting bonds of Christ's forgiveness, that provides the link from past to present so that the church is freed for its future. It is in repentance that sins of many are fully reckoned as the sins of the church. This preserves the link between sin and responsibility, and responsibility and repentance. Through repentance in the Spirit, the church is thereby conformed ever more to the body it is called to be.

In addition to arguments about how ecclesial repentance already implies the sinfulness of the church, there are several pastoral reasons why this theological concept ought to be developed in order to realize the aims expressed by the church's penitence. The

---

[65] Especially John Paul II, *Reconciliatio et Paenitentia: Apostolic Exhortation on Reconciliation and Penance* (1984), no. 16.

pastoral function of doctrine – how it helps the church to be faithful in the twenty-first century and effectively communicate what it has received from Christ – is implicit in the public character of ecclesial repentance. If one of the underlying assumptions of the emergence of ecclesial repentance in recent decades is the recognition that the church's identity and mission is embodied in particular historical contexts, and that acknowledging when and where it has failed to read the signs of the times better equips it to do so in the future, then the idioms in which its repentance is communicated cannot be separated from its meaning. The reason that Christ sanctifies the church by uniting himself with it, is so that the church as whole and all its members produce a 'shining witness' to the world.[66]

Whether consciously or not, penitent churches are addressing at least four audiences: a wider world suspicious of insulated, self-assured, totalizing institutions; communities with whom concrete reconciliation is sought (other churches, the Jewish people, racial/ethnic groups); the church's own often disillusioned members; and its members whose consciences the church seeks to form (a constituency that will be considered further in Chapter 7). In each of these cases, there are compelling practical reasons why the term 'sinful church' opens the space in which the church may give testimony to the nature and source of its holiness.

A key feature of postmodernity is the recognition of the limits of any perspective. In such a context, the church's grand claims about its access to the truth encounters significant resistance. Yet, faith in Jesus Christ as the truth, and in the Spirit's abiding presence in the church is not inconsistent with an embodied humility that regards this presence as not a possession but a continually received gift, mediated by a variety of 'others'. In addition to its set-apartness, the 'otherness' of the holy church may also refer its own brokenness, limitedness, and thus the need for voices from outside of itself. Lieven Boeve argues that in such a postmodern context 'only those narratives which admit to the specificity and limitedness of their own perspective and which witness to the impossibility of integrating the remainder are worthy of any claim to legitimacy'.[67] The church's acknowledgement of its sinfulness church suggests not only that the church is listening, but recognizes its need to listen. By truthfully

---

[66] *Lumen Gentium*, no. 39.

[67] Lieven Boeve, *Interrupting Tradition: An Essay on Christian Faith in a Postmodern Context* (Leuven: Peeters Press, 2003), 91.

naming its sinfulness, the church proclaims that since it is not the Kingdom come, it must actively discern where and how the Spirit is speaking, guiding and correcting it.

If reconciliation is a goal, then neither the intention of the church nor the way acts of corporate repentance and accompanying documents are received by those who have been harmed are incidental. The Catholic Church's insistence that its conduct as a church was without sin during the Holocaust was widely criticized as self-justifying. Ascribing errors to rogue individuals only reinforces the perception that the church constantly redefines itself to remain morally pure. By and large, Jewish people did not hear in *We Remember* a church truly contrite about its historical past, throwing itself on God's mercy. Unless this is heard by others, the mutual understanding towards which ecclesial repentance aspires, and within which the more subtle distinctions of how the church's holiness is related to sin, will not be received.

Finally, church members themselves may become disillusioned with the church when there is a disconnection between the church as it ought to be and the church as it is. The connection may be bridged by 'sinful church' language that portrays the often disappointing reality of church life, together with the affirmation that the Spirit nevertheless works through the church. Disillusionment with the church, particularly its institutional dimension, is not a new pastoral challenge. Michael McCarthy proposes drawing on how Augustine addressed this issue to help the contemporary Catholic Church respond to those disillusioned by the recent sexual abuse scandal. The problem with the ecclesiology of the sinless church, according to McCarthy, is that it 'not only underplays the full symbolic reality of the Church but invites idealization, and in doing so reinscribes the conditions of disillusionment'.[68] The disconnection between the proclamation of the moral purity of the church and the experience of the actual church accelerates disillusionment and abandonment of the church. Augustine's teaching about the eschatological grounding of the church's holiness gave him conceptual tools for embracing the ambiguity of the earthly church. Furthermore, Augustine would warn against the danger that a formal distinction of the church and its members might function to mask sin, rather than confess it.[69]

---

[68] Michael C. McCarthy, 'Religious Disillusionment and the Cross: An Augustinian Reflection', *Heythrop Journal* 48 (2007), 584.

[69] *Ibid.*, 588. McCarthy is therefore critical that *Memory and Reconciliation* interprets

Disillusionment due to the church's hypocrisy is minimized where there is a recognition that the church's ambivalent performance is nevertheless a fact of the church's life. The pastoral intention is not to thereby lower ethical standards, though it has been charged that such was Augustine's effect, but to form the church to see its actual holiness only in relation to the cross, God's perfection in humility.

Finding the Penitential Body in History

The repentance texts under consideration rarely reflect directly on what their action implies about the holiness of the church in general. Their purpose is rather to signal a practical turning of the church in a new direction concerning anti-Semitism and relations with the Jewish people, for instance. However, two implicit assumptions in these texts are worth identifying and testing. First, churches assume that whatever past sin is being confessed, it did not render the church something other than the church. Thus, the West German Bishops stated that even the church in need of conversion is to be honoured as mystery. And if it was the church, then it was the holy church of God. Though some critics may claim that such a betrayal renders the church no church at all, this is not the perspective implicit in church's practice of repentance.

Second, if sin does not extinguish the very existence of the church, then neither does the acknowledgment of that sin in repentance. A church may debate the advisability of particular statement of repentance, whether such an action will shake the faith of some in the church or whether the act of repentance will contribute to practical healing. But churches that have embarked on a course of repentance typically talk about how fidelity to the gospel mandates their action. This is usually stated negatively, in terms of the necessity to turn from the sin that is contrary to or undermines the calling of the church. The very identity of the church demands that the church make a radical change of direction, repent, and resolve to act differently. In this conviction the church holds that it is being obedient to Christ whose body it is, and whose Spirit vivifies it at all times. In the circumstances in which a church finds itself, repentance may be an expression of the very nature and mission of the church, and thus of its holiness.

There is then a temporal dimension to the question of holiness

---

Augustine's reminder that the church prays daily for forgiveness as evidence for a distinction between church and members, rather than as a pointer to God as the fount of all forgiveness, 585–6.

as it pertains to repentance for sins past. In the previous chapter, I developed an account of how the church in history is inextricably linked to God's triune action. I proposed that to the extent that ecclesial repentance is an action of the Holy Spirit, such repentance constitutes the continuity with the church's sinful past and its present whereby it is freed for its future. Developing further this notion of the historical career of the church, I pay particular attention to how the church's holiness is an implication of the promise of the Spirit to abide with the church and lead it into all truth.

That the church exists to repent, and actually does repent, is already an implicit affirmation that the church has not made a decision so irrevocable that it has ceased to exist.[70] It makes the scandalous claim that the Spirit was abiding with the church even as it espoused anti-Jewish theology, blessed racism, and sanctioned religious violence. The nature of the Spirit's presence in that church must not be taken to imply any minimization of the seriousness of those offences, let alone their justification. The crucial question is *how* the Spirit abides with a sinful church. The argument of the previous chapter suggests that the Spirit may be active in its leading the church into greater faithfulness by means of a practice of public repentance.

For example, the holiness of the slaveholding Church of England may be identified with the repentance for this sin that lay in its future. It is through its repentance and repudiation of this sin that the church's history of holiness encompasses its history of slaveholding. This holiness is not the church's 'progress' in understanding, but the way in which it subjects itself to the Spirit's action. As Rowan Williams writes, 'We can only be grateful that even a slave-owning Church had just enough sensitivity to the challenge of the gospel for a protest to be generated (however slowly) ... '[71] The church's openness to the action of the Spirit may indeed be mediated by a prophetic voice, the recovery of a long-obscured biblical truth, or the cry of an oppressed people. The key is that the holiness of the church has an irreducibly

---

[70] Dealing with a different set of issues, Robert W. Jenson examines the reversibility and irreversibility of ecclesial decisions, the latter being when the church 'bets her future self-identity' such that 'if the choice were faithless to the gospel there would be no church thereafter extant to reverse it'. *Systematic Theology: The Works of God*, vol. 2 (Oxford: Oxford University Press, 1999), 239. A penitent church, however, exists to repent.

[71] Rowan Williams, *Resurrection: Interpreting the Easter Gospel*, rev. ed. (Cleveland: Pilgrim Press, 2002), 58–9.

temporal dimension in which a present act of repentance relates to the past within the economy of the Holy Spirit.

Though there remains a temptation to see holiness as a supplement to the church's historical dimension or as the transcendence of it, Jesus Christ is not holy despite the incarnation, but in and through it. By implication, the church does not find itself in history nor does it find itself full of sinful members accidentally. The holiness of the church is grounded in the fact that this church exists where it is, as the body of Christ, because there God intends it. My point is not that the church is made holy by repentance. Just as ecclesial repentance reminds the church that a long view is required in order to judge its action, so a long view is required to determine even the faithfulness of repentance. Rather, repentance for past wrongs by the church that Christians already confess as holy may help us to better understand how the church's historicity is precisely its nature and mission – its place in God. To say that the church is holy in its historical identity is an affirmation of faith that cannot be confirmed by empirical observation. At the same time, since God has already chosen the church as the place where the body of Christ is, a body that God has already made visible in the incarnation, it is possible that the Holy Spirit is making holiness visible in and through ecclesial repentance. This provides the framework within which to consider more closely how the church's holiness might be reframed in light of the actual sinful history that churches have confessed.

IDENTITY OF A PENITENT CHURCH IN RELATION TO JUDAISM

The recognition of the sinful dimensions of traditional Christian teaching on Judaism has profound implications for Christian theology and practice. As discussed in Chapter 1, churches have acknowledged connections between their theologies of Judaism and anti-Semitism, violence against Jews and complicity in the Holocaust. This recognition led to renewed dialogue with Jewish people, new lenses for the interpretation of scripture and a rejection of supersessionist theology.[72] One church declared that only as the church repents and

---

[72] The ten theses of the Christian Scholars Group on Christian–Jewish Relations succinctly expresses this theological reorientation, 'A Sacred Obligation: Rethinking Christian Faith in Relation to Judaism and Jewish People', in *Seeing Judaism Anew: Christianity's Sacred Obligation*, ed. Mary C. Boys (Lanham, MD: Sheed & Ward, 2005), xiii–xix.

converts does it discover the common witness of Christians and Jews.[73] In this section, I examine the implication of the fact that churches have repented of a sinful relationship to Judaism and suggest one aspect of the common witness that comes into focus. I argue that an inadequate understanding of the church's holiness is related to its inadequate understanding of Judaism. As the church repents and corrects its supersessionist theology, it deepens its own account of what it means to be holy.

As traditions such as the Presbyterian Church (USA), the United Church of Canada, the Evangelical Lutheran Church in America, the Evangelical Church in Germany and the Roman Catholic Church each pledged commitment to a non-supersessionist theology, they proclaimed that the Holy Spirit is calling for more than just tinkering, but a reorienting of doctrinal, liturgical, ethical and missionary lives. However, just how this commitment may be held together with traditional Christian confessions about the person and work of Jesus Christ, for example, is not always entirely clear, a situation acknowledged in one denominational text.[74] As a result, Christian theology must anticipate disorientation and practice patience. Writing in the early twentieth century, theologian James Parkes estimated that it might take 300 years for such changes to be digested and integrated.[75] The church is not a finished product, not only because the church dwells in the midst of history, but because in the midst of that history God's Spirit continues to do a new thing.

Repentance statements that begin to forge new theological understandings are underwritten by the practice of Christian-Jewish dialogue, and in turn call for further dialogue. The challenge for the church is to meet itself differently in conversation with the Jewish people. Though mutual understanding may be a fruit of this encounter, it is required theologically. If Christians and Jews worship the same God, and find themselves in different covenantal relationships with that God, then the faithfulness of each requires the testimony of the other. That is, each side is called to truly hear God through the beliefs and practices of the other.

---

[73] Evangelical Church of the Rhineland, 'Towards Renovation of the Relationship of Christians and Jews' (1980), no. 4.

[74] Presbyterian Church (USA), 'A Theological Understanding of the Relationship Between Christians and Jews', (1987), nos. 2, 4.

[75] Alice L. Eckardt, 'Revising Christian Teaching: The Work of the Christian Scholars Group on Christian–Jewish Relations', in *Seeing Judaism Anew: Christianity's Sacred Obligation*, ed. Mary C. Boys (Lanham, MD: Sheed & Ward, 2005), 264.

Rabbi Irving Greenberg, addressing Jews but also Christians, writes that theology after Auschwitz must continually wrestle with its own brokenness and limit as necessary elements in its witness to truth.[76] Theology itself must embody a provisionality and an inadequacy befitting of the human condition before God:

> The one thing we know for sure is that a satisfactory or even a full resolution of the tormenting questions raised by the Shoah, in any direction, is wrong. It is almost certainly achieved by not taking some aspect of this surd sufficiently seriously. After the Holocaust, there should be no final solutions, not even theological.[77]

Thus, it may be most important for the church to be self-conscious of the ways in which it *cannot* fully articulate the relationship of the two covenants.

For the church to be unable to give a final account of itself in relation to Judaism, and thus of its nature and mission as church, is a fitting display of the church amidst the brokenness in which it participates. Thus, the church in time, and theology as the church's speech, find themselves under judgement. An appropriate theology will be a penitent theology which 'supremely resists the urge to finish and close what is being said'.[78] Cultivating such discourse opens the church to the epochal changes to its self-identity, demanded by a renewed relationship with Judaism. Though history is characterized by brokenness, it is not uniform or homogeneous. Rather, as the sphere in which the Spirit works, some present convictions will be unsettled while others are deepened. The non-closure of theology is the condition that it might in fact refer to the church whose mission is in and among the broken.

The relation between God's holiness and God's judgement emerges especially in the prophetic literature. The holy God of Israel demands the faith and obedience of a people who turn constantly to both idolatry and injustice. Israel's purity is violated not only by failures of its cultic obligations, but also in its obligations to all aspects of the law. Though rarely a theme in discussions of holiness as a mark of the church, ecclesial repentance points to the importance of the church hearing a word of judgement and submitting to the judgement and

---

[76] Irving Greenberg, 'Theology After the Shoah: The Transformation of the Core Paradigm', *Modern Judaism* 26 (2006), 227.

[77] Irving Greenberg, 'The Church as Sacrament and as Institution: Jewish Reflections', in *Ethics in the Shadow of the Holocaust: Christian and Jewish Perspectives*, ed. Judith H. Banki and John T. Pawlikowski (Franklin, WI: Sheed & Ward, 2001), 74.

[78] Rowan Williams, *On Christian Theology* (Malden, MA: Blackwell, 2000), 5.

justice of God. There is a renewed opportunity for the church to receive what John Webster calls 'an alien holiness'. This holiness is not any achieved perfection, nor even the church's moral self-discovery but is 'visible as humble acknowledgement of sin and as prayer for forgiveness'.[79] However, in order to know how to pray, this acknowledgement of sin must be rooted in the particularity of blindness to God's promises to the Jewish people and of reserving to the church God's exclusive interest. The church cannot deny that the preponderance of the supersessionist theological tradition is part of its historical identity, even if it now confesses the belief as incompatible with the God it worships. The church whose alien holiness is displayed in the acknowledgment of God's particular judgement and prayer for forgiveness is not an ideal church, but the actual church. The ideal church is not the holy church. There is no continuity between the two because the holy church exists in history while the ideal church, lacking members in the flesh, is as such not the church at all.

Several repentance statements point out that wrong interpretation of scripture contributed to supersessionism, though it is also the case that supersessionist convictions shaped the reading of scripture. R. Kendall Soulen demonstrates how supersessionism became intertwined with the church's 'standard canonical narrative'. As variously expressed by authors such as Justin Martyr, Ireneaus, Schleiermacher, Barth and Rahner, the net effect was a framework for interpreting the biblical story that proceeds from creation and fall to redemption in Christ and final consummation. The idea that Genesis 1–3 is all that is essential in the Old Testament for the history of salvation is woven deeply into Christian consciousness. In this model, God's identity as the God of Israel in covenant with a particular people is rendered 'ultimately indecisive for understanding how God's works as Consummator and as Redeemer engage creation in lasting and universal ways'.[80] The result is a flight from history. The particularity of God's enduring relationship with actual Jewish bodies is rejected in favour of imagining a universal humanity standing in relationship to God.

The inability to see the shape of God's relationship with the people of Israel as decisive for shaping conclusions about who God is is certainly parallel to, if not a cause of, a similar inability with respect

---

[79] John Webster, *Holiness* (London: SCM Press, 2003), 73.

[80] R. Kendall Soulen, *The God of Israel and Christian Theology* (Minneapolis: Fortress Press, 1996), 16.

to the actual history of the church. To conceive of God as primarily engaged with a universal humanity reinforces the idea of the church as essentially abstract and spiritual, standing over against its imperfect historical shadow. Supersessionism draws the eyes of faith away from historical particularity and towards an unmediated relationship of humanity with God. Such a framework supports both the Protestant preference for the fact of repentance over its historical content, and the Catholic inclination to distinguish a sinless institution from its actual members. Neither sees history as the ineluctable sphere in which God has a differentiated yet ongoing relationship with the Christian community.

Along similar lines, George Lindbeck argues that the core of the misreading has been in the church's failure to interpret Israel as the *people* of God, and thus to see itself in the mirror of the entire history of the people Israel. Widespread Christian practice interpreted the good elements in Israel's history as prefiguring Christ, while the bad elements were taken to reflect Jewish and general human sinfulness. By this interpretive strategy, elements of the story are isolated and abstracted from their proper place in the narrative construal of a whole people in relation to God. This not only misreads particular episodes, such as Abram's response to God's call or the golden calf, but fails to depict the identity of the people through its history of *both* faithfulness and unfaithfulness. To read the history of the people is to consider their entire, often ambiguous, history. Supersessionism therefore does not even view salvation as the replacement of one people by another, but rather the emergence of a new religion from a rejected Israel. As the church comes to see itself in relation to Israel – statements of ecclesial repentance repeatedly pledge the church to do so – it ought to see its own peoplehood in the mirror of the entirety of Israel's covenantal history, and more importantly to see God's faithfulness to Israel in light of Israel's unfaithfulness..[81]

A key premise of supersessionism is that Israel's election is revocable, because it has in fact been revoked for unfaithfulness. A church convicted of this sees its own faithfulness or moral achievement rather than election as the basis for its identity in God. This logic of revocability recurred in the Reformation charge that a sinful Roman Church ceased to be the church at all. Lindbeck points out how this

---

[81] George Lindbeck, 'The Church as Israel: Ecclesiology and Ecumenism', in *Jews and Christians: People of God*, ed. Carl E. Braaten and Robert W. Jenson (Grand Rapids: Eerdmans, 2003), 78–94.

perceived precariousness of the church's identity, exacerbated by the solidification of Reformation-era divisions, led churches to construe faithfulness in terms of specific 'segregated aspects' of its life – such as apostolic succession, true doctrine, conversion experiences, or various forms of moral purity – as evidence that, unlike Israel, it has not been rejected by God for unfaithfulness.[82] In this polemical context, appeals by one church to typify 'Israel' were limited to the Old Testament framework in which a faithful remnant (church) remained, but rivals were rejected. But the typology did not extend to Israel's continued existence beyond the coming of Christ. According to this logic, since Israel as whole ceased to be God's covenant partner after one decisive act of unfaithfulness – the rejection of Jesus as Messiah – therefore no church would acknowledge a historically particular act of corporate disobedience lest a similar judgement be rendered to it. Lindbeck concludes, 'Unless election is irrevocable for Israel, Christians cannot see their communities as the prophets saw Israel, as the adulterous spouse whom the Lord God may cast off for a time but has irreversibly promised never to cease loving, never to divorce'.[83]

The vicious circularity in this logic is precisely the point. Refusing to repent communally, the church cannot see itself as the people Israel; yet without seeing itself in this way it will not repent. On the Catholic side, it will not repent as church, and on the Protestant side it may do so as a consequence of universal sinfulness but not due to a particular history. The implication for how the church understands holiness follows. The church refuses to see itself under judgement, and concludes that it is holy because it is not judged negatively.

So how was a vicious cycle broken? I am not equipped to answer as a historian, but as a theologian I suspect the church will eventually come to its own account. To say it was the Spirit may be one answer the church will eventually give, though it ought to do so in a way that resists a simple idea of progress. Nevertheless, it may be by an intervention of the Holy Spirit that in repentance for offences against the Jewish people, several churches have reexamined their theology and affirmed what turns out to have been a condition of their repentance in the first place: God's promises to the Jewish people have not been revoked. If God's promise to Israel is not revoked, then the Spirit's presence in the church need not be removed for forgetting this

[82] *Ibid.*, 92–3.
[83] *Ibid.*, 94.

promise. That the church's holiness is tied to the election of the church as a people, in the entirety of their history of faithfulness and unfaithfulness, frees the church to see how repentance for any sin is possible, even required, *within* this election. But the fact of the church's doubt in God's trustworthiness does not signal the end of the Christian covenant.

The status of Jesus Christ remains a difficult point of conversation between Christians and Jews. The traditional charge that the Jews killed Jesus has justified in practice Christian violence against Jews throughout Christian history. In light of this legacy, there is an important way that the churches ought to claim the cross in the very moment they repent of misusing the cross against Jews. A recovery of the Jewishness of Jesus and the significance of this fact for the interpretation of his life and ministry has already been a key contribution of biblical scholarship for decades. There is a broad recognition that Jesus' life and ministry was thoroughly Jewish in context and that he preached a message of renewal to the people of Israel. However, there is a need to extend the analysis further, to remember the Jewishness of Jesus on the cross together with the identity of the Second Person of the Trinity.

The cruciform shape of the church's repentance is particularly vivid to the extent that Jesus is made the victim of the disciples' own crime. Jesus' followers abandoned him and became complicit in his death. Jesus' resurrection glorified the victim of precisely those who heard his message and then preached it. Rowan Williams cautions against seeing in God's choice of Jesus a merely abstract preference for the poor or the victim. This preference is particular and self-involving; it is 'our' victim that as God's chosen becomes the basis for hope. 'To hear the good news of salvation, to be converted, is to turn back to the condemned and rejected, acknowledging that there is hope nowhere else ... [S]alvation does not bypass history and memory of guilt, but rather builds upon it and from it'.[84]

Williams does not deny the universal dimension of human sin against Jesus, nor Jesus' assumption of that sin. Rather, the universality of human sin is expressed in particular forms not limited to the actions of the disciples but extended to all who encounter the risen Jesus as living lord. In just this way, Jesus is always 'our' victim. In light of the history of theologically 'justified' religious violence against Jews and the church's denial of God's faithfulness to the Jewish

---

[84] Williams, *Resurrection*, 6.

people, the image of a Jewish man on a cross assumes new poignancy. On the cross, Jesus suffers the sin of the church. On the cross, Jesus suffers the sin of the church against his own people, the Jews. In confessing its sin against the Jewish people, the church must see on the cross its own sin against the particular flesh of Jesus, and thus its hope in direct relation to the gracious promises of God attached to that flesh.

The encounter with this Jesus who suffers at the hands of his first followers, and now the church, contains the promise of the forgiveness of this sin. In this case, conversion is the turning to the actual victim, the Jewish Jesus crucified, now glorified.

> The formulation, 'Repent and believe', stresses that God's forgiveness cannot be abstract and general: the authentic word of forgiveness, newness and resurrection is audible when we acknowledge ourselves as oppressors and 'return' to our victims in the sense of learning who and where they are.[85]

Thus, the turning to Jesus implies and includes the simultaneous turning to the history of Christian betrayal, and the turning to those present Jewish communities who embody what was seemingly denied on the cross but vindicated in the resurrection.

Conforming the Body of Christ Over Time

The church does not secure its own future, not even in repentance. Yet, given the fact of repentance, the theological task is to examine what the possibility that repentance is a work of the Spirit implies for both the church and its understanding of God's action in and through the church. In the previous chapter, I argued that the Christologically mediated bonds between Christians were the condition for communion over time such that the present church is identical with the church that undertook the crusades or gave a theological defence for slavery. Since these bonds bear a particular promise, forgiveness in Christ, the temporal shape of the church is oriented by (among other things) this forgiveness and the repentance for which it calls. The arrival of the Spirit through ecclesial repentance animates these bonds and establishes the identity of the church by granting it a future in God. It makes possible the church's future by anchoring it in the vicissitudes of history, and opening it to being healed by the Spirit. In this final section, I argue that the church's holiness has to do with the shape of God's presence in the midst of sin. This presence and its effectiveness is promised, though its form

---

[85] *Ibid.*, 14.

requires continual discernment. Ecclesial repentance gives a glimpse at the way in which the Holy Spirit transforms sinful human beings into a body, the church, which as Christ's body bears sins for the sake of overcoming them.

Rowan Williams, who has both written about ecclesial repentance and led the Church of England in repentance, preached about the church's holiness in this way:

> The church is holy – and this congregation here present is holy – not because it is a gathering of the good and the well-behaved, but because it speaks of the triumph of grace in the coming together of strangers and sinners who, miraculously, trust one another enough to join in common repentance and common praise – to express a deep and elusive unity in Jesus Christ, who is our righteousness and sanctification. Humanly speaking, holiness is always like this: God's endurance in the middle of our refusal of him, his capacity to meet every refusal with the gift of himself.[86]

Sinners express unity in Jesus Christ through 'common repentance' by becoming that body that *is* God's endurance of sin: the body of Jesus Christ on the cross. In a variety of ways, one of which I propose is ecclesial repentance, the Spirit renders the church in history precisely this body and thus the bearer of God's promised victory over sin. The holiness of the church is indeed grounded in its being the body of Christ on which the Spirit descends, but it must not see its holiness as glory. Conforming the temporally extended church to Jesus Christ cannot circumvent humiliation and death.

In light of both the call for ecclesial repentance, and its actual fact, theologians have examined church tradition for adequate biblical and theological categories. Hans Urs von Balthasar traces the theme of the church as the 'chaste harlot' and her obligation to repent, throughout the patristic period and into the middle ages. For the church fathers, 'sinful' women throughout the Bible – Eve, Rahab, the prostitute Hosea marries, Delilah, even (more problematically) Bathsheba – typify the church as the bride of Christ, made holy only by union with him. The 'Church-bride can be "beautiful" only when she does penance' and is forgiven, according to Hippolytus.[87] In some cases, the conversion of the church is a singular event, mirroring the singular baptism of an individual, or the transformation of the synagogue into the primarily Gentile church. Thus, Origen regards Mary Magdalene's anointing of Jesus' feet as a type of the penitent

---

[86] Williams, *A Ray of Darkness*, 114–15.

[87] Hans Urs von Balthasar, '*Casta Meretrix*', in *Spouse of the Word: Explorations in Theology*, vol. 2 (San Francisco: Ignatius Press, 1991), 246.

church just prior to its conversion.[88] In other cases, the ongoing reality of sin in the church is expressed in terms of the church's harlotry to which Christ has humiliatingly bound himself. The purity of the church is an eschatological promise not of its members' making. While Balthasar does not find warrant to call the church a sinner per se, he concludes that the 'Church, abstracted from all her members, is no longer Church'.[89] The destiny of the church and its members are intertwined. Joined to Christ the bridegroom, the church is called to contrition and penitence.

In Bonaventure's apologetic for church reform, he identifies the church with Christ's body undergoing the passion,[90] an image I regard as particularly constructive. The church is not an entity over against its members, but rather consists of their being conformed to the body of Christ. Bonaventure argues that reform is necessary because the church has always succumbed to sin, especially 'legalism' as its original and ongoing sin. This basic sin of the church may be understood as its failure to identify itself with the humility manifest in the passion of Christ. According to Bonaventure, legalism flourishes where the clergy treat church offices as private property to be bought and sold, or regard ecclesial privileges as rights, even if canon law justifies such claims. Under legalism, the bonds between members are characterized not by self-emptying love but rather by self-interest. To reform the church in response to this sin is to identify the church with the self-emptying love of Christ on the cross. However, in his call for church reform and renewal, Bonaventure also warns that legalism resurfaces in the expectation that any particular reform will finally perfect the church.[91] No reform of church structures, nor any act of repentance for that matter, finally leverages the church out of its historical situation into eschatological perfection. In history, the church remains Christ's wounded body, and for the sake of its salvation must recognize this and respond accordingly.

Repentance is a gift for which the church continually prays, and for this reason holiness and repentance are linked. Neither repentance, nor the reform which may follow, are the work of the church in the sense of its human effort to make itself holy. The church is not the

---

[88] *Ibid.*, 224.

[89] *Ibid.*, 261.

[90] C. Colt Anderson, 'Bonaventure and the Sin of the Church', *Theological Studies* 63 (2002), 680.

[91] *Ibid.*, 682.

cause of its healing; it is the subject of Christ's healing, a healing accomplished by the church's being the body of Christ whose resurrection is promised. Neither is the church the cause of its own repentance, but rather in repentance it is conformed by the Spirit to Christ's humiliated body on the cross. Here is one meaning of Paul's assertion that God made Christ to be sin (2 Cor. 5.21). In repentance, the Spirit renders Jesus Christ the body on the cross whose members comprise the penitent church. In this conformance, the church does not assume an alien sin, since Christ is on the cross on account of the sin of the church. But the church confesses a sin uniquely and particularly its own, presupposing that its very basis for being in the first place is the promise that this sin is overcome. In this way, the church's embodiment of the humility and suffering of Christ on the cross expresses what the church already truly is.

A problem with the construal of the church as holy mother who assumes the sins of her children in order to forgive them and to purify itself, an image prominent in *Memory and Reconciliation*, is that the church's assumption of sin reinscribes a discontinuity between the church and its members. Despite a sense in which mother church cannot help but be wounded by the sin of her children in this model, the church's assumption of sins remains a free and *voluntary* action of compassion.[92] This betrays an ecclesiology in which the church, in itself, is not truly the concrete body of sinners, but rather faces a choice about whether to condescend to that level. On the one hand, since it assumes sins not its own, the church is virtually identified with Christ. On the other hand, in the possibility that the church might not assume these sins, it is in fact radically disconnected from Christ who has in fact *already* assumed these sins. Given that God has, in Christ, already condescended to the human condition, the church finds its identity only in and through that condescension. Its acknowledgement of sins truly its own cannot be optional, though I hasten to warn against a mere confession of universal sin apart of the church's actual sinful history. The church cannot teach penitential humility to its members if it does not itself repent from the core of its being. It cannot exemplify the mutual bearing of burdens within the body if the church does not find itself a humiliated body which must pray for its healing and restoration. In its 'imperfect holiness' the church wrestles with its failure to fully signify Christ in history,

---

[92] *Memory and Reconciliation*, no. 3.4.

though in its 'genuine holiness' this sin is eschatologically overcome in the church's being the body of Christ.[93]

A radical picture of the implications of the church's conformity with the life and death of Jesus is drawn by Ephraim Radner, which may initially appear at odds with my constructive pneumatological account of repentance. Radner argues that the post-Reformation divided churches ought to understand themselves as under God's judgement. Rather than supposing with the ecumenical movement that the Spirit is working on all sides towards a reconciled diversity (a supposition which can proceed without acknowledging the sinfulness of division), or concurring with Catholic or Protestant apologists that the Spirit is presently on their side (whether visibly confirmed in episcopal succession or true doctrine) and absent in the other, the church ought to contemplate whether the Spirit's presence has been providentially withdrawn from the church. The scriptural figure for this situation is the divided kingdom of Israel which suffered God's judgement, exile, and ignorance of its need of repentance.[94]

A figural reading of scripture that sees history through the mediating reality of Christ himself stands at the centre of Radner's argument.[95] In the first place, this requires attention to the particular sins of the church, and the ways in which these sins 'inform the very nature of "church" as the providential "body of Christ"'.[96] History must be taken seriously because there are true mutations in the church's historical life which must be discerned, in order to see the concrete church as the body of Christ. The very possibility for a figural reading, particularly of the church's history, has been obscured by the condition of division in which the divided body cannot see itself for what it is. And if it cannot see its situation for what it is, it will not see its need of repentance. Parts of this body may regard themselves alone as the whole church, or may regard each separated church as an unproblematic diversity whose unity is merely 'spiritual'. But it cannot see that it is despite itself one in Christ, and yet given its actually divided state, it is in Christ only as broken, divided, and dead. How can a 'dead' church repent?

---

[93] The allusion is to *Lumen Gentium*, no. 8.
[94] Ephraim Radner, *The End of the Church: A Pneumatology of Christian Division in the West* (Grand Rapids: Eerdmans, 1998), 35–9.
[95] *Ibid.*, 32.
[96] *Ibid.*, 1.

The providential purpose of the Spirit's absence is crucial. It is not that human sin has triggered a mechanism that automatically banished a passive Spirit. The Spirit's absence is not what supersessionism claims happened to the Jews. Nor does the Spirit's providential withdrawal mean that the church is no longer the church. Rather, Radner proposes that the Spirit has withdrawn for the sake of the church's new life in Christ, to conform the church to a judgement for a sin it has lost the ability to recognize and to bring it to a repentance it does not know is required. The Spirit acts through its absence by bringing the church into conformity with its own death in the form of Christ's death. By the Spirit's withdrawal, the church dies with Christ, though of course Christ's death is precisely for the ongoing sin of the church. In this sense 'the Church suffers Jesus' suffering for the Church'.[97] The crucifixion is 'a pneumatic abandonment of the first order',[98] in which the loss of the Spirit is identical with Christ's suffering the rejection of love. '[A] pneumatically abandoned Church will be the Church of Jesus Christ insofar as it is the body of the Son whom the Spirit abandons to the Father's sacrifice of love'.[99]

As Radner calls the church to repent of its 'denominated' condition, his provocative point is that the divided church cannot perceive its own sin and death and is thus in no condition to repent. 'For inasmuch as the power of repentance derives from the presence of the Spirit, and that Spirit expresses itself in the unity of the body, repentance as an act depends upon a perception of wholeness now obscured'.[100] Repentance is not a programme or a strategy that the church employs in order to heal itself. It is not a quick fix. Like biblical Israel, the church can only 'await repentance ignorantly'[101] while dwelling amidst its ruins. The repentance for which the church awaits is a recognition of its sins as the cause of its own death. Nevertheless, the *Spirit*'s conforming the church to the (divided, dead) body of Christ opens the church's future to resurrection. The church's hope for new life, and for the repentance in which this new life would be expressed, is in its adherence to Christ's own history.

---

[97] *Ibid.*, 317.
[98] *Ibid.*, 342.
[99] *Ibid.*, 343.
[100] *Ibid.*, 283.
[101] *Ibid.*, 282.

Radner rightly warns against making programmatic or general statements about the function of repentance in the life of the church. This danger is certainly present in my own attempt to think about the ecclesiological implications of ecclesial repentance, though hopefully mitigated by giving disciplined attention to the repentance of actual churches. Abstract pronouncements about the 'sinful church' direct the church's attention away from the particularities it needs to see in order to discern the Spirit and its own history of sin. Even the category of the church's 'historical existence' can become an abstract cipher if it is not attentive to the actual twists and turns of that existence, and the possibility that new things happen in this historical church. Radner's book is a penitential history of a particular ecclesial sin, and as such a display of this discipline. This history is not a homogeneous mess of indistinguishable sinfulness. There is faithfulness and sin in varying degrees which ought not to be flattened out by general confessions of sin. The illogic of church divisions generates blind spots in the church's life which may well be different than the blind spots that attend the church's confession of anti-Jewish theology or racism. Precisely as history it cannot be predicted in advance but must be interpreted as it unfolds.

The church that awaits repentance, or even the church that repents, may be unable to discern the precise shape, character and manifestations of the Spirit. (Radner devotes an entire chapter to the narration of how specifically Catholic and Protestant discourses of division have debilitated the discernment of holiness in the form of miracles, saints, and martyrs.[102]) Repentance is not a formula for holiness, nor a strategy for seizing the Spirit. Indeed, it is always possible that the church's repentance is misplaced or itself sinful. Churches that have confessed their anti-Semitism, racism or sexism must guard against moral superiority towards those who have not.[103] Whether guilty of a particular sin or not, the church does not thereby cease to be the church, and thus remains subject to God's holiness.

Radner does not seriously contemplate the actual repentance of churches. Thus, while he claims to write a penitential history that traces the travails of the actual church, and argues that the divided church fails to be a unified body capable of repentance, it is unclear

---

[102] *Ibid.*, Chapter 2.

[103] Thus, in its submission to the TRC, the (Anglican) Church of the Province of Southern Africa confessed its attitude of moral superiority towards those churches that did not repent of complicity in apartheid.

how he might account for the concrete history of repentance. Does not the fact that divided churches are repenting prove that it is possible for them to do so, and necessitate some reorientation of theology? His premises require consideration of the possibility that the Spirit has withdrawn, but does not assert that this is necessary or that the Spirit is somehow obligated by this state of affairs. Of course, it may be that some acts described in Chapter 1 above are not true repentance, and thus will not bear fruit of new life in the Spirit. However, it may be that given the unprogrammatic course of any penitential history, true repentance (a work of the Spirit, despite its absence or even through its absence) may precede specific reforms worked out over decades or centuries. That is, it is plausible that the recent emergence of ecclesial repentance is in fact a new contingent reality that informs the very nature of the church as the body of Christ.

The different answers to whether the church sins, the Protestant 'always' or the Catholic 'never', are each underwritten by a logic that deflects the church away from its historical character and identity. On the Protestant side, the church may see its sin in the mirror of the confession of the universality of sin rather than the particularities of its own culpability. For Catholic theology, a strong distinction of the sinless church and sinful members construes an abstract church that, without members, can hardly be the historical agent is appears to be and claims it is. Yet, the fact of ecclesial repentance itself is shifting the terrain of the debate about holiness and sin in the church. As the various church documents indicate, Catholic theology is moving towards the recognition of the sinfulness of the church, while still affirming the Spirit's abiding in the holy church. In their practice of wrestling with particular pasts, Protestant churches are doing the same.

The reorientation of theology entailed by the repentance of the churches for anti-Jewish theology, itself stimulated by repentance for sins of commission and omission during the Holocaust, provides an opportunity for the church to view God's gift of holiness in a new light. Acknowledging the depths of their denial that God is indeed faithful to his covenant with the Jewish people, penitent churches may recognize that their holiness is also a supreme gift, given unconditionally in spite of their unfaithfulness. Finally, linking the account of the Christological grounding of the church over time, and the pneumatological character of ecclesial repentance developed in the previous chapter, I sketched some ways that a penitent, sinful, holy church may understand itself as bound to the entire life of Christ's body. By the Spirit's action, through absention and death, or the production of penitential humility for its sins, the church is conformed ever more intimately to the body of Christ and the cross that bears that body. The church's holiness is fully in Christ, and fully bound to its historical character and identity.

Chapter 7

FORGIVENESS AND RECONCILIATION

In the native way, apologies are not 'accepted', they are acknowledged. [This is because] an apology must be lived out if it's to be a real apology. (The Reverend Alf Dumont, United Church of Canada)[1]

The United Church of Canada's 1986 'Apology to First Nations' was dramatic in many ways and continues to be remembered as such. In 1984, an Aboriginal member of the UCC General Council Executive, Alberta Billy, concluded a report to that group with a request: 'It is time you apologize to Native people'. Observers described it as a *kairos* moment for which no one was prepared. Billy had not followed the rules that required all such reports and requests to be submitted two months in advance, requirements that enabled the executive 'to control what came before them'.[2] Nevertheless, the agenda was set aside and discussion began on what such an apology would mean. Staff were assigned to develop a resource to be sent to congregations that both educated them about the need for such an action and sought their feedback.[3]

Two years later, Alberta Billy repeated the request for an apology at the General Council meeting in Sudbury, Ontario and then led the Aboriginal commissioners outside to a gravel parking lot to drum, dance, and wait for a response. Stanley McKay, who later became

---

[1] Quoted in Russell Daye, 'An Unresolved Dilemma: Canada's United Church Seeks Reconciliation with Native Peoples', *The Ecumenist* 36, no. 2 (May 1999), 12, square brackets in source.

[2] Stanley McKay and Janet Silman, 'A First Nations Movement in a Canadian Church', in *The Reconciliation of Peoples: Challenge to the Churches*, ed. Gregory Baum and Harold Wells (Maryknoll, NY: Orbis Books, 1997), 174.

[3] The resulting pamphlet included some history, a brief theology of repentance, and responses to possible objections to such an apology. United Church of Canada, 'Apology to Native Congregations', pamphlet (Toronto, 1986).

the first Aboriginal person to serve as moderator, explains that they decided 'not to take part in General Council's reflection on the issue or be cross-examined about [their] purposes'.[4] As they debated the wording of an apology, the General Council commissioners 'needed to assure themselves that it had not been wrong to bring the Gospel – but it had been wrong not to hear the Gospel from the Native people'.[5] After a text was approved, Moderator Robert Smith led a procession out to where about 300 Aboriginal members were waiting. He entered the tepee set up in the parking lot and delivered the apology to the 20 elders gathered there, and then repeated it to the much larger crowd outside.[6]

The full statement read:

> Long before my people journeyed to this land your people were here, and you received from your Elders an understanding of creation and of the Mystery that surrounds us all that was deep, and rich, and to be treasured. We did not hear you when you shared your vision. In our zeal to tell you of the good news of Jesus Christ we were closed to the value of your spirituality. We confused Western ways and culture with the depth and breadth and length and height of the gospel of Christ. We imposed our civilization as a condition for accepting the gospel. We tried to make you be like us and in so doing we helped to destroy the vision that made you what you were. As a result you, and we, are poorer and the image of the Creator in us is twisted, blurred, and we are not what we are meant by God to be. We ask you to forgive us and to walk together with us in the Spirit of Christ so that our peoples may be blessed and God's creation healed.[7]

Though some individuals immediately expressed forgiveness towards the church,[8] the elders said they would take this apology back to their congregations before responding. The All Native Circle Conference responded two years later by 'joyfully receiving' and acknowledging the apology but not accepting it. The Rev Alf Dumont explained that, 'In the native way, apologies are not "accepted", they are acknowledged. [This is because] an apology must be lived out if it's to be a real apology. The church is being asked to live out its real apology'.[9] On the advice of Elder Art Solomon, a stone cairn was erected on the

---

[4] McKay and Silman, 'A First Nations Movement in a Canadian Church', 174.

[5] Donna Sinclair, 'Of Course We Forgive You', *United Church Observer*, October 1986, 11.

[6] The story of the apology is recounted in Nancy Devine, 'Reflections on an Unfinished Journey: Three People Reflect on the Apology', *Mandate*, May 2005, 3–6, and Dean Salter, 'Twenty Years Beyond the Apology', *Mandate*, May 2005, 8–10.

[7] United Church of Canada, 'Apology to First Nations' (1986).

[8] Sinclair, 'Of Course We Forgive You', 10–11.

[9] Daye, 'An Unresolved Dilemma', 12.

exact spot where the apology was delivered to symbolize the unfinished and ongoing requirements of the apology. Stones were to be added as signs of healing and progress in the relationship.[10] To mark the twentieth anniversary of the apology, Moderator Peter Short repeated it in the very same spot. Several stones were added to the still unfinished cairn to mark concrete steps: the establishment of the All Native Circle Conference, programmes of aboriginal theological education, a Healing Fund especially for the legacy of residential schools, and an initiative to explore the relationship of Traditional and Christian spiritualities.[11]

According to Stanley McKay, the 1986 apology only marked the beginning of reconciliation. A true sharing of power and gifts has not yet been realized.[12] A sample sermon distributed to congregations to help them remember the apology acknowledged that '[f]ull reconciliation may not happen in my lifetime or in yours', yet affirmed the many ways in which an apology is a gift that occasions transformation, grace, and true relationship.[13]

The biblical vision of reconciliation centres on the conviction that 'in Christ God was reconciling the world to himself' and 'entrusting the message of reconciliation to us' (1 Cor. 5.19). Reconciliation is about the restoration or repair of broken relationships, first with God and by implication with fellow human beings and the entire world. The reconciliation of human communities is often named as the overarching goal towards which statements of repentance for Christian disunity or racism are directed. The UCC did not use the word 'reconciliation' in 1986 (nor did it use 'sorry' or 'apology' other than in its title), but it did ask forgiveness and subsequently framed the meaning of the apology in the very relational terms of reconciliation.

Joseph Liechty observes that forgiveness, together with concepts like repentance, apology, and reconciliation, are often defined idiosyncratically, as virtual synonyms or as sequentially related in various ways.[14] In a single volume of essays, for example, one author argues that an apology is an implicit request for forgiveness, while

[10] Devine, 'An Unfinished Journey', 3.

[11] The Rt Rev Peter Short, United Church of Canada, 'A Letter on the 20th Anniversary of the Apology to First Nations' (2006).

[12] McKay and Silman, 'A First Nations Movement in a Canadian Church', 182.

[13] James Scott, 'The Gift in Apology', Sermon for First Nations Day of Prayer, United Church of Canada (2006).

[14] Joseph Liechty, 'Putting Forgiveness in Its Place: The Dynamics of Reconciliation',

another claims that a true apology must not ask forgiveness.[15] This discrepancy is not addressed, it simply stands. And if such terms are not consistently used by theorists, neither are they used in actual practice of crafting church statements and engaging in actual relationships. However, I will follow Liechty's basic suggestion that repentance and forgiveness are typically two actions, by offender and offended respectively, which are conditions for reconciliation.[16] When churches repent or apologize, they frequently ask for forgiveness, especially if there is a definable group that may respond. This places repentance, my primary focus, together with forgiveness in an overarching framework of reconciliation.

The great danger of the discourse of forgiveness and reconciliation is the imposition of terms of settlement by the penitent and a premature declaration of reconciliation. The authors of the South African *Kairos* document forcefully stated in 1986 that 'it would be totally unChristian to plead for reconciliation and peace before the present injustices have been removed'.[17] Because God's gift of forgiveness stands at the centre of the Christian tradition, those who have been victimized may feel pressure to declare forgiveness before they are ready to do so. Where church apologies are framed as putting the past to rest and moving on, an offer of forgiveness may be expected, though such an expectation may well reflect a failure to understand the ongoing dimensions of pain and suffering, and the longer process in which the church must engage. True reconciliation, however, cannot bypass the question of justice.

Whether human or divine, forgiveness is always a dialogue and, as such, it presupposes the genuine voices of all involved. The non-acceptance of the 1986 UCC Apology may therefore be a sign of a greater exercise and recognition of the moral agency of Aboriginal persons in the church. A measure of justice, however small, is already embodied when Aboriginal members of the UCC say what justice entails and this is truly heard by the entire church.

---

in *Explorations in Reconciliation: New Directions in Theology*, ed. David Tombs and Joseph Liechty (Aldershot, UK: Ashgate, 2006), 59.

[15] In Mark Gibney, Rhoda Howard-Hassmann, Jean-Marc Coicaud, and Niklaus Steiner, eds., *The Age of Apology: Facing up to the Past* (Philadelphia: Pennsylvania University Press, 2008).

[16] Liechty, 'Putting Forgiveness in Its Place', 60.

[17] Cited in John W. de Gruchy, *Reconciliation: Restoring Justice* (Minneapolis: Fortress Press, 2002), 35.

In this chapter, one traditional practice of forgiveness – the Catholic sacrament of reconciliation – is the lens through which I examine the situation in which the church is the penitent. By attending to how ecclesial repentance is an application to a communal setting of a long-standing practice at the personal level, otherwise implicit dimensions of the former may be delineated. Through acts and statements of repentance for racism, slavery and sins against Aboriginal people, I explore how penitent churches participate in God's promise of reconciliation, especially with those the church has harmed.

Yet, in important ways a penitent church is quite unlike a penitent individual. Looking more closely as the differences highlights the particular challenges a church faces as it confronts its past sin and seeks to be both a reconciled community and a reconciling one. How does the church examine its conscience? How does the church express contrition, or sincerely resolve to not repeat an offence? An individual is absolved by a pastor, acting on behalf of the church; but how is a church absolved? I propose that answers to these questions require of the church a radical openness to those harmed by the church and caution the church against thinking about forgiveness solely on its own familiar terms.

SACRAMENT OF RECONCILIATION

Though Protestant theologians and church statements are discussed throughout this chapter, I begin with the Roman Catholic sacrament of reconciliation, or sacrament of penance (both names are appropriate though the former has become more widely used,[18]) because it provides an ordered and embodied framework for reflection on the role of repentance and forgiveness. Though the individual person is the primary subject of the sacrament, the rite presupposes and develops the social and ecclesial dimensions of reconciliation. James Dallen argues that the recent reforms of the rite attempt to recover early church conceptions of a penitent church which is both a reconciled and a reconciling community.[19] Moving from the logic of the sacrament of penance to the practice of ecclesial repentance is possible because both point to ways in which the church embodies

---

[18] See David M. Coffey, *The Sacrament of Reconciliation* (Collegeville, MN: Liturgical Press, 2001), xvi–xvii.

[19] James Dallen, *The Reconciling Community: The Rite of Penance* (New York: Pueblo Publishing, 1986), 259, also 303.

the reconciliation to which it is called. This helps to illuminate both the divine initiative in reconciliation, and the corresponding charge to human beings in and through the church.

The revised 1973 'Rite of Penance' implemented the general framework proposed by the Second Vatican Council. Reconciliation is explicitly located within the trinitarian history of salvation that embraces the church and its sacramental ministries. God's everlasting mercy is expressed in Jesus' ministry and in his death, which is the victory over sin and death and the reconciliation of the world to God. With the sending of the Spirit at Pentecost, the apostles were called to preach repentance and to bind and loose sins in Jesus' name.[20] God's saving intention defines the mission of the church, whose ministry of reconciliation includes but is not exhausted by the sacrament of penance.

The 'Rite' describes sin primarily in relational terms, as 'offence against God which disrupts our friendship with him', the effects of which always harm others in the community. Because 'men frequently join together to commit injustice ... they should help each other in doing penance so that they who are freed from sin by the grace of Christ may work with all men of good will for justice and peace in the world'.[21] In this perspective, the means and end of reconciliation are the repairing of relationships with God, church, world and self. It is not that the church 'dispenses' forgiveness, but the church 'must be the reconciliation, the welcome home of the Father expressed by the family of God, which makes the repentance and conversion possible'.[22] All forms of the rite of penance are liturgically structured as a human-divine dialogue. The church is thus called to embody God's reconciling embrace and through its practices make this reconciliation visible, available and attractive to others.

The 'Rite of Penance' describes three sacramental forms. The first involves an individual penitent, the second is for several penitents with individual confession and absolution, while the third involves several penitents with general confession and absolution. A fourth non-sacramental form does not entail all the elements such as absolution, but is a penitential service of worship intended 'to foster

---

[20] 'Rite of Penance', in *The Rites of the Catholic Church as Revised by Decree of the Second Vatican Ecumenical Council*, trans. The International Commission on English in the Liturgy (New York: Pueblo Publishing, 1976), nos. 1–2.

[21] *Ibid.*, no. 5.

[22] Monika K. Hellwig, *Sign of Reconciliation and Conversion: The Sacrament of Penance for Our Times*, rev. ed. (Wilmington, DL: Michael Glazier, 1984), 24.

the spirit of penance within the Christian community'.[23] The introduction of a liturgy for general absolution of a group of penitents (the third sacramental form) has elicited a great deal of interest, though it has been clarified that it is permitted only under conditions of 'grave necessity'.[24] While this third form is not repentance for social sin but personal repentance in a communal setting, Dallen argues it nevertheless discloses key convictions underlying the revision about the ecclesial and social character of sin, conversion and reconciliation.[25] David Coffey, by contrast, points out several anomalies in the third rite which may lead to confusion about its nature and meaning. For example, it presupposes that each participant makes an inner confession during the service. However, since no confessor has heard individual confession, the penance given to the congregation will have to be very general, potentially unrelated to the individual situations for which absolution is publicly announced.[26]

Contrition and Confession: The Examination of Conscience

The four movements in the sacrament are contrition, confession, penance or satisfaction, and absolution. Contrition is described as 'heartfelt sorrow and aversion for the sin committed along with the intention of sinning no more'.[27] This inner conversion is already a movement of the Holy Spirit to conform the person more closely to Christ. In his consideration of whether repentance is a prerequisite for God's forgiveness, Coffey points out that if reconciliation is considered the restoration of mutual friendship with God, then the human acceptance of God's continual offer of forgiveness is an indispensable element of that restoration.[28] It is not that forgiveness is earned by repentance, but that the relationship with God, neighbour or self cannot be restored apart from repentance and all that is implied by it. The intention to amend one's life is thus integral to repentance, the church's support of which is represented in various ways throughout the sacrament itself, for example examining conscience, discerning concrete ways to repair a relationship, and

---

[23] 'Rite of Penance', no. 37. Sample penitential services are outlined in Appendix II, 428–460.

[24] Coffey, *The Sacrament of Reconciliation*, 135–9. The clarifications were codified in canons 960–964 of the 1983 *Code of Canon Law*.

[25] Dallen, *The Reconciling Community*, 230.

[26] Coffey, *The Sacrament of Reconciliation*, 141–8.

[27] 'Rite of Penance', no. 6a.

[28] Coffey, *The Sacrament of Reconciliation*, 86.

bearing the promise of God's grace and mercy. Penance is genuine, and thus reconciliation possible, only in light of true contrition.

The confession of sins, the second part, 'comes from true knowledge of self before God and from contrition for those sins'.[29] That is, only by knowing oneself a sinner before the God who desires communion is one able to name the particular ways that relationships with God and with others have been distorted and damaged. If sin is primarily broken relationships, then the traditional distinction between venial and grave sins together with its emphasis on the objective dimension of sin (in its crudest form, naming sins from a list) recedes in favour of a more subjective spiritual discernment of how particular sins have disrupted these relationships. This does not mean that there is no objective sin, nor that the distinction of sins has no place, but rather that the effect on one's relationships of any particular sin cannot be determined in the abstract.[30] The confession of sins is thus not a technique but a spiritual practice that follows from an examination of conscience.

Dallen emphasizes that there is no formula for the examination of the personal conscience.[31] The liturgical structure of the sacrament, which is especially evident in communal services, places this examination following a reading of the Word and homily. According to the rite, readings should be chosen that illustrate the call to conversion, reconciliation in Christ and God's judgement on sin.[32] The recognition of oneself as a sinner, the step of contrition, cultivates the openness to hear God's Word addressed to a particular situation as both judgement and mercy. While mercy is God's final response, it should not be heard apart from the concrete judgement and condemnation of sin that renders mercy a true gift.

In preparation for the Day of Pardon, Pope John Paul II called for an examination of conscience by the entire church for the sins that have wounded its witness. Though he proposed that the sins such examination may discover will be those of individuals, these were to be discovered through an examination of the *church*'s conscience, implying the sins would be seen only in light of the whole. Yet, unless the church itself is contrite, it will not be in a suitable posture to

---

[29] 'Rite of Penance', no. 6b.

[30] Kenneth R. Himes, 'Human Failing: The Meanings and Metaphors of Sin', in *Moral Theology: New Directions and Fundamental Issues*, ed. James Keating (New York: Paulist Press, 2004), 154–6.

[31] Dallen, *The Reconciling Community*, 274.

[32] 'Rite of Penance', no. 24.

examine its conscience. And if it is truly contrite, then it cannot in advance determine that it will find only the sins of 'others' and not its own. A church open to the truth about itself is, in turn, the condition for the church guiding its members to name and confess those sins in which they are unknowingly implicated in virtue of being members of a sinful church. This significant transposition to the ecclesial of a concept that has been primarily a personal one raises several questions about how the two levels are related. First, how does an individual discern their specific patterns of sinfulness, and how might this apply to the ecclesial level? Second, what are the assumptions about how consciences are formed in the first place, particularly through participation in this sacrament, and what are the implications for repentance, forgiveness and reconciliation for the church as a whole?

Sin often entails blindness to the fact and to the consequences of sin. Since the individual penitent does not possess all the tools needed for discernment, the sacrament of reconciliation provides that the examination of conscience not be merely narcissistic introspection. It must entail a prayerful dialogue with God and with the church, represented in the person of the minister. The role of the confessor is not to cross-examine, but to listen, and engage in dialogue about the Word of God and the situation of the penitent. Appendix III in the 'Rite of Penance' provides some structure for this dialogue, ordered first to one's relationship with God, and then to neighbour, then to self.[33] The underlying presupposition is that with the mediating help of the church the spiritual blindness of the penitent can be overcome and the state of the relationships in need of repair confessed. However, while the template encourages an examination of strictly personal sins, rather than larger systems of injustice, it proposes a dialogical framework within such questions might be asked.

However, the church may not be competent in dialogue about the confession to which the church is called. The pasts that many churches are confronting are those in which the church itself failed to name as sin what it only later came to recognize as sin. Collective blindness is a theme that recurs throughout ecclesial repentance statements. The UCC confessed that what it now names as 'cultural and religious imperialism', it once undertook as faithfulness to the gospel. How can the church examine its conscience if its sin takes

---

[33] 'Form of Examination of Conscience', in 'Rite of Penance', 441–5.

the form of blindness that afflicts not only individuals, but a range of church practices endorsed as faithful, including, not incidentally, discourse on the nature of sin as strictly individual?

Kenneth Himes argues that sin as collective blindness 'refers both to the ways in which our personal sin becomes incarnated in unjust social practices and institutions, as well as to the power that these structures, having come into existence, exert upon us as heir to the sins of those who have gone before us'.[34] The manifestation of sin in structure and institution creates contexts in which individuals become implicated even despite their best intentions. Gregory Baum's typology of social sin also emphasizes collective blindness. Group false consciousness leads members to believe they are acting justly, a belief which legitimates and perpetuates oppression. Baum emphasizes that false consciousness does not release persons from their own culpability, though responsibility is differentiated among those whose eyes are simply closed, those who wilfully close their eyes, and those who intentionally perpetuate a sinful structure.[35]

What is the communal analogue of the individual penitent in dialogue with a confessor? How can a blind church see its sin? Who is the church's confessor? How does the church receive spiritual direction? The richness of the church's liturgical, catechetical, doctrinal, moral, and prayer practices are all ways that the Spirit preserves the church and binds it to the truth. Yet, it is instructive to observe how churches give an account of how they came to see and hear what they once did not.

Alberta Billy interrupted the UCC's 'business as usual' to raise the issue of apology. Archbishop Michael Peers of the Anglican Church of Canada began his apology by acknowledging the stories he heard about pain and suffering in residential schools. In confession to the heirs of the Anabaptists, the Reformed Church of Zurich noted, 'The persecuted do not forget their history; the persecutors by contrast would prefer to do so'.[36] Because the sinner prefers to forget, the wider church must listen to the prophetic voices whose experiences of suffering or of struggling to undo oppression gives them vivid perception of its causes, even though prophets may be dissonant, angry and unable or unwilling to speak in the conventional idioms

---

[34] Himes, 'Human Failing', 159.

[35] Gregory Baum, *Religion and Alienation: A Theological Reading of Sociology* (New York: Paulist Press, 1975), 201–2.

[36] Evangelical-Reformed Church of Zurich, 'Statement of Regret' (2004).

of good church order. At the same time, these voices must be heard together with the testimony of scripture, including both the suffering of Jesus and his victory over all suffering and sin. The polyphony that makes dialogue possible and necessary already exists in the voices found in scripture, tradition, theology, liturgy, collegial forms of ministry and the witness of the whole people of God. If the church makes itself vulnerable to marginalized voices within and without, the resulting disorientation may shape the church's imagination and conscience to see previously unnamed injustices and the church's complicity in them.

The Church of England's 'Walk of Witness' (24 March 2007) expressed its apology for slavery authorized the previous year. The participants paused for reflection at various London landmarks connected with the slave trade and the abolitionist movement and concluded with a penitential liturgy at Kennington Park. An explicit examination of conscience consisted of six declarations by the Anglican Primates of West Africa and the West Indies, representing new eyes on the Church of England's complicity in the slave trade. They reminded the assembled walkers, for example, that churches tolled their bells in celebration when a 1791 bill to outlaw the trade failed to pass parliament.

Archbishop Rowan Williams delivered a brief homily on the theme of blindness and sight following the gospel reading of Luke 4.16–21:

> The people caught up in running the slave trade were people who, in many ways, may have been decent, responsible people, but they couldn't see, and that's why we've just heard that reading from the gospel that's sometimes called Jesus' manifesto. 'He sent me to proclaim release to the captives, and recovery of sight to the blind'. And the release of the captives doesn't happen unless some people open their eyes to see, by God's grace and by the work of some extraordinary human beings 200 years ago people began to see ... Jesus tells us that when the Spirit of the Lord comes, those two things happen, release and vision, release and vision. Where he is there is release, and where he is there is vision.

Williams then asked those gathered to consider what sins are presently blinding the church. 'Who is not released today because of your unwillingness to open your eyes?' Until we see, he said, we must pray for vision to be granted by the Spirit and continue to examine our conscience.[37]

At a service a few days later to commemorate the abolition of slavery, with the Queen and Prime Minister in attendance, Archbishop

---

[37] Archbishop Rowan Williams, Reflections at Kennington Park, 24 March 2007.

Williams developed this theme further. Celebrating the achievement of abolition may lull Christians into thinking they are free, he said. But while humans are born for freedom they are bound by sin. Learning how to be free requires 'asking others to tell us the truth we can't see for ourselves' and hearing in that testimony both judgement and mercy.[38]

A protester then disrupted the solemn service. He ran to the front and shouted, 'You should be ashamed ... I want all Christians who are Africans to walk out'. After he was escorted outside, Toyin Abgetu explained that 'The monarch and the government and the church are all in there patting themselves on the back ... . The nation has never apologised'.[39] Though completely 'out of order', this outburst illustrates that institutional blindness may not be overcome by institutional means, but by prophetic disruption that may eventually be received as the work of the Spirit to lead the church into the truth. The assembled congregation ought to have been roused from any comforting notion of moral progress. Even an act of repentance is tainted by blindness and sin, and the vision of those who may see it as such is vitally important.

Examination of the church's witness cannot be done apart from the testimony of those who experienced the distortion of that witness and its life-denying effects. The practice of listening is absolutely crucial for the sake of forgiveness and reconciliation in Christ. The Walk of Witness did not retell the horrors of slavery in a way that invoked debilitating guilt, but named it as precisely the sin that Jesus heals. Through this healing process, Jesus frees the church by granting it vision. If the church is seriously contrite it must embrace an ongoing task. It must seek more actively to hear the voices of those both within and without who are currently suffering because of the church. The church which thus continually examines its conscience must reform its structures to be more open to hearing prophetic interruption.

The United Methodist Church's service of repentance for racism against African-Americans, held at its General Conference in 2000, reflected several dimensions of the examination of conscience.[40] Two symbols were introduced and presented as signs of prophetic

---

[38] Archbishop Rowan Williams, Sermon to Commemorate the Abolition of the Slave Trade, 27 March 2007.

[39] 'Protester Disrupts Slavery Commemoration', *the Guardian*, 27 March 2007.

[40] United Methodist Church, 'Act of Repentance for Racism', 4 May 2000. Some material from this section is drawn from the streaming video of the service, available at www.gc2000.org/audiovideo/videoevents.htm.

judgement on the church: a plumb-line (Amos 7.7–9) by which the people are to measure their actions in light of God's righteousness, and salt as a sign of covenant obligations (Num. 18.19; Mt. 5.13) which are broken when racism divides the church and renders its witness unsavoury. In fact, it was the scandal of disunity within Methodism that led UMC leaders to address the issue of racism as the underlying cause. The service was the initiative not of the Commission on Religion and Race, but the Commission on Christian Unity. Recognition of the sin of disunity led to the recognition and confession of the sin of racism.

One speaker addressed the assembly in the voice of Richard Allen, who was born a slave in 1760, bought his freedom, and became a Methodist preacher in Philadelphia. While most white Methodists at that time and place favoured emancipation, they did not treat African-Americans as equal. Worship services were often segregated, and blacks could not be buried in many church cemeteries. To reconcile his commitment to Methodism with his African identity, Allen formed a congregation which ultimately led to a separate denomination, the African Methodist Episcopal Church. Though Methodism's founder, John Wesley, vehemently denounced slavery, racism fractured and divided American Methodism.

Next in the UMC service, Bishop Woodie White 'performed a miracle', declaring all white members of the assembly persons of colour. He asked all to consider the implications of this in a church where racism still exists. 'Most of you pastors who came to this General Conference white ... no longer have an appointment ... even though you have the same gifts and spiritual depth'. In this way, he invited all persons to begin to see the sin of which the church was repenting.

The petition for forgiveness proceeded on two distinct but interrelated levels. Each of the approximately 3,000 persons in the assembly was called to silent personal confession of the sin of racism before God, publicly symbolized by receiving a piece of sackcloth (to be pinned to one's clothes) and the imposition of ashes on the wrist (because the chains were placed on the wrists of slaves). Then followed a common confession for racism perpetuated by structures of the church. Led by one of the bishops, the assembly prayed: 'Christ, our mediator, we acknowledge the sin of racism within the body, against those who left and against those who stayed ... We are heartily sorry and we humbly repent ... We petition for God's forgiveness, and solemnly ask the forgiveness from those we have wronged ...'

Through its corporate repentance, the church recognized its role in bringing individual members to repentance before God. Ecclesial repentance does not absolve individuals of their own responsibility, but rather forms them to examine themselves more deeply. At the same time, in order to issue this call to individuals and truly model repentance, the church had to name the sin of racism and identify its corporate complicity in sins that were once unseen, at least by those at the centre of power. Yet, the dialogue of persons and community is complex: the church itself was moved to confession because of the prophetic witness of individuals.

The fact that there is no linear sequence to this process discloses the way in which the church is simultaneously a reconciled and a reconciling community. The 1971 Synod of Catholic Bishops expressed this by declaring: 'While the Church is bound to give witness to justice, she recognizes that everyone who ventures to speak to people about justice must first be just in their eyes. Hence we must undertake an examination of the modes of acting and of the possessions and lifestyle found within the Church itself'.[41] As Dallen puts it:

> Only a converting community, one that recognizes and struggles to overcome the collective sin that has taken root in it, knows how to welcome and work with penitent sinners. A disincarnate, transcendent, and perfect institution, standing apart from its members, may channel an abstract forgiveness and grace, but it is unlikely to be a community that supports conversion and promotes reconciliation.[42]

At the Walk of Witness service, reflection on past blindness led to the recognition that racism continues in the church but left open the question of what other specific blind spots may exist. Sins other than racism and the consequent division of Christian churches were not named in the UMC service itself, but in the larger context of that General Conference an obvious link existed for some: the church's teaching and policy on homosexuality. The 2000 General Conference ultimately decided to uphold the status quo in which openly gay and lesbian persons could not be ordained, and same-sex unions would not be blessed by the church. There was vigorous debate on these issues, including demonstrations and civil disobedience by those urging the church to take a more inclusive position. Bishop Melvin

---

[41] Cited in Margaret R. Pfeil, 'Social Sin: Social Reconciliation?' in *Reconciliation, Nations and Churches in Latin America*, ed. Iain S. Maclean (Aldershot, UK: Ashgate, 2006), 187.

[42] Dallen, *The Reconciling Community*, 259.

Talbert explained that, as black man, he knew what discrimination in the church felt like, and he hoped such discrimination would end for gays and lesbians.[43] Historian John McEllhenney asks:

> Does history predict that future General Conferences will observe acts of contrition for the General Conference of 2000's antigay stance, just as the General Conference of 2000 observed a time of repentance for the way its predecessors acquiesced in slavery and racism? ... The answer: historians can identify parallels but cannot make predictions.[44]

The church continues to examine its conscience.

Penance

Penance is the third element in the sacrament of reconciliation: 'True conversion is completed by acts of penance or satisfaction for the sins committed, by amendment of conduct, and also by the reparation of injury'.[45] One of the objectives in the revision of the rite was to move away from a common misconception of penance as an imposed punishment or tariff for the sin committed. This association arose in part because the words of absolution were typically given before penance was done, making it seem extrinsic to the sacrament. According to Dallen, the revised rite aimed to recover the ancient sense that penance exhibit 'the depth and sincerity of repentance by externalizing it and shaping a life centered on God rather than on creatures'.[46] Thus, in the logic of the sacrament, penance precedes absolution, even though the order is typically reversed chronologically. Coffey explains that while absolution completes the sacrament, it is penance (or satisfaction) that completes conversion by embodying the intention to sin no more and to restore the relationship that was damaged.[47] Absolution is a gift. However, the conversion which truly seeks this gift is not complete without concrete acts of reparation.

How can a church express sincerity? Is it determined by the sum of individual dispositions? Or, is the sincerity of a collective expressed through particular practices and reformed structures? What penance is appropriate for a penitent church, and how might it be assigned? The rhythm of the sacrament in which penance is assigned by the confessor in dialogue with the penitent and services of ecclesial

---

[43] John G. McEllhenney, 'Contention, Contrition, Celebration, Caution: The 2000 General Conference in Historical Perspective', *Methodist History* 40 (2001), 32.
[44] *Ibid.*, 42.
[45] 'Rite of Penance', no. 6c.
[46] Dallen, *The Reconciling Community*, 283–4.
[47] Coffey, *The Sacrament of Reconciliation*, 111, 117.

repentance suggests constructive directions. If an examination of conscience has discerned distorted relationships, then addressing these relationships will be at the centre of penance.

Penance embodies the intention to not sin by amending one's way of life. For the church, this must involve commending particular practices for individual spiritual formation, and reforming structures to unmask and undo a sin's hold over the church itself. The formation of individuals conscientized to the insidiousness of a particular sin involves the 'evangelization and ecclesialization' of consciences[48] that discerns evil even in the church, names it as contrary to the gospel, and resolves to resist it actively. Services of repentance contribute to this end by examining conscience at a collective and personal level. They highlight the prominence of a particular sin in the church's life past and present, but also search the scriptures and hear the stories of those who have suffered the consequences of sin. Concrete programmes of action, such as the Church of England's commitment to the 'Stop the Traffik' anti-slavery coalition, not only attempt to repair damage in the world, but also form the consciences and habits of those who participate directly in them. Since official acts of repentance happen at the highest levels of the church, often initiated by key leaders (though at other times responding to the grassroots), there is usually a pressing need for an act to be received throughout the church. Giving priority to the education and formation of individual members on an issue is significant evidence of a church's intention to break its pattern of sinfulness.

A church partially blind to institutionalized racism must develop structures by which the voices of those who see how racism is manifest are genuinely heard. Collective sincerity is manifest in the reform of structures so as to detect a particular sin or blindspot more readily. As a result of some steps the UCC took in the 1970s to learn more about Aboriginal spirituality, the church sought greater involvement of Aboriginal people in decision-making structures. Alberta Billy was in the right decision-making body at the right time a decade later in order to interrupt business-as-usual. The UMC institutionalized its commitment to hearing the voices of those Methodist churches historically separated from it by race by mandating representation from them on UMC governing boards.[49] Though criticized by some as

---

[48] Dallen, *The Reconciling Community*, 274.

[49] 'Churchwide Boards Will Include Pan-Methodist Members', *United Methodist News Service*, 12 May 2000.

tokenism, welcoming the gifts of all members is essential to what the church is and how it is enabled by the Spirit to carry out its mission.

This is not to suggest that marginalized groups must bear the responsibility of exposing the blindness of the dominant group, but that for the sake of the witness of the church, the church must create structures by which the Spirit may convict it of sin and lead it to new ways of speaking, training its leaders, making decisions, allocating funds and engaging in social ministries. Which reparative actions a church takes ought to be shaped largely by the histories and relationships in question. For ecumenical repentance, it may involve the formal removal of canonical restrictions or mutual recognition of ministries. In relation to Judaism, it might entail reform of liturgy and theology, or commitments to dialogue. Material reparations, education, opportunity for members of marginalized and dominant groups in the church to talk to each, or advocacy of particular public policies may be judged appropriate in cases of institutionalized discrimination or racism. The key question for all penitent churches is whether it has truly opened itself to hear those voices that will guide it towards further justice.

There is no sharp distinction between the penance that expresses the intention to turn away from a particular sin, and the penance which seeks to repair a damaged relationship (or, to establish a relationship of respect in the first place). They overlap. The response of the Aboriginal leaders to the UCC apology, to acknowledge but not accept it, may be understood as assigning a very significant kind of penance to the church. The UCC discovered that a true amendment of life may not fit neatly into existing its expectations, structures or practice, but may demand their transformation. A commitment to a new relationship is not like an item on a business meeting agenda to be dealt with and dispensed. Thus, one penance assigned to the church was to live with an unfinished cairn of stones in its midst, and all that it represents. The UCC was assigned the task of *not* being able to put this painful past behind them, but to face the ongoing implications of their cultural imperialism. Symbolically at least, the church participates in the unhealed pain of Aboriginal people, within and without the church. Aboriginal leaders implicitly declared that a recognition of the true state of the relationship is a necessary condition on which genuine attempts to repair the damage must build. The lack of closure also aims to mitigate against complacency and continue to generate actions that live out the apology.

An apology is an offer of humility, vulnerability and respect for the other. The possibility that it might not be accepted shifts some power to those who, in this case, have held very little. The Aboriginal leaders were clear that by acknowledging but not accepting it, they were not disputing the UCC's intention, but creating the condition in which that intention might be realized in future actions and relationships of respect. In the new pattern of relationship already intimated by the response to the apology, terms cannot be unilaterally determined by the more powerful. Embracing more deeply a loss security and control is a significant penance that the church can perform. In the face of lawsuits that threatened to bankrupt the Anglican Church of Canada, draining its earthly means of security, Archbishop Michael Peers reminded the church that it does not know where the path of conversion will lead. Relinquishing control is difficult, and it may mean the end of 'our present form as a national church'.[50]

Loss of security and control are not good in themselves, but only insofar as they reflect the journey of the church in the way of the cross. And Peers concluded by reminding the church that only through the cross does it become a community of reconciliation. What penance means for a penitent church cannot be specified according to a general rule, but must be discerned in the context of the particular sin it has confessed, and together with those people sinned against. The challenge is thus for the church to reorient itself such that the assignment of penance is not external to itself, but intrinsic to a new set of reconciled relations the church is called to embody.

Absolution

Who absolves a penitent church? And what is the relationship between being forgiven by God, and seeking the forgiveness of others? Ecclesial repentance suggests a significant connection between these themes. The 'Rite of Penance' is clear that only God can forgive sins and restore right relationship with the penitent.[51] By the words of absolution, the minister absolves the penitent from his or her sins in the name of the *triune* God: the mercy of the Father, whose Son's death and resurrection reconciled the world to himself, and whose

---

[50] Archbishop Michael Peers, sermon preached at St James Cathedral, Toronto, 24 September 2000, 'Apologies' file (General Synod Archives, Anglican Church of Canada, Toronto).
[51] 'Rite of Penance', no. 8.

Spirit brings human beings to repentance.[52] The rite claims God's promise of forgiveness for the individual penitent, and many ecclesial repentance statements do the same for the church.

It is consequential that the church is not assigned to simply 'dispense' forgiveness, but to bring its members into a state of reconciliation with God and the church. The minister who declares absolution thus acts not only in God's name but also in the church's. On behalf of the church, a minister announces God's absolution precisely as the basis on which penitents are called to embody their forgiveness and to do so with others who are forgiven. To receive and embody forgiveness entails, as Gregory Jones puts it, 'habits and practices that seek to remember the past truthfully, to repair the brokenness, to heal divisions, and to reconcile and renew relationships'.[53] In other words, being forgiven presupposes a larger process of reconciliation. Stanley Hauerwas speaks about learning how to be a forgiven people as the practice of learning to not be in control. To be forgiven is to receive wholeness from another, ultimately from God in Christ, but also from the release given by those one has wronged.[54]

For this reason, the church cannot be the *unilateral* mediator of its own absolution. The Evangelical Church in Germany which declared that by its confession knows itself to be absolved[55] was not saying something untrue about God, but it was not telling the whole story about itself. While unilateralism is a sign of control, the task of the church is to seek ways that a porous ecclesial reality mediate absolution in ways that are indicative of the sin being forgiven. That is, the church ought to discern ways in which God's absolution makes it possible for the church to embody reconciliation.

Rowan Williams comments that: 'Once we grasp that forgiveness occurs not by a word of acquittal but by a transformation of the world of persons, we are not likely to regard it as something which merely refers backwards'.[56] Along these lines Jon Sobrino speaks of the significance of the church letting itself be forgiven by the poor whose presence calls the church to repent of those structures which have

---

[52] *Ibid.*, no. 46.

[53] L. Gregory Jones, *Embodying Forgiveness: A Theological Analysis* (Grand Rapids: Eerdmans, 1995), xii.

[54] Stanley Hauerwas, *The Peaceable Kingdom: A Primer in Christian Ethics* (Notre Dame, IN: Notre Dame University Press, 1983), 135–6.

[55] Evangelical Church in Germany, Darmstadt Statement (1947).

[56] Rowan Williams, *Resurrection: Interpreting the Easter Gospel*, rev. ed. (Cleveland: Pilgrim Press, 2002), 45.

caused their poverty in the first place. This requires that the poor not only be treated as full persons, but as those whose forgiveness represents to the church the possibility that what it proclaims and embodies is truly the gospel itself.[57]

In the UMC service, Bishop Charlene Kammerer led a prayer to God for absolution. She prayed to God for forgiveness and pardon, but also for the strength and courage 'to right both our personal sins and the wrongs of the church', recognizing that God's promised pardon is expressed in how the church embodies reconciliation. It is certainly significant that these words were spoken by a bishop who throughout much of Methodist history would have been excluded from leadership on account of her gender (though as a white woman, not on account of her race). By her leadership in the service, and that of numerous bishops, ministers, and laypersons of colour, absolution is not just announced but expressed in the transformation of personal relations. God forgives the church so that by being the community in which all gifts are recognized as from the Spirit, the church is freed to be the light to the nations and the reconciliation of the world.

Canadian Anglican Bishop Gordon Beardy spoke an unexpected word of 'absolution' to the Primate, Archbishop Peers, at a meeting of the National Council Executive, seven years after the initial apology. He said:

> From my heart, I would like to say that I forgive you and I want to forgive your church which has become my church. I forgive your people who have become my people. I accept your apology because you have worked so hard to break down the barriers ... Where once we were outsiders, today we are with you, as a friend, as a leader, as a brother. So, I extend my hand.[58]

With this dramatic gesture, Beardy responded to the 1993 apology with forgiveness that straddled the personal and the ecclesial. He said that he spoke not as a bishop but as an Anishinabe person who went to a residential school. However, since he attended a Presbyterian-run school, not an Anglican one, his voice was not only personal but representative of those Aboriginal people who did go to those schools the Primate apologized for his church having run. Furthermore, it is unlikely that his remarks would have been considered an 'absolution'

---

[57] Jon Sobrino, *The Principle of Mercy: Taking the Crucified People from the Cross* (Maryknoll, NY: Orbis Books, 1994), 100.

[58] Leanne Larmondin, 'Native Bishop Forgives Church and Primate', *Anglican Communion News Service*, 12 July 2001. Beardy unexpectedly resigned as bishop two weeks later.

had he not had the authority as a bishop to absolve. Beardy's action may thus be understood as both the forgiveness which can be offered only by one who has been sinned against, and an expression of God's ministry of reconciliation entrusted to the whole church, which in his role as bishop was able to announce and make visible by embracing the primate. This suggests that there is a role for the church to mediate God's absolution of the church. However, this absolution is not a word the church can claim apart from concretely transformed practices, and repudiating that aspect of its past identity that would not have consecrated an Aboriginal person as bishop.

I must clarify that I do not intend to paint an overly positive picture of the transformation of relations in any of these churches. I am not assessing the current state of affairs, but pointing to what is imagined and promised through these acts of apology and repentance. Ecclesial repentance is a *glimpse* at a promised future, but it is not in itself the realization of that promise.

Contributions of Repentance and Apology to Reconciliation

I do not intend to impose a definitive conceptual scheme on the many ways that concepts of forgiveness and reconciliation are used in actual practice. However, the practice of ecclesial repentance, both in its explicit claims outlined in Part 1, and in the implicit claims I have argued for in Part 2, contribute to the theological development of several key concepts. In this section, I examine the condition within which the church repents (collective responsibility) and the subject of its repentance (social sin). I briefly explore forgiveness and the reconciliation of human communities.

Collective Responsibility

The question of whether there is such a thing as collective guilt, collective responsibility, or collective moral agency is widely debated in the literature on political apologies and political forgiveness. The fourfold typology of guilt proposed by German Philosopher Karl Jaspers after World War II continues to resonate within the contemporary discussion. According to Jaspers, criminal guilt belongs to those individuals who have broken the law. Political guilt accrues not only to leaders who instituted unjust policy, but to citizens who may have supported the government or the general system of government, or acquiesced to government decisions. Moral guilt is determined solely by individual self-condemnation for the promotion or toleration of injustice or evil. Finally, the solidarity of all human beings is the basis for metaphysical guilt, particularly in the failure to do everything possible to stop evil. The consequences of the first two types of guilt are legal (prison) and political (such as reparations), while the latter types involve processes of repentance and self-transformation before God.[59]

Some argue that it is a category mistake to speak of collective guilt, and thus of collective apology or repentance. Former Australian Prime Minister John Howard refused to apologize for the 'Stolen Generation' policies because he claimed that to do so would imply that all contemporary Australians are personally and criminally liable. To make that accusation would be an injustice to Australians, he argued.[60] Jaspers' typology provides a tool for distinguishing personal guilt, which does not reasonably apply in this case, from political or moral guilt which may have a collective dimension. The consequences of political or moral guilt are rightly addressed by a political process or by a shared framework for personal introspection and response.

Several theorists argue that collective apologies are problematic because they assume a collective guilt or responsibility (a distinction I develop later) which does not exist.[61] David Martin's argument along these lines is instructive since it is aimed specifically at those Christians who advocate for national apologies for historical wrongs. He maintains that contrition and forgiveness are only possible at the individual level, between persons or before God. The idea of collective responsibility, the condition for a collective apology to make any sense, is based on the idea that guilt can be transmitted through blood (ancestry) or the idea of affiliation with one's nation as fundamental to one's identity, both of which he claims ought to be repulsive to Christians. Martin's point is that the Christian idea of forgiveness supersedes biological and national notions of corporate membership (to which he contends the Jews are still bound) and

---

[59] Karl Jaspers, *The Question of German Guilt*, trans. E. B. Ashton (New York: Capricorn Books, 1961), 31–6.

[60] Danielle Celermajer, 'The Apology in Australia: Re-Covenanting the National Imaginary', in *Taking Wrongs Seriously: Apologies and Reconciliation*, ed. Elazar Barkan and Alexander Karn (Stanford, CA: Stanford University Press, 2006), 157–9.

[61] See Michel-Rolph Trouillot, 'Abortive Rituals: Historical Apologies in the Global Era', *Interventions: International Journal of Postcolonial Studies* 2 (2000), 171–86, and Anthony Bash, *Forgiveness and Christian Ethics* (Cambridge: Cambridge University Press, 2007), Chapter 7.

renders the basic relation to be that of the individual before God, redeemed of sin by Christ.[62]

Martin objects to the idea of collective guilt because he denies that a communal mechanism transmits guilt to individuals. While Martin is writing about collectives such as a nation, not the church, he claims that Christians are bound to believe that no communal mechanism compromises the individual's stance before God. But is this individual relationship the only one that matters? Israel as a whole frequently stood before the God in judgement and in repentance (for example, Judg. 10.10–15, Ezra 9.7 and Dan. 9.4–19). Regardless of whether there is biological or national transmission of guilt to the individual (Martin's problematic distinction of carnal Israel and spiritual church fails to consider that God's election of both, in distinct ways, is the true constitution of peoplehood), Israel is not judged solely for an accumulation of personal sins, nor is its collective repentance before God on Yom Kippur strictly for such sins. If the church has a mission, then it stands before God with respect to that mission. Is it not possible for a community such as the church to be in a particular moral relationship with God that does not preclude the fact that each individual also stands before God in a differentiated and unique way but is not entirely reducible to it?

The association of the concept of collective guilt with indiscriminate application renders it highly problematic and unhelpful. Collective guilt was infamously ascribed to all Jews for the death of Christ and justified Good Friday violence against them.[63] Collective guilt for World War I was assigned to Germany by the Treaty of Versailles (1919). The concept dilutes the responsibility of the very guilty, and is manifestly unjust to the innocent, especially with respect to the related concept of collective punishment. In all of these cases, collective guilt is an accusatory label applied by others.

The concept of collective responsibility by contrast is a helpful one for several reasons. It acknowledges that 'the individual is, to a significant degree, folded into the communities and groups with which she/he identifies and, further, that group members have a responsibility for the actions of others who identify (or have identified)

---

[62] David Martin, 'A Socio–Theological Critique of Collective National Guilt', in *Reflections on Sociology and Theology* (Oxford: Clarendon Press, 1997), 207–24.

[63] The concept of collective guilt appears rejected for this reason in *Memory and Reconciliation*, no. 1.2.

themselves in the same way'.⁶⁴ This does not obliterate personal agency, but links it to identities and actions not reducible to the individual. Whereas guilt may lead to paralysis, revenge, or despair; collective responsibility, if genuinely confessed, entails both a truthful perspective on the past and the possibility of a truly new start through a commitment to act differently in the future.⁶⁵

The sociological and philosophical debates about whether collective responsibility exist are important, but existence in an 'objective' sense is not the only consideration. There may be good moral reasons to embrace the concept. Political scientist Danielle Celermajer argues that the national apology process in Australia is best understood not primarily as an act of remorse and regret for past policies and actions against the Aboriginal people, but as a 're-covenanting of the national imagery'. Here collective responsibility has its primary sense in a positive commitment to reconciliation rooted in communal identity. Despite Prime Minister Howard's refusal to apologize on behalf of the nation, many citizens participated in 'Sorry Day' events. Celermajer argues that what mobilized public interest and fostered a sense of collective responsibility was shame for the whole colonial project as the context in which bad policy was made and repressive actions were taken. Average citizens may have agreed with the prime minister that they did not hold direct personal liability for since-repealed laws or the excessive practices of individual government agents. But they desired an Australia in which such acts and policies would not happen because they were contrary to the nation's identity. Embodying *this* identity required taking collective responsibility. They thus embraced an examination of how Australia's 'collective norms formed the necessary conditions for particular wrongs to occur', expressed 'shame for those ethical flaws', and expressed hope for a new collective identity in which adherence to 'alternative norms ... would preclude wrongful acts'.⁶⁶ While these actions may appear to be simply the aggregate of individual sentiments, their culmination in an official apology on behalf of the nation by Prime Minister Kevin Rudd, who campaigned on the promise of such an apology, reveals them to be more.

---

⁶⁴ Elazar Barkan and Alexander Karn, 'Group Apology as Ethical Imperative', in *Taking Wrongs Seriously: Apologies and Reconciliation*, ed. Elazar Barkan and Alexander Karn (Stanford, CA: Stanford University Press, 2006), 26.

⁶⁵ Donald W. Shriver, Jr, *An Ethic for Enemies: Forgiveness in Politics* (New York: Oxford University Press, 1995), 114.

⁶⁶ Celermajer, 'The Apology in Australia', 155.

Celermajer's account locates the concept of collective responsibility in a process of reconciliation undertaken as an expression of collective identity, even as a nation wrestles with a particular past. She points out the way in which collective responsibility is assumed by a nation that wishes to embrace attitudes and patterns that are different from those in its past. Moreover, she links the nature of collective responsibility with the particular character and identity of the apologizing or penitent community. This does not mean that a collective is not responsible for a past that it has not already acknowledged. Nor does it mean that collective responsibility is just a mirage conjured up by a benevolent nation. The church must also wrestle with its failure as a corporate agent to fulfil its mission; these are not just alien failures the church claims though might chose not to. What Celermajer's account does show is how the very processes of repentance and reconciliation strengthen and focus the contested category of collective responsibility. This forms a kind of secular parallel to my argument in Chapter 5 about the sense in which the continuity of the present church with a sinful history is constituted by the Spirit's role in bring the church to repentance for that history.

The foregoing examination of collective responsibility within the discourse on apologies by nations is instructive for the church because while the church has a theological account of its identity, the frameworks of meaning established by other collective apologies impinge on the meaning that ecclesial repentance has in the public sphere. At the same time, the church is not bound by the results of the discussion about whether institutions like nations have collective responsibility or not. Unlike Australia, the collective moral identity to which the church aspires is not just a result of the collaboration of its membership or the decisions of its institutions. The identity of the church is given to it by Christ, and is received through scripture, tradition and the ongoing work of the Spirit in the practices of the church. And given that this identity relates to the reconciliation of all things in Christ, the church must discern with all seriousness how making use of the category of collective responsibility assists it to be more faithful in its mission. I propose that it does. By embracing ecclesial repentance, churches are signalling that they do indeed have a form of collective responsibility.

Social Sin

The logic of my method in this project is to ask: which notion of sin is presupposed by the fact that churches are repenting and pursuing penance for that which has compromised its mission? I argue that the sin that ecclesial repentance confesses is, by and large, social sin. This social sin is the church's sin. This may not appear to be saying anything new. The concept of the sinful church was developed in Chapter 6 within the discussion of the church's holiness more generally. In this brief section, I reflect on the fact that many repentance statements explicitly or implicitly invoke the concept of social sin. (Though there are subtle distinctions between them, I use the terms social sin, structural sin, and structures of sin interchangeably.) The point is not to develop an elaborate hamartiology per se, but to observe how the practice of ecclesial repentance can advance that discussion. By situating the language of social sin within that of repentance, I follow the theological rule which says that only by the light of the remedy for sin do we get a true glimpse at what sin really is. I emphasize that sin is known as sin in light of what overcomes it. I then move from sin back to ecclesiology. The sin of the church, which is social given the nature and mission of the church, refers to the church's disobedience to its mission.

In recent decades, Protestant and Catholic theologians, as well as the Catholic magisterium, have developed the discourse of social sin.[67] The concept is rooted in the facts that human beings are social and interdependent, and that human agency makes a difference in the world, creating and maintaining social structures. Social sin names the ways that sin becomes embodied and manifest in human institutions. Mark O'Keefe makes helpful distinctions between four ways the concept of social sin is employed:

> (1) social sin represents the social effects of individual personal sin; (2) social sin is the embodiment of personal sin and injustice in social structures; (3) social sin and personal sin are co-essential components of a comprehensive view of sin; and (4) social sin is the primary meaning of sin of which individual, personal sin is the manifestation.[68]

The first category, in which the sinful subject is strictly the individual, already recognizes that sinful structures might be created by manifold personal sins. The middle two categories wrestle with the degree to which social sin is a reality not reducible to personal sin. Personal sin

---

[67] See Derek R. Nelson, *What's Wrong with Sin? Sin in Individual and Social Perspective from Schleiermacher to Theologies of Liberation* (London: T & T Clark, 2009); Margaret R. Pfeil, 'Doctrinal Implications of Magisterial Use of the Language of Social Sin', *Louvain Studies* 27 (2002), 132–52.

[68] Mark O'Keefe, *What Are They Saying About Social Sin?* (Mahwah, NJ: Paulist Press, 1990), 17.

and responsibility remain in the account of how such structures came to be, but personal sin also arises from participation in the structures. Moltmann describes the vicious circle in which the dispositions and actions of individuals create structures, which in turn ensnare and implicate others as agents of sinful structures. While people are in many ways determined by the structures in which they live, they remain responsible for how they use their freedom within them, as well as whether they use their freedom to overcome them.[69]

The widely recognized problem with the fourth category is that personal agency is diminished or eliminated. This position is rejected in official Catholic teaching,[70] as well as by a strong advocate of the language of the social sin, Jon Sobrino. The nature of personal responsibility in a given situation must always be discerned, but individuals are not absolved simply because of social sin. Sobrino argues that keeping attention on the sinful *dimension* of structures, rather than on structures in isolation, highlights human disobedience and responsibility at both the personal and social levels.[71] The UMC service of repentance for racism, for example, explicitly confessed both corporate and personal responsibility, repentance and resolve to repair.

Controversy about ecclesial repentance often constellates around the anachronism or presumption to make judgements on individual Christians long dead, and especially to accuse them of particular sins. However, churches consistently clarify that their repentance does not presume such judgement but rather addresses the conditions in which the church was unable to form Christians to see the injury caused by even their best intentions. The structures of racism or colonialism are such that they blinded the church, especially those with the power to speak on behalf of the church, which as a result failed to form its members to avoid and oppose these sins.

The first document authoritative for the entire Roman Catholic Church which discussed social sin, *Reconciliatio et Paenitentia*, was preceded by a Synod of Bishops. There several bishops argued that this language resonated with the pastoral realities they encountered.

---

[69] Jürgen Moltmann, *The Spirit of Life: A Universal Affirmation*, trans. Margaret Kohl (Minneapolis: Fortress Press, 1992), 138–40.

[70] Pope John Paul II, *Reconciliatio et Paenitentia: Apostolic Exhortation on Reconciliation and Penance* (1984), no. 16.

[71] Sobrino, *The Principle of Mercy*, 85.

Archbishop Angelo Fernandes of India said, 'A theology of sinful social structures had best start from the agonizing cries of the victims of oppression, collective egoism, cultural prejudices, racism, communalism, etc'.[72] A UMC study guide on racism declared: 'Because our sin of racism was built into the systems and patterns of our United Methodist church, and because White privilege has been institutionalized over hundreds of years, our repentance for racism is corporate'.[73]

As argued in Chapter 5, the church's collective agency is grounded in the Christological and pneumatological identity of the communion of saints. The forgiveness which binds together the communion of saints does not just constitute the church as an institution, but already constitutes it as a body with a soteriological end. The church's 'collective responsibility' is its witness to Christ and the embodiment of reconciliation in him. The church's failure in this task, whether by fragmenting the body of Christ, denying God's covenant with the Jews, or violating human dignity through racial discrimination, is not only sin but sin of a necessarily structural kind. The inability of the churches to recognize the sin of their actual condition is itself a structural sin, impeding that which the church ought to do.

In his encyclical on ecumenism, Pope John Paul II wrote:

> All the sins of the world were gathered up in the saving sacrifice of Christ, including the sins committed against the Church's unity: the sins of Christians, those of the pastors no less than those of the lay faithful. Even after the many sins which have contributed to our historical divisions, *Christian unity is possible*, provided that we are humbly conscious of having sinned against unity and are convinced of our need for conversion. Not only personal sins must be forgiven and left behind, but also social sins, which is to say the sinful 'structures' themselves which have contributed and can still contribute to division and to the reinforcing of division.[74]

In this text, disunity is clearly rooted in personal sins, sins that Christ assumes. But there are also social sins which have a real and structural effect in the church, and are not simply reducible to many individual sins. Sinful structures do something; they contribute to division. This text notably locates social sin within the church, a step towards ascribing the sin of disunity to the church itself.

---

[72] Quoted in Pfeil, 'Doctrinal Implications of Magisterial Use of the Language of Social Sin', 139.

[73] *Steps Towards Wholeness: Learning and Repentance*, study guide (United Methodist Church, n.d.), 31.

[74] Pope John Paul II, *Ut Unum Sint*, no. 34, italics in original.

However, it may not be clear how the pope's claim can be reconciled with *Unitatis Redintegratio*'s insistence that 'one cannot impute the sin of separation to those who at present are born into' the divided Christian communities.[75] Hormis Mynatty observes that '[s]omeone can be really guilty of participating in sinful social structures or social sin only to the extent that he/she consciously and willfully does that'.[76] This particular passage in *Ut Unum Sint* does not address the personal situation of each individual in the presently divided church. The sinful reality of division, which has roots historically in many personal sins, does not in turn simply and indiscriminately distribute guilt to all individuals. The pope acknowledges that there are dimensions of repentance for Christian disunity which refer to communities as a whole. However, as *Memory and Reconciliation* warns, individuals do become responsible if they are 'pleased to remain bound to the separations of the past', or fail to work against it.[77]

Social sin is sometimes considered a dubious category because individuals within structures may be ignorant about the sinful quality of their actions. Yet, as the discussion throughout this chapter has shown, the structure of racism and other social sins promotes collective blindness. Social sin often entails entrenched structural barriers to its recognition. But if this is so, then the assignment of individual culpability is either entirely jettisoned from the concept of sin, or inappropriately assigned.

At this point, the practice of ecclesial repentance is illuminating, because the process of repentance names a sin as a sin. Even if the sin remains, ignorance cannot be an excuse. Ecclesial repentance presupposes the process of being conscious of a sin, and it helps persons and institutions recognize their own complicity. Precisely through this acknowledgment of agency are these structures called not just evil, but sinful. The church thus repents of what it *now* recognizes as a social sin. John Noonan's account of how the Catholic Church 'discovered' the sin of slavery sounds odd, because having discovered it, the church then affirms that it was always a sin.[78] But this is exactly the point. The caution in *Unitatis Redintegratio* that 'social sin' not serve as the mechanism by which to judge the

---

[75] *Unitatis Redintegratio*, no. 3.
[76] Hormis Mynatty, 'The Concept of Social Sin', *Louvain Studies* 16 (1991), 19.
[77] *Memory and Reconciliation*, no. 5.2.
[78] John T. Noonan, Jr, *A Church That Can and Cannot Change: The Development of Catholic Moral Teaching* (Notre Dame, IN: University of Notre Dame Press, 2005), 36–123.

subjective moral standing of individuals does not mean that the confessional process in which social sin is 'discovered' cannot serve the church (as communities, as members, and as a 'whole') in its present commitment to unity.

Of course, slaves knew their injustice experientially but their experience did not inform the official discourse of the church which is precisely the point. Joseph McKenna points out that the prophetic voices who called attention to a structural evil before it was widely recognized is one condition for the possibility of social sin.[79] The pope pointed to the need to become *conscious* of sinning against unity. In its confession for residential schools, the Presbyterian Church in Canada also confessed that it failed to hear the cries of injustice in its midst. Of course, not all dissenters are true prophets, and many truths the prophet proclaims may not be recognized for some time. For this very reason, the penance to which a sinful church is called may entail reforms and practices to attune the church to prophetic voices within and without.

While my method moves from the fact of ecclesial repentance to the kind of sin presupposed by such a practice, Pope John Paul II has invited examination of the opposite movement. He asked: 'Which penance and which social reconciliation must correspond to this analogical [social] sin?'[80] With this question as her point of departure, Margaret Pfeil connects social sin and ecclesial repentance in an instructive way.[81] She encourages her Roman Catholic Church to develop forms of social penance and reconciliation such as a Christian Day of Atonement along Jewish lines,[82] or to retrieve the ancient practice of an 'order of penitents'.[83] She gives considerable attention to the ways in which truth and reconciliation commissions provide a communal analogue to sacramental reconciliation.

---

[79] Joseph H. McKenna, 'The Possibility of Social Sin', *Irish Theological Quarterly* 60 (1994), 132–3.

[80] Pope John Paul II, 'The Value of This Collegial Body', in *Penance and Reconciliation in the Mission of the Church* (Washington, DC: United States Catholic Conference, 1984), 65.

[81] Pfeil, 'Social Sin: Social Reconciliation?'

[82] Peter E. Fink, 'Alternative 3: Liturgy for a Christian Day of Atonement', in *Alternative Futures for Worship: Reconciliation*, vol. 4, ed. Peter E. Fink (Collegeville, MN: Liturgical Press, 1987), 127–45.

[83] See Joseph A. Favazza, *The Order of Penitents: Historical Roots and Pastoral Future* (Collegeville, MN: Liturgical Press, 1988); Cardinal Joseph Bernadin, 'Proposal for a New Rite of Penance', in *Penance and Reconciliation in the Mission of the Church* (Washington, DC: United States Catholic Conference, 1984), 41–4.

A truth commission wrestles with the examination of conscience, the connection of personal responsibility and structural sin, the intersection of personal conversion and structural transformation, as well as the demands of justice through legal accountability, symbolic actions such as apologies and reparations. Though the relationship between a particular church and truth commission may be complex, the truth commission remains a model for naming social sin and engaging in social/political practices of reconciliation for a church implicated in the former and committed to the latter.

Forgiveness

This book focuses on the words and deeds of the penitent church. While I have been arguing that such penitence requires a vulnerable engagement with those who have been harmed, there is not space to examine the many issues around how particular groups or individuals have responded to acts of repentance, apology, requests for forgiveness and what these responses might mean. Nor do I touch on how the church might respond to requests it receives for forgiveness. However, in the process of repentance, churches reflect key assumptions about forgiveness. Some statements ask forgiveness primarily of God, as in the Day of Pardon. Many address both God and a human community. Some ask forgiveness only from persons, as in the UCC 1986 apology to Aboriginal people. Others do not use the language of forgiveness of all, though an apology is sometimes taken to be an implicit request for human forgiveness, and repentance before God a request for divine forgiveness.

In his work on the 'political forgiveness' that is possible among collectives such as nations and ethnic groups, but also churches, Mark Amstrutz writes that forgiveness is

> a demanding ethic that calls on political actors to confront their culpability and responsibility through the acknowledgement of truth, the expression of remorse, and a willingness to offer reparations and accept punishment. For their part, victims must refrain from vengeance, express empathy, and respond to repentance by reducing or eliminating the offenders' debt or the deserved punishment or both.[84]

Forgiveness does not imply that the offence was not wrong, but it revises the judgement on the offender, and promises to remember the past in a different way.

---

[84] Mark R. Amstutz, *The Healing of the Nations: The Promise and Limits of Political Forgiveness* (Lanham, MD: Rowman & Littlefield, 2005), 5.

One of the challenges of forgiveness between groups is to clarify the roles and obligations of each side. At the extreme ends, forgiveness can neither be a self-enclosed process in which a penitent church, assured of God's forgiveness, has no reason to engage with those persons hurt by their actions, nor a process in which the victims are expected to do all the work to restore the relationship. Anti-racism literature in particular emphasizes the self-reflective work that a church that confesses racism needs to do. Yet, for churches, the temptation to remain insulated may be abetted by the conviction that God's forgiveness, claimed in faith, closes the chapter and enables all to move on. From the outside, such a process appears to be narcissistic. One newspaper columnist complained that the Catholic Church's Day of Pardon, like other public apologies, 'seemed designed to make the apologiser feel far better than the people to whom the apology is aimed'.[85] Critics of the Australian apology movement point to a narcissistic desire by the dominant society to imagine a unified and harmonious Australia without truly engaging the otherness of Aboriginal people, or ongoing differences.[86]

The danger of narcissism can extend to a request for forgiveness from victims as well. Matt James argues that an authentic political apology (he writes about those of Canada) refrains from asking forgiveness.[87] When power is unequal, a request for forgiveness may become a demand for it, and the moral agency of group that grants it under those conditions is disrespected and diminished. The community which has publicly asked forgiveness may be perceived to have the moral high ground, turning the tables on a community that may be labelled spiteful, ungrateful, or stuck in the past if it does not grant forgiveness. Yet, it is unjust to assign victims the task of assuaging the guilt of their oppressors and expecting them to declare a state of affairs they do not believe exists.

In ecumenical situations discussed in Chapter 1, there tends to be a measure of mutuality. Both parties share a basic Christian

---

[85] Simon Heffer, 'This Pathetic Urge to Keep Saying Sorry', *Daily Mail*, 14 March 2000, 12.

[86] Haydie Gooder and Jane M. Jacobs, "On the Border of the Unsayable': The Apology in Postcolonizing Australia', *Interventions: Journal of Post-Colonial Studies* 2 (2000), 131–2.

[87] Matt James, 'Wrestling with the Past: Apologies, Quasi-Apologies, and Non-Apologies in Canada', in *The Age of Apology: Facing up to the Past*, ed. Mark Gibney, Rhoda Howard-Hassmann, Jean-Marc Coicaud and Niklaus Steiner (Philadelphia: University of Pennsylvania Press, 2008), 138.

framework, and past grievances, however bitter, are not usually present in the form of overt, ongoing oppression. Thus, the pope and ecumenical patriarch could declare in 1965 that some mutual forgiveness had already occurred, as could the Mennonites and the Reformed Church of Zurich in 2004.

However, members of minority ethnic or racial groups continue to experience marginalization. The 'past' that a church wishes to put behind it may not be truly past. Does a request for their forgiveness signal an assumption by the dominant group that mutuality is realized? Or, does it signal a desire by a church to move towards a goal? And which constituency is addressed by a church penitent about its relationship with Aboriginal people, for example – those within its churches, those in other churches, and/or those in society at large?

The Anglican Church of Australia chose to address Aboriginal Anglicans, as represented by the Aboriginal Bishop, in a 1998 service in response to the *Bringing Them Home* report. Speaking explicitly on behalf of non-Aboriginal members of the church, the primate asked forgiveness from God and the Aboriginal Bishop on behalf of his people. Aboriginal Bishop Arthur Malcolm declared that though his people have suffered much, 'it is through the message of Jesus Christ that we have learned to be willing to forgive. We have received his forgiveness, and now in turn we must also forgive'.[88] Though tone is difficult to detect in any document, the statement implies as much obligation as it does freedom or new relationship. Is such forgiveness automatic, and does asking it from a bishop of the church raise the expectation that it be granted? The fact that Bishop Martin in turn asked forgiveness for 'some suffering' caused by Aboriginal people may indicate a framework of general sinfulness in which the past is viewed through a lens of balance, rather than in terms of acknowledgment of a particular and unique history. Though Bishop Malcolm said he spoke only for Aboriginal members of the Anglican Church, healing a rift within the church is not yet the same as addressing the church's role in the wider social and political context. The key question is not by what authority Bishop Malcolm spoke, but whether the 'non-Aboriginal' part of the church, or the church as a whole, takes this forgiveness to be a sign of fully realized reconciliation.

---

[88] Anglican Church of Australia, *Standing Committee Report: General Synod 2007*, Appendix E.

If churches do decide that their repentance requires asking forgiveness from others, it is important that they do not have a preconceived idea of what that means, but are truly open to the response they receive. When the Mennonites were asked for forgiveness by the Reformed Church of Zurich for persecution centuries earlier, they replied that they were somewhat embarrassed to be asked forgiveness, since they no longer feel like victims. The women who responded the UCC's apology for the Disjoining Rule emphasized that they did not speak for anyone else. There is no constituted 'body' of those affected by this policy; the church would need to relate to each woman individually. As discussed above, the All Native Circle Conference of the UCC did not accept the 1986 apology, effectively deferring forgiveness until such time as it can be made by equals within a truly healed relationship. A tour of Canadian church and Aboriginal leaders in 2008 to promote healing for residential schools sought to hear the stories of survivors. But even as the Presbyterian request for forgiveness in 1994 was regularly restated, some flatly rejected it, others embraced it and still others are waiting to see what will follow. One church leader warned, '[W]e should not expect residential school survivors to make it easy for us, by offering comforting words of forgiveness along with a depiction of the pain and trauma they have suffered. We need to be prepared to be exhausted by the process'.[89]

Jewish groups have been the most outspoken about the belief that *only* victims themselves, not proxies or representatives, can forgive. Even God cannot forgive on behalf of victims who cannot speak for themselves. This objection has been most forcefully articulated with respect to whether Jews who survived the Holocaust may forgive those who were active or complicit in the Holocaust. Simon Wiesenthal tells of being asked to forgive a dying SS officer who had asked to speak to a Jew on his deathbed. Though the Nazi officer offered sincere repentance, Wiesenthal replied that only the victims can forgive and he cannot do so on their behalf.[90] Since the victims are dead, the crime is unforgivable.

Jewish philosopher Elliot Dorff writes, 'God's forgiveness, however extensive, only encompasses those sins which a person commits directly against him; those in which an injury is caused to one's fellow human being are not forgiven, according to the rabbis, until

---

[89] Lori Ranson, 'Remembering Forward', *Presbyterian Record*, May 2008, 21.
[90] Simon Wiesenthal, *The Sunflower* (New York: Schocken Books, 1976).

the injured party has personally forgiven the perpetrator'.[91] Solomon Shimmel argues that the Christian expectation of God's forgiveness undermines the premise of sincere contrition and repentance.[92] These three claims – that only victims can forgive the offences against them, that God alone cannot forgive offences against others,[93] and that forgiveness from God ought to be sought without entitlement or expectation – are serious challenges for churches whose actual practice appears to deny them.

The church rightly has its own convictions about God's forgiveness of sins, and it ought to act from within that framework. The Christian tradition confesses that God in Christ forgives precisely the 'unforgiveable', though I do not thereby suggest that there is a single Christian view of forgiveness and its implications. But whatever these beliefs are, they form the context for seeking forgiveness and reconciliation with those who may well hold very different understandings of the nature and implications of forgiveness.

At the same time, churches must guard against expecting communities to respond based on the church's assumptions about forgiveness. A church is an ambassador of reconciliation as it receives responses to its request for forgiveness on the religious, philosophical or cultural terms of the other. It may be that the church ought to seek forgiveness from the Jewish people because such a request is thinkable on Christian grounds, and then hear from them why it cannot be (fully) extended. Numerous texts do make explicit requests to the Jewish people for forgiveness.[94] On explicitly Jewish grounds, Dorff himself argues that while only the victims of the Holocaust can offer *full* forgiveness, existing Jewish communities can and should offer 'some lesser form of it', when asked to do so by a truly penitent

---

[91] Elliot N. Dorff, 'Individual and Communal Forgiveness', in *Autonomy and Judaism: The Individual and the Community in Jewish Philosophical Thought*, ed. Daniel H. Frank (Albany, NY: SUNY Press, 1992), 196.

[92] Solomon Shimmel, *Wounds Not Healed by Time: The Power of Repentance and Forgiveness* (Oxford: Oxford University Press, 2002), 212.

[93] One particularly clear statement of the position that God forgives only where preceded by human forgiveness is Mark Dratch, 'Forgiving the Unforgivable? Jewish Insights Into Repentance and Forgiveness', *Journal of Religion and Abuse* 4, no. 4 (2002), 7–24.

[94] For example, Reformed Church of Hungary, 'Declaration on the Persecution of the Jews and the Mission to the Jews' (1946), Lutheran World Federation, Løgumkloster Report (1964), West German Catholic Bishops, 'The Church and the Jews' (1980), Swiss Catholic Bishops, 'Confronting the Debate about the Role of Switzerland During the Second World War' (1997).

church. This forgiveness, oriented to reconciliation and acceptance, can be given on the basis of the enduring communal Jewish identity through time.[95]

The church should not ask forgiveness only of other Christians, even though in such an exchange it will most clearly recognize the response. Churches confronting their past are bound to engage with whomever they have sinned against. Furthermore, the church may lay claim to God's promised absolution, but as in the sacrament, absolution is truly received and completed only in light of penance. For the church to engage in the reception of forgiveness on the terms of another community may well be one of its appropriate penances for historical wrongs. As an expression of the church's desire to reconcile, the church may need to bear the fact that the living community of Jewish people can grant only partial forgiveness for past offences. The church may need to live with an unfinished cairn of stones in its midst, and all that represents. In its own way, the church can therefore take seriously Shimmel's conviction that repentance entails throwing oneself on God's mercy without expectation. While the church knows that Christ's death makes forgiveness possible and certain, the church cannot know how those it has wronged will respond. Indeed, the certainty of God's ultimate forgiveness makes bearable the deferred reconciliation on the human historical level. For a church whose identity is, in Christ, extended through time as a single agent, the duration of penance may extend through time as well.

Furthermore, since the church circumvents true reconciliation by *expecting* human communities to grant instant and absolute forgiveness (though I do not suggest that this is impossible within ordinary time), the church may need to wait until what Miroslav Volf calls the 'eschatological transition', for full forgiveness to be extended and reconciliation achieved. Christian theology affirms that in this transition to the world to come, a world of perfect love, all things are judged and reconciled in Christ. Sins are exposed and judged for what they are, but sinners are judged by the one who has taken the judgement of all sins upon himself. True encounters are possible because all persons are brought together across time and space without the problems posed by representative forgiveness, or the death of the victim or perpetrator. (Volf does not consider social or ecclesial sins, but it seems reasonable that the particular complex-

---

[95] Dorff, 'Individual and Communal Forgiveness', 203–6.

ities of how communal agents interact in ordinary time and space are likewise overcome.) Yet, the overcoming of offences is not yet the world of perfect love. That occurs when wronged and wrongdoer 'see each other and themselves with the eyes of Christ' and respond with full forgiveness and embrace.[96] This can be a thoroughly Christian view of forgiveness that does not require all parties to have the identical understandings of what forgiveness means. While the concept of eschatological transition need not become an explicit part of dialogue between Christians and Jews, or the church and non-Christian Aboriginal groups, it is one in which the church may hold a vision of (deferred) forgiveness and reconciliation in Christ together with a true openness to the response it receives from another.

Apology and Reconciliation

Acts of repentance alone do not constitute the whole of a reconciliation process. Essential questions of justice, reparations or reform might be implied or promised in a statement of repentance, but their realization pursued in other ways. A separate study is required to examine the range of practices that have actually preceded and followed ecclesial repentance and their practical effect. However, sincere statements of repentance or apology not only point to future reconciliation elsewhere but as performative speech-acts, already anticipate and embody it. While this must not license complacency, it counters those who say that *only* actions matter, and that words are not important. Bearing in mind that repentance statements ought not to stand in isolation, they further a goal of social reconciliation in several ways.

First, a statement of repentance or apology by an institution puts something on the public record. It acknowledges an interpretation of the past that may have been denied or disputed. The way in which the acknowledgement of a past wrong can contribute to the healing of relationships has been widely noted.[97] Trudy Govier and Wilhelm

---

[96] Miroslav Volf, *The End of Memory: Remembering Rightly in a Violent World* (Grand Rapids: Eerdmans, 2006), 180.

[97] For example, Nicholas Tavuchis, *Mea Culpa: A Sociology of Apology and Reconciliation* (Stanford, CA: Stanford University Press, 1991), 109; Trudy Govier, 'What is Acknowledgement and Why is It Important?' in *Dilemmas of Reconciliation: Cases and Concepts*, ed. Carol A. L. Prager and Trudy Govier (Waterloo: Wilfrid Laurier University Press, 2003), 65–89; Michael Henderson, 'Acknowledging History as a Prelude to Forgiveness', *Peace Review* 14 (2002), 265–70.

Verwoerd identify acknowledgment as crucial to the 'mystery' of how an apology can actually bring about a shift in attitudes on all sides. Acknowledgment includes admitting that an act or pattern of behaviour was wrong, acknowledging the moral status of the victim who did not deserve the treatment they received, and finally, recognizing the legitimacy of feelings of hurt or anger by those wronged.[98] Injustices towards minority groups are often compounded by denying their stories, and their legitimate resentment towards the source of their oppression. The recognition of the dignity and moral worth of victims, through the acknowledgment of their violation, may in itself be considered one form of reparation or amend. Acknowledgment for the public record may stimulate debate about the interpretation of the past and its significance. Such debates may surface lingering prejudices or stereotypes, or may reveal layers of complexity that cannot be fully reflected in any concise, official, statement. As a Chilean human rights lawyer noted, 'Truth doesn't bring the dead back to life ... but it brings them out of silence'.[99]

Second, repentance or apology may begin to correct imbalances of power. As in the case of the refusal of Aboriginal leaders to accept the UCC apology, the invitation to respond is an act of respect towards those who have often not been respected. Legal scholar Martha Minow argues that the 'mystery of apology depends upon the social relationships it summons and strengthens; the apology is not merely words. Crucial here is the communal nature of the process of apologizing. An apology is not a soliloquy'.[100] Dialogue about the terms and content of an apology may already began to manifest new social relations. But this does not mean that the dominant group can simply say, 'write the words and we'll say them', if the receiver of the apology does not wish to do so or if the request is an attempt to circumvent true engagement in the issues.

Political philosopher Janna Thompson argues the power of an apology lies partly in the way it displays the *inadequacy* of all efforts to redress past wrongs. In the case of slavery, it is impossible to imagine any process meaningfully restoring what the victims and their successors have suffered. While this fact ought not to preclude

---

[98] Trudy Govier and Wilhelm Verwoerd, 'The Promise and Pitfalls of Apology', *Journal of Social Philosophy* 33 (2002), 68–9.

[99] Cited in Robert R. Weyeneth, 'The Power of Apology and the Process of Historical Reconciliation', *Public Historian* 23, no. 3 (Summer 2001), 33.

[100] Martha Minow, *Between Vengeance and Forgiveness: Facing History After Genocide and Mass Violence* (Boston: Beacon Press, 1998), 114.

material or political reparations, the point is that such gestures seek to repair and reconcile, but cannot restore. Not only does the passage of time render the idea of an original state nonsensical, the moral nature of the offences make precise calculation of damages impossible. Thompson argues that a collective apology for such a historical wrong should be understood as a forward-looking negotiated consensus about what constitutes a present relationship of respect and power precisely in light of the inability of any word or act to restore what was lost. Churches have done sinful things and acknowledging their own inability to undo the damages expresses respect for victims.[101]

Third, new relationships and commitments require and presuppose new stories. Every church is shaped by the stories it tells about God, Jesus Christ and the journey of the church through history. A church is challenged to tell a more truthful story about itself by an act of repentance which may be a milestone in a revision of the identity-forming narrative. The UMC as a whole was reminded that the experience of African-American churches who left the dominant church is not a alien history, but a common painful history. As Canada embarks on a national Truth and Reconciliation Commission, the framework within which individual testimony will be received has already been determined by a narrative declared through apologies by churches and by the government about the harm of residential schools.

The scope and tone of a narrative determine whose identity is shaped by it, and in what way. The development of a shared narrative by groups once estranged is particularly important for how it redefines the identity of the powerful. Will a church be able to see itself through the eyes of those it has marginalized? Writing about his Australian context, Peter Lewis advocates a hermeneutic of 'relocation' by which the churches learn to relinquish their power and find their identities in and through Aboriginal narratives of pain and in solidarity with the tellers of those stories. Yet, he also cautions: 'Dialogue may have replaced misguided "protection" as the normative mode of mission but, apart from some level of acknowledgment and apology, the churches have a long way to go in their solidarity with Indigenous peoples'.[102]

---

[101] Janna Thompson, *Taking Responsibility for the Past: Reparation and Historical Injustice* (Cambridge, UK: Polity Press, 2002), 38–53.

[102] Peter Lewis, 'After Sorry: Towards a Covenant of Solidarity and Embrace',

The confession of war responsibility by the United Church of Christ in Japan is another example. Since the Protestant churches in Japan were unified by the government in order to support its war aims, a disavowal of those aims could not be anything but a reshaping of ecclesial identity. While the confession that its support for the war was sinful reflected a change in perspective that had already been manifest in the church's peace advocacy in the 1960s, it also enacted that change by telling a new solemn and public story, culminating in a confession, about the discontinuity of its founding and its future mission.[103]

Fourth, acts of collective repentance or apology promote social reconciliation by fostering practices to avoid repetition. In this chapter I have already pointed to ways by which penitent churches may form individual consciences, listen to marginalized voices, and develop structures of accountability. An apology is also a public ethical commitment for the future. By acknowledging a violation of moral norms, the substance of those norms is affirmed. By doing so publicly, the church is visibly accountable for how it fulfils its commitments. An apology also provides an interpretive framework for research and education about the past in a variety of substantive and symbolic ways. Commemoration of an act of repentance, such as marking an anniversary or erecting a monument, serves as a beacon of a future that is not the same as the past. This future orientation, expressed in terms of an attitude of lament and responsibility for the past, is fitting for a collective which cannot change that past but can commit to not repeating it.

The logic of the sacrament of reconciliation reveals the social and ecclesial dimensions of the forgiveness of sins. With the help of the church, the individual penitents name the distorted shape of their relationships with God, and others, and are guided into a way of life that seeks to repair and overcome them. This is possible through the promise of God's mercy and expressed in the individual's reconciliation with the church. The church is thus a community of reconciliation. Yet, the church cannot help its members see the reality of their sins if it is blind to its own sins. Personal repentance presupposes ecclesial repentance.

Pacifica 22 (2009), 16. See also Gary Redcliffe, 'The Residential Schools and Narrative Identity: A Pastoral Analysis', *Toronto Journal of Theology* 19 (2003), 53–67.

[103] See Iwao Morioka, 'Japanese Churches and World War II', trans. Akira Demura, *Japan Christian Quarterly* 34 (1968), 75–85.

When the penitent is the church, the goal is similarly a realization of reconciliation but the process looks different. The penance which seeks to set relationships right includes a reform or transformation of structures to enable the church to hear the stories of those who have experienced the church as something other than a community of reconciliation. Through these voices, the church may see what it has not seen before, enabling it to truly confess the sins which have infected its communal life. The church lives out its repentance and seeks forgiveness as gifts intrinsic to its mission and its historical identity. Demonstrating true repentance, the church is called to cultivate those practices by which it is open to receiving the forgiveness of God and those it has harmed, along the way towards a full eschatological reconciliation.

CONCLUSION

For history is not something exterior, it is part of the particular identity of the Church.
(Catholic Bishops of West Germany, Berlin, and Austria)[1]

This book began with the testimony of survivors of Indian Residential Schools run by the Anglican Church of Canada and the primate's apology at the second National Native Convocation in 1993. At the sixth Indigenous Sacred Circle (successor to the Native Convocations) 16 years later, that apology continued to serve as a definitive point of reference in the developing relationship of Aboriginal Anglicans with the rest of the church. Archbishop Fred Hiltz, the current primate, noted that conversations at the Sacred Circle shifted away from the pain of residential schools toward spiritual renewal and self-determination, a sign perhaps of some advance toward healing.[2]

Shortly after the 1993 apology, the Anglican Church of Canada adopted a covenant that spoke about the equal partnership of Aboriginal people in the church. This led to structures of self-determination within the church, most notably the institution of a National Indigenous Bishop. Reflecting on the Sacred Circle, the incumbent National Indigenous Bishop, Mark MacDonald, said, 'We have begun to be what we hoped to be. We're on a trajectory towards becoming a vital, vibrant set of churches and ministries'.[3] The church has followed its apology with an attempt to make real changes in its structure, in its attitudes, and in its pattern of relationships.

Nevertheless, the devastating effects of residential schools are present and raw for many survivors, and legacies of abuse and dysfunction continue within family systems. Racism and inequality persist in the church. When Archbishop Hiltz spoke at a public event of remembrance and healing in Winnipeg, Manitoba, a woman

---

[1] 'Accepting the Burden of History' (1988).

[2] Marites N. Sison, 'Sacred Circle a Pivotal Moment "In a Positive and Life-Giving Way",' *Anglican Journal*, October 2009, 3.

[3] "We Have Begun to Be What We Hoped to Be", *Anglican Journal*, online edition, 19 August 2009.

interrupted him, yelling that he was telling lies.[4] As Canada's Truth and Reconciliation Commission begins its work of receiving testimony from former residential school students, the role of churches will be revisited once again and questions asked about how churches now are repairing the effects of its past actions.

I have argued in Part 2 that the doctrinal tradition of the church provides resources to make sense of acts of apology and repentance such as this one, just as an apology occasions some reshaping of those doctrines. For example, the communion of the saints provides the framework within which the presently penitent Anglican Church of Canada is the same one that ran residential schools, starting more than 100 years ago. To say, 'I didn't run the schools', does not relieve the church of responsibility. Moreover, the church's holiness is defined not by asserting that whatever was sinful must have been done by those acting outside the structures of the church, but in seeing God's presence in the midst of sin – this church's particular sin – and in the church as a forgiven community. The church embodies reconciliation as it hears the cries of marginalized people, overturns power imbalances and addresses ways to heal individuals and communities, while developing structures to ensure voices are in the future heard and the wrong is not repeated.

Furthermore, I have proposed a specifically trinitarian account of ecclesial repentance. Within the communion of saints, forgiveness in Christ is what binds the church together as a single community through time and space. Ecclesial repentance may be understood as an act of the Holy Spirit to constitute the temporal continuity of the church by binding the church and its history of sin to its singular source of forgiveness, and to free the church for its future by granting forgiveness for the sins of its past. By extension, the holiness of the church may be understood in a specifically Christological way. In the midst of the church's own sin, the Holy Spirit acts to conform the penitent church evermore to Christ's body – that body on the cross which is God's endurance of sin and victory over it. In this way, the church is a profoundly forgiven and reconciled community, and just so given the ministry of reconciliation. However, reconciliation is not only a list of programmes or new initiatives the church undertakes, as indispensible as these are within the contingencies of history, but also the very condition by which the church embodies the reconciliation it has from Christ, for the sake of the world. Underlying this all is a

[4] Judith Farris, 'The Weight of Sin', *Presbyterian Record*, May 2008, 27.

conviction about the irreducibly historical dimension of the church within God's economy of salvation. With Robert Jenson, I contend that God intends that there be a church, and that this be exactly the one that exists.

The theologian studying ecclesial repentance studies the church studying itself. Theology disconnected from the life of the church will fail to help the church be faithful to its calling. It will not discern where the community is falling down, nor will it gain inspiration and insight from acts of faithfulness. At the same time, reflection on church practice pursued in isolation from God's saving self-disclosure will reduce the church to strictly human processes. Rejecting both of these options, I have demonstrated throughout this book a way of doing theology disciplined by what actual churches are doing and in faithful dialogue with the theological tradition. If the emergence of ecclesial repentance points to the irreducibly and properly historical identity of the church, then theologizing attentive to the actual practices and histories of the churches is the discourse appropriate to this subject. By such discipline may the theologian be granted the ears to hear what the Spirit is saying to the church.

BIBLIOGRAPHY

Books, journal articles, chapters, dissertations, church documents. (The sources of ecclesial repentance texts are provided in the Appendix.)

Accattoli, Luigi, 'A Pope Who Begs Forgiveness: John Paul II and His "Mea Culpa" at the Turn of the New Millennium'. In *John Paul II: A Pope for the People*, 89–115. New York: Abrams, 2004.
——, *When a Pope Asks Forgiveness: The Mea Culpa's of John Paul II*. Translated by Jordan Aumann. Boston: Daughters of St. Paul, 1998.
Alberts, Louw and Frank Chikane, eds., *Road to Rustenburg: The Church Looking Forward to a New South Africa*. Cape Town: Struik Christian Books, 1991.
Amstutz, Mark R., *The Healing of the Nations: The Promise and Limits of Political Forgiveness*. Lanham, MD: Rowman & Littlefield, 2005.
Anderson, C. Colt, 'Bonaventure and the Sin of the Church'. *Theological Studies* 63 (2002), 667–89.
Anderson, H. George, J. Francis Stafford and Joseph A. Burgess, eds., *The One Mediator, the Saints, and Mary: Lutherans and Catholics in Dialogue VIII*. Minneapolis: Augsburg Fortress Press, 1992.
Anderson, Terry, 'Lessons from the Residential Schools: Some Beginning Reflections'. *Touchstone* 16, no. 2 (May 1998), 22–8.
Augustine, *City of God*. Translated by Henry Bettenson. London: Penguin, 1984.
——, *Confessions*. Translated by Henry Chadwick. Oxford: Oxford University Press, 1991.
Balthasar, Hans Urs von, '*Casta Meretrix*'. In *Spouse of the Word: Explorations in Theology*, vol. 2, 193–288. San Francisco: Ignatius Press, 1991.
Banki, Judith H. and John T. Pawlikowski, eds., *Ethics in the Shadow of the Holocaust: Christian and Jewish Perspectives*. Franklin, WI: Sheed & Ward, 2001.

Barkan, Elazar, *The Guilt of Nations: Restitution and Negotiating Historical Injustices*. New York: Norton, 2000.
Barkan, Elazar and Alexander Karn, 'Group Apology as Ethical Imperative'. In *Taking Wrongs Seriously: Apologies and Reconciliation*, edited by Elazar Barkan and Alexander Karn, 3–30. Stanford, CA: Stanford University Press, 2006.
——, eds, *Taking Wrongs Seriously: Apologies and Reconciliation*. Stanford, CA: Stanford University Press, 2006.
Bash, Anthony, *Forgiveness and Christian Ethics*. Cambridge: Cambridge University Press, 2007.
Baum, Gregory, *Religion and Alienation: A Theological Reading of Sociology*. New York: Paulist Press, 1975.
Baumann, Michael, ed., *Steps to Reconciliation: Reformed and Anabaptist Churches in Dialogue*. Zürich: Theologischer Verlag Zürich, 2007.
Bavelas, Janet B., 'An Analysis of Formal Apologies by Canadian Churches to First Nations'. Centre for Studies in Religion and Society, Occasional Paper. Victoria, BC: University of Victoria, 2004.
Bellitto, Christopher M., 'Teaching the Church's Mistakes: Historical Hermeneutics in *Memory and Reconciliation: The Church and the Faults of the Past*'. *Horizons* 32 (2005), 123–35.
Bergen, Jeremy M., 'Problem or Promise? Confessional Martyrs and Mennonite–Roman Catholic Relations'. *Journal of Ecumenical Studies* 41 (2004), 367–88.
——, 'Reconciling Past and Present: A Review Essay on Collective Apologies'. *Journal of Religion, Conflict, and Peace* 2, no. 2 (Spring 2008). Online journal: www.religionconflictpeace.org/node/52.
Berkouwer, G. C., *The Church*. Translated by James E. Davison. Grand Rapids: Eerdmans, 1976.
Bernadin, Joseph, 'Proposal for a New Rite of Penance'. In *Penance and Reconciliation in the Mission of the Church*, 41–4. Washington, DC: United States Catholic Conference, 1984.
Bernauer, James, 'The Holocaust and the Catholic Church's Search for Forgiveness'. Paper presented at Boisi Centre for Religion and American Public Life, Boston College, 2002. Online: www.bc.edu/research/cjl/meta-elements/texts/cjrelations/resources/articles/bernauer.htm.
Biffi, Giocomo, *Casta Meretrix: 'The Chaste Whore': An Essay on the Ecclesiology of St. Ambrose*. Translated by Richard J. S. Brown. London: Saint Austin Press, 2000.

Boeve, Lieven, *Interrupting Tradition: An Essay on Christian Faith in a Postmodern Context*. Leuven: Peeters Press, 2003.

Bonhoeffer, Dietrich, *The Cost of Discipleship*. Translated by R. H. Fuller. New York: Macmillan, 1963.

——, *Ethics*. Translated by Neville Horton Smith. New York: Macmillan, 1955.

——, *Sanctorum Communio: A Theological Study of the Sociology of the Church*. Translated by Reinhold Krauss and Nancy Lukens. Minneapolis: Fortress Press, 1998.

Borromeo, Agostino, ed., *L'Inquisizione: atti del simposio internazionale*. Vatican City: Biblioteca Apostolica Vaticana, 2003.

Boston Globe Investigative Staff, *Betrayal: The Crisis in the Catholic Church*. Boston: Little, Brown, 2002.

Botman, H. Russel, 'The Offender and the Church'. In *Facing the Truth*, edited by James Cochrane, John de Gruchy, and Stephen Martin, 126–31. Cape Town: David Philip, 1999.

Bouteneff, Peter C., 'Ecumenical Ecclesiology and the Language of Unity'. *Journal of Ecumenical Studies* 44 (2009), 352–60.

Braaten, Carl E. and Robert W. Jenson, eds., *In One Body Through the Cross: The Princeton Proposal for Christian Unity*. Grand Rapids: Eerdmans, 2003.

Braham, Randolph L., 'Remembering and Forgetting: The Vatican, the German Catholic Hierarchy, and the Holocaust'. *Holocaust and Genocide Studies* 13 (1999), 222–51.

Brockway, Allan., 'Assemblies of the World Council of Churches'. In *The Theology of the Churches and the Jewish People: Statements by the World Council of Churches and Its Member Churches*, 123–39. Geneva: WCC Publications, 1988.

Brooks, Roy L., ed., *When Sorry Isn't Enough: The Controversy Over Apologies and Reparations for Human Injustice*. New York: New York University Press, 1999.

Burgess, Andrew, 'A Community of Love? Jesus as the Body of God in Robert Jenson's Trinitarian Thought'. *International Journal of Systematic Theology* 6 (2004), 289–300.

Buscher, Frank M. and Michael Phayer, 'German Catholic Bishops and the Holocaust, 1940–1953'. *German Studies Review* 11 (1988), 463–85.

Bush, Peter G., 'The Presbyterian Church in Canada and the Pope: One Denomination's Struggle with Its Confessional History'. *Studies in Religion/Sciences Religieuses* 33 (2004), 105–15.

Caner, Ergun Mehmet and Emir Fethi Caner, *Christian Jihad: Two*

Former Muslims Look at the Crusades and Killing in the Name of Christ. Grand Rapids: Kregel, 2004.

Capizzi, Joseph E., 'For What Shall We Repent? Reflections on the American Bishops, Their Teaching, and Slavery in the United States, 1939–1961'. *Theological Studies* 65 (2004), 767–91.

Carmichael, Kay, *Sin and Forgiveness: New Responses in a Changing World*. Aldershot, UK: Ashgate, 2003.

Cassidy, Edward Idris, 'The Vatican Document on the Holocaust: Reflections Toward a New Millennium'. In *Ethics in the Shadow of the Holocaust: Christian and Jewish Perspectives*, edited by Judith H. Banki and John T. Pawlikowski, 5–22. Franklin, WI: Sheed & Ward, 2001.

Castro, Daniel, *Another Face of Empire: Bartolomé de Las Casas, Indigenous Rights, and Ecclesiastical Imperialism*. Durham, NC: Duke University Press, 2007.

Cavanaugh, William T., *Torture and Eucharist: Theology, Politics and the Body of Christ*. Oxford: Blackwell, 1998.

Celermajer, Danielle, 'The Apology in Australia: Re-Covenanting the National Imaginary'. In *Taking Wrongs Seriously: Apologies and Reconciliation*, edited by Elazar Barkan and Alexander Karn, 153–84. Stanford, CA: Stanford University Press, 2006.

——, *The Sins of the Nations and the Ritual of Apologies*. Cambridge: Cambridge University Press, 2009.

Chircop, Lionel, 'Remembering the Future'. In *Reconciling Memories*. Enlarged ed., edited by Alan D. Falconer and Joseph Liechty, 20–9. Dublin: Columba Press, 1998.

Christian Scholars Group on Christian–Jewish Relations, 'A Sacred Obligation: Rethinking Christian Faith in Relation to Judaism and Jewish People'. In *Seeing Judaism Anew: Christianity's Sacred Obligation*, edited by Mary C. Boys, xiii–xix. Lanham, MD: Sheed & Ward, 2005.

Chryssavgis, John, ed., *Cosmic Grace, Humble Prayer: The Ecological Vision of the Green Patriarch Bartholomew I*. Grand Rapids: Eerdmans, 2003.

Clifford, Catherine E., *The Groupe Des Dombes: A Dialogue of Conversion*. New York: Peter Lang, 2005.

Cochrane, James, John de Gruchy and Stephen Martin, 'Faith, Struggle and Reconciliation'. In *Facing the Truth*, edited by James Cochrane, John de Gruchy and Stephen Martin, 1–11. Cape Town: David Philip, 1999.

Coffey, David M., *The Sacrament of Reconciliation*. Collegeville, MN: Liturgical Press, 2001.

Commonwealth of Australia, *Bringing Them Home: Report of the National Inquiry Into the Separation of Aboriginal and Torres Strait Islander Children from Their Families*. Sydney: Human Rights and Equal Opportunity Commission, 1997.

Communio Sanctorum: The Church as the Communion of Saints, Official German Catholic–Lutheran Dialogue. Translated by Mark W. Jeske, Michael Root and Daniel R. Smith. Collegeville, MN: Liturgical Press, 2004.

Conradie, Ernst M., *The Church and Climate Change*. Pietermaritzburg, South Africa: Cluster Publications, 2008.

Conway, John S., 'How Shall the Nations Repent? The Stuttgart Declaration of Guilt, October 1945'. *Journal of Ecclesiastical Studies* 38 (1987), 596–622.

Copeland, E. Luther, *The Southern Baptist Convention and the Judgment of History*. Rev. ed. Lanham, MD: University of America Press, 2002.

Cottier, Georges, *Mémoire et repentance: Pourquoi l'Église demande pardon*. Saint-Maur: Parole et Silence, 1998.

——, 'Repentance in an Ecumenical Context'. *Theology Digest* 47 (2000), 103–8.

Coyne, George V., 'The Church's Most Recent Attempt to Dispel the Galileo Myth'. In *The Church and Galileo*, edited by Ernan McMullin, 340–59. Notre Dame, IN: University of Notre Dame Press, 2005.

Croner, Helga, comp. and ed., *More Stepping Stones to Jewish – Christian Relations*. Mahurah, NJ: Paulist Press, 1985.

Dallen, James, *The Reconciling Community: The Rite of Penance*. New York: Pueblo Publishing, 1986.

Daye, Russell, 'An Unresolved Dilemma: Canada's United Church Seeks Reconciliation with Native Peoples'. *The Ecumenist* 36, no. 2 (May 1999), 11–15.

de Gruchy, John W., *The Church Struggle in South Africa*. 25th anniversary ed. Minneapolis: Fortress Press, 2004.

——, *Reconciliation: Restoring Justice*. Minneapolis: Fortress Press, 2002.

Ditmanson, Harold H., Introduction to the Løgumkloster Report. In *Stepping Stones to Further Jewish–Lutheran Relationships*, edited by Harold H. Ditmanson, 18–25. Minneapolis: Augsburg Fortress, 1990.

Dokecki, Paul R., *The Clergy Sexual Abuse Crisis: Reform and Renewal in the Catholic Community*. Washington, D.C.: Georgetown University Press, 2004.

Dorff, Elliot N., 'Individual and Communal Forgiveness'. In *Autonomy and Judaism: The Individual and the Community in Jewish Philosophical Thought*, edited by Daniel H. Frank, 193–218. Albany, NY: SUNY Press, 1992.

Dratch, Mark., 'Forgiving the Unforgivable? Jewish Insights Into Repentance and Forgiveness'. *Journal of Religion and Abuse* 4, no. 4 (2002), 7–24.

Dulles, Avery, 'A Half Century of Ecclesiology'. *Theological Studies* 50 (1989), 419–42.

——, 'Should the Church Repent?' *First Things*, no. 88 (December 1998), 36–41.

Durocher, Alain Paul, 'Between the Right to Forget and the Duty to Remember: The Politics of Memory in Canada's Public Church Apologies'. Unpublished Ph.D. dissertation. Graduate Theological Union, 2002.

Eckardt, Alice L., 'Revising Christian Teaching: The Work of the Christian Scholars Group on Christian–Jewish Relations'. In *Seeing Judaism Anew: Christianity's Sacred Obligation*, edited by Mary C. Boys, 263–71. Lanham, MD: Sheed & Ward, 2005.

Emery, Pierre-Yves, *The Communion of Saints*. Translated by D. J. Watson and M. Watson. London: Faith Press, 1966.

Erb, Peter C., ed., *Martyrdom in an Ecumenical Perspective: A Mennonite–Catholic Conversation*. Kitchener, ON: Pandora Press, 2007.

Euart, Sharon, 'A Canonical Perspective on the Sexual Abuse Crisis'. *Origins* 37, no. 8 (5 July 2007), 113–19.

Farrow, Douglas, David Demson and J. Augustine Di Noia, 'Robert Jenson's *Systematic Theology*: Three Responses'. *International Journal of Systematic Theology* 1 (1999), 89–104.

Favazza, Joseph A., *The Order of Penitents: Historical Roots and Pastoral Future*. Collegeville, MN: Liturgical Press, 1988.

Fette, Julie, 'The Apology Moment: Vichy Memories in 1990s France'. In *Taking Wrongs Seriously: Apologies and Reconciliation*, edited by Elazar Barkan and Alexander Karn, 259–85. Stanford, CA: Stanford University Press, 2006.

Fink, Peter E., 'Alternative 3: Liturgy for a Christian Day of Atonement'. In *Alternative Futures for Worship: Reconciliation*, vol. 4, edited by Peter E. Fink, 127–45. Collegeville, MN: Liturgical Press, 1987.

Finocchiaro, Maurice A., *Retrying Galileo, 1633–1992*. Berkeley, CA: University of California Press, 2005.

Forte, Bruno, 'The Church Confronts the Faults of the Past'. Translated by Adrian Walker. *Communio: International Catholic Review* 27 (2000), 676–87.

Frawley-O'Dea, Mary Gail, *Perversions of Power: Sexual Abuse in the Catholic Church*. Nashville: Vanderbilt University Press, 2007.

Funk-Unrau, Neil, 'Re-Negotiation of Social Relations Through Public Apologies to Canadian Aboriginal Peoples'. *Research in Social Movements, Conflict and Change* 29 (2008), 1–19.

Gaillardetz, Richard R., *Teaching with Authority: A Theology of the Magisterium in the Church*. Collegeville, MN: Liturgical Press, 1997.

Gibney, Mark, Rhoda Howard-Hassmann, Jean-Marc Coicaud and Niklaus Steiner, eds., *The Age of Apology: Facing up to the Past*. Philadelphia: Pennsylvania University Press, 2008.

Goldhagen, Daniel Jonah, *A Moral Reckoning: The Role of the Catholic Church in the Holocaust and Its Unfulfilled Duty of Repair*. New York: Knopf, 2002.

Gooder, Haydie and Jane M. Jacobs, ' "On the Border of the Unsayable": The Apology in Postcolonizing Australia'. *Interventions: International Journal of Post-Colonial Studies* 2 (2000), 229–47.

Govier, Trudy, 'What is Acknowledgement and Why is It Important?' In *Dilemmas of Reconciliation: Cases and Concepts*, edited by Carol A. L. Prager and Trudy Govier, 65–89. Waterloo: Wilfrid Laurier University Press, 2003.

Govier, Trudy, and Wilhelm Verwoerd, 'The Promise and Pitfalls of Apology'. *Journal of Social Philosophy* 33 (2002), 67–82.

Greenberg, Irving, 'The Church as Sacrament and as Institution: Jewish Reflections'. In *Ethics in the Shadow of the Holocaust: Christian and Jewish Perspectives*, edited by Judith H. Banki and John T. Pawlikowski, 61–80. Franklin, WI: Sheed & Ward, 2001.

——, 'Theology After the Shoah: The Transformation of the Core Paradigm'. *Modern Judaism* 26 (2006), 213–39.

Gunton, Colin, ' "Until He Comes": Towards an Eschatology of Church Membership'. *International Journal of Systematic Theology* 3 (2001), 187–200.

Hanke, Lewis, *All Mankind is One: A Study of the Disputation Between Bartolomé de Las Casas and Juan Ginés de Sepúlveda in 1550 on the Intellectual and Religious Capacity of the American Indians*. DeKalb, IL: Northern Illinois University Press, 1974.

Hauerwas, Stanley, *The Peaceable Kingdom: A Primer in Christian Ethics*. Notre Dame, IN: Notre Dame University Press, 1983.

Healy, Nicholas M., *Church, World and the Christian Life: Practical–Prophetic Ecclesiology*. Cambridge: Cambridge University Press, 2000.

——, 'Practices and the New Ecclesiology: Misplaced Concreteness?' *International Journal of Systematic Theology* 5 (2003), 287–308.

Hebbelinck, Thérèse, 'Le 30 septembre 1997: L'église de France demande pardon aux juifs'. *Revue d'histoire ecclésiastique* 103 (2008), 119–60.

Hellwig, Monika K., *Sign of Reconciliation and Conversion: The Sacrament of Penance for Our Times*. Rev. ed. Wilmington, DL: Michael Glazier, 1984.

Helmreich, Ernst Christian, *The German Churches Under Hitler: Background, Struggle, and Epilogue*. Detroit: Wayne State University Press, 1979.

Henderson, Michael, 'Acknowledging History as a Prelude to Forgiveness'. *Peace Review* 14 (2002), 265–70.

Henry, Patrick, 'The French Catholic Church's Apology'. *The French Review* 72 (1999), 1099–105.

Himes, Kenneth R., 'Human Failing: The Meanings and Metaphors of Sin'. In *Moral Theology: New Directions and Fundamental Issues*, edited by James Keating, 145–61. New York: Paulist Press, 2004.

Hinze, Bradford E., 'Ecclesial Repentance and the Demands of Dialogue'. *Theological Studies* 61 (2000), 207–38.

Hockenos, Matthew D., *A Church Divided: German Protestants Confront the Nazi Past*. Bloomington, IN: Indiana University Press, 2004.

Horton, Michael S., *People and Place: A Covenant Ecclesiology*. Louisville: Westminster John Knox Press, 2008.

Howard, Keith and Gaye Sharpe, 'Were You There?' *Touchstone* 16, no. 2 (May 1998), 16–21.

Hunsinger, George, 'Robert Jenson's *Systematic Theology*: A Review Essay'. *Scottish Journal of Theology* 55 (2002), 161–200.

Huysmans, Ruud G. W., 'The Inquisition for Which the Pope Did Not Ask Forgiveness'. *The Jurist* 66 (2006), 469–82.

International Theological Commission, 'Memory and Reconciliation: The Church and the Faults of the Past'. *Origins* 29, no. 39 (16 March 2000), 625–44.

James, Matt, 'Wrestling with the Past: Apologies, Quasi-Apologies, and Non-Apologies in Canada'. In *The Age of Apology: Facing up to the Past*, edited by Mark Gibney, Rhoda Howard-Hassmann, Jean-Marc Coicaud and Niklaus Steiner, 137–53. Philadelphia: University of Pennsylvania Press, 2008.

Jaspers, Karl, *The Question of German Guilt*. Translated by E. B. Ashton. New York: Capricorn Books, 1961.

Jenson, Robert W., *Systematic Theology: The Triune God*. Volume 1. Oxford: Oxford University Press, 1997.

——, *Systematic Theology: The Works of God*. Volume 2. Oxford: Oxford University Press, 1999.

——, *Unbaptized God: The Basic Flaw in Ecumenical Theology*. Minneapolis: Fortress Press, 1992.

John Paul II, Pope, 'Incarnationis Mysterium: Bull of Indiction of the Great Jubilee of the Year 2000'. *Origins* 28, no. 26 (10 December 1998), 445, 447–52.

——, 'Orientale Lumen: Apostolic Letter to Mark the Centenary of *Orientalium Dignitas* of Pope Leo XIII'. *Origins* 25, no. 1 (18 May 1995), 1, 3–13.

——, 'Reconciliatio et Paenitentia: Apostolic Exhortation on Reconciliation and Penance'. *Origins* 14, no. 27 (20 December 1984), 432, 434–58.

——, 'Tertio Millennio Adveniente: Apostolic Letter on Preparation for the Jubilee of the Year 2000'. *Origins* 24, no. 24 (10 December 1994), 401, 403–16.

——, 'Ut Unum Sint: Encyclical Letter on Commitment to Ecumenism'. *Origins* 25, no. 4 (8 June 1995), 49, 51–72.

——, 'The Value of This Collegial Body'. In *Penance and Reconciliation in the Mission of the Church*, 61–68. Washington, D.C.: United States Catholic Conference, 1984.

John Paul II, Pope and Ecumenical Patriarch Bartholomew I, 'Common Declaration on Environmental Ethics, 2002'. In *Growth in Agreement III*, edited by Jeffrey Gros, Thomas F. Best and Lorelei F. Fuchs, 184–86. Geneva: WCC, 2007.

Jones, L. Gregory, *Embodying Forgiveness: A Theological Analysis*. Grand Rapids: Eerdmans, 1995.

Jüngel, Eberhard, 'The Church as Sacrament?' In *Theological Essays*, edited and translated by John B. Webster, 191–213. Edinburgh: T & T Clark, 1989.

Kelly, J. N. D., *Early Christian Creeds*. 3d ed. London: Longman, 1972.

Klenicki, Leon, 'Commentary by Rabbi Leon Klenicki'. In *The Holocaust, Never to be Forgotten: Reflections on the Holy See's Document We Remember*, 23–46. New York: Paulist Press, 2001.

Koesten, Joy and Robert C. Rowland, 'The Rhetoric of Atonement'. *Communication Studies* 55 (2004), 68–87.

Komonchak, Joseph A., 'Preparing for the New Millennium'. *Logos: A Journal of Catholic Thought* 1, no. 2 (1997), 34–55.

Kress, Robert, '*Simul Justus et Peccator*: Ecclesiological and Ecumenical Perspectives'. *Horizons* 11 (1984), 255–75.

Kuperus, Tracy, *State, Civil Society, and Apartheid in South Africa: An Examination of Dutch Reformed Church–State Relations*. Houndmills, UK: Macmillan, 1999.

Lakeland, Paul, 'Roman Catholicism After the Sex Scandals'. In *Faith in America: Changes, Challenges, New Directions*, vol. 1, edited by Charles H. Lippy, 45–61. Westport, CT: Praeger, 2006.

Lapomarda, Vincent A., 'Reckoning with Daniel J. Goldhagen's Views of the Roman Catholic Church, the Holocaust, and Pope Pius XII'. *The Journal of the Historical Society* 3 (2003), 493–502.

Laszlo, Stephen, 'Sin in the Holy Church of God'. In *Council Speeches of Vatican II*, edited by Hans Küng, Yves Congar and Daniel O'Hanlon, 44–8. Glen Rock, NJ: Paulist Press, 1964.

Lazare, Aaron, *On Apology*. Oxford: Oxford University Press, 2004.

Lewis, Keith D., *The Catholic Church in History: Legends and Reality*. New York: Crossroad, 2006.

Lewis, Peter, 'After Sorry: Towards a Covenant of Solidarity and Embrace'. *Pacifica* 22 (2009), 1–19.

Liechty, Joseph, 'Putting Forgiveness in Its Place: The Dynamics of Reconciliation'. In *Explorations in Reconciliation: New Directions in Theology*, edited by David Tombs and Joseph Liechty, 59–68. Aldershot, UK: Ashgate, 2006.

Lind, Jennifer, *Sorry States: Apologies in International Politics*. Ithaca, NY: Cornell University Press, 2008.

Lindbeck, George, 'The Church as Israel: Ecclesiology and Ecumenism'. In *Jews and Christians: People of God*, edited by Carl E. Braaten and Robert W. Jenson, 78–94. Grand Rapids: Eerdmans, 2003.

Lutheran World Federation and Roman Catholic Church, 'Joint Declaration on the Doctrine of Justification, 1999'. In *Growth in Agreement II: Reports and Agreed Statements of Ecumenical Conversations on a World Level, 1982–1998*, edited by Jeffrey Gros, Harding Meyer and William G. Rusch, 566–82. Geneva: WCC Publications, 2000.

Madigan, Kevin, 'A Survey of Jewish Reaction to the Vatican Statement on the Holocaust'. *CrossCurrents* 50 (2000–2001), 488–505.

Mannion, Gerard, *Ecclesiology and Postmodernity: Questions for the Church in Our Time*. Collegeville, MN: Liturgical Press, 2007.

Marrus, Michael R., 'Papal Apologies of Pope John Paul II'. In *The Age of Apology: Facing up to the Past*, edited by Mark Gibney, Rhoda Howard-Hassman, Jean-Marc Coicaud and Niklaus Steiner, 259–70. Philadelphia: University of Pennsylvania Press, 2008.

Martin, David, 'A Socio–Theological Critique of Collective National Guilt'. In *Reflections on Sociology and Theology*, 207–24. Oxford: Clarendon Press, 1997.

McCarthy, Michael C., 'An Ecclesiology of Groaning: Augustine, the Psalms and the Making of Church'. *Theological Studies* 66 (2005), 23–48.

——, 'Religious Disillusionment and the Cross: An Augustinian Reflection'. *Heythrop Journal* 48 (2007), 577–92.

McDonnell, Kilian, 'The Ratzinger/Kasper Debate: The Universal Church and Local Churches'. *Theological Studies* 63 (2002), 227–50.

McDonough, William and Catherine Michaud, 'Papal Apologies Embody and Advance Vatican II on the "Tradition Poured Out in the Church".' In *Revelation and the Church: Vatican II in the Twenty-First Century*, edited by Raymond A. Lucker and William McDonough, 103–22. Maryknoll, NY: Orbis Books, 2003.

McEllhenney, John G., 'Contention, Contrition, Celebration, Caution: The 2000 General Conference in Historical Perspective'. *Methodist History* 40 (2001), 29–42.

McFarland, Ian A., 'The Body of Christ: Rethinking a Classic Ecclesiological Model'. *International Journal of Systematic Theology* 7 (2005), 225–45.

McGoldrick, Patrick, 'Sin and the Holy Church'. *Irish Theological Quarterly* 32 (1965), 3–27.

McKay, Stanley and Janet Silman, 'A First Nations Movement in a Canadian Church'. In *The Reconciliation of Peoples: Challenge to the Churches*, edited by Gregory Baum and Harold Wells, 172–83. Maryknoll, NY: Orbis Books, 1997.

McKenna, Joseph H., 'The Possibility of Social Sin'. *Irish Theological Quarterly* 60 (1994), 125–40.

Meiring, Piet, 'The Dutch Reformed Church and the Truth and Reconciliation Commission'. *Scriptura* 83 (2003), 250–57.

Melton, J. Gordon, *The Churches Speak on – Women's Ordination: Official Statements from Religious Bodies and Ecumenical Organizations*. Detroit: Gale Research, 1991.

Metz, Johann-Baptist, 'Facing the Jews: Christian Theology After Auschwitz'. In *Faith and the Future: Essays on Theology, Solidarity, and*

Modernity, Johann-Baptist Metz and Jürgen Moltmann, 38–48. Maryknoll, NY: Orbis, 1995.

Meyer, Harding, 'Christian World Communions'. In *A History of the Ecumenical Movement, 1968–2000*, vol. 3, edited by John Briggs, Mercy Amba Oduyoye and Georges Tsetsis, 103–22. Geneva: WCC Publications, 2004.

Miller, J. R., *Shingwauk's Vision: A History of Native Residential Schools*. Toronto: University of Toronto Press, 1996.

Minow, Martha, *Between Vengeance and Forgiveness: Facing History After Genocide and Mass Violence*. Boston: Beacon Press, 1998.

Moltmann, Jürgen, *The Church in the Power of the Spirit*. Translated by Margaret Kohl. Minneapolis: Fortress Press, 1993.

———, *The Spirit of Life: A Universal Affirmation*. Translated by Margaret Kohl. Minneapolis: Fortress Press, 1992.

Monter, William, 'The Roman Inquisition and Protestant Heresy Executions in 16th Century Europe'. In *L'Inquisizione: atti del simposio internazionale*, edited by Agostino Borromeo, 539–48. Vatican City: Biblioteca Apostolica Vaticana, 2003.

Morioka, Iwao, 'Japanese Churches and World War II'. Translated by Akira Demura. *Japan Christian Quarterly* 34 (1968), 75–85.

Mynatty, Hormis, 'The Concept of Social Sin'. *Louvain Studies* 16 (1991), 3–26.

Nelson, Derek R., *What's Wrong with Sin? Sin in Individual and Social Perspective from Schleiermacher to Theologies of Liberation*. London: T & T Clark, 2009.

Neudecker, Richard, 'The Catholic Church and the Jewish People'. In *Vatican II: Assessment and Perspectives*, vol. 3, edited by René Latourelle, 282–323. New York: Paulist Press, 1989.

Niebuhr, H. Richard, 'The Disorder of Man in the Church of God'. In *Man's Disorder and God's Design: The Amsterdam Assembly Series*. World Council of Churches, First Assembly, 78–88. New York: Harper & Brothers, 1949.

Noonan, John T. Jr, *A Church That Can and Cannot Change: The Development of Catholic Moral Teaching*. Notre Dame, IN: University of Notre Dame Press, 2005.

Novak, David, 'Jews and Catholics: Beyond Apologies'. *First Things*, no. 89 (January 1999), 20–5.

O'Collins, Gerald and Mario Farrugia. *Catholicism: The Story of Catholic Christianity*. Oxford: Oxford University Press, 2003.

O'Keefe, Mark, *What Are They Saying About Social Sin?* Mahwah, NJ: Paulist Press, 1990.

Parkinson, Patrick, Kim Oates and Amanda Jayakody, 'Breaking the Long Silence: Reports of Child Sexual Abuse in the Anglican Church of Australia'. *Ecclesiology* 6 (2010), 183–200.

Paul VI, Pope, 'Ecclesiam Suam: Encyclical Letter on the Church'. In *The Papal Encyclicals 1958–1981*, vol. 5, compiled by Claudia Carlin, 135–60. Wilmington, NC: Grath, 1981.

Pfeil, Margaret R., 'Doctrinal Implications of Magisterial Use of the Language of Social Sin'. *Louvain Studies* 27 (2002), 132–52.

——, 'Social Sin: Social Reconciliation?' In *Reconciliation, Nations and Churches in Latin America*, edited by Iain S. Maclean, 171–89. Aldershot, UK: Ashgate, 2006.

Phayer, Michael, 'The German Catholic Church After the Holocaust'. *Holocaust and Genocide Studies* 10 (1996), 151–67

Pope, Stephen, 'Accountability and Sexual Abuse in the United States: Lessons for the Universal Church'. *Irish Theological Quarterly* 69 (2004), 73–88.

Prusak, Bernard P., 'Theological Considerations – Hermeneutical, Ecclesiological, Eschatological Regarding *Memory and Reconciliation: The Church and the Faults of the Past*'. *Horizons* 32 (2005), 136–51.

Radner, Ephraim, *The End of the Church: A Pneumatology of Christian Division in the West*. Grand Rapids: Eerdmans, 1998.

Radner, Ephraim and Philip Turner, *The Fate of Communion: The Agony of Anglicanism and the Future of the Global Church*. Grand Rapids: Eerdmans, 2006.

Rahner, Karl, 'The Church of Sinners'. In *Theological Investigations*, vol. 6, translated by Karl-H. Kruger and Boniface Kruger, 253–69. Baltimore: Helicon Press, 1969.

——, 'The Church of the Saints'. In *Theological Investigations*, vol. 3, translated by Karl-H. Kruger and Boniface Kruger, 91–104. Baltimore: Helicon Press, 1967.

——, 'The Sinful Church in the Decrees of Vatican II'. In *Theological Investigations*, vol. 6, translated by Karl-H. Kruger and Boniface Kruger, 270–94. Baltimore: Helicon Press, 1967.

Ratzinger, Joseph, 'The Church's Guilt'. In *Pilgrim Fellowship of Faith: The Church as Communion*, translated by Henry Taylor, 274–83. San Francisco: Ignatius Press, 2005.

——, *Principles of Catholic Theology: Building Stones for a Fundamental Theology*. Translated by Mary Frances McCarthy. San Francisco: Ignatius Press, 1987.

Rausch, Thomas P., *Towards a Truly Catholic Church: An Ecclesiology for the Third Millennium.* Collegeville, MN: Liturgical Press, 2005.

Redcliffe, Gary, 'The Residential Schools and Narrative Identity: A Pastoral Analysis'. *Toronto Journal of Theology* 19 (2003), 53–67.

Research Institute on Christianity in South Africa, 'TRC Faith Communities Report [RICSA Report]'. In *Facing the Truth*, edited by James Cochrane, John de Gruchy, and Stephen Martin, 15–80. Cape Town: David Philip, 1999.

Rhonheimer, Martin, 'The Holocaust: What Was Not Said'. *First Things*, no. 137 (November 2003), 18–27.

Rigali, Norbert J., 'Moral Theology and Church Responses to Sexual Abuse'. *Horizons* 34 (2007), 183–204.

Rikhof, Herwi, 'The Holiness of the Church'. In *A Holy People: Jewish and Christian Perspectives on Religious Communal Identity*, edited by Marcel Poorthuis and Joshua Schwartz, 321–35. Leiden: Brill, 2006.

Riley-Smith, Jonathan, 'Rethinking the Crusades'. *First Things*, no. 101 (March 2000), 20–23.

'Rite of Penance'. In *The Rites of the Catholic Church as Revised by Decree of the Second Vatican Ecumenical Council.* Translated by The International Commission on English in the Liturgy, 341–448. New York: Pueblo Publishing, 1976.

Rossetti, Stephen, 'Renewal of the Priesthood in the Post-Dallas Era'. *Origins* 33, no. 15 (18 September 2003), 243, 245–8.

Roth, John D., 'Forgiveness and the Healing of Memories: An Anabaptist–Mennonite Perspective'. *Journal of Ecumenical Studies* 42 (2007), 573–89.

Ruddy, Christopher, 'Ecclesiological Issues Behind the Sexual Abuse Crisis'. *Origins* 37, no. 8 (5 July 2007), 119–26.

Schönborn, Christoph, 'The 'Communion of Saints' as Three States of the Church: Pilgrimage, Purification, and Glory'. Translated by Walter Jüptner. *Communio: International Catholic Review* 15 (1988), 169–81.

Second Vatican Council, *The Documents of Vatican II.* Edited by Walter M. Abbott. New York: America Press, 1965.

Senn, Frank, 'Confession of Sins in the Reformation Churches'. In *The Fate of Confession*, edited by Mary Collins and David Power, 105–16. Edinburgh: T & T Clark, 1987.

Shea, William R. and Mariano Artigas, *Galileo Observed: Science and the Politics of Belief.* Sagamore Beach, MA: Science History Publications, 2006.

Sherman, Franklin, 'The Road to Reconciliation: Protestant Church Statements on Christian–Jewish Relations'. In *Seeing Judaism Anew: Christianity's Sacred Obligation*, edited by Mary C. Boys, 241–51. Lanham, MD: Sheed & Ward, 2005.

Shimmel, Solomon, *Wounds Not Healed by Time: The Power of Repentance and Forgiveness.* Oxford: Oxford University Press, 2002.

Shore, Megan, *Religion and Conflict Resolution: Christianity and South Africa's Truth and Reconciliation Commission.* Farnham, UK: Ashgate, 2009.

Shriver, Donald W. Jr, *An Ethic for Enemies: Forgiveness in Politics.* New York: Oxford University Press, 1995.

Smith, Nick, *I Was Wrong: The Meanings of Apologies.* Cambridge: Cambridge University Press, 2008.

Sobrino, Jon, *The Principle of Mercy: Taking the Crucified People from the Cross.* Maryknoll, NY: Orbis Books, 1994.

Soetens, Claude, 'The Ecumenical Commitment of the Catholic Church'. In *History of Vatican II*, vol. 3, edited by Giuseppe Alberigo and Joseph A. Komonchak, 257–345. Maryknoll, NY: Orbis, 1995.

Soulen, R. Kendall, *The God of Israel and Christian Theology.* Minneapolis: Fortress Press, 1996.

Stephens, Prescot, *The Waldensian Story: A Study in Faith, Intolerance, and Survival.* Lewes, UK: Book Guild, 1998.

Stormon, E. J., ed., *Towards the Healing of Schism: The Sees of Rome and Constatinaple.* New York: Paulist Press, 1987.

Sullivan, Francis A., 'Do the Sins of Its Members Affect the Holiness of the Church?' In *In God's Hands: Essays on the Church & Ecumenism in Honour of Michael A. Fahey, S.J.*, edited by Michael S. Attridge and Jaroslav Z. Skira, 247–68. Leuven: Peeters, 2006.

Swartley, Keith E., ed., *Encountering the World of Islam.* Atlanta: Authentic Media, 2005.

Szablowinski, Zenon, 'Apology Without Compensation, Compensation with Apology'. *Pacifica* 18 (2005), 336–48.

Taft, Robert F., 'The Problem of 'Uniatism' and the 'Healing of Memories". *Logos: A Journal of Eastern Christian Studies* 41–2 (2000–2001), 155–96.

Tavuchis, Nicholas, *Mea Culpa: A Sociology of Apology and Reconciliation.* Stanford, CA: Stanford University Press, 1991.

Thompson, Janna, *Taking Responsibility for the Past: Reparation and Historical Injustice.* Cambridge, UK: Polity Press, 2002.

Torpey, John C., *Making Whole What Has Been Smashed: On Reparations Politics*. Cambridge, MA: Harvard University Press, 2006.

——, 'The Pursuit of the Past: A Polemical Perspective'. In *Theorizing Historical Consciousness*, edited by Peter Seixas, 240–55. Toronto: University of Toronto Press, 2004.

Trouillot, Michel-Rolph, 'Abortive Rituals: Historical Apologies in the Global Era'. *Interventions: International Journal of Postcolonial Studies* 2 (2000), 171–86.

The Truth and Reconciliation Commission of South Africa Final Report. Volume 4. Cape Town: Juta, 1998.

Tutu, Desmond, *No Future Without Forgiveness*. New York: Doubleday, 1999.

Visser't Hooft, W. A., ed., *The New Delhi Report: The Third Assembly of the World Council of Churches 1961*. London: SCM Press, 1961.

Volf, Miroslav, *The End of Memory: Remembering Rightly in a Violent World*. Grand Rapids: Eerdmans, 2006.

——, 'The Final Reconciliation: Reflections on a Social Dimension of the Eschatological Transition'. *Modern Theology* 16 (2000), 91–113.

Weakland, Rembert G., 'Images of the Church: From "Perfect Society" to "God's People on Pilgrimage"'. In *Unfinished Journey: The Church 40 Years After Vatican II*, edited by Austen Ivereigh, 78–90. New York: Continuum, 2003.

Webster, John, *Holiness*. London: SCM Press, 2003.

Welch, Claude, *The Reality of the Church*. New York: Scribner's, 1958.

Weyeneth, Robert R., 'The Power of Apology and the Process of Historical Reconciliation'. *Public Historian* 23, no. 3 (Summer 2001), 9–38.

Wiesenthal, Simon, *The Sunflower*. New York: Schocken Books, 1976.

Williams, Rowan, *On Christian Theology*. Malden, MA: Blackwell, 2000.

——, *A Ray of Darkness: Sermons and Reflections*. Cambridge, MA: Cowley Publications, 1995.

——, *Resurrection: Interpreting the Easter Gospel*. Rev. ed. Cleveland: Pilgrim Press, 2002.

——, *Why Study the Past? The Quest for the Historical Church*. Grand Rapids: Eerdmans, 2005.

World Council of Churches, *The Evanston Report: The Second Assembly of the World Council of Churches, 1954*, London: SCM Press, 1955.

——, *The Nature and Mission of the Church: A Stage on the Way to a Common Statement*. Revised Faith and Order Paper no. 198. Geneva: WCC, 2005.

——, 'Towards a Confession of the Common Faith, 1980'. Faith and

Order Paper no. 100 in *Documentary History of Faith and Order, 1963–1993*, edited by Günther Gassmann, 171–77. Geneva: WCC Publications, 1993.

Yeago, David S., '*Ecclesia Sancta, Ecclesia Peccatrix*: The Holiness of the Church in Martin Luther's Theology'. *Pro Ecclesia* 9 (2000), 331–54.

Yetzer, Bernard E., 'Holiness and Sin in the Church: An Examination of *Lumen Gentium* and *Unitatis Redintegratio* of the Second Vatican Council'. Unpublished STD dissertation. Catholic University of America, 1988.

Yoder, John Howard, 'Walk and Word'. In *Theology Without Foundations*, edited by Stanley Hauerwas, Nancey C. Murphy and Mark Nation, 77–90. Nashville: Abingdon Press, 1994.

Yutaka, Shishido, 'The Peace Movement of Postwar Japanese Christians'. *Japan Christian Quarterly* 51 (1985), 215–24.

APPENDIX

Ecclesial repentance: acts, documents and sources

THE DISUNITY OF CHRISTIANS

1920	Lambeth Conference of Anglican Bishops	'Appeal to All Christian People', resolution 9	Roger Coleman, ed., *Resolutions of the Twelve Lambeth Conferences, 1887–1998* (Toronto: Anglican Book Centre, 1992), 45–8; www.anglicancommunion.org/acns/archive/1920/1920-9.htm.
1927	Faith and Order Conference, Lausanne	'The Nature of the Church', adopted report	Lukas Vischer, ed., *A Documentary History of the Faith & Order Movement, 1927–1963* (St. Louis: Bethany Press, 1963), 30–3.
1937	William Temple, Archbishop of Canterbury	Opening sermon	*The Second World Conference on Faith and Order: Held at Edinburgh* (London: Student Christian Movement Press, 1938), 15–23.
1947	Church of South India	'Order of Service for the Inauguration of Church Union'	Unpublished text provided by Geoffrey Wainwright, Duke University Divinity School.
1948	World Council of Churches, Amsterdam Assembly	'The Universal Church in God's Design: Report of Section 1', adopted report	Vischer, *Documentary History*, 75–81.
1952	Faith and Order Conference, Lund	'Final Report: Lund'	Vischer, *Documentary History*, 85–130.

Year	Body	Document	Source
1954	World Council of Churches, Evanston Assembly	'Our Oneness in Christ and our Disunity as Churches', Faith and Order paper	Vischer, *Documentary History*, 131–43.
1960	General Conference Mennonite Church	'Centennial Study Conference Statement to Mennonite Brethren'	*Yearbook of the General Conference of the Mennonite Brethren Church of North America* (Hillsboro, KS, 1960), 38; Mennonite Heritage Centre (MHC) Archives, Winnipeg, MB.
1960	General Conference of the Mennonite Brethren Churches	Response to Greeting and Statement of Regret	*We Recommend . . . Recommendations and Resolutions of the General Conference of Mennonite Brethren Churches* (Fresno, CA, 1978), 20–1; MHC Archives.
1961	World Council of Churches, New Delhi Assembly	'Report of the Section on Unity', adopted report	W. A. Visser't Hooft, ed., *The New Delhi Report: The Third Assembly of the World Council of Churches* (London: SCM Press, 1961). 116–34.
1963	Roman Catholic Church, Pope Paul VI	Speech at the Opening of the Second Session of Vatican Council II	*The Vatican Council and Christian Unity* (London: Darton, Longman & Todd, 1966), 271–3.
1964	Roman Catholic Church, Second Vatican Council	*Unitatis Redintegratio: Decree on Ecumenism*, no. 7	Walter M. Abbott, ed., *The Documents of Vatican II* (New York: America Press, 1965), 341–66; www.vatican.va/archive/hist_councils/ii_vatican_council/documents/vat-ii_decree_19641121_unitatis-redintegratio_en.html.
1965	Roman Catholic Church and Ecumenical Patriarchate (Orthodox Churches)	'Joint Catholic–Orthodox Declaration'	E. J. Stormon, ed., *Towards the Healing of Schism: The Sees of Rome and Constantinople* (New York: Paulist Press, 1987), 126–8; www.vatican.va/holy_father/paul_vi/speeches/1965/documents/hf_pvi_spe_19651207_common-declaration_en.html.

1970	Church of North India	Service of Inauguration	Reference in W. J. Marshall, *Faith and Order in the North India/Pakistan Unity Plan* (London: Friends of CNI, 1979), 38–9.
1970	Lutheran World Federation	Statement on the visit of Cardinal Willebrands	*Sent Into the World: Proceedings of the Fifth Assembly of the Lutheran World Federation* (Minneapolis: Augsburg, 1971), 156–7.
1972	United Reformed Church (UK)	'Basis of Union'	David M. Thompson, ed., *Protestant Nonconformist Texts*, vol. 4 (Aldershot: Ashgate, 2007), 378–84; www.urc.org.uk/what_we_do/the_manual/the_basis_of_union.
1983	Roman Catholic Church, Pope John Paul II	Letter to Cardinal Willebrands for the Fifth Centenary of the Birth of Martin Luther	Luigi Accattoli, *When a Pope Asks Forgiveness: The Mea Culpa's of John Paul II*, trans. Jordan Aumann (Boston: Daughters of St. Paul, 1998), 195–6.
1983	World Alliance of Reformed Churches/Reformed Church of Zurich	Confession of sin	*Baptists and Reformed in Dialogue* (Geneva: World Alliance of Reformed Churches, 1983), 47.
1983	Baptist World Alliance/Swiss Union of Baptist Churches	Confession of sin	*Baptists and Reformed in Dialogue*, 47–8.
1985	Roman Catholic/Lutheran Joint Commission	Joint and separate statements of confession	*Facing Unity: Models, Forms and Phases of Catholic-Lutheran Church Fellowship* (New York: Lutheran World Federation, 1985), nos. 48–54.

1986	Canadian Conference of Mennonite Brethren Churches	Greetings and request for forgiveness	*CMC Yearbook* (Winnipeg, MB: Conference of Mennonites in Canada, 1986), 81.
1990	Lutheran World Federation	Statement on Lutheran Confessions and Baptists today	*Baptists and Lutherans in Conversation: A Message to the Churches* (Geneva: Baptist World Alliance; Lutheran World Federation, 1990), 38–41.
1990	Baptist World Alliance	Statement on Lutheran Confessions and Baptists today	*Baptists and Lutherans in Conversation*, 38–41.
1990	Reformed–Roman Catholic Dialogue	'Towards a Common Understanding of the Church', Second Phase, nos. 117–18	*Growth in Agreement II* (WCC: Geneva, 2000), 780–818.
1991	Roman Catholic Church, Pope John Paul II	Meeting with the Orthodox, Bialystock, Poland	Accattoli, *When a Pope Asks Forgiveness*, 194; www.vatican.va/holy_father/john_paul_ii/speeches/1991/june/documents/hf_jp-ii_spe_19910605_incontro-ecumenico-bialystok_it.html.
1991	Roman Catholic Church, Pope John Paul II	Ecumenical Celebration, Synod of Europe	Accattoli, *When a Pope Asks Forgiveness*, 98–9; www.vatican.va/holy_father/john_paul_ii/homilies/1991/documents/hf_jp-ii_hom_19911207_sinodo-vescovi_it.html.
1995	Roman Catholic Church, Pope John Paul II	*Ut Unum Sint: Encyclical Letter on Commitment to Ecumenism*, nos. 33–5.	*Origins* 25, no. 4 (8 June 1995), 49, 51–72; www.vatican.va/edocs/ENG0221/_INDEX.HTM.

1995	Roman Catholic Church, Pope John Paul II	*Orientale Lumen: Apostolic Letter to Mark the Centenary of Orientalium Dignitas*, nos. 17–21	*Origins* 25, no. 1 (18 May 1995), 1, 3–13; www.vatican.va/holy_father/john_paul_ii/apost_letters/documents/hf_jp-ii_apl_02051995_orientale-lumen_en.html.
1995	Roman Catholic Church, Pope John Paul II	Canonization of Jan Sarkander	Accattoli, *When a Pope Asks Forgiveness*, 146.
1995	Roman Catholic Church and Ecumenical Patriarchate (Orthodox Churches)	Common declaration	Accattoli, *When a Pope Asks Forgiveness*, 225–6.
1996	Roman Catholic Church, Pope John Paul II	Ecumenical celebration, Paderborn, regarding Martin Luther	Accattoli, *When a Pope Asks Forgiveness*, 194.
1997	Roman Catholic Church, Pope John Paul II	Baptismal Vigil, World Youth Day, reference to St. Bartholomew's Day Massacre	*Origins* 27, no. 4 (4 September 1997), 185, 187–9; www.vatican.va/holy_father/john_paul_ii/speeches/1997/august/documents/hf_jp-ii_spe_19970823_youth-vigil_en.html.
1997	Italian Catholic Bishops	'We Can Heal the Wounds of Memory', statement to Italian Protestants	Unpublished text provided by the Waldensian Evangelical Church, Italy.
1999	Roman Catholic Church, Pope John Paul II	Address to an International Symposium on John Hus	www.vatican.va/holy_father/john_paul_ii/speeches/1999/december/documents/hf_jp-ii_spe_17121999_jan-hus_en.html.

Year	Body	Title	Source
2000	Roman Catholic Church, Pope John Paul II	Universal Prayer, Day of Pardon	*Origins* 29, no. 40 (23 March 2000), 645–8; www.vatican.va/news_services/liturgy/documents/ns_lit_doc_20000312_prayer-day-pardon_en.html.
2000	United Methodist Church	'Letter to Pope John Paul II Asks Forgiveness', approved by General Conference	*Origins* 30, no. 2 (25 May 2000), 30.
2001	Roman Catholic Church, Pope John Paul II	Address to His Beatitude Archbishop Christodoulos, Primate of Greece	*Origins* 31, no. 1 (17 May 2001), 1, 3–4. www.vatican.va/holy_father/john_paul_ii/speeches/2001/documents/hf_jp-ii_spe_20010504_archbishop-athens_en.html.
2001	Roman Catholic Church, Pope John Paul II	Address at the arrival in Kiev	*Origins* 31, no. 8 (5 July 2001), 145–6. www.vatican.va/holy_father/john_paul_ii/speeches/2001/documents/hf_jp-ii_spe_20010623_ucraina-arrival_en.html.
2003	Mennonite World Conference and Roman Catholic Church	'Called Together to be Peacemakers', joint and separate statements, nos. 198–206	*Growth in Agreement III* (Geneva: WCC, 2007), 206–67; www.bridgefolk.net/dialogue2003/calledtogether.htm.
2004	Evangelical-Reformed Church of Zurich	'Statement of Regret', to the Amish, Mennonites, and Hutterites	Michael Baumann, ed., *Steps to Reconciliation: Reformed and Anabaptist Churches in Dialogue* (Zürich: Theologischer Verlag Zürich, 2007), 81–2.
2004	Swiss Mennonite Conference	Response to Evangelical-Reformed Church of Zurich	Baumann, *Steps to Reconciliation*, 83–4.

2004	Roman Catholic Church, Pope John Paul II	Welcome Address to the Ecumenical Patriarch Bartholomew I	www.vatican.va/holy_father/ john_paul_ii/speeches/2004/ june/documents/hf_jp-ii_ spe_20040629_bartho lomew-i_en.html.
2006	Evangelical Lutheran Church in America	Declaration on the Condemnation of Anabaptists	Draft text: 'Right Remebering in Anabaptist-Lutheran Relations', Report of the ELCA and Mennonite Church USA Liason Committee (Chicago, 2004), 13–16; final text: www.elca. org/~/media/Files/Who%20 We%20Are/Ecumenical%20 and%20Inter%20Religious%20 Relations/Declaration_ Condemnation_Anabaptist.ashx.
2008	Evangelical Protestant Church of Westphalia	Greetings to 300th Anniversary of Brethren Movement	Copy provided by the Board of Directors, Brethren Encyclopedia, Inc.
2009	Lutheran World Federation Council	Statement on Lutheran-Mennonite relationships, resolution recommended for adoption at LWF assembly 2010	Copy provided by LWF Office for Ecumenical Affairs.

OFFENCES AGAINST THE JEWISH PEOPLE

1946	Reformed Church in Hungary	'Declaration on the Persecution of the Jews and the Mission to the Jews'	Rolf Rendtorff and Hans Hermann Henrix, eds., *Die Kirchen und das Judentum*, vol. 1 (Paderborn: Bonifatius-Druckerei, 1988), 443–4.
1947	International Council of Christians and Jews	'An Address to the Churches' [Seelisberg Address]	*Die Kirchen*, vol. 1, 646–7; www. jcrelations.net/en/?item=983.

1948	World Council of Churches, Amsterdam Assembly	'The Christian Approach to the Jews', report	W. A. Visser't Hooft, ed., *The First Assembly of the World Council of Churches* (London: SCM Press, 1949), 160–4.
1948	Evangelical Church in Germany	'Message Concerning the Jewish Question'	Matthew D. Hockenos, *A Church Divided: German Protestants Confront the Nazi Past* (Bloomington, IN: Indiana University Press, 2004), 195–7; *Die Kirchen*, vol. 1, 540–4.
1950	Evangelical Church in Germany	Berlin-Weissensee Statement	Hockenos, *A Church Divided*, 199; *Die Kirchen*, vol. 1, 548–9.
1964	National Council of the Churches of Christ (US)	'Resolution on Jewish-Christian Relations'	Helga Croner, comp., *Stepping Stones to Further Jewish-Christian Relations* (London: Stimulus Books, 1977), 87.
1964	Lutheran World Federation	'The Church and the Jewish People', [Løgumkloster Report]	Harold H. Ditmanson, ed., *Stepping Stones to Further Jewish-Christian Relations: Key Lutheran Statements* (Minneapolis: Augsburg Fortress, 1990), 25–32.
1974	American Lutheran Church	'The American Lutheran Church and the Jewish Community'	Ditmanson, *Stepping Stones: Lutheran*, 67–74.
1975	West German Catholic Bishops	'A Change of Attitude Towards the Jewish People's History of Faith'	Croner, *Stepping Stones*, 66.
1975	Lutheran World Federation	'The Oneness of God and the Uniqueness of Christ' [Oslo Report]	Ditmanson, *Stepping Stones: Lutheran*, 52–9.
1977	Lutheran Church-Missouri Synod	'To Share the Gospel with Jews', resolution	Ditmanson, *Stepping Stones: Lutheran*, 77–8.

1978	Evangelical Church in the DDR (East Germany)	'Statement to the congregations on the occasion of the 40th anniversary of what is known as *Kristallnacht*'	*Die Kirchen*, vol. 1, 588–90.
1978	Evangelical Church in Germany	'Statement for the 40th anniversary of the Jewish pogroms of 9/10 November 1938'	*Die Kirchen*, vol. 1, 591–2.
1980	Evangelical Church of the Rhineland	'Towards Renovation of the Relationship of Christians and Jews'	*Die Kirchen*, vol. 1, 593–6; www.jcrelations.net/en/?item=1005.
1980	West German Catholic Bishops	'The Church and the Jews'	*Die Kirchen*, vol. 1, 260–80; www.bc.edu/research/cjl/meta-elements/texts/cjrelations/resources/documents/catholic/german_church_jews.html.
1983	Lutheran World Federation	'Luther, Lutheranism, and the Jews'	Ditmanson, *Stepping Stones: Lutheran*, 99–103.
1987	Presbyterian Church (USA)	'A Theological Understanding of the Relationship Between Christians and Jews', report	*Minutes, 199th General Assembly*, Part I (1987), 417–24; www.pcusa.org/theologyandworship/issues/christiansjews.pdf.
1987	United Church of Christ	Relationship between the United Church of Christ and the Jewish Community, General Synod resolution	*Minutes of the Sixteenth General Synod* (1987), 67–8; www.ucc.org/assets/pdfs/87-gs-jewish.pdf.

Year	Body	Title	Source
1988	Catholic Bishops of West Germany, Austria, and Berlin	'Accepting the Burden of History'	Hans Hermann Henrix and Wolfgang Kraus, eds., *Die Kirchen und das Judentum*, vol. 2 (Paderborn: Bonifatius, 2001), 355–65; www.bc.edu/research/cjl meta-elements/texts/cjrelations/ resources/documents/catholic/ burden_of_history.html.
1988	Evangelical Church in the DDR	'Statement on the 50th Anniversary of the Pogrom of 1938'	*Die Kirchen*, vol. 2, 580–1.
1990	Reformed Church in Hungary	'Statement of the Synod on its Relations with the Jews'	*Christian Jewish Relations* 23, no. 1 (1990), 43–5.
1992	Spanish Catholic Bishops	On the 1492 expulsion of Jews and Muslims	Accattoli, *When a Pope Asks Forgiveness*, 122.
1994	Evangelical Lutheran Church in America	'Declaration of the ELCA to the Jewish Community'	ELCA Church Council, Minutes April 16–18, 1994, 89; ELCA Archives, Elk Grove Village, IL; www.jcrelations.net/ en/?item=1003.
1994	Hungarian Bishops and Ecumenical Council of Churches in Hungary	'Joint Statement on the Occasion of the 50th Anniversary of the Holocaust'	*Catholics Remember the Holocaust* (Washington DC: United States Catholic Conference, 1998), 7–8; www.bc.edu/research/cjl/ meta-elements/texts/cjrelations/ resources/documents/catholic/ hungarian_joint_statement.html.
1995	National Conference of Catholic Bishops (US)	'Commemorating the Liberation of Auschwitz'	*Origins* 24, no. 34 (9 February 1995), 561, 563–4.
1995	German Catholic Bishops	'Opportunity to Re-examine Relationships with the Jews'	*Origins* 24, no. 34 (9 February 1995), 585–6; www.jcrelations.net en/?item=1035.

Year	Body	Title	Source
1995	Polish Catholic Bishops	'The Victims of Nazi Ideology'	*Origins* 24, no. 34 (9 February 1995), 586–8; www.jcrelations.net/en/?item=1034.
1995	Dutch Catholic Bishops	'Supported by One Root: Our Relationship to Judaism'	*Die Kirchen*, vol. 2, 263–6; www.jcrelations.net/en/?item=1033.
1995	Alliance of Baptists	Statement on Jewish-Christian Relations	*Die Kirchen*, vol. 2, 502–3; www.jcrelations.net/en/?item=1002.
1996	United Methodist Church	'Building New Bridges in Hope', reaffirmed 2004	*The Book of Resolutions of the United Methodist Church 1996* (Nashville: United Methodist Publishing House, 1996), 189–97; www.jcrelations.net/en/?item=999.
1997	Episcopal Church	'Reaffirm Interfaith Dialogue and Acknowledge Prejudice Against Jews', General Convention resolution D055	*Journal of the General Convention of the Protestant Episcopal Church in the United States of America* (1996), 216.
1997	French Catholic Bishops	'Statement of Repentance' [Drancy Declaration]	*Origins* 27, no. 18 (16 October 1997), 301, 303–5; www.jcrelations.net/en/?item=1030.
1997	Swiss Catholic Bishops	'Confronting the Debate about the Role of Switzerland During the Second World War'	*Catholics Remember the Holocaust*, 25–6; www.jcrelations.net/en/?item=1031.

1998	Roman Catholic Church, Commission for Religious Relations with the Jews	*We Remember: A Reflection on the Shoah*	*Origins* 27, no. 40 (26 March 1998), 671–5; www.vatican.va/roman_curia/pontifical_councils/chrstuni/documents/rc_pc_chrstuni_doc_16031998_shoah_en.html.
1998	Italian Catholic Bishops	Letter to the Jewish Community of Italy	*Catholics Remember the Holocaust*, 38–40; www.jcrelations.net/en/?item=1029.
1998	Evangelical-Lutheran Church in Bavaria	'Christians and Jews'	*Die Kirchen*, vol. 2, 805–12; www.jcrelations.net/en/?item=993.
1998	Evangelical Church in Austria (Augsburg and Helvetian Confessions)	'Time to Turn'	*Die Kirchen*, vol. 2, 522–5; www.jcrelations.net/en/?item=994.
1998	Slovakian Catholic Bishops	'Declaration on the Vatican Document *We Remember: A Reflection on the Shoah*'	*Die Kirchen*, vol. 2, 292–6.
2000	Roman Catholic Church, Pope John Paul II	Day of Pardon; Prayer of the Holy Father at the Western Wall	*Origins* 29, no. 40 (23 March 2000), 647; www.vatican.va/holy_father/john_paul_ii/travels/documents/hf_jp-ii_spe_20000326_jerusalem-prayer_en.html.
2000	Polish Catholic Bishops	Letter on the Occasion of the Great Jubilee of the Year 2000	*Die Kirchen*, vol. 2, 334–9; www.bc.edu/research/cjl/meta-elements/texts/cjrelations/resources/documents/catholic/polish_bishops_2000.htm.

2000	Evangelical Church in Germany	'Christians and Jews: A Manifesto 50 Years after the Weissensee Declaration'	*Die Kirchen*, vol. 2, 939–41; www.jcrelations.net/en/?item=991.
2001	United Church of Christ	Resolution on Anti-Semitism	*Minutes of the Twenty-Third General Synod* (United Church of Christ, 2001), 12; www.ucc.org/assets/pdfs/synod/gs23.pdf.
2003	United Church of Canada	'Bearing Faithful Witness: Statement on United Church-Jewish Relations Today', General Council resolution	*Record of Proceedings* (UCC, General Council, 2003), 213–14.

OFFENCES AGAINST ABORIGINAL PEOPLE

1970	Conference of Mennonites in Canada	'A Litany of Confession'	*Conference Bulletin* 6, no. 3 (4 September 1970), 10; MHC Archives.
1986	United Church of Canada	'Apology to First Nations'	*Record of Proceedings* (UCC, General Council, 1986), 85; www.united-church.ca/beliefs/policies/1986/a651.
1989	General Conference Mennonite Church	'Resolution on the 500th Anniversary of Colombus'	*Minutes of the 45th Triennial Sessions*, Normal, IL (1989), 17; MHC Archives; www.mennonitechurch.ca/about/foundation/documents/1989-columbus.htm.
1991	National (Canadian Catholic) Meeting on Indian Residential Schools	Statement	www.cccb.ca/site/images/stories/pdf/apology_saskatoon.pdf.

1991	Missionary Oblates of Mary Immaculate (Canada)	'An Apology to the First Nations of Canada'	*Origins* 21, no. 11 (15 August 1991), 183–4; www.cccb.ca/site/images/stories/pdf/oblate_apology_english.pdf.
1991	[Oblate Provincials]	Apology to members of the order	*Kerygma* 26 (1992), 27–9.
1992	Roman Catholic Church, Pope John Paul II	General audience, 21 October	Accattoli, *When a Pope Asks Forgiveness*, 158–9; www.vatican.va/holy_father/john_paul_ii/audiences/1992/documents/hf_jp-ii_aud_19921021_it.html.
1992	Mennonite Central Committee	'Statement to the Aboriginal People of the Americas'	*The Teachable Moment: A Christian Response to the Native Peoples of the Americas* (Winnipeg: MCC Canada, 1992), 11.
1992	United Methodist Church	'Confession to Native Americans', resolution	*The Book of Resolutions of the United Methodist Church 2008* (Nashville: Abingdon, 2008), 436–7.
1992	General Conference Mennonite Church	'Statement of Confession', litany	*Program Book, 46th Trienniel Sessions*, Sioux Falls, SD (1992), 28–30; MHC Archives.
1993	Society of Jesus (Jesuits), Fr. Peter-Hans Kolvenbach, Superior General	'Apology to Native Americans for Past Mistakes'	*Origins* 23, no. 3 (3 June 1993), 36–7.
1993	United Church of Christ, President Paul Sherry	'An Apology to the Indigenous Hawaiian People', implementing General Synod resolution	*New Conversations*, Spring 1993, 5–6; United Church of Christ Archives, Cleveland, OH.

1993	Anglican Church of Canada, Archbishop Michael Peers, Primate	'A Message to the National Native Convocation'	*Anglican Journal*, September 1993, 6; www.anglican.ca/rs/apology/apology.htm; *Dancing the Dream*, videocassette (Anglican Church of Canada, 1993).
1994	Presbyterian Church in Canada	'Our Confession', General Assembly resolution	*Acts and Proceedings of the General Assembly of the Presbyterian Church in Canada*, 120th General Assembly (1994), 376–7; www.presbyterian.ca/webfm_send/1510.
1996	United Methodist Church	Sand Creek Apology, General Conference resolution	*Book of Resolutions 1996*, 395–6; http://archives.gcah.org/GC96/PETS/PET/TEXT/p22781.html.
1997	United Church of Canada	'Residential Schools Apology/Repentance', resolution	*Record of Proceedings* (UCC, General Council, 1997), 893–4; www.united-church.ca/beliefs/policies/1997/r271.
1997	Episcopal Church	'A Covenant of Faith', worship service, covenant signing, Jamestown, VA; implementing General Convention resolution	Report: *Episcopal Life*, December 1997, 1, 5; covenant text: www.episcopalarchives.org/cgi-bin/ENS/ENSpress_release.pl?pr_number=97-2011; *The New Covenant at Jamestown*, videocassette (New York: Episcopal Church Centre, 1997).
1997	Religious Orders of Australia (Catholic)	Apology to Indigenous People	*Social Justice Report 1998* (Sydney: Human Rights and Equal Opportunity Commission, 1999), 52; www.humanrights.gov.au/pdf/social_justice/sjreport_1998.pdf.

1998	United Church of Canada, Moderator Bill Phipps	'Apology to Former Students of United Church Indian Residential Schools, and to Their Families and Communities', oral statement authorized by General Council Executive	General Council Executive Minutes, October 23–6, 1997; www.united-church.ca/beliefs/policies/1998/a623.
1998	Quakers in Australia	Sorry Statement to the Indigenous People of Australia	*Social Justice Report 1998*, 50.
1998	Australian Catholic Bishops	Statement on National Sorry Day	Excerpt: *Social Justice Report 1998*, 50–1; full text: www.catholic.org.au/index.php?option=com_docman&task=doc_download&gid=660&Itemid=309.
1998	Anglican Church of Australia	'*Bringing Them Home* Report', General Synod resolution	Excerpt: *Social Justice Report 1998*, 51; full resolution, and presentation: www.anglican.org.au/docs GS07B3a7EJointAffirmation.pdf.
2000	Australian Catholic Bishops	Statement of Repentance	*Origins* 29, no. 40 (23 March 2000), 655–6.
2000	Brazilian Catholic Church	500th Anniversary of First Mass in Brazil, apology to Indians and Blacks	*National Post*, 27 April 2000, A15.
2001	Synod of Catholic Bishops for Oceania	'Post-Synodal Apostolic Exhortation Ecclesia in Oceania', no. 28	*Origins* 31, no. 35 (14 February 2002), 573, 575–96; www.vatican.va/holy_father/john_paul_ii/apost_exhortations/documents/hf_jp-ii_exh_20011122_ecclesia-in oceania_en.html.

2008	United Methodist Church	'Healing Relationships with Indigenous Persons', resolution pledging Act of Repentance in 2012	*Book of Resolutions 2008*, 437–9; http://calms.umc.org/2008/Text.aspx?mode=Petition&Number=153.

SLAVERY AND/OR RACISM

1975	World Council of Churches, Nairobi Assembly	'Structures of Injustice and Struggles for Liberation', adopted report	*Breaking Barriers: Nairobi 1975*, Official Report (London: SPCK, 1976), 109–13.
1990	Alliance of Baptists	'A Call to Repentance'	*Baptists Today* 9, no. 17 (1991), back page.
1992	Roman Catholic Church, Pope John Paul II	Visit to the House of Slaves, Goree, Senegal	Accattoli, *When a Pope Asks Forgiveness*, 241; www.vatican.va/holy_father/john_paul_ii/speeches/1992/february/documents/hf_jp-ii_spe_19920222_maison-esclaves_fr.html.
1992	Roman Catholic Church, Pope John Paul II	Message to Afro-Americans, Santo Domingo	Accattoli, *When a Pope Asks Forgiveness*, 243; www.vatican.va/holy_father/john_paul_ii/messages/pont_messages/1992/documents/hf_jp-ii_mes_19921013_afroamericani_sp.html.
1992	Roman Catholic Church, Pope John Paul II	General audience	Accattoli, *When a Pope Asks Forgiveness*, 244; www.vatican.va/holy_father/john_paul_ii/audiences/1992/documents/hf_jp-ii_aud_19921021_it.html.
1995	Roman Catholic Church, Pope John Paul II	Ad limina visit of Brazilian Bishops	Accattoli, *When a Pope Asks Forgiveness*, 245–6; www.vatican.va/holy_father/john_paul_ii/speeches/1995/april/documents/hf_jp-ii_spe_19950401_brasile-ad-limina_po.html.

Year	Body	Action	Source
1995	Southern Baptist Convention	Resolution on Racial Reconciliation	*SBC Annual* (1995), 80–1; www.sbc.net/resolutions/amResolution.asp?ID=899.
1999	United Church of Christ	Public service of repentance	*Minutes of the Twenty-Second General Synod* (United Church of Christ, 1999), 53–4.
1999	Presbyterian Church (USA)	'Facing Racism: A Vision of the Beloved Community', General Assembly approved policy statement	*Minutes, 211th General Assembly*, Part I (1999), 274–86.
2000	United Methodist Church	'Act of Repentance for Racism', worship service, mandated by resolution of General Conference	Order of service: www.gc2000.org/music/repentance/; resolution: *The Book of Resolutions 2008*, 464–5; streaming video: www.gc2000.org/audiovideo/videoevents.htm.
2000	Church of Norway [Lutheran]	'The Relationship between the Roma people and Church of Norway', General Synod decision	Church of Norway Information Service, 11 July 2002; www.kirken.no/english/news.cfm?artid=5851.
2000	Roman Catholic Church, Pope John Paul II	Universal Prayer, Day of Pardon, discrimination due to race, ethnicity, religion	*Origins* 29, no. 40 (23 March 2000), 645–8.
2000	Australian Catholic Bishops	Statement of Repentance	*Origins* 29, no. 40 (23 March 2000), 655–6.
2001	Roman Catholic Church, Pontifical Council for Justice and Peace	*The Church and Racism*, updated text, nos. 6–12	*The Church and Racism: Towards a More Fraternal Society*, updated ed. (London: Catholic Truth Society, 2001).

Year	Body	Action	Source
2001	Christian Church (Disciples of Christ)	'An Act of Repentance calling the [Disciples] to be an Anti-Racist, Pro-Reconciling Community', resolution	*Year Book & Directory 2002 of the Christian Church (Disciples of Christ)*, (Indianapolis, 2002), 259; www.disciples.org/Portals/0/PDF/ga/pastassemblies/2001/resolutions/0121.pdf.
2003	Christian Church (Disciples of Christ)	'An Apology for the Sin of Slavery', resolution	*Year Book & Directory 2004*, 261; www.disciples.org/Portals/0/PDF/ga/pastassemblies/2003/resolutions/0314.pdf.
2006	Moravian Church, Southern Province	Racial Reconciliation, resolution	*Synod 2006 Moravian Church in America, Southern Province* (Resolutions, Reports, and Elections), June 2006; www.mcsp.org/Synod2006/res_synod_resolutions26_58_2006.htm.
2006	Moravian Church, Northern Province	Racial Reconciliation, resolution	*Resolutions of the Moravian Church, Northern Province on Social Issues* (Bethlehem, PA, 2008), 83–4; www.mcnp.org/synod/resolutions/Racial%20Reconciliation.pdf.
2006	Episcopal Church	'The Sin of Racism: A Call to Covenant', bishops' pastoral letter	*Journal of the General Convention* (Episcopal Church, 2006), 806–8; www.episcopalchurch.org/3577_73047_ENG_HTM.htm.
2007	Church of England	'Walk of Witness', public action fulfilling 2006 resolution of General Synod	*Walk of Witness: London.24.03.07*, programme book (2007); www.makingourmark.org.uk/downloads/Final_WalkofWitness_15march.pdf; resolution: www.cofe.anglican.org/news/gspm0802.html.

2007	Baptist World Alliance	Service of Memory and Reconciliation	Order of Service, Cape Coast Slave Castle, Ghana, 5 July 2007, provided by the Office of the General Secretary, Baptist World Alliance; resolution: www.bwanet.sitewrench.com/bwaresolutions2007.
2007	Baptist Union of Great Britain	'An Apology for the Transatlantic Slave Trade'	www.bwanet.sitewrench.com/bugbapology.
2008	Episcopal Church	'Day of Repentance', mandated by resolution A123 of 2006 General Convention	Order of Service, African Episcopal Church of St. Thomas, Philadelphia, 3–4 October 2008, provided by the Anti-Racism Office of the Episcopal Church; resolution: www.episcopalarchives.org/cgi-bin/acts/acts_resolution.pl?resolution=2006-A123.

APARTHEID IN SOUTH AFRICA

1982	World Alliance of Reformed Churches	'Racism and South Africa', resolution	John W. de Gruchy and Charles Villa-Vicencio, eds., *Apartheid is a Heresy* (Grand Rapids: Eerdmans, 1983), 168–73.
1990	Dutch Reformed Church (South Africa)	'Resolution on Apartheid', General Synod	*The Story of the Dutch Reformed Church's Journey with Apartheid, 1960–1994: A Testimony and a Confession* (General Synodal Commission, 1994), 21–2; http://web.uct.ac.za/depts/ricsa/commiss/trc/drc_sub.htm.
1990	National Conference of Church Leaders in South Africa	'Rustenburg Declaration'	Louw Alberts and Frank Chikane, eds., *Road to Rustenburg: The Church Looking Forward to a New South Africa* (Cape Town: Struik Christian Books, 1991), 275–86.
1997	25 national church entities	Official written and/or oral submissions to the Truth and Reconciliation Commission	Research Institute on Christianity in South Africa, University of Cape Town, http://web.uct.ac.za/depts/ricsa/commiss/trc/trc_subm.htm.

Clergy Sexual Abuse

Year	Source	Document	Reference
1996	Catholic Church in Australia	*Towards Healing*, revised and apology reiterated in 2010	www.catholic.org.au/index.php?option=com_docman&task=doc_download&gid=952&Itemid=158.
1999	Christian and Missionary Alliance	'Statement Regarding Abuses from Mamou Alliance Academy'	Christian and Missionary Alliance Archives, Colorado Springs, CO.
2000	Australian Catholic Bishops	Statement of Repentance	*Origins* 29, no. 40 (23 March 2000), 655–6.
2001	(Catholic) Synod of Bishops for Oceania	'Ecclesia in Oceania', no. 49	*Origins* 31, no. 35 (14 February 2002), 573, 575–96.
2002	Cardinal Bernard Law of Boston	'Statement apologizes for clergy sexual abuse of minors'	*Origins* 31, no. 32 (4 January 2002), 525, 527–8.
2002	Bishop Wilton Gregory, President of US Conference of Catholic Bishops	Presidential address, Dallas meeting	*Origins* 32, no. 7 (27 June 2002), 97, 99–102.
2002	US Conference of Catholic Bishops	'Charter for the Protection of Children and Young People, revised'	*Origins* 32, no. 25 (28 November 2002), 409, 411–15.
2009	Archbishop Diarmurd Martin of Dublin	'Reaction to Dublin Archdiocese Abuse Report'	*Origins* 39, no. 27 (10 December 2009), 437–8.

2010	German Catholic Bishops	Statement on Revelations of Sexual Abuse against Minors within the Church's Sphere of Influence	www.vatican.va/resources/ resources_german-bishops-2010_ en.html.
2010	Roman Catholic Church, Pope Benedict XVI	Letter to the Catholics of Ireland	*Origins* 39, no. 42 (1 April 2010), 682–7; www.vatican.va/ holy_father/benedict_xvi/ letters/2010/documents/ hf_ben-xvi_let_20100319_church-ireland_en.html.
2010	Catholic Bishops of England and Wales	Statement regarding child abuse	www.catholic-ew.org.uk/ catholic_church/media_ centre/press_releases/ press_releases_2010/statement_ by_the_catholic_bishops_of_ england_and_wales.

WAR, CIVIL WAR, CRUSADES

1945	German Catholic Bishops	Fulda Pastoral Letter	*The Catholic Mind* 43 (November 1945), 691–6.
1945	Evangelical Church in Germany	Stuttgart Declaration of Guilt	Hockenos, *A Church Divided*, 187.
1947	Evangelical Church in Germany	Darmstadt Statement	Hockenos, *A Church Divided*, 193–4.
1967	United Church of Christ in Japan	'Confession on the Responsibility During World War II'	Lukas Vischer, ed., *Reformed Witness Today* (Bern: Evangelische Arbeitsstelle Oekumene Schweiz, 1982), 64–5.
1971	General Conference Mennonite Church	'Resolution of Repentance', regarding war in Southeast Asia	*Minutes of the 39th Trienniel Sessions*, Fresno, CA (1971), 22–3.

1986	Roman Catholic Church, Pope John Paul II	Day of Prayer for Peace in the World, Assisi	Accattoli, *When a Pope Asks Forgiveness*, 141; www.vatican.va/holy_father/john_paul_ii/speeches/1986/october/documents/hf_jp-ii_spe_19861027_prayer-peace-assisi-final_en.html.
1994	Archbishop George Carey of Canterbury	Sermon in Christ Church Cathedral, Dublin	'Anglican Archbishop Ends Visit with Ecumenical Service', *Irish Times*, 19 November 1994, 5.
1995	Cardinal Cahal Daly of Ireland	'Forgiveness: Necessary Condition for Peace'	*Origins* 24, no. 33 (2 February 1995), 545, 547–9.
1996	Anglican Communion in Japan	'Statement on War Responsibility', General Synod resolution	*Anglican and Episcopal History* 65 (1996), 489–91.
1996	Argentine Catholic Bishops	Statement on National History	Accattoli, *When a Pope Asks Forgiveness*, 90–2.
1996–1999	Reconciliation Walk	Statement of Apology	C. Lynn Green, prod., *The Reconciliation Walk: From Europe to Jerusalem*, videocassette (A Reconciliation Walk and JEMS/Skunkworks Production, 1999); www.religioustolerance.org/chr_cru1.htm.
2000	Roman Catholic Church, Pope John Paul II	Universal Prayer, Day of Pardon, for hatred and the desire to dominate others	*Origins* 29, no. 40 (23 March 2000), 645–8.

WOMEN

1995	Society of Jesus	'Jesuits and the Situation of Women in Church and Civil Society', General Congregation decree	*Documents of the Thirty-Fourth General Congregation of the Society of Jesus* (St. Louis, MO: The Institute of Jesuit Sources, 1995), 171–8.

1995	Roman Catholic Church, Pope John Paul II	'Letter to Women'	*Origins* 25, no. 9 (27 July 1995), 137, 139–43; www.vatican.va/holy_father/john_paul_ii/letters/documents/hf_jp-ii_let_29061995_women_en.html.
2000	Roman Catholic Church, Pope John Paul II	Universal Prayer, Day of Pardon	*Origins* 29, no. 40 (23 March 2000), 645–8.
2006	United Church of Canada	'A Service of Apology and Appreciation to Women in Ministry Affected by the Disjoining Rule'	Documents provided by the Office of Faith Formation and Education, United Church of Canada.

HOMOSEXUAL PERSONS

1997	Episcopal Church	'Apologize for the Church's Rejection of Gays and Lesbians', General Convention resolution	*Journal of the General Convention* (Episcopal Church, 1997), 278; www.episcopalarchives.org/cgi-bin/acts/acts_resolution-complete.pl?resolution=1997-D011.
2000	Church of the Province of Southern Africa (Anglican)	Apology to Homosexual Persons	Noel Bruyns, 'Southern Africa's Anglican Bishops Apologise to Homosexual People', *Ecumenical News International* bulletin 97–0123 (1997).
2001	Bishop Michael Ingham (Anglican)	Apology to Gays and Lesbians	*Anglican Journal*, General Synod Supplement, September 2001, 4.
2006	Episcopal Church	'Express Regret for Straining the Bonds of the Church', General Convention resolution	*Journal of the General Convention* (Episcopal Church, 2006), 339; www.episcopalarchives.org/cgi-bin/acts/acts_resolution-complete.pl?resolution=2006-A160.

Other

Year	Body	Title/Subject	Source
1992	Roman Catholic Church, Pope John Paul II	Address to the Pontifical Academy of Sciences, regarding Galileo	Accattoli, *When a Pope Asks Forgiveness*, 132–5; www.vatican.va/holy_father/john_paul_ii/speeches/1992/october/documents/hf_jp-ii_spe_19921031_accademia-scienze_fr.html.
2000	Roman Catholic Church, Pope John Paul II	Universal Prayer, Day of Pardon, sins in the service of truth; against the poor, weak, or disadvantaged	*Origins* 29, no. 40 (23 March 2000), 645–8.
2004	Roman Catholic Church, Pope John Paul II	Letter to Cardinal Roger Etchgaray on the Occasion of the Presentation of the Volume *L'Inquisizione*	*The Pope Speaks* 50 (2005), 23–4; www.vatican.va/holy_father/john_paul_ii/letters/2004/documents/hf_jp-ii_let_20040615_simposio-inquisizione_en.html.
2004	World Alliance of Reformed Churches	'The Accra Confession'	www.warc.ch/documents/ACCRA_Pamphlet.pdf.
2008	United Methodist Church	'Repentance for Support of Eugenics', General Conference resolution	*Book of Resolutions 2008*, 340–6; http://calms.umc.org/2008/Text.aspx?mode=Petition&Number=1175.

INDEX

Aboriginal people (incl. repentance for offences against) 2, 58–70, 243–5, 259–60, 275, 285–6
absolution 100, 260–3
American Lutheran Church 42
Anglican Church of Australia 66, 69, 88, 275
Anglican Church of Canada 1–3, 61–2, 107, 252, 260, 262–3, 285–6
Anglican Communion in Japan 101
anti-Judaism (*see also* supersessionism) 36, 119–20
anti-Semitism (incl. repentance for) 36–9, 41–2, 44–56, 119–20, 142, 143, 209
apartheid (incl. repentance for) 80–5
apology (*see also* ecclesial repentance)
  definition 6, 61, 70–1
  distinction from repentance 6, 18, 52–3, 64, 69–71
  public perception shapes meaning of 17–18, 61, 68, 90, 110–11, 124, 137–8, 141–2
  reconciling elements of 279–82
apologies, national/state 3–4, 49–50, 60, 67–8, 266
'Apology to First Nations' (UCC 1986) 59–60, 243–6, 259–60
Argentine Catholic Bishops 102
Augustine 175–6, 189, 223–4
Australian Catholic Bishops 69, 144

Balthasar, Hans Urs von 117, 234–5
Baptist churches
  Alliance of Baptists 45, 73

Baptist Union of Great Britain 73–4
Baptist World Alliance 26, 27, 73
Southern Baptist Convention 72–3, 170, 180–1
Barth, Karl 160
Bartholomew I, Ecumenical Patriarch 111–12
Benedict XVI, Pope 61, 94–6, 217
  Ratzinger, Cardinal Joseph 124, 128, 132–3, 134, 168
Biffi, Cardinal Giocomo 121–3
blindness to sin 75, 218–20, 237–9, 251–4
  overcoming blindness 250–7, 258–9, 271–2
Bonaventure 235
Bonhoeffer, Dietrich 206–8

Cassidy, Cardinal Edward 52, 121, 134
Catholic Church in South Africa 84
Celermajer, Danielle 266–7
Christian and Missionary Alliance 88
Christian Church (Disciples of Christ) 75–6
Church of England 78–9, 102–3, 110–11, 169, 253–4, 258
Church of Norway (Lutheran) 74
Church of South India 22
Church of the Brethren 33
Church of the Province of Southern Africa (Anglican) 83–4, 107
church
  concrete historical particularity of 9, 145–6, 156, 163–4, 193–4, 205, 209, 215–17, 226, 229–33, 237–40, 286–7

church (*continued*)
  continuity not biological 170–1, 264–5
  continuity over time 5, 13, 56, 65, 73, 79, 150, 154–5, 161–72
  distinction from members 48, 52–3, 117–19, 138, 210–21, 223–4, 235, 236
  marks (*see* holiness)
  simul justus et peccator 20, 203–4
  as singular agent 128, 130, 220, 267, 270
church, images of
  body of Christ 117, 164–5, 201, 202
  body of Christ on the cross 234–41, 286
  bride 117, 122, 201, 234–5
  mother 117, 122–3, 126, 148, 236
  people of God (with Israel) 148, 201, 230–1
  pilgrim 117–18, 148, 211, 212–13
  sacrament 214
clericalism 96–7, 105
collective guilt 127, 263–6
collective representation, debates over 60, 61, 62–3, 65–6, 76–7, 82, 84–5, 103–4
collective responsibility 64, 220, 263–7
communion of saints 13, 150, 172–83, 286
  Christ's forgiveness as basis of 174–77, 180–1, 187, 194–6
  scope of 180–2
condemnations between churches (incl. repentance for) 24, 27, 31–4, 168, 185–7
Congar, Yves 211
conscience
  examination of 28, 51, 129–30, 144, 250–6
  formation of 48, 122, 219, 256, 258
contrition (sincerity) 81, 97, 249–50
  actions demonstrate collective contrition 59–60, 65, 81–2, 96–8, 141, 257–9
conversion/*metanoia* 19, 28, 35, 174

Cottier, Fr. Georges 119, 121–3
crusades (incl. repentance for) 103–4, 153–4

Dallen, James 247, 249, 256, 257
Darwin, Charles (alleged apology to) 110–11
Day of Pardon (Roman Catholic Church 2000) 3, 54, 104, 115–49, 250, 274
  reception in tradition 142–9
  response/reaction 136–42
  Universal Prayer 133–5
development of doctrine 5, 142–3, 147
dialogue(s)
  ecumenical 19, 24–7, 32, 184–6
  Jewish–Christian 36, 42, 44, 143, 227
disunity of Christians (incl. repentance for) 19–35, 112, 134, 146, 147, 169–71, 174–5, 213, 240
Drancy Declaration (French Catholic Bishops 1997) 47–50, 217–19
Dutch Reformed Church, South Africa (NGK) 80–2, 84–5

ecclesial repentance
  absence of 106, 139–40, 147
  acceptance/response 29–30, 31–2, 49, 51–3, 59, 62, 82, 105–6, 146–7, 180–1, 223, 244–5, 262–3, 275–8
  as accusation 23, 28, 50, 125
  as acknowledgement 92–5, 279–80
  as authorized teaching 142–3, 147
  in Book of Revelation 126, 146
  calls for 19–21, 80–1, 100, 107–8, 111–12, 145
  conditional 23, 90, 99, 105
  criticism (general) 11–12, 53, 63, 104, 111, 121–3, 140–1, 150, 154, 170, 264–5, 274, 276–8
  criticism (specific instances) 50, 51–4, 58, 61, 64–5, 72, 77, 81–2, 84–5, 89–92, 95–6, 104, 138–42, 254
  definition 3, 6–7, 17–18

ecclesial repentance (*continued*)
  dialogical form of 24–8, 93, 125–6, 143–4, 244–5, 251–4, 278–9
  expresses church's mission/future commitments 60, 75–6, 78–9, 97, 101, 112–13, 122–3, 135, 145, 149, 174–5, 178–80, 181, 222–4, 266–7, 281–2
  expresses respect for/acknowledges agency of victims 93, 125, 246, 259–60, 274, 280–1
  as God's gift (*see also* Holy Spirit, ecclesial repentance as work of) 165–7, 175, 235–6, 238–40, 245
  humility 19, 24, 112, 133, 143, 181–2, 222–4, 235–6, 241, 260
  new identity 22, 27, 186–7, 209, 230, 267, 281–2
    both individual and collective 255–6, 258, 272–3, 282
  as public record 83, 279–80
  qualified 58, 89–92, 94–6, 99
  relational dimensions 31, 62, 65, 70–1, 82, 169–70
  scope/classification 8–10, 17–19
  for sins of members 126–8, 182, 220–1
  for sins of nation/world 74, 99, 102–3, 206–8
  unfinished 259–60
  vulnerability/loss of security 259–60, 261, 278–9
ecclesiological method 5, 7, 9–10, 287
economic injustice (incl. repentance for) 112
environment (incl. repentance for) 111–13
Episcopal Church 44, 68, 77–8, 107–8, 182
eschatology 159–60, 164, 178, 191–4, 196, 278–9
eucharist 173, 194–5
eugenics (incl. repentance for) 108–9
Evangelical Church in Austria 43
Evangelical Church in Germany (EKD), incl. regional churches 33, 37–8, 43–4, 98–100, 208–9, 261
Evangelical Lutheran Church in America 32–4, 45
Evangelical-Reformed Church of Zurich 31–2, 186–7, 252

Faith and Order, conferences and papers 19–21, 34–5, 200–2
figural reading 237
forgetting 40, 129, 184, 191–3
forgiveness 6, 28, 245–7, 273–9
  being forgiven 261, 283
  debate about who may offer 52–3, 82, 105–6, 276–8
  expectation of 53, 246, 274–8
  of future generations 113
  inappropriate to ask 53, 274, 276
  political forgiveness 273
  relation of divine and human forgiveness 23, 24, 28, 53, 54, 63, 125–6, 150, 260–3, 273–9
  relation to repentance 245–6
French Catholic Bishops 47–50, 217–19

Galileo (incl. repentance for treatment of) 109–10
German Catholic Bishops (including West Germany, East Germany) 38–9, 40–1, 46–7, 100, 199–200, 217
God
  Father 117, 156
  Trinity 5, 155, 157–64, 194–5, 200–2, 212, 260–1, 286
Goldhagen, Daniel Jonah 141–2

Hauerwas, Stanley 261
Healy, Nicholas M. 5, 9–10
heresy 80–1
Hinze, Bradford 143–4, 219–20
history
  contested interpretations of 53, 54, 63, 75, 104

history (*continued*)
  ecclesial repentance gives new perspective on 27, 41, 85, 121, 125, 184–7
  role of historian/historical research 51, 119–20, 130–2, 148–9, 184–7, 190
holiness (mark of the church) 13, 55–6, 150, 200–41, 286
  ecclesial repentance gives new perspective on 228–41
Holocaust/Shoah (incl. repentance for) 35, 36–9, 40–4, 45–56, 137, 141, 199–200, 236
Holy Spirit 9, 10, 113–14, 117, 139, 156, 157, 159–69, 171–2, 173, 180–2, 209, 212–13, 215–16, 221, 223, 231, 240, 286
  absence of 237–40
  ecclesial repentance as work of 5, 10, 156, 161–5, 172, 221, 233–4, 238, 240
  renders penitent church continuous with its sinful past 161–70, 225
homosexual persons (incl. repentance for offences against) 106–8, 139

Indian Residential Schools, Canada (incl. repentance for) 1–2, 60–6, 181, 285–6
inquisitions (incl. repentance for) 120–1, 143
intercession/prayer 162–5, 177–80, 193
International Council of Christians and Jews 36–7, 140
Irish Catholic Church 95–6, 102–3
Italian Catholic Bishops 29, 46

Jaspers, Karl 263–4
Jenson, Robert W. 155–72, 179, 194–5
Jesuits (Society of Jesus) 104–5
Jesus Christ 116–17, 133, 159, 162, 163, 187, 188, 206–8, 232
  distinction of Christ and church 164, 166, 171, 207, 236
  head of the church/*totus Christus* 157, 162, 164–5, 168, 172, 175–8
  suffers the sin of the church 232–3, 236, 238
Jewish People (incl. repentance for offences against), 35–56, 134, 218–19, 226–7
  evangelization of 37–8, 42–3
  as people of God 230–1
  revised theology of Judaism 39, 43–5, 55–6, 209, 226–33
John Paul II, Pope 27–30, 53, 54, 69, 71–2, 74, 94, 101–2, 105, 109–10, 112, 115, 118, 119–21, 133–8, 153–4, 167–8, 174, 217, 250, 270, 272
'Joint Declaration' (Catholic–Orthodox, 1965) 24, 29, 167, 184
Journet, Charles 122, 210–11
judgement of God 135, 156, 165, 167–8, 174, 217, 250, 270, 272
judgement on the past
  anachronistic/illegitimate 49, 61, 104, 131–2, 154, 269
  legitimate 182–3, 216
justice 11, 78, 135, 190–3, 205, 229, 246, 256, 259, 273

Lambeth Conference of Anglican Bishops 21–22, 108
Law, Cardinal Bernard 88–90, 93
legal liability 63–4, 91
Lindbeck, George 230–1
Lumen Gentium (Vatican II) 117, 209–13
Luther, Martin 25, 41, 204
Lutheran Church–Missouri Synod 42–3
Lutheran World Federation 25, 32–4, 41, 170–1, 186

Martin, David 264–5
McCarthy, Michael 175–6, 223–4

Index

memory 54–5, 127–8, 183
  healing/purification of
    memories 27, 51, 129–31, 183–8, 191–7
  and identity 189–91
  relation of memory to history 130–1, 184–6, 190
Memory and Reconciliation
  (Catholic) 116, 123–33, 220, 236–7, 271
Mennonite churches
  General Conference Mennonite Church (including CMC) 30–1, 67, 102
  Mennonite Brethren 30–1, 169–70
  Mennonite World Conference 27, 147, 170–1
  Old Order, Amish 32
  Swiss Mennonite Conference 31–2, 187
'Message to the National Native Convocation' (Anglican Church of Canada 1993) 2–3, 61–2, 262–3, 285–6
Missionary Oblates of Mary Immaculate 61
Moltmann, Jürgen 204, 205–6, 269
Moravian Church (Southern and Northern Provinces) 76
Muslim–Christian relations 103–4, 127, 140, 146–7, 184

Niebuhr, H. Richard 20, 182
Nostra Aetate (Vatican II) 39–40, 51, 129
Novak, David 52–3, 70

Orthodox Churches 147
  Ecumenical Patriarchate 24, 154, 157–9
  Greek Orthodox Church 29, 153–4, 168
  Ukrainian Orthodox Church 30

pastoral function of doctrine 221–4
Paul VI, Pope 23–4, 125, 211, 217

penance 143, 187–8, 257–60, 272–3, 278, 283
Pius XII, Pope 39, 50, 130–1, 137, 140
Polish Catholic Bishops 46–7
Presbyterian Church in Canada 33, 62–3, 65, 181
Presbyterian Church (USA) 44, 75

racism (incl. repentance for) 71–7, 79–80, 134, 254–5
Radner, Ephraim 237–40
Rahner, Karl 213–16, 220
reconciliation 7, 14, 71, 125, 150, 191–3, 223, 245–6, 261, 267, 272–3, 279–83, 286
  church embodies reconciliation 247–9, 261–3, 286,
'Reconciliation Walk' (1996–99) 103–4
reform 97, 141–2, 143–4, 164, 211, 235, 254, 258–9
Reformed Church in Hungary 36, 43
reparations 65, 77–8, 141–2, 258–9
repentance for previous act of repentance 61
Roma (incl. repentance for offences against) 74
Roman Catholic Church (*see also* individual popes, specific official documents, national conferences of bishops)
  CDF/International Theological Commission 116, 123–4
  Commission for Religious Relations with the Jews 50–2
  Pontifical Council for Justice and Peace 71
  Pontifical Council for Promoting Christian unity 25–6, 27
  Synod of Bishops 269–70, 256

sacrament of reconciliation (also sacrament of penance) 89, 247–63
  truth and reconciliation commissions as analogous to 272–3

saint 173, 177–80, 215
scriptural interpretation (incl. repentance for) 43, 45, 46, 51, 229
'Service of Repentance for Racism' (UMC 2000) 75, 254–7, 262, 269
sexual abuse by clergy (incl. repentance for inadequate response by bishops) 87–98
sin
   of church/sinful church 13, 41, 48–9, 96, 144–5, 148, 150, 164, 176, 194–6, 200, 203–24, 270
   of church as failure in its mission 48–9, 63, 165, 195–6, 213, 214, 218–19
   definition 219, 248
   of individuals harming the church 27, 118–19, 123, 139, 201, 211–15, 218, 270
   universal sinfulness 91–2, 99, 203–5, 207–9
sinless church 53, 112, 117, 148, 122–3, 164, 201, 209–12, 223, 230
slavery (incl. repentance for) 58, 72, 74–80, 169, 253–4, 255, 271
Sobrino, Jon 261–2, 269
social sin 79–80, 219–21, 252, 267–73
   and responsibility 127, 221, 268–9
'Stolen Generation', Australia (incl. repentance for) 68–9, 265–6, 275
Stuttgart Declaration (EKD 1945) 18, 36, 99–100
subjective moral responsibility 127–8, 131–2, 135, 220–1, 270–2
Sullivan, Francis 138–9, 220
supersessionism 38, 39–40, 41, 43, 44–50, 55, 229–31
   shaped Christian perspective on holiness 227
Swiss Catholic Bishops 46, 217

teachings of the church (repentance for) 37, 43–5, 48, 53, 112, 138–9

time, theological account 156–61
Truth and Reconciliation Commission, South Africa 82–5
Tutu, Archbishop Desmond 82, 84

Unitatis Redintegratio (Vatican II) 23, 210, 211, 213, 271–2
United Church of Canada 45, 59–60, 105–6, 147, 243–6, 251, 252, 258, 259–60
United Church of Christ 45, 67–8, 75
United Church of Christ in Japan 100–1, 282
United Methodist Church 45, 66–7, 75, 108–9, 146–7, 254–7, 258–9, 262, 269, 270
US Catholic Bishops 46, 88–94, 96, 98
Ut Unum Sint (papal encyclical) 28–9, 174, 270–1

Vatican II, speeches 23, 39, 211
Vietnam war 100, 102
voices of victims
   leading to repentance 1–2, 12, 66, 93, 243–4, 252–5
   reform structures to hear 97, 143–4, 222, 254–7, 272, 286
Volf, Miroslav 178, 188–94, 196, 278–9

'Walk of Witness' (Church of England 2007) 78, 253–4
We Remember: A Reflection on the Shoah (Catholic) 40, 50–4
Williams, Rowan 169, 171, 182, 225, 232–3, 261
   Archbishop of Canterbury 70, 78–9, 253–4
women (incl. repentance for offences against) 104–6, 134
World Alliance of Reformed Churches 26, 27, 80–81, 112
World Council of Churches, assemblies and statements 20–2, 35, 37, 72
   WCC general secretary W. A. Visser't Hooft 99–100
World War II 36, 98–102